The Cancer Stage of Capita

John McMurtry

The Cancer Stage of Capitalism

Pluto Press
LONDON • STERLING, VIRGINIA

First published 1999 by Pluto Press
345 Archway Road, London N6 5AA
and 22883 Quicksilver Drive,
Sterling, VA 20166–2012, USA

British Library Cataloguing in Publication Data
A catalogue record for this book is available from
the British Library

ISBN 0 7453 1352 3 hbk

Library of Congress Cataloging in Publication Data
McMurtry, John, 1939–
    The cancer stage of capitalism/John McMurtry.
      p.   cm.
    Includes bibliographical references.
    ISBN 0–7453–1352–3
    1. Capitalism—Moral and ethical aspects. 2. Economics—
Sociological aspects. 3. Economic history. 4. Marxian economics.
I. Title.
HB501.M555   1999
332.12'2—dc21   98–45475
                                       CIP

Designed and produced for Pluto Press by
Chase Production Services, Chadlington, OX7 3LN
Typeset from disk by Stanford DTP Services, Northampton
Printed in the EC by T.J. International, Padstow

Contents

Preface

The title of this book is not a provocative metaphor. It is the conceptual outcome of long personal experience and deep-structural social investigation over 30 years of research across disciplinary boundaries. During this period, I have been involved with my brother, a medical researcher, in ongoing co-investigation of pathogenic patterns at the highest level of abstraction. I have also been the husband of the mother of my four children who was overwhelmed by a deadly anaplastic cancer, and a serious student of a non-lethal carcinogenic invasion of my own body. These prolonged events of learning life and death sequences of disease and immune response have led to the deepening recognition of common principles of growth and disease between social and cellular life-organization.

At the most general level, both social and cellular levels of life-organization are subject to states of disease (i.e., systemic reductions of their life function). Both have endogenous capabilities to recognize these dysfunctional states (i.e., immune systems) and to respond to them by selecting against what causes them. Both either succeed at this life-protective immune recognition and response to invasive growth sequences with no committed function to the larger life-host, or they suffer an advancing deterioration of their life capacities. Each is vulnerable to immune-system failures in which the aggressive growth of a not-self agent within the host body increasingly appropriates its nutriments for its own self-multiplication, with no protective response by the incrementally depredated host life-organization.

Between these poles of survival and development on the one hand and systemic degeneration on the other are countless degrees of possibility within the common life-requirements of social and cellular bodies. Both levels of life-organization, for example, must have food, water, and air to live, and require each of these in exact compositions, distributions and quantities to survive. Each suffers reduction of life range in precise proportion to their deprivation, a law of diminishing returns which we can observe as clearly in human as in cellular communities.

The most fundamental and significant difference between the cellular and social planes of life-organization is that social bodies are not genetically determined in their healthy or their pathogenic sequences of function and reproduction. Social bodies, unlike cellular bodies, reproduce in every moment through underlying value codes and decision structures which are, as human, subject to conscious modification. This foundational distinction between genetic and decision codes as regulating structures of cellular and social life systems is the philosophical and observed basis upon which this analysis depends. Its standpoint therefore rejects reductionist theories of societies' being determined in their histories by 'economic laws' or 'genetic blueprints' which rule out significant social-organizational alternatives to the status quo.

Pathogenic patterns at the social level of life-organization are analysed in this study as *value programme mutations*. These regulating sequences are not genetically fixed, but are *sets of presupposed principles of preference* which mutate beneath notice and which, when diseased, come to select for exchanges within the the social body that invade, deplete and strip the society's vital resources and functions. These mutating social value programmes underlie ideologies, which are merely their rationalizing disguises. They come, if not arrested, to be system deciders for the entire social host's reproduction and decline. They may appear law-like in their blind operations and even 'inevitable'. But they are in fact conditioned preference-programmes conforming to a gridlocked social paradigm which has delinked from the requirements of its social and environmental life-hosts and become a virulent system depredating and consuming them.

The first chapter of this study is devoted to laying bare the operation of closed value programmes across the history of civilized thought, each eventually recognized and overcome as societies learn to flag them as virulent. The second, third and fourth chapters expose and track the dominant value programme of the last three centuries, the mutating market paradigm, into its recent carcinogenic eruption and metastasis. The concluding chapter considers the evolution of the unseen substructure of history, the civil commons, as the bearer of the underlying life ground, and the regulating foundation of a life economy on the local or the global level. The core interface throughout is the 'life-sequence economy' versus the 'money-sequence economy', whose conflict and resolution have been lost to view.

This investigation's framework of social self-understanding adopts a wider lens than the currently received models of social explanation – in particular, the engineering model of neo-classical economics from which life value has been expelled. It is a telling symptom of our condition that no established school, discipline or general theory of social analysis has grounded itself in life requirements as such. Instead, some social construct is invariably adopted as the ultimate reference body – a set of ideas, the state, the market, a class, technological development, or some other factor than the life-ground itself. Or social ideologies have found their independent variable of determination in an already given structure of the world – God's plan, human nature, a racial type, archetypal memories or psychostructures, genetic reproduction, geographical conditions, and so on. Once this closed reference-set decouples from the vital, highly specific and interconnected requirements of the life-ground itself, and becomes an autonomous system of selection and exclusion overriding all claims of life to expand itself, it becomes a lethal value programme. The degree of its deadliness, in turn, is borne by its technical powers of manufacture, communication and destruction, and their pervasion. The 'self-regulating' global market system presents us with a totalized paradigm of such a programme at the end of the twentieth century. Its technical powers and morbidities of effect have propelled the wholly unprecedented crisis of global life deterioration and collapse that emerges today.

The investigation ahead tracks this dominant economic paradigm and the mutating value sequences and consequences it bears as the underlying determinant of an unrecognized and progressively deepening transnational disease. The analysis identifies the historically recurrent problem of life-blind social value programmes from ancient slave society on, but focuses systematically on the causation, the effects and the resolution to the global market disorder. This disorder has progressed by unseen money-sequence mutations and by systematically blocked connections to their life-destructive consequences. Throughout the planetary cancer's advance, it has found its pathways of opportunistic invasion in an undetected 'pathogenic money code' whose mutating sequences have assumed forms unrecognized by economic theory and never seen by Karl Marx. These life-attacking money sequences have typically invaded their social and environmental life-hosts by the non-living vehicles of corporate conglomerates, and have become dominant through leveraged and credit money-demand without a gold standard or legal-tender reserve requirement to inhibit their decoupled and borderless circuits of self-multiplication. They have been propelled and metastasized by ever more deregulation, velocities and volumes of cross-boundary transaction advancing and spreading in new and proliferating vehicles and forms of self-increase. They have been precipitously deregulated, insured, expedited and escalated by captured governments and corporation-dictated trade and investment treaties. They have fed throughout on engineered public debts that are not repayable in principal but demand ever rising compound-interest payments which strip evolved social sectors and defence-systems. And these pathogenic money sequences are served around the clock by globe-girding weapon-systems of mass life destruction which siphon public accounts and have themselves become dominant commodities in the global market.

None of these conditions or 'capital sequences' existed in full invasive opportunity until the fall of the Berlin Wall. All took their current footings after the Vietnam War – unregulated 'Eurodollar' tides to pay US military debt, the abandonment of the gold-standard anchor for floating-peg US dollars, surplus windfalls of US and Arab petrodollars flooding into dictator-created Third-World debts, trillions of highly leveraged Japanese loans pervading the world's markets, and ever rising deluges of borderless pension and mutual funds, uncommitted capital flows and vast currency and stock speculations entering and exiting societies overnight with no function but their own self-increase.

The world economic meltdown that looms at the end of the millennium is not unexpected if the macro-indicators have been observed. But as we find ahead, the money-into-more-money sequences driving the carcinogenic circuits have no reference-body beyond themselves in the global market system which allocates and disposes of the wealth of nations. All the coordinates of global environmental, social and economic meltdown are in fact connected, and their common cause lies in proliferating mutant sequences of money-demand whose defining principle – as the dominant economic paradigm that houses them – is not to serve, but to feed on life-hosts.

A clear understanding of the aetiology, determinants and effects of this global disease, and the underlying life sequences which resist it, are required to stave it. Recognition of a disease is always the necessary pre-condition of the successful response to it, at the social level of life-organization no less than the cellular. But at this stage, the resources of social immune systems and the civil commons that bear them are life bases of successful response which have not yet been fully understood or mobilized.

Acknowledgements

The long project of this analysis has, as might be expected, received little official support. The academy and its vehicles of funding have become largely ancillary to the global market corporate occupation. The investigation has thus had to arise, develop and grow on a wider ground. Many deep lenses of inquiry have assisted in the cross-disciplinary tracking. Two medical researchers in particular, Dr Robert McMurtry and Dr Allan Connolly, have shared their rich medical understanding over countless hours of discussing the connection of the principles of scientific medicine to the larger life-organizations of society. Dr Robert Gould and Pat Sutton of San Francisco invited me to contribute the prototype of this research to a special issue on public health of *Social Justice*, and challenged me to meet counterarguments to its model. William Krehm, editor of *Economic Reform* and chair of the Committee on Economic Reform, published pivotal portions of the work as it was written, and gave unstintingly of his deep knowledge of banking and support of an alternative paradigm of economic value. G.A. Cohen of All Souls, Oxford, encouraged the project and responded with peerless analytic rigour in probing and interrogating my most general arguments. Susan George of the Transnational Institute, France and Holland, whose work in demonstrating the disease of social injustice is legendary, connected the project to Pluto as publisher and encouraged the work throughout, not least in translating a portion on the Multilateral Agreement on Investment into French for submission to the National Assembly of France. Terisa Turner provided a wealth of research to show the applicability of my concepts of the 'civil commons' and the 'life-sequence economy' to gendered class struggle in Africa. Ed Finn of the Canadian Centre for Policy Alternatives selected, edited and published pieces of the text as it was written in a primary source of the book's research, the *CCPA Monitor*. Bernard Hodgson valuably referred me to sources on the physics model of neo-classical economics when I presented, on his co-invitation, the Bank of Montreal Distinguished Visitor Lecture at Trent University under the title, 'The Banks and the Cancer Stage of Capitalism'. Robin Mathews, Douglas Kellner, David Korten, Tony Clarke and Jean Bergevin were acutely supportive at key moments of the work crystallizing out of a 1200-page manuscript entitled 'The Invisible Prison'. Many others have been helpful in ways too numerous to cite here. But my partner Jennifer Sumner's tireless proofreading, inputting and encouragement in dark times was a pillar of the study throughout. Pluto's Director, Roger van Zwanenberg, was searching, responsive and focused on getting the investigation into print, while his Managing Editor, Robert Webb, expeditiously cleared the way to publication.

In the end, this work evolved from the civil commons as an expression of its social immune system and the shared life goods it bears which, I trust, will form across borders against the global corporate market disorder which at this historical juncture grinds the world.

John McMurtry
August 1998

1

The Ancient Taboo

When people come to examine any way of life in the world, they are conditioned not to expose their own social order to the same critical eye with which they view a different or opposed social order. This is because they identify with their own way of life as normality, and thus the other as abnormality. If the other is not only different but also *opposed* to the home order, then to abnormality is added the offence of enmity.

Accordingly, members of the 'free world' competed with one another in denouncing the Soviet Union for the 75 years it existed. But at no time was 'the free world' exposed to such criticism by the same criteria of people murdered, killed, starved, persecuted, silenced or dispossessed. Yet its operations were no less subject to humane concern – for example, over two million Vietnamese, over a million Latin Americans, over one million Indonesians and over three million Algerian and sub-Sahara Africans killed by 'the forces of the free world' during the same period.[1]

The twentieth century has come to be known as the Age of Massacre, but the mind-bias at work in blocking out one side of the massacre has been repressed from view. There is not only a rule against recognizing the monstrous in one's own social system, but a rule against recognizing that there is such a rule. This mind-lock is as old as civilization itself.

Philosophy is its intended antidote. Thus one of the most insistent questions asked of our politicians and public figures is, 'What is your *philosophy* on this matter?' or 'Could you tell us about your philosophy here?' They are not asked, 'What is your science on the matter?' or 'What is your religion?' or even 'What are your politics?' They are asked for something deeper: the shape of their overall idea of what a society is and ought to be.

For a belief-system to qualify as reasonable rather than mere dogma, it must be *open to question*: exposed to analysis of its presuppositions and arguments, and the consequences which follow from believing in them.

Critical thought takes on the recognized power of a tradition from Socrates in the West and Lao Tzu in the East. It's a kind of 'systematic irreverence', to use Richard Wollheim's phrase. Or, more dialectically, it builds by negations: going back on its predecessors, stepping out past them, picking up stitches, losing them, rejoining divergent lines in a larger whole, then falling apart again into some potential regrouping that will, in the end, allow us a wider and deeper view of what deserves belief. The fundamental block in this whole process, however, is that certain critical questions are very dangerous to ask. For example, the question, what are the arguments against the relationship assumed between God's will and the powers of the State?, has been traditionally dangerous to ask in any of its various forms.[2] It exposes unexamined assumptions which the hierarchy of state-investitured interests normally prefer to leave unasked. Indeed such questions have long invited attack upon their authors as disturbers of social order who ought to be silenced for breach of manners, if not social treason.

Conventional philosophical questions, in contrast, are accompanied by no such peril. At their purest, they offend no-one and no interest. Compare the inquiry, 'What is wrong with the empiricist metaphysic?' to '*What is wrong with the private property system?*' The former question has been put by almost every major philosopher since Parmenides, while the latter has not been pressed by any main philosopher outside the early Rousseau and Marx, both of whom were publicly maligned and persecuted for doing so.

So strong is the resistance to deep questioning of established social relations that it is difficult to think of any settled form of societal life that is rationally challenged in the history of philosophy before 1750. Socrates, for example, despite his reputation as an inveterate interrogator of conventional opinion, never went so far as to seriously query his society's belief in enslaving other people to do its work, nor did he ever think to question the system of aggressive war and imperialism upon which this enslavement was based. Like his fellow citizens, he benefited from such arrangements, and however they might cry out for the philosophical *daemon* he held so dear, he left them unexamined. His questions stopped short precisely where one might have hoped for his gadfly bite – where repression of the light of intellect was at its worst.[3]

But the lasting significance of Socrates was that he raised questions about the nature of social relations at all. The Pre-Socratics had prudently relaxed in speculations about natural phenomena,[4] and it was an accepted view even amongst the reputedly wise that social custom and role constituted fate, or Moira. Indeed, transgressing one's assigned lot in the social order was conceived as the root of all tragedy: an ancient outlook that continued through Shakespearean times and remains *au courant* today in denunciation or death to those who are perceived as 'subversives' or 'communists' or repudiators of the social given of some kind. Socrates distinguished himself in this framework by being sceptical enough of Athenian social forms as to be executed for his impiety and questions (though he accepted without question the laws by which he was condemned).[5]

Socrates was executed because his interrogation of established values was considered too radical even so far as it went. The great generality of the charges against him – 'corrupting the minds of the young and believing in deities of his own invention instead of the gods recognized by the state' – indicate that it was because Socrates was thought to be undermining the very structure of social life his fellow citizens lived and identified with that he was charged with a capital crime. Had he stuck to inquiries into the natural elements as the Pre-Socratics who had safely preceded him, or had he questioned within the framework of deference to power as the sophists who coexisted with and followed him, he would doubtless have been left to philosophize on, 'minding his own business' as his triers put the option to him. But Socrates, though never venturing so far as to debate the value of the laws or the state, had his 'divine command' to inquire without stint into the rationality of conventional belief. His indifference and even disdain for the price of offending the socially accepted in this quest was considered too subversive of established authority and order to tolerate.[6] In consequence, as in all classical tragedy, where the social order is Fate and its upset by even unwitting non-compliance bears in its wake the sentence of death, Socrates was condemned to the hemlock. In fact if not in intention, he might be called the first martyr of social philosophy.[7]

After Socrates, social philosophy, as if in tribute, is made respectable by *The Republic*, but more in name than in influence, because it is the ontological and mainly epistemological arguments within *The Republic*'s sociopolitical framework that are taken seriously by Plato's successors. The really burning questions of social philosophy that it raises seem essentially ignored until they become conventionally acceptable to debate (for example, its arguments on the equality of women). Or they are kept at arm's length indefinitely, as with the position that disinterested government requires communist governors. (Consider how many Plato scholars have defended that position on the rule of reason.) Plato does not really emphasize these arguments in his work, it is true, and he accepts the refuge of the cave along with approved social thinkers in general who stay clear of such inflammatory issues as a matter of professional survival. But he does give them a critical role in his discussion, as the tradition from Aristotle on does not, even though he may avert his rational inquiry from such other established social forms as mass slavery, Greek hegemony and competition for victory spoils.

In the Eastern philosophical tradition, there is still less explicit critical reflection on the social given than in ancient Athens, and the same persistent structures of caste, conquest, sexism, blind obedience to superiors, intolerance of alternative, paternal absolutism, disabling punishment, material inequality, and degradation of other life-kinds continue more or less unquestioned as a prioris of normal thought. Consider that catalogue of violently repressive forms of life again, and how each is repugnant to civilized Western consciousness today. But all were and in many places still are thought to be inevitable and proper. We will see how, in fact, quite as violent and repressive forms of life in a different guise are thought to be perfectly acceptable, and indeed 'free' today.

In the ancient East, however, the shape of fate is different. What remains of social philosophy, other than justifications of the social given as part of the moral order of the universe, is hidden in code. In every case of social critique which survives for us, criticism of the socially accepted is concealed behind the protective face of paradox, symbol and cipher. Lao Tzu's brilliant dismantlings of Confucian orthodoxies, warlordism, and human chauvinism in the *Tao-te-Ching*, for example, and Krishna's dialogical surpassment of the values of competition for reward and caste maintenance in the *Bhagavad-Gita*, are classics of such covert social philosophy.[8] But always the profound criticisms of the social status quo are maintained on a level corresponding to some purely personal or metaphysical level, thereby yielding the escape-route of alternative sense to shield the message and its author from official attention. Here, as elsewhere, questioning the forms of social life within which one lives is regarded as a kind of blasphemy against the Absolute of which these forms are seen as the sanctified expression.

Criticizing the social order is a very dangerous business. For example, the Carvaka, an ancient materialist, anti-caste doctrine in India, was hunted to virtual extinction, and its proponents burned alive;[9] while any philosophical work in China which did not feature the Five Relations of social subordination as its cornerstone given – whether by implicit challenge (as with Mo Tzu's 'universal love without distinctions') or by omission (as with Buddhism) – was inexorably condemned as a threat to society itself. Even the Taoism of Lao Tzu, almost inscrutable to conventional intelligence, was soon emptied of its anti-Confucian and antinomian content by the transcendentalism of Chuang Tzu. Eventually, it was assimilated into Neo-Confucianism, where the doctrines of filial piety and the Five Relations that Lao had scorned were re-established more strongly than ever on Lao's metaphysical basis of universal harmony.

We may conclude, in short, that there is from the very beginnings of reflective consciousness a systematic selection against critical questioning of the social status quo. It is by ancient tradition an essentially forbidden subject.

But coming up from the ground, there is always a countervailing current representing the common life interest. Like a social-immune response to the internal disorders of oppression which attack the living bodies of its members, critical recognition of the more invasive forms of social life still persist, even when its bearers suffer the loss of their own existence in flagging the pathological constructions. Socrates is, it is true, successfully repressed in his aged body, but he springs up more lastingly than before in the dialogical explorations of his student Plato which push back the margins of thought *as* thought, which can no longer be simply prohibited as an offence against the gods. The range of socially shared consciousness is extended and deepened permanently. Socrates is soon succeeded by the far more robust and unpersecuted anti-conventionalism of Diogenes the Cynic, 'Socrates run mad'.[10] Elsewhere, it is the same mixed story of loss in the particular, gain in the field of life that lives on. The Carvaka, Mohism, and Lao's mockery of all social regulation arise and are discredited and attacked in their respective societies, sometimes in the most vicious ways. But they survive in the long run through the tests of millennia, opening the span of human self-consciousness still wider, if only by tortuous historical route.

A not dissimilar pattern occurs in Judeo-Christian thought. The more socially critical Prophets of Israel are deprived of their security and threatened from above for their fiery criticism of the wealthy and powerful who 'tread upon the faces of the poor.[11] Nonetheless, their words outlast by epochs the works of the social orders they condemn.

Their culminating figure, Yeshua, is crucified for his antinomian criticism, whose radical break with every vested interest of the day ends in his execution as a political criminal.[12] But however mystified and distorted his attack on oppressive institutions has subsequently been, it still stirs to life-sacrifice critics of exclusionary social orders across the globe.[13]

Even the Stoics, who form one of the most enduring establishment philosophies in history with their abdication of Cynic iconoclasm for submission to the social given as Natural Law, generate by this concept of universal right one of the most influential normative traditions in history: namely, the idea that there is one law to which all alike are subject. The implication of this universalization of law to rulers and subjects alike is that whoever violates this principle of equality before law is ipso facto unnatural, and against the order of the universe. From the view of received legal doctrine itself develops a tradition that special privilege is no longer a self-certifying given.

In short, we see a kind of dialectic at work here, between, on the one hand, the tribalism of established social habit and the vested interests it protects and, on the other hand, the opening space of consciousness that can conceive of criticisms of and alternatives to conventionalized oppressions and socially constructed reductions of vital life. On the level of social as well as individual life-organization, the system which develops evolves through experience and trial to more comprehensive compasses of understanding and habit.

The long silence of social thought in the Dark Ages is a period in which recorded social reflection is more or less confined to speculative moral theology as sanctioned by Church authority. It is the one post-classical period in which this dialectic seems to cease. Given social relations are either kept out of discussion altogether, as an unspoken taboo of the day's media, or they are accorded mere apologetic and justification. We call this 'the Dark Ages' for good reason. But dark ages can happen again. Do today's media ever question the corporate capitalist relations of the global market? Do they not pervasively describe all of significance that occurs as accountable to the market, which is itself accountable to nothing? Do we not confront a new absolutist theology, only with laws of commerce rather than God as the omniscient 'invisible hand'?

The last dark age can be seen from a distance. We can discern its culture of imposed silence that brooks no criticism of the ruling order as a kind of collective delirium in which the mind is submerged as in a dream. We may see it around us again today – after the fall of a world empire, after the unravelling of civil fabrics by barbarians overrunning all resisters and looting whatever is at hand, and in the thrall of a global end-of-history ideology. The last dark age is easily recognizable to us now. Not once in a millennium of philosophy does rational challenge of a significant form of its ruling social order occur: not of slavery nor serf bondage, not of hierarchical command nor sovereign absolutism, not of capital punishment nor killing of heretics, not of trial by battle nor rule by military lords, not of economic inequality nor living off the work of others, not of sexist relations nor childbeating: not, in short, of any form that might seem worthy of critical recognition. With the conquest of the controls of thought by the Church in return for its theological support of the temporal order, the entire institutional fabric of society is apotheosized as the Will of God, with any criticism of it a blasphemy punishable by ostracism or the fire.

Society's worshipping of itself as totem, a transcultural tendency as ancient as human groups, is in any dark age a monocultural form. There is only one God or System, an all-powerful One, whose prescriptions endow all established relations of the world's social order with the authority of the final and inevitable order of man. Therefore, to criticize or to challenge any constituent of it is to challenge the laws and necessity of the invisible hand itself. In the last dark age, one can search the inquiries of this era's preserved thinkers, from Augustine and Aquinas to Scotus and Ockham, and fail to discover a single page of criticism of the established social framework, however rationally insupportable feudal bondage, absolute paternalism, divine right of kings and the rest may be.[14] In the current final order, is it so different? Can we see in any media or even university press a paragraph of clear unmasking of a global regime that condemns a third of all children to malnutrition with more food than enough available, or that strips the biosphere of species at 1000 times the average rate?

In such a social order, thought becomes indistinguishable from propaganda. Only one doctrine is speakable, and a priest caste of its experts prescribes the necessities and obligations to all, with loss of livelihood or life the punishment for disobedience. Endless sacrifices are called for across borders, from one site of harsh discipline to the next. The laws of prescription and penalty are without alternative. Their disciplines are inevitable and necessary for the promise of future prosperity in a time and place that recedes as the terrors of insecurity increase. Social consciousness is incarcerated within the role of a kind of ceremonial logic, operating entirely within the received framework of an exhaustively prescribed regulatory apparatus protecting the privileges of the privileged. Methodological censorship triumphs in the guise of scholarly rigour, and the only room left for searching thought becomes the game of competing rationalizations.

In an era of such captivity of the social mind, systems of abstraction are obliged to avoid this-worldly fact. In philosophy itself, the original dark age has never been clearly overcome. John Locke may atypically write a treatise on government that is used by revolutionary movements elsewhere, but his work fails to see the light of day until after the removal of the regime he criticizes from social sovereignty, and the clear takeover of the bourgeois property-holders for whom he has since stood as the prime philosophical defender. Hobbes may write social and political philosophy based on a metaphysic which is also social and political philosophy in an unconscious form, but one can look in vain for a line of it that does not remain within obedient deference to the ascendant powers of his place and time. Of which well-known English-speaking philosophers today are we able to say different? In general, social thought is avoided for detail which is subserved to a system-justifying metaphysic that is given – the ruling paradigm of how societies are to live that is never itself questioned.

This tendency prevails from the Continental Rationalists on. Leibniz, Spinoza, Descartes, Berkeley, Kant, and Hegel, for example, more or less entirely presuppose the social regime of their day and its constituent forms as in some way the expression of a divine Mind, which they see it as their rational duty only to accept or to justify. They confine their attention to purely philosophical, that is, a-social issues – being as such, the conditions of knowing as such, and so on. Or they rationalize the social given as the manifestation of some kind of perfect Reason.[15]

Even Hume, perhaps the West's greatest subverter of conventionally accepted assumptions since Socrates, refrains from his vaunted scepticism altogether, as do his successors, when it comes to thinking deeply about the validity of the social order within which he prospers. He rides on received opinion with an absolutist's faith in repression of their contrary, calling for the crushing of dissent against accumulations of private property as a robberous crime:

Fanatics may suppose that dominion is founded on grace and the saints alone inherit the earth; but the civil magistrate very justly puts these sublime theorists on the same footing with common robbers.[16]

It is made explicit in what follows that what Hume and 'mankind' are struck with 'horror' at is the suggestion of certain seventeenth-century English non-conformists that there be 'an equal distribution of property'. Hume asserts without any argument for the status quo he prefers that such equality would 'destroy all subordination' and 'weaken extremely the authority of the magistracy'. He then concludes that its very proposal is 'pernicious' and deserving of the 'severest punishment'.

There is no point refuting the question-begging virulence of Hume's position here. Its disorder is all too evident. But what does deserve emphasis is the invisible prison of dogma within which even an arch sceptic is incarcerated when the surrounding forms of social rule with which he identifies are criticized. It is a mental block which few escape, but upon which the open future of life depends. David Hume as others is as riveted to their acceptance as fixedly as any tribesman to his totem. When the English-speaking world's very paragon of understatement and assumption uncovering acuity reels into intolerant unreason when confronted with the challenge of social alternative, he reveals by his example the hold of the social given on even philosophical consciousness. With Hume, as elsewhere, thought is confined by the force of social habit and rule within a social value programme that regulates understanding to expel whatever does not conform to it.

What we find as a more systematic form of censorship in the global market's corporate media is, at a deeper level, a profoundly rooted structure of humanity's still evolving capacity to think. As we will see, the need arises at a certain stage of blindness in a ruling paradigm of society to see *past* its indoctrination, or expose planetary life itself to progressive depredation by its automatized operations.

Rousseau is perhaps the first major modern philosopher to criticize the social given within which he lived; and he does so with respect to its most primary forms: exclusionary property, the 'chains' of the law, and upbringing of the young. That he quarrelled violently with Hume is hardly a surprise, and perhaps more due to Rousseau's philosophical scruples than philosophers have hitherto allowed in their defence of his less troublesome colleague. Compare his trenchant position on privatized property and the civil order with that of Hume:

The first man, who after enclosing a piece of ground, took it into his head to say, *this is* mine and found people simple enough to believe him, was the real founder of civil society. How many crimes, how many wars, how many murders, how many misfortunes and horrors would that man have saved the human species, who pulling up the stakes or filling up the ditches should have cried to his fellows: Beware of listening to this imposter: you are lost, if you forget that the fruits of the earth belong to us all, and the earth itself to nobody.[17]

After Rousseau, philosophy is never again the same. It awakes us to the social problematic and the underlying structures, principles and values which it is philosophy's vocation to disclose and to surpass. The revolutionary ideas Rousseau advances of freedom by self-given law, participant democracy, reduction of material inequality, non-authoritarian education, and social sovereignty of the 'common interest' are philosophical advances of the first order, explanatory and evaluative principles by which human forms of social life are better understood and surpassed by a more comprehensive way of thought. Not only do these ideas set the stage for the later moral and epistemological theories of Kant and Dewey, for example, and radical political thought ever after, but they establish a core of critical standpoints for social philosophy that to an important extent provides the modern foundations of the subject. Rousseau's work begins the release of philosophy from its long slumber within the social status quo.

Needless to say, Rousseau paid dearly for his philosophical courage. He was afflicted with financial worries, church and state persecution, notoriety, and ill-health. Social philosophy is still a dangerous subject after him, but less so because of his refusal to exchange compliant thought for personal privilege and position. Yet even here we must not overlook the social impediments to critical inquiry by which even a Rousseau is cognitively blocked. He drops his anti-property line soon after his *Origin of Inequality*, refuses after he is persecuted by the Parliament and the Archbishop of Paris for *Emile* to talk about an educational system for the Polish Constitution he is commissioned to pen, and by the time of the *Social Contract* endorses as just such forms as the exclusion of women from public life, special honours and privileges for rank, state censorship, and the execution of anyone who no longer believes in 'the dogmas of civil religion'.[18]

What breaks open the reflective space for critical analysis of the social given once and for all is the unprecedentedly penetrating work of Karl Marx. Though refused a post within the University, expelled from France, calumniated by the popular press, and tried for treasonous conspiracy, he manages to survive to give to philosophy's long acquiescence with the economic status quo an historical *coup de grace* from which it never fully recovers. Going far beyond Socrates or Rousseau, he exposes to systematic criticism the material power structure of all hitherto existing civil society: the ruling class system wherein, he argues, a self-serving minority owns most of the society's means of producing the necessities of life, and to which, therefore, the majority is constrained to subordinate its life-interests. No philosopher in history before this had dared to go so far. Ever since, Marx's work has been a critical reference point on the philosophical landscape: a landmark beyond the normal limits of thought beckoning to philosophers whose concern for underlying structures extends to social forms, and not merely natural and conceptual ones.

The second major critical blow Marx gives to the continued repression of philosophical thought within a framework of implicit or explicit acceptance of the social given is his latent theory that mainstream philosophy is *determined by the social order within which it arises, to remain within the latter's accepted bounds of cognition.* That is, Marx suggests, the social order is of x-character, and the reason philosophers in general will not discern or criticize it is because they are bounded by its x-character *not* to discern or criticize it: as, say, players of a game do not see or criticize the game's structure as long as they are playing inside it. They are, in other words, determined by the requirements of their position in the game not to question its nature, as a price of holding and advancing their own places in it.

Marx, however, was not much concerned about the reflective space of philosophy, or its methodological self-contradiction: on the one hand, claiming to interrogate received positions at the deepest level of critical examination, yet on the other hand, failing to do precisely this where the social order is concerned. His disturbing general idea that human consciousness is *determined* to remain within the parameters of acceptable inquiry permitted by the society's ruling class ownership structure is one that people had to reject to understand themselves as free, or to wrestle with, which put them at odds with the ruling structure they sought to be free of.[19] Most people preferred the easier option. As always, the outcome *selected against recognition of any pathological structure of the received regime of power.* This is the invisible prison of most historical social orders, and the hidden basis of their incapacity to adapt to the challenges of self-transcendence which are posed to all thinking systems of life-organization.

Mill's *On Liberty*, perhaps the English-speaking world's greatest classic of acceptable social philosophy, can be understood as one of the first, implicit struggles with the thought of Marx. Of course, it is also at the same time an independent move towards releasing social consciousness from imprisonment within the social given: arguing step by step for the right to think and speak in divergence from customary belief to any extent whatever so long as it does not interfere with the rights and liberties of other individuals. Herein lay a pushing back of the margins of acceptable discourse whose opening up of the reflective space for social criticisms was of momentous importance. But, interestingly, it is against the very force of the collective whose interests Marx is concerned to advance that Mill directs his case for individual liberty; and it is on behalf of the very privileged classes that Marx attacks that Mill's arguments are consistently, if often unconsciously, made (that is, in defence of British imperialism, racism, unequal voting, and disregard for the lot of the oppressed).[20]

This is not to say that Marx's social philosophy was not also undergirded by the uncritical presumptions and biases of the same social order. On the contrary, however vast his contribution to their critical examination, his work remains within the grips of accepted forms of social life in ways that Marxists a century since have not yet confronted nor surpassed: his absolute human chauvinism, his blindness to the totalitarian disenfranchisements of the young, his Euro-supremacism, and his conception of ever more social centralization and machine technology as laws of development not subject to choice. These regimenting forms of social consciousness have been shared across cultures and classes for centuries, and they are underlying principles of judgement regulating normalized thought, even the thought of history's greatest social revolutionary.

What distinguishes Marx and even Mill from the preceding and succeeding mainstream of social thinkers, however, is their critical readiness to debate and to evaluate existing social structures and patterns, even if they still continue to take many of them for granted. And what distinguishes Marx from Mill, in turn, is that Marx probes far more deeply and systematically into the inner logic of the prevailing social order, and so is correspondingly more adequate and coherent in his understanding and assessment of it, as well as its alternative possibilities.[21] Whatever his shortcomings, he is closer to realizing the still evolving human project of social self-knowledge than any philosopher before him.

By the second half of the twentieth century after the Marxian awakening, social thought *seemed* to be moving beyond the systematic repression by which it had traditionally been confined. Even according to the determinist theory of Marx, the colossal growth of society's productive forces had enabled a new internationalism of communications and outlook, an extension of literacy and information resources, and an organization of democratic power which together enabled, or appeared to, a far wider range of social critical possibility than in any previous period. The knell of the old imprisoned social consciousness seemed to have sounded. The principal foundations of a liberated social self-criticism seemed to have been laid.

In the brief era of unlimited social interrogation which emerged between 1965 and the early 1970s, humanity witnessed the most fundamental, far-reaching and transcultural questioning of the social-structural given in human history. An unprecedentedly encompassing challenge of life-repressive forms swept across national and cultural borders. The mass-killing mode of resolving social conflicts, the systematic torture and destruction of other species and creatures by human systems, the oppression of sexual freedom between consenting adults, the abuse of children as the right of parental and school authorities, patriarchal and sexist rule over smaller humans, and even the capitalist structure of controlling society's means of existence were all and at once exposed to a world-wide re-evaluation. After a few years of this 'raising of consciousness', a still undiscussed counter-revolution occurred. Its nature will be the topic of the rest of this study. Its consequences, however, went far beyond what could have been the intention of its advocates. It was hardly less than a reversal of history.

The appearance cultivated by both mass communications and mainstream intellectuals in the years since the mid-1970s has, as we know, been the opposite of 'a reverse of history'. The 'new reality' has been presented as one of the triumph, rising material prosperity and democratizing universalism of capitalism. We will expose this view to the deep-structural diagnosis its claim and the life reality of its consequences deserve. Here we simply observe that the substructural pattern we have come to recognize at work in other social orders and times is now at work by the presupposition of another form of social paradigm which has deployed the sciences instead of repressing them.

But the regulating paradigm of our epoch has peculiar features of self-representation. It is deemed to be freedom and, at the same time, there is said to be 'no alternative'. It is declared to be what people want, and, at the same time, what they must accept as 'inevitable'. It is what delivers prosperity to the world, but what simultaneously requires ever more sacrifices.

What always holds social understanding back from critical comprehension of its object is *the law-like tendency of social systems to select against the reproduction of those views which expose and criticize their constituent forms.* This is a transcultural mental block. We have traversed the history of its unseen hold on human thought since the beginnings of social reason. But what may hold social intelligence back now more than ever before is an unprecedented regime of mass communications regulating public consciousness across cultural and physical boundaries. It is very complex and rapidly developing in its technical capacities to reach around the globe instantaneously to all peoples, and at levels of the psyche of which they are not conscious. But all of its 24-hour-a-day manifestations in all of its bewildering variety of reproductive forms are governed by a single master principle: *Nothing which contradicts the value or necessity of transnational corporate control of all that exists for self-maximizing returns to shareholders will be reproduced in any of these mass media.*[22] This is a diagnostic claim at the highest level of generalization. It deserves the most searching scrutiny before we accept its truth. But what exception can we find to its meta-assertion? The exceptions – if we find any – will indicate the rule. If this meta-principle of censorship holds up to examination, then humanity has come to a limit that few suspect, the totalitarian moment of the ancient taboo. It includes the control of what is inscribed in learned texts, as well as what is sat before in one-way imprinting for an average of three-to-five hours a day across the world. It follows from the meta-principle of exclusion at work that whatever happens in the real world which could provoke doubt about the prevailing regime's capacity to rule – say, an ozone layer that no longer filters the carcinogenic rays of the sun or world fish-stocks and forest covers that have been stripped across continents – will never be referred *back* to the profit-maximizing programme of this regime itself, even if there is a clear causal linkage.

Surely, we might think, the most educated population in history with more public-sector intellectuals than any epoch preceding it would exercise their disciplinary and individual capacities so as to expose the underlying pattern. But as we will now find, there are structural impediments built into the practice of these disciplines themselves, which are even less exposed to the light than corporate media censorship across all public domains of image, word or sign.

Methodological Censorship in the Academy

Let us suppose that the ruling programme of value which we live within has become *so* entrenched underneath conscious thought and reflection that its system of values is presupposed as 'immutable law', even by those mandated by society to understand them. The 'laws' may be assumed as prescribed by human nature or by economic necessity or by God – all three conceptions are current in variations on the global market paradigm. But what is common to the conception and to its adherents in economic science is that this structure of values is understood as without alternative.

As Philip Mirowski observes from a standpoint which does not follow up the consequences of the misconception,

> The imperatives of the orthodox research programme [of economic science] leave little room for maneuver and less room for originality. ... These mandates ... Appropriate as many mathematical techniques and metaphorical expressions from contemporary respectable science, primarily physics as possible. ... Preserve to the maximum extent possible the attendant nineteenth-century overtones of "natural order" ... Deny strenuously that neoclassical theory slavishly imitates physics. ... Above all, prevent all rival research programmes from encroaching ... by ridiculing all external attempts to appropriate twentieth century-physics models. ... All theorizing is [in this way] held hostage to nineteenth-century concepts of energy.[23]

Mirowski's concern as an avant-garde economist is that the *right kind of physics* is not being appropriated. The deeper concern is that any model of physics *leaves us comprehending human life as not human*. If even economist *critics* of the dominant paradigm remain imprisoned within a framework that comprehends the most basic co-operative structure of human life in the same manner as we understand the movement of inanimate particles, there seems little hope that the contemporary economics can help us understand what has gone wrong.

Once the social structures of humanity's life are framed in the same way as inanimate objects and forces, and their modes of life are conceived as governed by laws as falling objects or heating gases are, then no choice is permitted entry into the structure of the system. This is, as we will see, why the model has been selected for reproduction and dominance within the larger society of actual economic ordering. It rules out the human capacity to be more than law-governed particles by the paradigm of understanding it imposes on what it regulates. In this way, economics' submission to the larger ruling order outside it becomes, in effect, a police function of it.

Economics is not, of course, the only site of this subservience as a disciplinary apparatus. Still, its leading members promulgate such notions as 'the invisible hand' and 'necessary sacrifices' with an aggressive certitude which gives their prescriptions special credibility in the corporate market. We might say that economics is to the corporate market what theology was to the medieval Church, the investitured deifier of the ruling order. We can certainly observe a similar pattern of thought subjugation in other academic disciplines; but more by silent premise than by an axiomatic metaphysics which conceives persons and societies as the objects of an engineering mechanics. Such incarceration of learned thought may follow from the rationalizing function by which disciplinary practitioners advance their careers. But one might have hoped for a little more critical doubt from a discipline that prides itself on its anti-metaphysics, and is assigned the publicly funded responsibility of comprehending the value system which it has invented.

But because mainstream neo-classical economists imagine the capitalist market system as given by the structure of reality like the law of gravitation – David Ricardo's very model for the labour market – they construe their study as 'value free'. They do this even while calling for its imposition on any society who rejects it. In this, the economists follow the larger ruling paradigm they serve. When peoples are then forced to obey 'value neutral' laws – as the indigenous peoples across the world have been over 500 years by invasion, mass murder, land clearances and criminal prosecution for resistance – their remainders are made eventually to submit. But once the reign of terror is perceived as a law of motion, like physics, then it is only a matter of necessity which no-one could rationally resist or criticize. Order thus found, the extraction of money profit can be regularized in such a way that its operations are quantified, plotted on graphs and made into equations, thereby appearing to their designers as laws of Newtonian physics at work in the world.

Successful coercion is in this way reflected in the regularities described by the theory as 'positive facts'. In answer to any objection to the people who are crushed by this system of physics-like laws, it can be confidently held that all that is being done is to attend to *the facts as they are, and not as others might like them to be*. This analysis can then be called 'value-free economics', and any who may disagree, in particular students of economics, can be categorized as 'insufficiently rigorous'.[24]

The question arises that a 'value-free' study of a forced-labour camp would yield the same results. The inmates obey, and the prison-camp labour yields predictable outputs and revenues from minimal cost inputs as long as there is no 'external interference' in the natural laws of the extraction process. Any who showed concern could be sternly admonished for imposing their own values on a system which must be studied with the strictest impartiality. 'These are the facts. We must study them as they are, and not as moralists would command us. We are scientists, and will stand against all who would subvert its method.' In this way, growing armies of economists can proudly repudiate questions of value as illegitimate, while presupposing with increasing certitude that the system of value whose effects they describe is as neutral and inviolable as the laws of motion studied by the natural sciences.[25] We are thus obliged to pose a very unsettling question. Is economics of this kind really an academic discipline or a science? *Does it anywhere open, as any authentic intellectual discipline or science must, its established paradigm to challenge and question?* Or has it become a monologic propaganda of this presupposed paradigm?

Mathematical economist, William Krehm, in reviewing earlier analysis along this line in *Economic Reform*, reminds us of an important general fact. Economics, he observes, 'has banished value theory from economic thinking'.[26] If value *theory* is banished from a subject whose every *object* of study *is* a value, then it is disordered at the base of its conceptions. Yet because economists have encoded their assumptions into formalist equations, they are no longer aware of what they have assumed. Their presupposed values have disappeared into a formal language of symbolic mathematics. We can see the bond here to earlier times. Just as ancient Latin operated in the medieval Church to reify dogmas into ritualized sequences untouchable by the vulgar or the passage of time, so econometrics functions in today's economics. It conceals the value judgements it assumes in an a-temporal algebraic apparatus that is severed from natural language, living referents and accountability to its effects.

The mathematicalization of economics began with a system-deciding metaphysical move which was not understood as one – the application of calculus to the buying-and-selling transactions of market economies in the last decades of the nineteenth century. Grounded in an engineering model of perfectly divisible inputs and outputs, life was in principle ruled out by a methodological reduction which substituted the borrowed model of an outdated physics for the ecology of human reality. Once the Procrustean machinery took hold, human choices and value sequences were necessarily conceived and frozen in the bloodless categories and functions of mathematical equations. *People* were, and still are, *presupposed by the model as, and only as, a-political atoms of automatically self-maximizing preferences.* The life-and-blood complexities and histories of society and social relations were, it followed, abstracted away as non-existent. Values and ethical concerns in disagreement with the system were excluded as unscientific. Whatever resisted such reduction in the flesh was, it also followed, none of the method's concern. Only the predictable sequences of mathematically rendered inputs and outputs could any longer compute as entrants to the calculus. Economics in this way moved beyond the conceptual apologetics of ideology to the mechanics of an engineer's paradigm.

This mechanistic paradigm was, of course, exactly suited to a value programme which processed human and environmental life forms as throughputs of global corporate machines maximizing money-profits for stockholders. Here we see the connection we might otherwise lose between the dominant economic paradigm's delinkage from the life-ground, while serving a ruling order of it at the same time. Once political and democratic interventions in the mega-machine's operations were expunged – by processes to be examined ahead – there were few footings left to resist the re-engineering of world life to disposable functions of the machine's advances. Regulated by such a model of how we must live, economists and the societies they prescribed to were bound to become increasingly obedient creatures of the unexamined value programme they reproduced and elaborated.

This is why we might conclude that economics ceased to be a science or an investigation once it presupposed an engineering physics model as its methodological given. It became instead the defining software of a machinal system with no place for life in its money-sequence operations. Like the received dogma of another epoch, its formulations decoupled from reality in a scholastic formalism, its priesthood would not acknowledge the right of any but trained believers to speak on issues designated by the subject, and its iron laws subsumed all that lived as material ready to be made productive by transformation into the system's service.

Yet it would be a very great mistake to simply reject economics as a resource of analysis. It provides an articulated lexicon of exact referents, operations and principles of the global market mechanism which it presupposes as the natural order. And its resources are invaluable in coming to understand the system of rule which the global market now implements across the world in its restructuring operations. One has to expose and understand the principles the doctrine assumes in order to examine and unmask their implications for life-organization. One has to follow the assumptions its theoreticians take as given to see the trail of consequences for reality which obedience to this unseen metaphysic unleashes on the world. One has to connect across the logical lattice of the covert value system the defining axioms and co-ordinates it bears to see what it means for the planetary life-web as an integrated whole. One has, in short, to do what the economist avoids as the explosion of his own identity – open up its value structure to examination.

This is what the study which follows does. In particular, those axioms and certitudes of this unrecognized moral doctrine which now rule public policy across the world will be diagnosed for two fateful blindspots – their unexamined assumptions and implications, and their consequent cost to people's lives. As we know from historical experience a programme of value is most dangerous when it is built on premises which exclude vital life needs and capacities from its calculi of what matters and what does not. This paradigm of how societies ought to live is closed on both counts. The consequences to life, we will see, have now taken the form of a systemic threat to its survival. But the paradigm exerts historically unprecedented influence and pervasion. It has developed countless switches and relays of technical and ideological circuits to move to and from in maintaining its theoretical equilibrium in the face of ever more alarming facts. But because it has never been tracked as a living, mutating system that can endanger its life-host as a systemic disease does, it is revealed here in a very different light than we are used to.

Lenses of value analysis, premise exposure, and connection to life requirement reveal unseen and disturbing deformations as soon as they are applied. Philosophy would seem the perfect antidote to this unexamined metaphysic regulating the world as an engineering mechanism. It alone among the disciplines and methods of the academy takes nothing for granted as a matter of methodological principle. It seems for this reason to be vocationally suited to the task of laying bare a presupposed value system, above all one whose principles are conceived as 'laws' whose operation is assumed to be 'necessary' and 'inevitable'. But here again, as we have seen before in philosophy's long history, we confront a methodological block. Even inside the systematic scepticism of its posture, philosophy's current practice indicates the hallmark closures of an unexamined value programme at work as an unstated premise of its investigations.

In a different way from economics, philosophy also repels critical examination of the dominant market system while at the same time assuming its order as a given. Its most influential figures not only tacitly assume the market system regulating world existence as a general fact they never question. More deeply, they posit its *first principle of self-maximization as the meaning of reason itself.* Thus the dominant contractarian model of both social philosophy and ethics begins in its most famous cases with this unexamined assumption of the commercial market – to relate with others so as to get as much as you can for yourself – as the first law of understanding justice and morality. John Rawls writes (emphasis added): 'I have assumed throughout that the persons in the original position [of seeking the principles of justice by a contractual agreement] are rational. ... [By this I mean] It is rational for the parties to suppose that they do *want a larger share* ... The concept of rationality invoked here is the standard one in social theory.'[27] David Gauthier extends this principle of rationality as calculated self-seeking to morality itself, assuming with the ruling market paradigm as well that rationality *means* 'maximizing the interests of the self'.[28]

This is not a new pattern of servitude to the ruling idea of an age. Philosophers have traditionally closed their eyes to the value paradigms ruling them, and considered safer prey. They have preferred to challenge *other* philosophers' concepts of truth, reality and goodness instead. Philosophy has become in this way a discipline of words about words, principally other philosophers' words, which pose puzzles not disturbing ruling social orders, however life-destructive they might be.

Fitting into the surrounding system of power is, one might say, a hallowed tradition of philosophical wisdom. Contemporary philosophy in this way complements its offspring of economics as a silent partner wherever questioning of the value programme of 'capitalism' or, as it is called nowadays, 'the global market' is concerned. Where its most eminent theorists *have* critically spoken to this or that aspect of the subject, they have done so by isolating a principle in antiseptic abstraction from practice, or by pursuing sequences of argumentation in counterfactual realms where the hard realities of the world do not intrude. Scepticism about actual structures of rule is thought to be 'not philosophical'. As so much of academic theory today, investigation becomes confined to self-referring circles of discourse. This permits exact deductive movement among system-defined abstractions without the confusions and complexities of the actual world to mislead thought into confusion.

With noble exceptions, as there always are, the hard realities of mass-child malnutrition, 80-hour weeks in global market sweat shops or stripping of social sectors and environmental protections to provide 'free circulation to capital' are issues which are not thought worthy of 'sophisticated' argument. One might wrongly conclude from this that even philosophy is useless to a serious investigation of the global market as a value system. But here again this conclusion would overlook the particularly invaluable resources philosophy offers to pursue this critical task. As Socrates first hinted, philosophy's method is to value dogmas as the physician's diagnosis is to disease.

Philosophical lenses are particularly helpful in seeing through the pretence of 'value-free' facts, or an economic paradigm which is imagined to be independent of human norm and choice. This is very important because the global market system is now standardly represented as an inalterable structure of the world to which societies must adapt whether they approve of its consequences or not. This costume of fate needs to be removed so we can see this regulating system of value without its sacerdotal clothing of necessity. Once seen and understood as a social construction, as a theoretically manufactured programme whose designations as good and exclusions as bad are not laws of nature or even of economic organization, we are better able to recognize and respond to its effects.

Another relevant method to understanding how we live in the face of blinkers against it is political science. Neither economics nor philosophy can help us much in this area because both avoid 'politics' as a methodological corruption. Political power and conflicts over power raise too vexed and dangerous issues of vested interests to stir too deeply. So these disciplines are in the main refined to exclude such contents. Methodological avoidance is more effective than prohibition in releasing a ruling social paradigm from critical contesting of it. This is how it hardens into a social value programme – prescribing and ordering people's lives as a settled framework of existence which is presupposed as given by even professional thinkers. As we know, a value regime imposes its patterns of behaviour as 'necessary', even if this necessity means killing your neighbour as with land-clearing operations in Rwanda-Burundi, or tacitly concurring in the impoverishment and malnutrition of your neighbours in the larger global market.

It is for these reasons that the dimensions of political science are especially essential to a study of the current world system. On the face of it, we can see that the mainstream practice of political science is as dead set against critical examination of the global market system as economics or philosophy. Examine any major journal of political theory or affairs to observe the pattern. Analysis invariably assumes the major premise that the global market is a '*free* market' with no reflection on the truth of this value affirmation, or on the use of a normative affirmation as a description. You will also observe that if and when any changes are recommended to this 'free market', they are measures to ensure its further implementation or its more efficient defence. On the other hand, whatever exposes or criticizes this world system is unlikely to be published. For it follows from the premise of 'the free market' that what opposes it must be *against* freedom. This may be a simplistically black and white value ground from which to base political analysis, but because it is not acknowledged or recognized, it remains presupposed in the apparently most scientific discussions.

For this reason, we might conclude that political science is another form of ideology, bound at its premise-base by an unexamined bias of what is socially good and what is socially bad. We would be mistaken again, however, to dismiss the resources it offers. Like economics and philosophy, political science has developed lenses of analysis without which it is not possible to comprehend the full dimension of the submerged metaphysic we are investigating. It may exemplify this unseen substructure in its mainstream expressions. But its underlying method enables understanding of what it is constrained by. Mainstream political science, for example, unmasked the structures of state power, the ruling special interests, and the justifying ideology whereby the value programme of 'Marxism-

Leninism' or 'communism' was inculcated in transnational populations. It never ceased to expose these underlying parameters of political rule over many decades. These general frames of analysis – *state power, ruling special interests, and ideology* – are central to its method. They help us to comprehend how any sociopolitical system is instituted, represented, contested, maintained, and overthrown.

With one exception. The exception is the sociopolitical system within which political scientists are themselves located. Here mainstream analysis becomes uncritical. It presupposes in our own sociopolitical field, for example, the nature of the 'liberal-capitalist' state as 'democratic', even if only business-financed parties are ever elected to national government office. It declines to examine government's relationship to these regulating financial interests to which its policies and institutions correspond. It passively internalizes the ideology of 'the free market' and 'globalization' at face value. Although no political scientist would ever examine an opposing sociopolitical order in this way, it is normal to do this with the order within which one seeks a career. But none of this can be noticed without appearing to be subversive. As with other symptomatologies of a social taboo, representations of reality are internalized as reality itself to remain acceptable. At this limit condition of its practice, political science ceases to be a science and becomes instead a rationalization of the taboo itself.

Sociology and anthropology are wider-lensed disciplines whose deepest methods are indispensable to comprehending a world system whose regulating principles have come to be presupposed as the physical structure of the globe. But again we must distinguish between these disciplines as accepted practices and their inherent capacities as methods. Here too, there is an unrecognized confinement of the mainstream discourse within the regulating value programme of the dominant culture. Here too, these subjects work best at a cultural distance. Indeed, traditional anthropology has normally functioned *only* at a distance from the society within which its practitioners live. 'I had to leave France to study man,' Levi-Strauss once said, apparently conceding that being a member of a social order made impartial comprehension of it impossible. Levi-Strauss flushed a peculiar fact to the surface without pursuing it. Presupposing and identifying with the value system one has been indoctrinated in day in and day out as a native member of a society creates a mental block against exposing its presuppositions and mind-sets. It is assumed as the structure of one's own being, and so critical observation *of* it risks the collapse of one's identity.

This block against exposing the habituated and socially constructed self, and more deeply the regulating order which has constructed it, is a transcultural problem. It militates against reflective thought the more that any alternative to it is inconceivable. Social members can be so constituted by this social system of which they are cultural products that each's *own very meaning and identity* is framed by the value order all have learned to think in terms of. Each sees and interprets within its frame of valuation as both onlooker and recipient. Each presupposes its goods of achievement and bads of failure as both evaluator of others and evaluator of *the self*. One cannot recognize its pathological structures without putting the self at risk. This is why I have chosen the term '*value programme*' as a designator. A value system becomes a *programme* when its assumed structure of worth rules out all thought of alternative to it as 'nonsense'.

When the Hindu does not think of a reality beyond caste dharma, and when the marketeer cannot value beyond market price, we see examples of value programmes at work. A social value programme is a jealous God. Consciousness and decision, preference and rejection are imprisoned within it. Whatever is against it is repelled as alien, evil, abnormal. The modalities of role and individuation, personal gratification and avoidance, become elaborations and differentiations of the programme internalized as the self. Lived alternative to the role-master is taboo. In the adolescence of the species, all members of the group see as the group sees. All experience as the group does. All affirm and repudiate as the group does. There is no reality beyond it save the Other.

We think in this time and age that we are beyond this subjugation to a closed programme: that we are no longer tribal, but cosmopolitan 'world citizens' in a global concourse of visibly contrasting ways of life and social belief-systems. But this typifies the delusion when, in fact, a single value system is presupposed as normal across all the expressions of it. What could such a value programme be, it may be replied, when we are all so different as individuals and peoples? *The test is*: Which of these different individuals and peoples does *not* now presuppose the global market value system as normal; its system of production and exchanges as what necessarily regulates one's work and afterhours; its goods as what one must seek more of; its functions as what one must perform to be accepted; and its requirements as what one must compete against others to fulfil?

When we approach the current market system in this way, we are drawing precisely on kinds of analysis which anthropological and sociological comprehension have evolved to understand individual identity-formation and group systems of social organization. What is essential in these disciplines is to comprehend human and social phenomena as *systematically interrelating wholes in terms of which individuals and groups are constituted as social roles and functions.*

This is certainly not the *whole* of human reality. For what is truly human is what can think and experience *beyond* the script of a given social system. If the script of the social system has come to be propelled by a value sequence which in fact attacks the life-fabric of its social or environmental life-host, moving beyond its invisible prison is a condition for collective survival. This is the choice-path that has in fact confronted societies in the past. We now live with little self-consciousness within a ritualized value-system sanctified by 'the invisible hand' regulating its distributions, 'market miracles' to beatify it, and never-ending 'sacrifices' to impose its discipline – in effect a new world theology on the level of representation. But none of this shakes the assumption that the system is scientific in nature. We know from anthropological and historical evidence that religious conceptions and world-views are the traditional organizing frameworks of self-conception in terms of which a social order standardly understands itself. Even the 'godless' order of Sovietism worshipped sanctified persona who did not exist, incanted phrases mesmerically to ward off critique, and invoked apocalyptic destruction of oppressors as a legitimating device. We know that since before the Old Testament and the Vedas, individual members of society have comprehended themselves in terms of these larger orders of meaning and fate. We may continue to imagine that we are beyond these collective superstitions which worship their surrounding social order as God. It is the global market we live in where 'all that is holy melts into air'. Here, surely, such religious mists of illusion and superstition, beliefs in divine plans and magical, invisible forces have finally dissolved and disappeared.

But as reflection on its phenomena from outside soon discloses, there is a theocratic character to the global market system not recognized by its adherents, even as they continually invoke religious categories and ghosts. It prescribes commandments that cannot be disobeyed without harsh punishments and terrors to the disobedient. It metes out rewards and tribulations in accordance with inexorable and immutable laws. Nothing that occurs from its fundamental principles of human ordering can be doubted, however many innocents may suffer death and destruction from their impositions. Those who presume to question or repudiate it are agents of the evil conspiracy known to all free humanity. Any who seek to defy or replace it are to be warred against until redeemed or eradicated.

The issue of 'economic theology' raises the question of religion itself as a level of analysis we require to comprehend the nature of the beast. Religion always has as its field of the sacred what is believed to be an eternal, universal and salvational order. A religion's principles are thought to express this divine order as morally obligatory requirements we cannot disobey without punishments or fires of tribulation. Religions can be understood to be higher or lower in value to the extent that they include, or exclude, people's access to their promised benefits of well-being. If a religion's life-benefits, or that of the social system claimed to represent it, are very narrowly accessible (for example, confined to a tribal or social elite, or to a skin pigmentation or gender), then it is a lower religion. To the extent that it embraces all of humanity and life in its circle of possibility and life-giving light, it is a higher, that is, universally embracing religion.

Some currently marginalized thinkers of the higher religious outlook have, interestingly, been among the most ethically explicit critics of the global market regime. They have focused on this system's deprivations of those with the least. They have in their 'preferential option for the poor' represented an ancient tradition of the Old Testament prophets and, in particular, the founder of Christianity himself. Recent 'social justice' and 'liberation theology' movements have emerged on this basis. To feed the hungry, protect the homeless, clothe the naked and, in general, care for those excluded by the market's distribution system has been the vital purpose of another kind of normative system that is grounded in social love. In the East too, there are selected contemporary Buddhist, Islamic, and Hindu voices who have spoken from the life-ground past their particular social systems to a universalist concern for all that breathes.

Here, one might argue, has been a vital source of criticism of the global market value code. Yet such voices are designated as 'economic meddlers' and even 'Marxists' or 'communists' by the categorizing operations of this system. Stigmatizing any and all critics of a social value programme as members of a demonic party or conspiracy is, as we know, a standard mechanism of social terror. It is the armour against thinking whereby an unexamined form of life remains unexamined. If a social system has become closed, one dare not criticize its accepted principles of assigning payoffs or deprivations, lest one be put in league with the system's designated mortal enemies.

Social paradigms of how to live are instituted and reproduced by this age-old reaction mechanism; which is, in turn, maintained by remaining unexposed to conscious reflection. This process of confining consciousness within the closed loop of a given frame of reference typically continues until it is recognized to be in contradiction with the needs of life and survival. Whether by violent upheaval or cognitive advance, the old mind-set is opened to question. Either its adherents adjust to life realities which the value programme has excluded from view, or they prolong the systemic destruction which collapsing value programmes are usually marked by. In the meantime, the reigning order of reproduction is promulgated as necessity to which there is no alternative, and judgement proceeds accordingly in terms of its given principles of prescriptive organization. Opposition, evidence or argument that does not fit its frame of reference is ruled out a priori. This is what makes it a value *programme* on the level of the regulating sequences of a machine. The Communist/Enemy/Unbeliever who falls outside or opposes it is bad. Those who repel from their minds all the Other stands for know they are positioned on the right side. All that disconfirms these givens of the real world is 'misinformation', 'lies', 'extremist'. Since there is no alternative to the system, whatever must be done to defend it is the unavoidable cost of protecting the known good. This is the closed circle which can lead to entire societies accepting a social lock-step that dismantles life-organization itself.

There is, of course, a distinction between a healthy value-set and a morbid one. What most importantly distinguishes the behaviour of a pathological value programme from a humanly intelligent ethic is that its affirmations and negations of value continue to be declared as absolute even if their operations systematically select against life's reproduction and growth. The damage can simply be denied as the lies of the enemy, or it can be acknowledged as a serious problem. But it is never traced back to the value programme as its cause. Always the value programme itself remains presupposed. It is this system-bound blindness to its life-destructive consequences which marks any value programme *as* pathogenic in its reproduction. The way in which it rules out comprehension of the harms it causes is by in *some* way blocking them out as outcomes of its own prescriptions. There are countless variations on this theme, and history is, one might say, a symptomology of them.

Life is a feedback system which grows from the feedback its previous structures could not accomodate. We know a life-organization is breaking down when it excludes or does not respond to the feedback that reveals its disorder, even though this failure may be exposing it to systemic destruction. On the social level of life-organization, for example, there may be evidence of contradiction between the *representations* of the value programme as 'free' or 'God's will' and the *reality* of progressive destructions of social or environmental life following from its imposition. In the social life-organization that is breaking down, the conflict between representation and feedback does not enter its accounts. Rather, *the problem is relocated in those who assert that it exists*. Its displacement is effected by the standard mechanism of stigmatization, which is always as an enemy of the values that the given order falsely imagines it embodies. This discourages dissent, and so the feedback pathways remain closed.

The relationship of intellectuals to the ruling value system around them is, in consequence of this closure, one of habitualized submission. This pattern, as we have seen, operates across epochs, and across secular and spiritual modes of understanding. Society's established value regime is *represented* as good and desirable, and all opposition to it is, therefore, construed as deplorable. Any reality which may contradict the received view is, in turn, ignored or blamed on the miscreants who expose it. Where the value system has hardened into an unfalsifiable programme, nothing can enter into it except what it is constituted to recognize. All else is excluded except what fits its programmed designations of what is acceptable and what is not.

Yet in the face of such dead-end circles of the indoctrinated social order, every discipline of understanding has developed *intrinsic* resources of comprehension which reach for deeper than the doctrinal limitations it is confronted by. These internal methodological resources can be mobilized, and *are* mobilized by the more critical-minded to pierce the veils of accepted appearance. They can and, eventually, do unmask any value programme and its covert structures of oppression. Integrity in the discipline's pursuit is always at work in *some* form because in every discipline there are long struggled-for standards of impartiality and interrogation which enable the researcher to get beyond the set-points of the received view. In every case, the deepest methods afford developed lenses for precisely this task – lenses to peel away the layers of pretence which value programmes encrust themselves in to block recognition of their systemic blind-spots and destructive consequences. With a value programme whose regulation of and effects on social and planetary life are pervasive, all of the established disciplines become relevant to comprehension of its operations and consequences.

Towards the Larger Whole: The Interdisciplinary Lens

To this point, we have focused on the rationalizing patterns *and* the deeper critical powers of four forms of inquiry into how we live – the meta-discipline of philosophy, the target discipline of economics, the power-mapping discipline of political science, and the spiritual discipline of theology. These are all lenses of the comprehensive method required for diagnosis of the contemporary global breakdown. By integrating their capacities across subject divisions, the many-sided object of our scrutiny can be exposed from all sides. In this way, we can avoid the confinement within narrow specialist blinkers which have long prevented the understanding of the whole as 'out of my field'. The real world does not obey the boundaries of specialists. If the larger whole we live within is to be understood in its systemic slippage of life indicators, if a global value-system regulates all levels of social and natural life-organization, and if every purpose of existence is increasingly accountable to only its demands, then we are dealing with a totality whose interrelated problematic cannot be understood from the standpoint of specialized formalisms. There is, in fact, no discipline of understanding not implicated in its rule.

By pursuing analysis across subject divisions, we return to what we seek as human beings – the meaning of the connected whole. Here the connected whole is already conceptualized as 'the global market'. It is a living system, but has not been comprehended as one because no one disciplinary method can accomodate it. But if it is an interrelated whole producing and reproducing itself daily, and is subject to crises, adjustments, growth or disease as all living systems are, then we need the life sciences more than engineering mechanics to comprehend its global processes. Of course, life-organization at the social level is not at all the same as at the cellular level on which the life sciences still exclusively focus. In this way, we are led into the realm of another field of understanding which is indispensable to following the impacts of this regulating system on its human and planetary life-hosts. I refer here specifically to the medical-biological paradigm of 'the immune system', and the patterns of 'pathogenic invasion' it recognizes and responds to.

On the surface, such categories and explanatory principles seem not to belong to an investigation of a socioeconomic system. But there are correlating structures of self-protective recognition and response here which are not yet recognized. This bridging across realms of the planetary life-web is not so risky a connection as may first appear. As we trace an ever clearer profile of systemic disorder in the global life-body, and at the same time observe the nature of the evolved social resources to combat it, the most basic principles of immune response and recovery can be seen to be challenged and already aroused in societies across the world. Once seen, the connections become so evident that we recognize they were there all along. But the analysis here is complex and must be deferred until Chapter 3 and after. By such reconnections of explanation and understanding across what is, in fact, one planetary system, the interlinked problems we face still in fragments come together in an intelligible whole we need to reground ourselves in before we can confront the global crisis's common cause.

In raising the issue here of a 'social disease' we may immediately wonder: What is 'normal' for a social body, and what is 'pathological'? Is there a principle of distinction between these conditions of life which is not merely subjective? Here again, the evolved value judgements of medical science between disease and health provide a life-ground for answering such questions. We know well, for example, the objective differences between being afflicted by a disabling disease and not being afflicted. And we have no difficulty in saying the former state is 'bad' for us. Such reliable value co-ordinates dispatch currently fashionable value relativisms which would have us believe that values are merely cultural perspectives or projections. The exact distinctions between healthy and diseased states provide uncontroversial value bearings *across* individuals and cultures.

Beneath medical science is a first major premise of value that all assume, but that the global market system is not regulated by – *the premise that health is preferable to disease.* Peoples of all places and in all social orders prefer to be alive, and they perform countless functions and avoidances to ensure they continue that way. There is no 'cultural relativism' about whether unpolluted water to drink, or freedom from hunger, or having a place to sleep is of value or disvalue. The universal values and disvalues bonding all human beings, and indeed all that lives, are quite undeniable once recognized. But in the strange loss of bearings of our time, these values are not recognized in the social sciences and humanities of the academy. Universal values are denied by post-modernism, needs are relativized by nearly all, shared grounds of value are lost. The disorientation reflects the deeper disorder by which we are afflicted in which disorientation is a known symptom. Only what is not alive, what is priced or generates a profit, still stands as uncontested value in our reproduction at the macro-level of societies. But if we go beneath the shadow play of this systemic loss of value bearings, we find the life-ground again, and it is, in the final analysis, all the conditions necessary to the preservation and growth of our embodied being.

Even the health sciences themselves have not comprehended the unifying principles that underlie every judgement that they make of what is 'healthy' or 'normal', on the one hand, and what is 'disease' or 'abnormal', on the other. Once the underlying principles at work in their assumptions are made conscious as ultimate yardsticks of value judgement, very different disciplines and mind-sets can be linked across boundaries by shared touchstones of value which give us solid common ground. As we begin to discern these deep connections of the life-ground and the life-sequence of value across levels of life-organization, we are propelled into still further disciplinary regions to comprehend what is happening to our global life-system as a whole.

Another challenge then arises in this context: How can we track this life-system's *historical* developments – and all post-tribal phenomena are historical, not cyclical – if we do not document by sources of record the ongoing facts of what is going on? The discipline of history, as we know, provides a recognized method for accurately recording historical trends, the documented co-ordinates of social patterns and changes. But since the discipline as it is standardly practised avoids any period more recent than a quarter of a century past, its method is of use here, but not its practice. The global market value programme which 'restructures' the world is very present. Its pattern is not yet 'history' in the professional historian's sense. For this reason, investigation of it must do its own history from this period's newspapers and journals of record.

Tracking and documentation of the corporate system's invasive pattern has been the most laborious task of the book, finding the causal pattern of the sea-change transforming the structure of social life in almost all nations at the same time. To penetrate behind the images and representations, the disconnected facts and phenomena to the underlying forms they express, and to diagnose the systemic consequences to social and planetary life-hosts to find the common pattern that propels them is an enterprise shared by all the sciences and humanities at the core.

The historian's resources of documentation and period-trend identification are indispensable to this mapping of humanity's unfolding condition. But mainstream historical practice is cordoned off from the living field. All disciplines are blocked in one way or another against recognizing deep systemic problems in the social order of rule within which they function. But history is further blocked by having to wait until the period of transformation is over before it can present its map of events and trends. Any entry of historical study into the present *while* historical patterns are set by the dominant powers of the day is ruled out as '*presentist*', a sin for historians – unless they speak for the dominant powers of their period. Then they are invited to pronounce on the current reality, and proclaim on matters about which they know nothing as historians, with no adverse criticism issuing from members of the profession.[29] The historical method required here, in contrast, must confront the navigational pattern of this world value-programme as it is steered, identifying the co-ordinates of its destruction as they trail in the wake of its implementation.

In tracing the implications of the global system and its relationship to the requirements of organic life, still other disciplines must be brought into play. Because the global market's value imperatives come, as we will see, into conflict with the very conditions of life's reproduction, the findings of the environmental sciences and ecology are also integrally required to understand the infrastructural life-bearings of the unfolding pattern. If, for example, only money-priced goods are recognized in the market value-system, the implications for the unpriced goods of, say, biodiversity and non-commercial species are profound. It follows from such a metric of value that selection for money value replaces natural selection as to what lives and dies, and how. Natural selection's evolved inter-connections of function and recycling of wastes to reproduce life are re-engineered to reproduce and grow money demand rather than ecosystems.

But this entailment is not noticed. It is an implication which crosses subject domains, disparate commercial interests and libraries of different disciplinary studies. That its unrecognized truth may be of fatal consequence to global life is, in consequence, not seen. Since ecologists and environmental scientists remain confined by their established specialties and practices to domains of analysis which exclude the market system as a determinant of harmful effects, their methodological lenses blinker out the deep structure of rapidly decreasing distribution and reproduction of the world's species. The fragmentary vision again fits global market selection very well. Systemic lines of harm following from economic system-deciders are blinkered out by methodology, and so cannot be seen.

It is reliably estimated that species extinctions now proceed at 1000 times their normal rate, and that up to 99 per cent of the materials used in the US production process end up as waste within six weeks. For every ton of garbage, in turn, there are five tons of materials to produce it, and 25 tons extracted from nature to yield these materials.[30] But these facts are not connected across the fields of expertise which track them. As the earth is thus stripped and polluted by ever more unfettered global market operations, the market paradigm of value that leads governments does not factor into its calculus the countless life forms, habitats and systems which are thus extinguished and poisoned. When objections are raised, the followers of the paradigm that rules sternly warn that all is necessary 'to keep the economy going'. Peoples increasingly observe that their life-ground is being devastated, but no 'new discovery' reports that every step of decision behind this process of life-destruction is taken to enact the global market programme.

Locked in the mind-set of the paradigm, politicians do not register the problem. If they do, like US Vice-President Gore, they block out its connection to the ruling value programme. Behind them, the disciplinary practices of the academy are confined to narrow and formalized professionalisms and their counsel cannot contribute what is required to public policy formation. Thus without causal bearings communicated from any quarter, political leaderships and university presidents themselves exhort societies to 'compete harder' at fulfilling the demands of the very paradigm of economic value that drives the increasing and systemic life-destruction. The auditing of life's deficits does not figure in this strategic plan. But if the global market metric nowhere registers these effects in its accounts, the media and public discourse rule out connection to their systemic determinant from discussion, and the academic disciplines that bear the cortex of the system are themselves confined by specialist and careerist blinkers, how are we to connect the consequences back to their cause, or even consider the question?

That no scientific literature yet relates the cumulative environmental collapse back to the preference structure driving its extractions, effluents and wastes is another marker of the closed circle of taboo, and, far deeper, of an unseen pattern of pathogenic reproduction at the level of social life-organization. As our compass of comprehension unavoidably broadens in the decoding of the market value programme, we are inevitably brought to 'the bar of the law' in our inquiry. If the environmental sciences can tell us of the *effects* of the system of extracting and using natural resources that the globe is regulated by, the gains or losses of the biophysical carrying capacity and species wealth of our common life-ground, the discipline of the law can provide us with the precise base-lines of society's enforceable structures of *prevention* (for example, by international protocols against transboundary pollution). The discipline of the law can also report to us what exactly *is* the law on such central dimensions of the global market value system as corporate constitution, liability avoidance, tax and banking legislation, trade regulation, and existing international law in human rights and environmental protection. Again we cannot comprehend the nature of this regulating world system unless we follow it with transdisciplinary lenses across national and international jurisdictions.

The law, to be sure, presupposes as given and inviolable the general structures of ownership and exchange it legitimates. It can, for this reason, be seen as an uncritical and ideological reflection of the market status quo it regulates, adjudicates and enforces. But just as economics is indispensable to laying bare the internal operations of the world market as a mechanism for allocating resources to society's production and distribution of priced goods, so the law is indispensable to understanding the codified framework within which these buying and selling operations of the money-economy are obliged to take place. Indeed, as we will see, the dynamic interface between these complementary disciplines is at the inner core of the global market system and its steering for good or ill.

There are deep general problems which emerge in the investigation of this relationship. The law in the main presupposes the market's distributive patterns and existing ownership rights as the given framework of its judgements, and typically asks no questions of fairness beyond these parameters of given rule. This relationship of the law to the 'economic base' is what led Karl Marx to claim that the law is a determined 'superstructure' of it whose function it is to maintain the capitalist system intact by both masking and protecting it.

In these times of global economic change and restructuring, then, we might expect laws to undergo some corresponding modifications. These modifications have indeed occurred, with even established laws of ancient jurisdiction erased, overridden and suspended to accommodate the new demands of international trade agreements by the World Trade Organization, the North American Free Trade Agreement, the European Union, the Multilateral Agreement on Investment, and so on. This is a deep and overlooked pattern to be delineated ahead. Although we hear very little about these structural changes in the rule of law from trade-lawyers rewriting the terms to which national and local legislation must conform, there is much that we can learn from the law's *deeper evolved norms of protecting life* which underlie all worth that the law has, and without which it is mere regulation for privilege and special interest. These underpinnings of life-protective norm are overlooked in the loss of bearings of our time, but they are the common ground for a lawful life-economy which are already codified and in place for an international system bound as it is not now by the rule of law. There are also regional and provincial statutes and jurisdictions which are being unilaterally overridden by national-level agreements which have not been constitutionally challenged. These bearings of law, given the force of law, can make the global market rule of money becoming more money for money investors accountable beyond itself.

If the law, as Adam Smith himself recognized in part, has long been used to protect the rich from the indignation of the poor, and is now being rewritten by transnational corporations to protect their money-to-more-money sequences from the claims of life itself, this is not a condition to which the rule of law as such condemns us. It is a usurpation of the rule of codified principles of mutual restraint by a despotic party against which progressive history is the struggle.

But here again, conscious awareness of this undergirding structure of the codified 'civil commons' has not yet emerged as a reference body for the times. The ordering framework of codified policy and law which has evolved beneath the class protection of those with property against those without is the core of what humanity has won to advance the shared interests of all against the private interests of the few. This written civil commons, in turn, has a source which reaches back before history and has been sustained as the silent guiding thread of humane civilization since. Its still evolving ground of both individual liberty and the common weal has most dramatically developed since the Great Depression and the Second World War of this century. But this deepest of all projects of humanity is now at risk of reversal by a more systemic threat than armed forces or nuclear explosion. What invades it, how, and the response to it is the subject of the remainder of this investigation.

Technological Determinism: A Symptom of the Taboo

Though we may seem to have touched all the bases of understanding we require to recognize and respond to the planetary value crisis we now face, there will be an objection. It may be thought that we have left out a basic field of analysis – the critique of *technology* as a prime mover of the globe's palpable degenerations of life diversity and ground. It is certainly true that the ever more pervasive invasions of technology in our lives form the drive wheels of the displacement and mechanization of the life-ground wherever we look. This vast pattern of life-reduction has led a number of eminent thinkers – Martin Heidegger, Jacques Ellul and George Grant, for example – to interpret capital-T 'Teknologie/Technologie/Technology' as our ultimate value challenge.

This comprehension of our predicament, however, does not penetrate deeply enough. In the global market, technology is in fact an *instrument* of the more basic value programme which it is taboo to expose or criticize. It is here that we strike to the inner wheel of the system, its iron programme of prescription and its thousand-armed tool of material power. The unifying principle of the programme and its vast instrument of motion and force can be crystallized into a single formula:

> *Behind the selection and the development of technology's advances over every step of its planning, design, assembly, manufacture and displacement of past ways and life regions stands one commanding value-decision: to maximize the difference between input and output of money demand in market investment sequences.*

We need to pause on this claim because, if it is true, then technological development is not our ultimate problem, but rather, again, its *effect*. That is, technology is blamed for what is, in truth, a decision-structure behind it which develops and employs technology for a *non-technological* purpose. This non-technological purpose is identified in the italicized lines. We need to find a significant exception to this general causal principle if we are to continue to think that 'out-of-control technology' is the source of contemporary humanity's loss of the life-ground. If we *cannot* find one significant case in the current world where technology is not used for the system-deciding goal of maximizing returns to the money investment sequence, we cannot coherently go on blaming technology for problems in which it has become only a programmed tool.

It may be objected that the Soviet system was not programmed by the sequence of maximizing the sum of money-value outputs over money inputs, but was nevertheless afflicted with an out-of-control technology which devastated natural environments and reduced people to detail-operations within industrial orders. Yet this objection would miss two related points. The first is that the Soviet system is no longer, and thus does not figure in the problematic we are examining. The second is that the extent to which the Soviet system was essentially *a derivative and imitative order* of industrial capitalism is overlooked. We might even say it was a parody order, mimicking industrial capitalism in its regulating logic prior to the latter's mutations into money-sequences delinked from production. Consider the analogues of ruling social programme-militarized public sectors, dictatorial management of the forces of production, Taylorist production systems disaggregating every natural movement and process into lock-step phases of uniform sequences, pervasive machine-culture as a desirable order for society, and systematic devastation of the environment for 'efficiency' and 'development'. Dominant expressions of the ruling paradigm of how to live had been altered, principally private proprietary *title*, but the most basic forms of the life-excluding social programme were not recognized or responded to. Rather, the Soviet system, as in all such competitive races, imitated the system it sought to replace the more furiously it strove *to win in its terms*. The common, ruling principles of industrialization, of absolute privileges and control of management over workers, of capital-output ratios as the final measure of efficiency, of aggregate GNP as society's collective value goal, of maximally wide projection of armed-force power, and, perhaps most deeply of all, of conversion of nature into products and waste of maximizing production systems – all continued in place as more absolute than before.

Technology and its development are not self-moving authors of their effects, but the instruments and expressions of a deeper value programme which now governs their every implementation and advance. To attribute autonomous determination to 'Technology' as the despot of our condition is, then, a mystifying fetishism: one more recoil of avoidance of confronting the regulating paradigm of how to live behind it. As we have seen again and again, the commanding value programme of a social order is the unquestioned substructure of its life-organization. So basic is its hold on consciousness in the corporate market that even our profoundest cultural critics fail to bring it into the light, seize on its effects as the problem instead, and reify what drives it as the given structure of the world. As long as its underlying frame of final preference is not exposed to critical reflection, it remains hidden and un-decoded.

In the case of the anti-technology critiques of contemporary culture by Heidegger, Ellul and Grant, the money-sequence programme behind the pervasive advances of machine technology is never uncovered. The value logic of 'development', 'investment' and 'profit' in which technology is always the means, is not itself examined. The ownership structure within which the hungry machines of technology are always the chattel of agents who deploy their powers for profit or command is a connection which is not penetrated. The regulating principles governing the private and state corporate bodies who plan, produce, implement and distribute machine technology of every kind are in this way left unexamined. What we see at work here is a classic case of blaming the tool for what the tool is used for, thereby evading the need to face the social rule behind it which always selects against the exposure of itself.[31] This is the way of unexamined social value programmes. They exclude from view what they presuppose.

All that is extracted, restructured or wasted in the global market system follows this investment sequence. One is the cause, the other is the consequence. Or, more exactly, technology stands to the programme of value selecting and applying it as the decision's implementation does to the value sequence of the decision. The critic of 'technological civilization' is properly appalled at the motor-driven destruction of a wilderness by the latest commodity invasion, or by the loss of people's control over their lives by the homogenizing culture of mechanical instrumentalism. But until understanding connects these phenomena back to the regulating value-system deciding them, it remains lost in symptoms, which leaves the underlying taboo against exposing and criticizing the assumed system of social rule unseen and intact.

In laying bare the logic of prescription which expresses itself in every development of modern technology, we are eventually brought back to the core interface of economics and the law. The global market economy is the world system of producing and distributing goods in short supply for competitive prices within and across borders to all who have the money-demand to purchase them. In contrast, the law embodies the diverse systems of nations, regions and municipalities which specify normative rules of conduct for the jurisdictions *within* which these globalized economic transactions take place. It is within these two primary and often conflicting structures that most of humanity now lives.

At first glance, all this may seem, as it is said to be, 'inevitable' for framing a new global order. *The traditional and local gives way to the new and more efficient wherever they conflict, and protects the property of investors wherever they are incompatible.* This is the inner logic of the transnational trade agreements now ringing the world. But as this analysis lays bare the pathogenic logic of reproduction advancing within this emerging global order, we will find there are more and more life-assaulting consequences of its implementation which are excluded from the regulating paradigm's view in accordance with the rules of its own reproduction. These problems are not resolvable by market principles because they are the effects of its structural biases and blocks. The 'value crisis' people sense but have not tracked to its systemic cause becomes lethal to the extent that this system seeks always to resolve the problems it causes by more pervasive implementation of the unexamined programme that generates them.[32]

Barring the unlikely event of successful revolution across the world, the normative constraints of the rule of life-protective law are required to regulate on behalf of the common life interest. Yet if the market value programme is precisely structured to reject 'government interference' or accountability to law as barriers to its 'freedom', and seeks only *more* 'deregulation' and 'self-regulation' of its operations, then we confront a problem of incalculable gravity. For there is no limit to the planetary life damage that can be done by such a closed system without accountability beyond itself. In such a predicament, we must connect the programme to the unseen harms which follow from it in a diagnosis resembling that of the physician understanding a systemic disease invading and attacking its life-host.

It is a commonplace that 'the rule of law' is civilization's sole regularized mode for safeguarding life across communities – despite the long manipulation of it by the privileged – and that no private interests or agents should be 'above the law'. But to what *life-protective* laws is the global market accountable? If the distinction *between* the requirements of the market and of society's common life-interest is not made, what basis remains to recognize or preserve the interests of life which are not computed in the market metric? These questions touch on the core of life security of every citizen and country in the global market – but are not yet publicly asked.

A Marxist standpoint might hold that this focus on unexamined social paradigms of value and the taboo against exposure of them is 'ideological'. This response, however, misses the point. For an ideology is an expression or rationalization of a social value programme which, in the case of the global market, regulates every moment of what is socially planned, instituted, implemented and enforced in its decision sequences. A social value programme is, in fact, more basic than what Marx called 'productive forces', for these – as we saw with technology – are themselves *instruments* of its regulating decision structure.

We will argue ahead that a social value programme is, in fact, the cultural counterpart of a genetic code on the level of social life-organization, but much more difficult to penetrate because it is taboo to lay bare or criticize its ordering structure. In order to demystify its transhistorical hold on social consciousness, a grip which remains as long as it is presupposed as given and without alternative, we conclude here with a ten-step anatomy of social paradigms of value in general, and the general mode of their life-protective transformation. Table 1.1 following this ten-step anatomy sets out the system of blocking out whatever contradicts the necessity or value of the global market value programme in particular, which bears in its mutating axioms and sequences an invasive disorder across the planetary life-system.

(1) A social value system can be expressed in an ideology which rationalizes and legitimates it; or, more deeply, it can be a programme of decision and action by which the critical mass of society actually lives;

(2) Analysis should not divorce these levels of operation of a social value system, but recognize that principles of worth can become so presupposed and instituted in a social formation that their operation is absolutized as a law of nature or history even by those who criticize them;

(3) Any social value system is, in truth, a social construction, and as such can be constructed differently by its members within the limits of material reality;

(4) Given (1) to (3), analysis needs to examine and expose the regulating value system or programme of a society to understand the meaning and reality of it as a society in the process of historical formation;

(5) Such examination and reflection on a regulating social paradigm of value proceeds by exposing its defining principles of affirmation and negation, designation and exclusion, representation and reality in disclosure of its stated and actually system-deciding principles of worth;

(6) In exposing a social value regime to diagnosis with no assumption of its inevitability or necessity, we release its repressed premises and implications into view which, in turn, enables us to penetrate their causal determination of systemic harms to civil and environmental life;

(7) Understanding the systemic harms which an unexamined, deep-structuring value regime causes or selects for is the same in principle as understanding the harms which an individual value system causes or selects for. In both, there is identifiable loss or destruction of life following from implementation of the value regime's principles;

(8) In a value system which is still open or 'healthy', there is a critical feedback loop between its principles of preference and its practice such that if harm or disability follows from the living out of its principles, then the two can be connected, and revision or restraint of the programme can proceed on this basis;

(9) In a value programme which is closed, such connections of value cause and effect are ruled out of view, and so the systemic harms or disabilities following from imposition of the value-set continue to build to higher levels of life reduction, unless communicated recognition

breaks through the fixity of the programme (by some variation on steps (2) through (8)).

(10) If recognition of disorder in a social value programme is to translate into prevention of its life reductions, then the system-deciders of society, such as its law and policy formation, must be rechannelled or reconstituted to protect and enable the civil and environmental life from its systemic harms.

Table 1.1   The basic value programme and its grammar of censorship

The Basic Value Programme (BVP)	
Principle I	There are large capitalist corporations which control production and distribution of social goods so as to maximize the money value of their stocks.
	What can be said
Principle II	This BVP sets the limits of the range of possibility of what can be publicly stated.
	What cannot be said
Principle III	Nothing can be publicly said which contradicts the necessity or value of the BVP.
	Operations of exclusion from the range
Principle IV	The degree of exclusion is in proportion to contradiction of the BVP.
Operations:	1. Ruled out (e.g., BVP is evil/replaceable) 2. Omitted (e.g., causal relation of BVP to systemic harms) 3. Selected out (e.g., successes of alternative orders) 4. Marginalized (e.g., known critics of BVP)
	Operations of selection within the range
Principle V	What validates BVP as necessary/moral *and* what invalidates opposition to BVP as impractical/immoral is selected for publication.
Operations:	1. Selection of point of view (e.g., first person/unindividuated mass) 2. Selection of events/issues (e.g., report/do not report degradations of life conditions) 3. Selection of descriptive terms (e.g., BVP imposers are 'pace-setting'/BVP modifiers are 'dictatorial')

The Pathologization of the Market Model

Those who bear the global market programme militantly denounce whatever does not comply with its dictates – at the mildest, as 'protectionism', at the most abhorred, as 'communism'. The terms are assumed to be sufficient to invalidate any opposition by pronouncing their syllables of stigmatization. If we consider them in the light of anthropological science, they are incantational epithets for the unclean. They may be enough to lead to the dismissal, persecution or death of those who are so labelled.[1]

We might say that such effects of a value programme on those who are deemed to dissent from it are proof of its pathology. Certainly there have been enough victims of anti-communist witch-hunts, pogroms and invasions over generations of this global system's march across the world to justify such a conclusion. But here I will take another, untravelled track. I will argue that the global market system is *itself* opposed to the free market it claims to embody. This exposure will go deeper than critique. It will argue that 'the global market' is, in fact, a profound perversion of the market we know as a place of living people exchanging for goods they need – much as a diseased cell formation is a perversion of a healthy cell formation, but succeeds in invading its host by masking its nature as the normal 'self' of the body.

The Real Free Market versus the Corporate System

The master term of the global system's representation of itself is the nominative subject, '*the market*'. 'The market' is always in control, always infallible, and always to be obeyed. It requires, demands, punishes and restructures societies' production, distribution and survival across the planet. With transnational corporate oligopolies as its moving parts, the immutable law-giver of humanity's material condition. Or so it believed.

In this Old Testament conception of 'the market', an invisible and unerring hand of stern judgement produces economic miracles one day, and economic meltdowns the next, usually of the same societies. It pushes stockmarkets to new highs, attacks government social spending, transforms social orders overnight, and generally comports itself in ways that are understood as once God was comprehended by the godfearing. It is always right, no more resistable than the laws of physics, and deviation from its rule must inevitably end in disaster.

Yet we find that whenever we go to any *real market*, we move within an entirely different world. We may be in central London or Paris, an Indian or African village, an older town of Canada or Germany on the weekend, a Latin American plaza or a Far Eastern backstreet on any morning – everywhere there is a real market, a living community gathering together to exchange what each needs to enable their and their families' lives.

This free market is not remotely like the oligopolist corporate system which now calls itself '*the* market'. It is not an hypostacized aggregate of borderless money investors focused solely on having more money demand, nor controlled by transnational corporations and financial syndicates entering and exiting societies in nano-seconds to increase profit margins as the single ruling objective of their being. There seems nothing in common between this real free market we enjoy in the flesh, and the corporate model which re-engineers societies across the world as 'the global free market'. How could such opposites be so pervasively called by the same name?

The free market we experience in real life needs to be remembered to recover from the cultural amnesia within which we are now submerged. The real free market is made up of ordinary people meeting in a publicly owned space, some looking and some buying and almost as many displaying and selling what they have made or grown. The goods are generally foodstuffs, mostly fresh, often live, grown typically by their sellers, with personally made handicrafts on the open tables or ground in between. No-one force-plays with a sudden invasion or desertion of money demand. All are friendly and jovial as on a festival day. The buyers and sellers inquire and talk with one another of the health of their families, their shared community, and local affairs. Not a place in the real free market can be privately owned, and the quality of goods is not hidden under wraps or chemically engineered for false appearances.

Goods are sold without packaging or in recycled paper. The articles for sale serve a need, not artificially contrived and ad-stimulated wants. People walk within a community space without blacktop expressways and fossil-fuel machines walling their lives in. Creation of desire by the continuous operant conditioning of sex and power images does not deform minds. There is no monopolist or oligopolist distortion of supply or demand for the competition of alternatives is open. Every good sold, unless the market is being undermined, expresses the local region's culture. Prices of different vendors are immediately comparable, directly negotiable with the owner, and hard sells cannot entrap buyers in the open public venue. Relations of community mediate everywhere, and no closed doors, big-box conditioning apparatuses and distant manipulation schemes by corporate head offices control transactions.

No non-contributing stock-owner can make a profit out of the real free market. Bank and credit cards do not structure the exchanges, nor appropriate a hidden margin from either vendor or buyer. Paper debts and interest charges cannot enter the producer-and-buyer-controlled process. No waste or pollution is generated by the direct transactions of individuals exchanging for what they need, and nothing is sold to harm people's lives. Because no-one from outside the market can get rich from producing nothing for it, it is democratic. Most profoundly, the sequence of exchanges serves the growth of life on both sides, not the growth of money as an end in itself.

The real free market was a great advance of the community's control of its own life when it was no longer subjugated to kings, lords or municipal monopolies for the privilege of its existence. It was an opening of liberty when ordinary individuals could freely exchange with each other in a public space to acquire the foods or crafts they chose to produce or buy. Money here was not a weapon to reduce others to instruments. Money in the real market is a universal medium of exchange that enables individuals to transact across differences of jobs and goods without incommensurables of worth standing in the way.

We might conclude that the real free market *is* truly 'individual', 'free' and 'democratic' as a social form of life. While these properties are also claimed by the global corporate 'market', its justifications draw on properties of its opposite, the real free market, to sustain the profound confusion between them. There is not an argument made by 'libertarian' theorists like Milton Friedman and Robert Nozick, for example, that does not in some way trade on the confusion between these completely different and radically incompatible forms of life. The fallacy of equivocation at work here would invite our hilarity as ideological pun if it were not so indoctrinated into the corporate culture *as a starting point of thought.*

Table 2.1 identifies these oppositions, but not their consequences to living people. We will move to these as the unmasking of the corporate system proceeds. But we can see from this summary figure of structural contrasts that the real free market and the 'global market' are opposed in every property they bear. Not even the medium of exchange they depend on is the same, any more than pocket money is the same as interest-and-financial-charge-bearing instruments without cash reserves – the drive-wheel of the global system. The question, then, arises again. How could these opposed forms of life be collapsed into identity without the notice of economists, political or social theorists, or practical logicians? How could they be so pervasively confused that no terms in the technical literatures of the social sciences distinguish between them? How could such an equation of contraries so control world culture that public policy decisions continue everywhere on the basis of what is, in effect, a systematic world lie?

The distinction here is so basic that it is not seen. It is hardly an exaggeration to say that it rivals an inability to distinguish dream-time and being awake. Yet the difference between the real and the unreal is not only repressed in the mass media, including in those regions of the world where the real free market is still a daily site of community life. It is also repressed in school texts, economics courses, and professional economic models themselves. Indeed, one finds that just about everyone justifies the global corporate market *in terms of* its opposite, the real free market, even though the consequences of doing so are like steering world life while asleep.

Table 2.1   The real free market and the corporate system: structural contrasts

	Real free market	Corporate system
Investor	Direct producer	Money investor
Product	Organic food and handicrafts	Any commodity that sells
Labour contribution	Labour of those who own and sell	Purchased labour of unrelated others
Methods of production	Skill-intensive integrated labour	Machine-intensive division of labour
Seller	Producer and/or associates	Separate retailer
Buyer	Local individuals	Global mass market
Product information	Personal knowledge	Media commercial
Medium of exchange	Cash or promise	Bill payment
Source of packaging	Recycled wrapping	Extraction of natural resources
Nature of demand	Natural need	Stimulated want
Price determination	Local negotiation	Fixed by external decision
Relation between producer and buyer	Face to face	Non-existent
Site of transaction	Open community meeting place	Segregated private property
Relation to local culture	Expression of its climate or arts	Normally none
Surplus value recipient	Principally producer	Non-producing stockholder
Expenditure of revenues	In local community	By corporate head office

The confusion here embodies, in the end, a collapse of opposed systems of life-organization into deformed homogeneity. Non-living corporations are conceived as human individuals. Desire to turn money into more money for unknown stockholders in nameless places is represented as personal production and service to fellow citizens. Consumers who are mass-conditioned under their conscious awareness are portrayed as freely choosing individuals. Continent-wide machine extractions of the world's natural resources, pollutive mass-manufacturing and throwaway packages are imaged as home-spun market offerings for the local community. Junk and unneeded commodities are made to appear as necessary for vital life as food to eat. Faceless corporate bureaucracies structured to avoid the liability of their stock holders are represented as intimate and caring family friends bearing the responsibility of the larger society. The exploited mass-labour of others is transformed into the manufacture of the corporation as 'the producer'. The very concept of 'the global market*place*' is made into a proper name when all of its primary agents and products are distinguished by the fact that they have no place that they are in, but are borderless operations and transactions directed from cyberspace.

If we walk through each of the properties of the real free market, in short, we find that not one of them belongs in fact to the global market system, but every one of them is appropriated by it as its own. 'The free market' which remains is, in truth, the systemic attack on the free market we experience, masking itself in the properties of what it destroys as its justification and flag.

Bear in mind a principle that will become increasingly important. The not-self of the medical model of disease only succeeds in its invasion of the host body when the self of the body's immune system does not recognize it as not-self. This is the model whereby oncologists and other disease diagnosticians distinguish between the pathogen and its life-host. Their conceptual schema, drawn from the most fundamental everyday disjunction we know, expresses a deep principle which operates as well at the social level of life-organization.

The Unseen Mutations of Adam Smith

It might be objected that what is called 'the free market proper' is the traditional market form, but not the classical form of the market first theorized by Adam Smith. The latter model of the market is what the global system expresses, this counterargument would hold, and it expresses this modern concept at the highest level ever.

Certainly, Adam Smith is universally accepted as the founder of the free market paradigm, and certainly global system advocates, defenders, corporate spokesmen, and economists standardly invoke Smith's name and the principles he identifies as what guides the market and our understanding of it. What dissent there may be is muted and undeclared. Rejecting Smith as a definer of the free market's guiding principles would be like an evolutionary biologist repudiating Darwin's theory of natural selection.

Yet Adam Smith's express concept of the free market and its properly regulating principles is no less opposed to the global system that societies have been 'restructured' by as the traditional market itself. This is not a recognized point. The silencing of the distinction is not unlike the quietude of heresy in the medieval church. Opposing Adam Smith to the global system now regulating the planet would challenge its moral and theoretical legitimacy at the foundations. 'Classical economic theory' is grounded on Smith, and 'neo-classical theory' is grounded on classical. Any normal 'free market' society, in turn, takes its economic counsel from neo-classical economics. Adam Smith is the founder and first saint of the free market paradigm. To expose the global system as a systematic *violation* of Smith's economic template would be, then, to undress it as a rogue programme.

In light of the argument of Chapter 1, it is not surprising that this ground of legitimacy is never seriously questioned or rebutted by those who might know enough to do so. The ruling social order cannot be challenged safely, least of all by exposing its fraudulence at the ground of its premises. But nevertheless there is a systematic contradiction between the current global economic order and the principles of Adam Smith. It reveals the false identity of the system at another level. As we uncover at another level the oppositions between what is so far assumed as *the same*, we should continue to bear in mind that the mask of the not-self as the self at the cellular level of life-organization is the way the pathogenic pattern invades the host body until it is recognized as a rogue occupier.

Let us begin with the first basic axiom of market theory and practice, the principle that *the pursuit of one's private interests in the market promotes the public good.* Smith put it this way:

> Every individual is continually exerting himself to find out the most advantageous employment for whatever capital he can command. It is his own advantage, indeed, and not that of society, which he has in view. But the study of his own advantage naturally, or rather necessarily leads him to prefer that employment which is most advantageous to society ... By directing that industry in such a manner as its produce may be of the greatest value, he intends only his own gain, and in this, as in many other cases, he is led by an invisible hand to promote an end which was no part of his intention.[2]

A master principle of value and causality has been inferred from this canonical text, and it is the regulating first principle of the global system. No-one has put it more straightforwardly than Milton Friedman, the global system's first mullah. As he has famously said: '*The one and only responsibility of business is to make as much money for stockholders as possible – The doctrine of social responsibility [for business] is a fundamentally subversive doctrine in a free society.*'[3] In the global system today, all doubt of this ruling principle of 'the free market' and 'the free society' is, accordingly, repudiated as subversive resentment. But when Adam Smith first introduced his concept, it was not yet a narrowed-down dogma of money selfishness for corporate stockholders.

Smith supposed a set of *powerfully qualifying conditions* to his principle of coincidence for investor and market gain. The market and its investors were assumed to have the following characteristics before the principle could apply. Smith did not assert these conditions for this specific principle, which has been blown far out of proportion to the one paragraph of text in which he expressed it. The conditions which follow were far more central to his theory, and they qualify all that he says in the *Wealth of Nations*.

First, there could be *no private monopoly or oligopoly of production or distribution.* Smith deplored monopoly and oligopoly above all – the Royal Charters of his day – because they undermined the normative ideal of the market: independent producers and sellers competing to undersell one another in a condition of equal inability to manipulate market supply, demand or price.[4] What Smith above all deplored, however, has largely come to pass in another form. Monopoly and oligopoly is not instituted by royal proclamation, but by processes of government-subsidized transnational corporations which by 1993 controlled market sales of over 70 per cent of market durables, 60 per cent of cars and trucks, airlines and aerospace (the latter so subsidized by governments that they are dependent on it for most of their capital formation), almost 60 per cent of electronic components and steel, and nearly 50 per cent of oil, computers, mass media and chemicals.[5]

Second, because of the unavoidable inconvenience, cost and insecurity of investing in foreign countries, Smith took it for granted that *domestic capital would not migrate to foreign nations* so long as the investor was able to receive 'ordinary' or 'not a great deal less than the ordinary profits of stock'.[6] Again, what Smith assumed as a natural disposition to retain investment in the host society has turned out to be the opposite in the global market. Small margins of higher returns across the globe propel tidal capital outflows from societies overnight where it has been earned with no more identification or commitment to the home society than one not living in it, even if the investment elsewhere leaves the majority of the society plunged into poverty. Indeed, the 'fiduciary duty to stockholders to maximize returns' has been absolutized as sole and final authority, thereby *ruling out* the minimal loyalty to one's country that Smith took for granted.

Third, Smith specified that investment which is 'productive' or 'wealth creating', the only kind of investment which he supported, *must manufacture 'some particular subject or vendible commodity which lasts for some time at least after that labour is past'.*[7] Note that Smith confines his idea of a market commodity to what has some lasting value and is made by human labour. As we will see in more detail ahead, this condition too has been reversed by the global market system. Commodities have an average life of 42 days, and most investment is in financial vehicles with no labour input and with no production of material commodity at all.

Fourth, Smith explicitly stated that *'the sole use of money is to circulate consumable goods, provisions, materials and finished work'*, thereby ruling out stock, bond and currency speculations where money is invested and multiplied as an end in itself in decoupled, reiterating circuits that circulate nothing of use or productive work whatever.[8] In this movement from *money as a medium of exchange* between people's work, their means of production and their consumables to money-demand as the beginning, middle and end of delinked sequences of self-multiplication with no committed function to production or use lies the pathway of mutation to which we devote much of Chapter 3.

Fifth, Smith strongly stipulated that *capital must be reinvested in productive jobs, or else it is 'perverted from its proper destination'.* As Smith put this foundational principle in fuller context (my emphasis): 'No part of private capital ... can ever afterwards be employed to maintain any but productive hands, without an evident loss to the person who *perverts* it from its proper destination. *By diminishing the funds destined for the employment of productive labour,* [such an investor] necessarily diminishes, so far as it depends upon him, the value of the annual produce of the land and labour of the whole country, tending not only to beggar himself but to *impoverish the country.'*[9] There is no principle more emphatically specified by Adam Smith, and no principle more completely in contradiction with the global market's systemic disemployment of productive workers by downsizing, job-shedding, and public sector dismantling as an automated choice-path.

Sixth, *government taxation must fall on citizens 'in proportion to their respective abilities' [to pay], and on those to whom 'the benefit is confined'.*[10] Flat taxation, taxation of the majority to pay for government services serving only transnational investors and corporations, competitive lowering of corporate taxation across the world, off-shore tax havens for the rich, and increasing reduction of income taxes on the wealthy for equal consumption taxes on poorer income groups are all dominant tendencies of the global market, and all clearly invert Smith's principle of fair taxation.

Seventh, *'no two characters seem more inconsistent than those of trader and sovereign* – the mean rapacity, the monopolizing spirit of merchants and manufacturers neither are, nor ought to be, the rulers of mankind'.[11] Smith thus implicitly prescribes against what has today become normalized – the rule of society by 'business methods' of 'efficiency' and 'productivity' which mean no more than the reduction of all money inputs to interests other than business so as to maximize money outputs to business, a law of partiality and greed ruling society with no limit recognized to its spheres of extension and appropriation.

In the contemporary reality of the global system now re-engineering all societies to its prescriptions, we may conclude, not one of these conditions Smith specified or assumed as 'the free market' is adhered to by global system theory or practice. On the contrary, as we can see the more deeply we examine the matter, *every one of Smith's classical principles of the free market has been turned into its effective opposite.*

Smith's famed principle of the invisible hand whereby capital investors' private profit promotes the social good has been, in these ways, stripped of every condition and qualification upon which it was based, and perverted into its contrary. In its place has emerged an unconditional absolute – that money-profit maximization is a final good in itself, whether or not it meets any of the founding doctrine's original provisos of social and productive accountability.

Smith's very different market model remains, of course, a ritual template portrayed in economics departments and corporate ideology. But it is, in fact, a mask of its opposite, the global corporate system, which has as with the traditional free market appropriated for its self-description what it opposes in every principle. Only self-maximizing money gain decoupled from every condition that made it acceptable to Adam Smith remains, and it is, as we will see, a programme for the systemic depletion and destruction of the wealth of nations rather than its provider.

What these contradictions with the classical market paradigm together reveal is a *'perversion'*, to draw on Adam Smith's term again. But the structural anaplasia has remained fatefully concealed. The assumption that the mask of this system is its reality, that it *is* indeed a 'free market' system, is the basis upon which self-multiplying money sequences committed to no life-host infiltrate and spread across social bodies.

Unfreedoms Masked as Freedoms

When we relate the global system to the free market principles of both the historical free market and the classical free market of Adam Smith, we find that its properties are not expressions or extensions of either or both. We discover, on the contrary, that the global system calling itself *'the* market' or 'the global free market' or 'the global marketplace' is deeply opposed to the reproductive logic of both. Yet the collapse of meanings and regulating codes is not observed as the global market paradigm prescribes across the world how all societies must live if they are not to suffer 'shock treatments'.

Let us now advance from the traditional free market and Adam Smith's model to the *'neo-*classical' concept of 'the free market' as expressed by its most prominent institutional advocate, Friedrich A. Hayek. Let us see whether even here *the principles of freedom* it espouses are what they seem to be, or also mask their contrary underneath what they assert. The rhetoric of freedom which from the 'neo-classical' stage on is declared as the system's ultimate justification has a meaning that is much narrower than first appears. As we will now find, it has no referent except the freedom of those exercising money demand.[12]

This deep-structural movement in the meaning of 'freedom', from the apparent universality of benefit we find in the exchanges among equals in the real-life marketplace to increasingly narrow partiality and debasement of sense, is allowed to occur by a combination of *conceptualization decoupled from reality*, and the simultaneous *massive change of reality within the concept's permissive licence.* Consider a simplified example. If I say to you, 'We are both free to disagree, and that is our shared principle of freedom', you may understandably concur. As long as both of our lives are such as to enable us both to speak, this rhetorical principle may suffice. But if I own all that can broadcast and reproduce speech, and you work a 12-hour day with a family you can barely feed, then this principle of our mutual freedom which has no qualification of definition or circumstantial substance to keep its bearings can mislead us into thinking we *are in fact* both free when, in truth, you are silenced and I am mega-volumed by our actual conditions of life.

If then these conditions of life become patterned across time and social populations, and the owners of the conditions of public speech keep asserting 'we all have the right and freedom to speak', while very few in fact have the means or conditions to do so, then the idea of equal freedom to speak has been deformed to stand for what is in effect the opposite. This is the underlying pattern of all of the principles of 'freedom' declared by the global system. Always they disguise a reality beneath which is the reverse. The not-self masquerades as the self of 'free society', but the membership of the society do not yet recognize the not-self which has occupied their life-organization. They continue to think that it *is* 'a free market' or even 'a free world' they live within, without confronting their actual condition. Even radical opponents accept both the term and the referent 'free market' when what they live within is not, in concept or in reality.

Hayek's canonical definition of 'the free market' is one of the few that exists. As in other social value programmes, the nature of the ruling order is *assumed* to be good or free, with no defined idea of what these pro-predicates mean. This is how social value programmes evade accountability to reason or fact. Hayek, however, provides some explanation. He writes:

> Parties in the market should be free to buy and sell at any price at which they can find a partner to the transaction – free to produce, buy and sell anything that can be produced or sold at all.[13]

As Hayek's formula emphasizes, the principal argument for the 'free market' is the freedom it grants producers, buyers and sellers: that is, freedom from any external control in the production and exchange of goods between buyers and sellers who agree to the transaction. Because this freedom applies to the basic spheres of people's lives – what they eat, drink, live in, travel by, read, are entertained by and so on – it appears on the face of it to be the most important and fundamental realm of freedom there can be. This is the great selling point of the doctrine.

But let us examine the argument more carefully. As we do so, let us keep a question before us throughout. Are any of the following problems of the free market ever raised in the mass media, or in economics courses? If not, why not?

Freedom to Consume

Let us assume for the moment a premise that we will later find to be dubious in fact: namely, that agents transacting in the corporate global market are free to buy or *not* to buy goods for sale in this market. With the mutations of the market system which we will come to examine ahead, however, even this most basic freedom of the traditional and classical market paradigm is no longer clear. Here is one example of many emerging. A Massachusetts law instituting the choice of the government not to buy products such as oil from businesses collaborating with the military dictatorship of Burma (on the grounds that its agents were international criminals under law for systematic crimes against humanity) was prohibited by World Trade Organization decree. The Massachusetts government was charged by the European Union and Japan with violation of World Trade Organization regulation for 'discrimination' on the basis of its 'process of production'.[14]

Let us for the moment set aside this mutation of the transnational corporate market, and focus instead on the normal 'freedom of the consumer' conceived by Hayek. Here as well there are limitations to this freedom which are not exposed because its implications are not followed through. If the consumer does not have the money required to pay for the good he or she needs or desires (for example, food or shelter), then the consumer cannot buy it, and thus cannot have it or consume it. In the free market, therefore, those who do not have enough money to pay for what they require to live have no right to food or shelter or any other required means of life which is produced and sold. To call this freedom for such people – an increasing number of our society and the world approaching a third – is therefore false in a deep way. Freedom cannot exist for those with no means to act freely. To say people are free to consume bread when they have none and can buy none, as market 'libertarians' imply, is a symptom of the paradigm's disconnection from life fact.

It is worthwhile considering the profile of money-demand and life-need which has emerged within global market conditions. 1.3 billion people of the world have less than a dollar a day to live on, twenty per cent of all people will die before 40 on this account, and a rising 100 million people in the most developed countries live below the absolute poverty line.[15] To declare the 'freedom of the consumer' in such life conditions, and to declare it as the acme of the global system's freedom which 'uplifts all peoples of the world to prosperity', reveals a pattern of doctrine which no longer engages with the reproduction of human life.

The reason the received market paradigm cannot recognize such problems is that under its rules, need without effective demand (that is, the purchasing power of money) is not recognized. It has no value, and counts for nothing. Need with no money to back it has no reality or value for this regulating structure in any of its forms. This is why developed societies introduced government interventions in the market over generations prior to the global system to provide government assistance to those who were without the money, mostly children of underemployed parents, to have enough life-goods to survive.

But such provisions have been under systematic attack for a decade or more by global system architects and ideologues as 'unaffordable' and 'government interferences in the free market'. Across the world, 'structural readjustments' to reduce or to eliminate food subsidies and social programmes have been imposed by the International Monetary Fund and the World Bank as a condition for new loans to pay back compounding interest on foreign bankers' past loans to governments instituted against or without taxpayers' consent.

The 'freedom of the consumer' in the free market, in other words, is more limited in the freedom it grants than it appears to be. It is, in truth, only the freedom of those who have enough money to demand what they want. For all those who do not possess enough money to consume what they require to be healthy or alive, there is no freedom of the consumer, even to eat. It follows, then, that people without the money to purchase the goods they need – a quarter who are starving and a third who are unemployed – do not have under the rules of the global system the right to live.[16]

Since the right to live which they may have possessed by *non*-market programmes of public assistance has been at the same time attacked by the global system, then this system opposes in a more invasive way the right of the poor to live. It increasingly deprives them while those with more money-demand than they need become richer through tax reductions by this deprivation. At the same time, this paradigm of how societies must live with 'no alternative' continues to declare the 'freedom of the consumer' as its universal liberty, with governments themselves substituting the concept of 'consumers' for citizens in their representation of the common interest. Again here we observe a deepening derangement and autonomization of an economic logic delinking from the life-ground.

Freedom of the Seller

People who must work most of their active hours to earn enough money to live must normally sell their work or service to a corporation or other employer in exchange for wages and salaries. The sale of their work is all of the value they have to sell in the corporate market(as distinguished from the traditional free market where exchangers are independent producers). The employer, in turn, having paid for their work or service, has the right by his property in their labour to prescribe or command everything they do, and how they do it. It is, as the saying declares, 'company time'.

But to be told what to do and how to do it during most of your active waking hours cannot be meaningfully called 'freedom'. It is for this reason that Marx called such a condition of life 'wage slavery'. He meant that most of one's active life is owned by another.

The lot of sellers of their work or service who can find no buyer – the unemployed – is more constrained still. They are left by the free market with no value. It is because one must normally sell oneself to a buyer in the marketplace that Henry Thoreau referred to the marketplace as a 'site of humiliation'. One is required to present oneself as an object for sale, and may still find no-one with money who is willing to buy one's work or service.

These conditions in which the 'freedom of the seller' of labour is hedged in are made less free the more that there are many more sellers than there are buyers of labour, the more that corporate employers can hire lower-wage workers elsewhere and still sell their commodities in the home market, the more that there are no alternative means of employment or life-support in public service, the more that technological devices replace human work, and the more that unions, minimum-wage laws and other labour-protective institutions are reduced or abolished. All of these trends are established, and all increase in the global market.

In other words the 'freedom of the seller' in this system does *not apply to those who are by far the most numerous sellers in it,* those who must sell their work or service to stay alive. 'Freedom of the seller' applies only to those who are not required to sell themselves or their work to survive, a small minority of society. As the global system replaces previous economic forms, what is said to be a general freedom becomes, again, the increasing unfreedom of an increasing majority.[17]

Freedom of the Producer

Because those who must sell their work or service to live must normally obey the orders of their employer most of their active hours, they do not have freedom as producers. Who, then, *is* free as a producer in the global system? Artists of all kinds have a special freedom of independence in their work. But they must create what buyers with enough money will purchase and, therefore, must shape their products so as to attract and not to offend those with sufficient money demand beyond need to buy. Their freedom as producers is thus limited to a small percentage of society who are able *and* willing to pay for their artistic creations.

The still smaller minority who have enough capital to employ others rather than work as employees also have more freedom than most, including their employees. But in the global system even they are compelled by its laws to invest only in economic activities that will net them money profit at the end of the production and exchange cycle. This means that they must relate to other people who work for them only as a means to make profit for themselves and their shareholders. This is the explicit morality of the global market, and it is called 'fiduciary duty to stockholders', an obligation which is prescribed in the charters of corporations and the terms of financial managers' contracts. They cannot, therefore, be concerned about the employment or conditions of their workers, about maintaining the host society's jobs or standards of life, or about anything but maximizing money profits for their firm or investors. If they act otherwise, they are being *unjust by this paradigm's rules.*

Those who produce value for others without having to sell what they make or do for someone else's profit, are, in contrast, independent as producers. Professionals of various kinds – doctors and professors, for example – are in this way free or self-governing in their work lives. Bear in mind that the meaning of freedom is *self-governing*, because this too is a meaning which has been lost in the inverted logic of the global system. But professionals remain free only because, and to the extent that, what they do for others is *not* for sale in a borderless market at a profit for corporate shareholders. For if they are, as doctors increasingly are in the US, in 'health maintenance organizations' where every diagnosis, finding and treatment is time- and cost-prescribed by corporate financial departments, then they are not free, but mere functions in externally prescribed money-sequence operations. Their independent professional judgement and commitment to the health of their patients as overriding is displaced by extrinsic corporate financial formulae whose regulating code is to maximize money returns.

We are thus constrained to face the opposite conclusion of what corporate market advocates claim. People are only free in their work when they are *not* bound by its rules of 'freedom'.

Freedom from Government Interference

Perhaps the strongest conviction of true believers in the global market programme is that its 'open competition ensures freedom from government interference'. In the context of the 'command economies' of past social orders, this argument had some meaning by contrast. But these conditions of contrast no longer exist, and so no longer can provide the basis of conviction. Let us then examine this assertion free of diversion to alien social orders.

Proponents of the global system fail to acknowledge that its productions and distributions continuously require very expensive government interventions to provide round-the-clock protection and services for its operations and for its private investors of money capital. These very costly government assistances to protect and serve private-profit seekers include domestic police forces guarding both foreign and domestic assets and exchanges, armed forces to protect private investments across home borders, and government diplomatic offices and personnel to continuously monitor, promote, and protect private business interests in other states. This global market system *is* certainly free in the sense of free of cost for transnational corporations. But it is not free, but a cost burden without returns, for those within host societies who must shoulder the tax burdens to pay for what they do not profit from.

The 'global free market' for transnational corporations also requires continuous government intervention to provide serviced roads and highways to transport privately owned and sold commodities to production and exchange sites, as well as school training and natural resources at little or no cost to supply them with whatever human and resource capital they require to produce the commodities they sell.[18] All of these protections, services and goods are provided by local governments supported by local citizens, nearly all of whom receive no revenues in return from these publicly subsidized transnational corporate activities. The idea of the global market being 'free of government' is, again, so contrary to fact as to be fantastic to anyone not programmed by its incantations.

Global system proponents really mean something that is never distinguished, and is the opposite in moral sense. They mean 'freedom from government' *that is not necessary or profitable to transnational corporate profits.* That is why they never talk about reducing government interventions that benefit these interests (for example, more police, weapons, prisons, roads, free employee training or public resource giveaways), but only demand reductions of government interventions that do not directly benefit private corporations, but people's lives (for example, universal social security and environmental regulations). That this very basic distinction is never made in the global market is a further symptom of the masking of its selection against public life protection and for private corporate growth from public funds.

At the same time, government tax loop-holes, deferments and subsidies to corporate investment sequences and their stockholders are increasingly demanded 'to compete in the global market', although they rapidly escalate the very government deficits these corporate agents attack.[19]

So it is not 'government interventions' or 'costly government programmes' that these 'free market' agents in fact deplore, but only those government interventions and programmes that do not directly subsidize private corporations. We are obliged to conclude that the only sense of 'free' which applies here is redistributions to corporate accounts of public revenues free of charge to corporations, which is, once again, the opposite of what is claimed.

But there is another side to government intervention in the corporate market economy. Under pressures of democratic accountability, governments have *also* over the last century come to serve the life interests of society as a whole with revenues not directed to subsidize and serve the private money sequences of corporations and their shareholders. It is always *these* functions which corporations and their political representatives seek to axe as 'interferences in the free market'. But if we assemble these functions as a whole, and consider their common nature, we discover that they constitute an evolving pattern of social life that defines the proper vocation of government – *to protect and enable the lives of its citizens*. Thus by a long and painful process of democratic movement, elected governments in the developed world have introduced legislation to limit the hours of the working day and week; to establish safety standards and environmental regulations for factories and businesses; to permit employees to organize in workers' unions; to provide unemployment insurance and income security for those without jobs; to institute programmes of health care available to all independent of ability to pay; to provide public education for everyone and university education to the qualified at a fraction of cost; and to construct publicly accessible transit systems, parks and cultural centres free of cost or at below-cost prices.

Go over this list of foundational life-functions for people, and consider whether even one of these basic social goods can be provided without government intervention. Go over it again to see if even one has not been attacked in the past and the present by corporate lobbies, newspapers and political organs. It is when we see the matter whole in this way that we begin to discern a sinister, underlying pattern. The corporate system is structured to attack the shared base of people's lives as a competitor against its programme of profitable control of all of societies' means of life.

However much they have been defamed as 'big government spending', all of these 'government interferences in the free market' have been achieved through public democratic process. None has ever been, or can be, provided by a for-profit system. All require government enforcement and taxation. They are evolving constituents of an age-old process of development which we will later analyse as 'the civil commons'. But each and all have been historically opposed by corporate business, in particular by transnational corporations, often homicidally (for example, by killing worker and community organizers in the 1930s US or 1980s

Central America). Furthermore, not one transnational trade or investment agreement protects or recognizes as binding one of these social infra-structures which protect and enable the lives of society's members. 'Freedom from government interference' under transnational corporate regulation, then, entails partial or entire *loss* of all of these freedoms for citizens to assured access to life goods.

In this light, we need to ask what is the ultimate meaning of the current intense campaign to 'reduce government regulations', 'privatize' public-sector goods, and 'cut social programmes'. Global market proponents argue that 'we can no longer afford' these high standards and social goods. But if this system is progressively more efficient and productive, as its essential legitimating argument claims, why must people be increasingly less free and secure the more efficient and productive it becomes? Why must they become so under its rules while transnational corporations, which are not alive, become ever freer and more secure at the same time? We see in these questions the hidden ultimate conflict, perhaps to the death, which has emerged between what protects and enables life, on the one hand, and what invades it on the other.

Lower Costs

The next argument implied by Hayek's canonical formulation for what is conceived as 'the free market' is that this system reduces the costs of production and distribution. The argument here is that in this system producers and sellers must compete to produce and sell their goods at the lowest price. In this way, the market ensures lower costs, and therefore lower prices for consumers. This is the common basis of the *efficiency argument* which has held sway since Adam Smith. Within limits of a life-protective framework effectively regulating and contextualizing such a system, this argument for reducing costs of production and sale is cogent and supported by much evidence. But then this market is not at all like the global system, which has no such framework, or even one constituent of it in place.

Delinked from accountability to host societies, as the borderless global system is, its agents seek to lower costs for corporations. This premise is generally accepted, but again its implications are not considered. For if costs go down for corporations while government infrastructures, security expenditures, debt payments and so on continue, then the costs must be borne instead by local citizenries and environments.

At the same time, home markets and resources are thrown open to transnational corporations with no conditions attached. All 'performance requirements' of job maintenance and creation, technology transfer, resource sustainability, or profit reinvestment are under transnational trade decree explicitly prohibited. Moreover, as we have just seen, transnational trade regimes like the WTO rule out 'discrimination' by host societies against the 'process' of production of commodities allowed into domestic markets free of charge. Released in this way from obligations to life-security or host societies, transnational corporations can lower their costs of production by disinvesting in them overnight and relocating for lower costs in places where there are no pollution controls, no minimum wages, no workers' benefits, no health and safety standards, and no government taxes to pay for the care and support of the sick and unemployed.

Armed with the new right to sell their products back to host societies, they can bleed both producing and buying populations at the same time. That is why under new international 'free trade' agreements private corporations and businesses have increasingly demanded that governments deregulate and lower taxes so that they are not obliged to pay the costs of sustaining the life of host-societies or their environments. This demand for lower costs for transnational corporations achieves its nadir in 'free trade zones' like the Maquiladora Zone on the border between Mexico and the United States. Here wages are a small fraction of what they are in Canada and the US, effective pollution controls are non-existent and taxes for public health and education have been abolished. With the unconditional right under this system to export and sell free of obligation the low-cost products back to Canadian and US markets, transnational corporations indeed 'lower costs' for themselves, but sap and destroy communities, environments and living conditions while doing so. They can avoid the costs of protecting people and the environment in their low-cost operations, while 'improving their profits for stockholders'.

The efficiency that exists here is the lower ratio of costs to revenues for transnational corporations. This once more is accepted as rational and good. But its implication is again not seen, that it *excludes costs to life.* On the life scale, this system is very inefficient. How monstrously inefficient we will discover as this diagnosis deepens.

Unemployment and loss of livelihood to people is a further *benefit* to transnational operations and businesses in general because it lowers the price of labour, and, therefore, the revenues that private employers are required to pay out to workers. With automated and electronic processes increasingly replacing workers of all kinds, and with the new 'free trade' right of private investment capital to move production to the lowest-wage areas, the price of labour therefore has no floor. Life's requirements do not figure in the paradigm. As we have seen in even Europe, whose countries are the most life-protected in the world by social legislation, unemployment rates and insecure life conditions have skyrocketed the more the global market system has been implemented – over 50 million people out of work and rising at a rate of two million a year in the late 1990s.

What is a disaster for *people's lives*, ratcheting-down their incomes or loss of their livelihoods, is a *monetary gain* for corporate investors. There is even less need to worry about workers' rebellions or uprisings as unemployment grows and wages and salaries drop. All that is required is to relocate investment to another region of the world where people compete to work for much less and in hazardous working conditions. There are always vast supplies of 'free' labour available for hire in other societies, and government-assisted mobility for instant cost-free departure if there are uprisings. That is why more developed societies are warned that they 'must adapt to the harsh new reality of the world market', and that 'shock treatments' are necessary for societies who do not adjust.

Low-cost 'free trade zones' across the world which do not have independent unions or human rights protections to raise the cost of labour have according to global market doctrine a *comparative advantage* in this condition, which is code for the fact that corporations can relocate to them to minimize their costs. The comparative advantage does not, in fact, rebound to the home country in this 'race to the bottom' as it has come to be called.[20] This is because the cost advantage is not reaped by the home country, but by the cost-reducing corporation which has no commitment to its social hosts, but solely to its bottom line wherever it can be most maximized.

It is only by government or other intervention that societies can prevent their standards of life falling to the lowest common denominator, which itself can keep falling to ever lower levels of poverty and pollution for the bottom half. But such minimum standards are protected in no free trade agreement, with the exception of the European Union. But the EU is under increasing pressure to reduce and remove these 'inefficiently costly barriers to continued investment'. The result is mounting European unemployment the longer that no-standard 'free trade' continues through and outside its borders. Life-protective standards are a liability in the global corporate system. There are thousands of pages of rules to protect corporate and business rights, over 20,000 pages of them in the most recent General Agreement on Tariffs and Trade (GATT), but no rules protect human rights or the quality of the environment.

A further major way of reducing costs in the free market is by 'economies of scale' where the greater the investment and purchasing power, the capital infrastructure of labour-saving machinery, the division of labour and specialization, the volume of goods produced, and the international linkages of production and distribution, the cheaper the per-unit costs of the commodities produced and sold. Since transnational corporations have the greatest economies of scale, they are best able to reduce their costs of production. Consequently, small producers and small businesses without these economies of scale – and without hidden government subsidies – may be unable to compete in the price of their goods. It was for this reason, for example, that the small Chiapas producers of corn in southern Mexico began a rebellion against 'the death sentence of NAFTA' on the day of its inception in January 1994.

At the same time, economies of large scale make for more and more uniformity of methods and goods – from monocultural farming and seeds to mass homogeneity of media products and books. Diversity raises prices. Vandana Shiva has called the outcome of this global market homogenization a 'monoculture of the mind'. With ever fewer multinational media conglomerates in the global free market monopolizing control of the production and distribution of television programmes, film, magazines, newspapers and even textbooks and learned journals, this 'monoculture of the mind' extends into the control of people's brain circuits themselves. This saves the costs of having to articulate products that enlist the thought of their consumers. The concept of 'dumbing down' has thus arisen as a common phrase to signify the loss of mental life. But such signifiers have signifieds, and so are seldom repeated in the media or academic print.

But are the lower costs for corporate bodies which proceed from these competitive advantages and economies of scale really lower costs for societies? What about increased poverty, pollution, unemployment, ill-health and environmental degradation which follow from such cost reduction methods? Or what of the loss of cultural diversity and autonomy of thought, more motor noise, and commercial occupation of life-space?

None of these negative consequences of the global system compute to its paradigm. Only what costs money computes. If such life reductions are observed and not denied, they are '*externalities*'. But it is difficult to think, short of armed invasion, of more important and drastic costs to the life of society's membership. While consumer goods may become marginally less expensive, though this is by no means assured with increasingly oligopolist conditions in the global market with no international anti-trust regulation,[21] the basic goods of life such as the air we breathe, the sun we move in, the social space around us and the security of children's futures deteriorate.

On closer examination, in short, we see that the argument for *lower costs* in the global market, its ultimate argument of efficiency, is the opposite of the truth from the perspective of life. If we review what this paradigm's concept of costs exclude, we find that there is a unifying principle. Life loss itself has no value. In truth, the destruction of life and life goods nets a sinister advantage to the global market's investment growth. This is because each good lost in the community or nature is at the same time a new opportunity for the manufacture of priced commodities to substitute for it – from pharmaceuticals to treat people's loss of peace of mind to travel industries to substitute for dead local environments.

The Free Market as Democracy

The most themal political argument for the global market system is the repeated generalization that it 'promotes democracy'. So standard is this view that heads of state in the developed world deploy it on a routine basis to answer criticism that they are expanding investment and trade, including the sale of lethal armaments, to gross violators of human rights and genocidal dictatorships. Heads of state reply that 'constructive engagement through building market ties will do far more good for democratic development than human rights criticism', or that 'international market relationships will seed democracy in the long term', or some variation on this assertion of a causal link between global market extension and increase of local democratic progress in other societies. It is hardly an exaggeration to say that this justification is cited by some government leader on a daily basis across the world.

The argument is rarely challenged. Rather, more pressing concerns are urged such as the justice or wisdom of appeasing mass murderers to boost corporate trade. But what of the democracy argument itself? Regrettably, there is in fact no evidence to substantiate the democracy linkage to increased foreign investment and trade. On the contrary, there is overwhelming evidence to refute it. For example, when societies like Guatemala, Iran, Indonesia, Chile, Mozambique, Angola, and Nicaragua were returned to 'the free market fold' by military coups or civil wars plotted and financed by the military and the CIA of the world's leading corporate state between 1954 and 1988, which *one* of these societies experienced a growth of democracy afterwards?

Consider the case of Nicaragua, the most recent beneficiary of democratization by 'the free market'. Before invasion, it was claimed by the US government to be a 'totalitarian dictatorship', 'a Soviet beach-head for Marxist dictatorship', 'a clear and present danger to the security of the United States', and so forth. The remedy to 'democratize society' here, as elsewhere, was proclaimed with certitude to be 'the institution of free market relationships'. What follows is a brief third-party report of the outcome in terms of increased democracy after US-armed and financed 'freedom fighters' succeeded in marketizing Nicaragua.

> Popular organizations in Nicaragua are struggling to find solutions to their worsening economic and social situation. Poverty has increased dramatically, and now affects over 70% of the population. Unemployment stands at 60%, while 80% of children do not finish primary school, and deaths from malnutrition have skyrocketed. Hunger, practically unknown throughout the 1980s is widespread.[22]

As with other conversions to foreign corporate rule by armed-force intervention to advance the cause of free market and democracy, Nicaragua was in fact being punished for offering a socioeconomic alternative to foreign corporate occupation. Its apparent market crime was to repatriate resource and market control from foreign corporate control, however insignificant in this case. But its real crime was to work better by doing so in the full view of other countries.

This is not to deny that a real free market can, in fact, 'promote democracy'. The real free market liberated both pre-corporate English villagers and post-Mao country-dwellers from the absolutist control of production and distribution by feudal and party autocracies. Adam Smith's market paradigm was later directed against the royal monopolies and self-serving business lobbies of his day which, as we have seen, he thought capable of any 'mean rapacity' and 'with an interest to deceive'. But neither of these classical structures of the free market has anything in common with the global corporate system. As we will see, the evidence is overwhelming that the global corporate market works systematically to *de*-democratize society as its necessity for continued growth and expansion.

The agents of the global system do not say this directly, of course, even though suspicion of democracy is strongly voiced in private. But in the arena of action, transnational corporations seek singly and together as a law of their self-regulated being to ensure a unifying and disguised goal: *to open all domestic markets, natural resources, built infrastructures and labour pools of all societies of the world to foreign transnational control without the barrier of self-determining governments and peoples in the way.* We will observe at the end of this chapter this underlying programme to de-democratise society in its pure form in the Multilateral Agreement for Investment secretly planned for the 29 developed countries of the OECD by the World Trade Organization.

In this wider programme of social management, societies must compete harder to be effective means of transnational investment, production and distribution, and not obstruct any 'free flow of capital and goods' by 'protectionist' or other obstacles, of which effective democracy is the most obdurate. That is why the Trilateral Commission founded in 1973 and composed of the world's leading corporate CEOs, past and future US Presidents and Harvard academics, frankly announced in a task-force paper entitled 'The Crisis of Democracy' prior to its initiation of the US–Canada 'Free Trade Agreement', that there was an '*excess* of democracy' in the Western world. It argued that what was needed was the 'apathy and non-involvement' of a 'governable' democracy, and more recognition of 'the inescapable attributes of government' – 'the legitimacy of hierarchy, coercion, discipline, secrecy and deception'.[23]

The same global market mind-set argued the case more explicitly 20 years later. The research voice of transnational business in Canada, the Fraser Institute, publicly asserted in defence of more 'free trade' that 'a trade deal simply limits the extent to which a government can respond to its citizens'.[24]

It is worth returning here to the market theory's founder, Adam Smith, on the connection between democracy and the market. Smith never presumed to assert the non-sequitur claim that the free market promoted democracy. He certainly exceeded the democratic commitment of the current global system in his foundational opposition to oligoply-controlled markets and commitment to investment in productive labour and goods. But he openly regarded 'the race of workers' as 'inferior', and asserted that the lives of their children were properly left without food when the supply of labour exceeded demand.[25]

The causal relation now declared between the market and democracy is not to be found in Adam Smith or any other economist until the advertising techniques of the 'new global market'. These function as the weavers of a mask for a programme of reproduction and spread which is precisely not accountable to any democratic interest. For actual democracy is the greatest possible danger to a borderless oligopolist regime which seeks unconditional or 'free' access to every society's local markets, resources and jobs. No society with democratic accountability of its leadership would, or has, ever given away all its bases of wealth free of cost or performance requirement as these transnational regimes prescribe.

Adam Smith *did* believe that workers were likely to be less impoverished if there were a free market, and reducing the poverty of the *demos* is certainly a basic democratic concern. Smith's free market model, however, rules out the oligopolist global market from qualifying *as* a 'free market' because it does not satisfy his condition that no producer or seller in a free market is able to affect the supply or demand of the good being sold.

Observe here as well that it is not only the increasingly oligopolist control of *supply* in the global market that undercuts the 'free market' condition its agents claim for democratic development. The global market's transnational system also controls *demand* – by the pervasive operant conditioning of buyers by its dominant corporations not available to other sellers, by financial and lobby steering of government policy and purchases (for example, of military security systems and armaments build-ups), and by excluding alternative goods from public access (for example, non-auto systems of urban transit, as in the case of US cities).

The founder of the classical free market paradigm also made an important observation about the *intrinsic nature* of corporations (or 'joint stock companies' as they were then called) which goes to the heart of the contradiction between democratic rule and rule by oligopolist corporations. Adam Smith said that the corporation is fit solely for '*uniformity of method ... of little or no variation*'.[26]

It is not easy to think of a more profoundly anti-democratic character than uniformity of prescription ruling out diversity. But this is how Smith himself characterized the nature of corporations. Presciently, the reason he thought corporations good only for homogeneous tasks was that he observed them to be effective solely at the routine, non-productive work of *financial accounting* – the very operation, through debt-financing, from which the major transnational corporations now extract most of their profits. As we will see, it is by the isolation and autonomization of these corporate money sequences that the global market has mutated to pathological forms of profit of which Adam Smith never conceived.

It is in this intrinsic nature of corporations that we find the core of their anti-democratic character. They are top-down bureaucracies whose stock-owning CEOs are vastly richer than the direct producers of the corporation, and wield absolute power over the livelihoods of thousands of hierarchically organized subordinates. They are only accountable to boards of directors and stockholders who are not elected, and no-one in these artificial bodies represents under law any interest beyond the self-maximization of the money-demand value of the corporation and themselves. In fact, their liability for damages to their social hosts or to other life interests of any kind are excluded by their limited-liability structure under law. The accountability here to shareholders may seem itself democratic, but shareholders vote by shares owned, and well under 10 per cent of any population has enough shares to purchase more than beer supplies by their dividends.

In short, the global market corporation is as anti-democratic an institution as exists next to the military bootcamp. Together its representative agents form what Plato or Aristotle would have called the extreme of plutocracy, a plutocracy across national borders which finances and advises political representatives and parties in all continents to represent transnational corporate positions as overriding in international affairs such as trade treaties, and in domestic affairs such as taxes. Lest there be any doubt about this transnational plutocracy's existence, we need to bear in mind that 98 per cent of all foreign direct investment for which governments compete as a first priority is by transnational corporations, and that over 80 per cent of this foreign investment is for takeover of domestic firms.[27] We need also to bear in mind that over 80 per cent of all world trade is controlled by the same transnational corporations, and that over 80 per cent of all land cultivated for export is similarly controlled.[28]

If we look at the matter from the individual standpoint, we might say that the democracy of the corporate market consists – as its advocates sometimes declare – *in dollars as votes*. According to United States Congressional statistics, the top 1 per cent of the population controls more dollar votes of private wealth than the bottom 90 per cent of the society.[29] This is a democracy, then, where 1 per cent have more voting power than 90 per cent.

Democracies are constrained to remain within the limits of this domestic and transnational control of humanity's means of existence, or face the risk of being singled out for 'market punishment'. As eminent economist Peter Drucker puts it with approval: 'Every country and every society must learn that the first question is not is this measure desirable, but what will be the impact on the country's competitive position in the world economy?'[30] Deconstructed, this sentence means, 'Democracy or other desirable states of affairs do not rank. What ranks is reducing costs and increasing revenues for corporations.'

All that can remain as democracy within such limits is the shell of democracy. This shell is worth examining in the light. *As long as democracy is confined to periodic elections of parties and politicians who never conflict with or challenge the control of the built, natural, market and human wealth of domestic economies by transnational corporations*, then this democracy will remain within this range of control.

The *de*-democratization of society is further managed on the level of public communications by corporate media chains whose publicity favours or discredits parties and candidates for all relevant public offices. The general unfreedom of the media in such conditions can be formulated in a straightforward, predictive principle: Nothing will be reproduced in these media which exposes or argues against private corporations' increasing control of domestic societies' means of life. The operations of selection and exclusion whereby this and other 'filterings' of democratic communication occur was set out at the end of Chapter 1.[31]

There are as well other, complementary methods for securing this control of democracy as a shell, especially in 'budding democracies' or 'societies seeking the democratic path'. These include low-intensity warfare, selective assassination, trade embargoes, military invasions, international propaganda wars and so on against local leaders and populations who resist the appropriation of their markets and natural resources by transnational corporations which require these resources of local life-hosts for their continued growth.

A free election cannot really exist in these conditions. If the parties, politicians and agenda of discussion are all hedged in by the same principle of control, and if whatever does not comply with it is silenced, then this too reduces democracy in ways that the Trilateral Commission and the Fraser Institute have recommended. We can let our own observation confirm or disconfirm the pattern described here. In what recent election across the world has critical exposure or debate of this corporate control of society's life been featured once in the mass media of any 'market democracy'?

In light of this underlying pattern, a general conclusion follows which is repressed from view. Ever more 'deregulation', 'privatization' and 'public sector cutbacks' to 'develop the free market' can only be called a move towards 'more democracy' from a programme of thought that inverts reality into its opposite. The more that public goods and regulations accountable to electorates and open to public criticism are transferred to 'the private sector', the more that democratic accountability is in fact abolished, and the more that control is transferred to those with accountability to no goal but the money profits of corporate investors.

In complement to this underlying general pattern which is not observed from the standpoint of the global market paradigm, a further general principle of inverse relation holds that is not recognized. The more unequal the possession of wealth is, the more people there are without the money to buy what they need, the more that unpriced goods of the community and nature are expropriated or destroyed, the more *un*freedom and *lack* of democracy there in fact are.

But this recoding of the traditional and classical market paradigm to systematic dispossession of the *demos* while proclaiming it 'democracy' was not all at once or unplanned.

The Global System's Covert War

In recent years, globe-girding information technologies and supranational trade-and-investment regimes accountable to no public authority have allowed transnational corporations and finance capital to break previous life-connections with or required commitments to their social hosts. Industrial and service workers of all kinds can now be displaced not only by workers elsewhere willing to work more cheaply, but – the other blade of the pincers – by new labour-replacing, computer-driven systems of production and communication. With no democratic input or consent required, corporations and investment capital can cancel or move their operations across the world with the speed of an electronic signal. The vast majority of the planet's people have in this way been radically disempowered, and the global corporate system, billed under the salable category of 'free trade', has in effect brought us to the age of disposable humanity.

It is predictable from this re-engineered life-condition that there will be maddened reactions among peoples who have been stripped of their life-security but do not know who to blame except people from other cultures among or around them. Thus ethnocentric conflicts and upheavals have been on the rise across the world since the world restructuring began. But the cause remains unspeakable in the corporate press which presents the effects of the restructuring as terrible reminders of our human nature. That the madness is the desperate reaction of dispossessed peoples to the land clearances, loss of livelihoods, stripping of social sectors, and the increasingly rootless command posts of international financial institutions and other corporations is not an hypothesis that will be allowed a public view, however well documented it may be.[32]

No problem which the global market paradigm can observe is exposed by these social tumours. On the contrary, many transnationally operating corporate bodies are bequeathed more international outlets for money-sequencing which such social crises provide: manufacturing and marketing more arms for dictatorships and combatants; selling more narcotic stimulants and violence-entertainment to all; producing and selling phar-maceuticals to the environmentally afflicted who are able to afford them; mass-marketing security devices and substitutes in many forms; and, in lawlike pattern that all can see but no government seeks to interfere with, making the rich fabulously richer in money-demand accumulation, fractioning the rations of the poor, and recreating the environment as more uniform and lifeless. But effects remain disconnected from cause.

Under these circumstances and in proportion to the movement in these directions, this global regime becomes a systemic threat to the life-ground itself. There is no need to be obscure about the basis for value judgement here. *The more a regime of social regulation increases/decreases its members' access to the produced and natural goods they need to live, the better/worse it is as a regime of social regulation.*

There is doubtless the justification for a world-wide workers' revolution against such a regime, and the restructuring of society's economic and political power so that it is democratically controlled to serve its direct producers. But this is a solution that has been difficult to make work. A more modest solution is to institute a rule-based international economy where the rules do not, as now, merely protect the interests of corporate investors turning their money inputs into maximally more money outputs in greater volumes, velocities and compounding returns. Minimum standards to protect workers' wages, health and safety, to safeguard the environment against pollution and degradation, and to ensure vital life goods for all as a basic contract of civil society was between 1945 and the mid-1970s, in fact, a rapidly evolving framework which inhibited the causes and effects of a corporate market system committed to an opposed goal.

But these protections of the reproduction and growth of people's lives rather than the money of money investors did not sit well with many agents of capital sequences. There was a long propensity to disregard all life requirements built into these sequences themselves. Thus their agents, who failed to recocognize their derivative role as these sequences' temporary functions, militantly opposed over centuries the introduction of maximum work hours, reduction of child labour, workplace safety, minimum wages, labour unions, public health-care, unemployment insurance, old-age pensions and social security support-systems. These protections of the members of society were always deemed 'too costly', 'unworkable', 'against private initiative', or – in the last 150 years – 'communist'.

But the reforms nevertheless came to pass in many jurisdictions through the mass struggle and support of social populations forming themselves as what will be later analysed as 'the civil commons', with waged workers at the fore in collective agencies representing shared life needs. As these very social infrastructures of life-protective standards and social programmes have been attacked or dismantled by the global market system in recent years, a clear message has increasingly emerged. The requirements of life fabrics and the corporate market system are not the same, and the latter is in fact programmed to attack any system which provides unpriced life-goods. Can one think of an exception to this fateful underlying fact?

Corporate money sequences in this condition are for the first time in history tied to no community of people. They can leave any society in which effective laws to protect human rights or the environment cost more than regions of investment elsewhere. Governments not only promote the corporate trade treaties permitting this transnational unaccountability to social hosts, but compete against one another to lower the costs of uncommitted corporations. Comparative advantage thus moves from producing goods more efficiently in classical free market terms of multiple local producers in fair competition, to dominant transnational corporations avoiding all standards which protect the lives of people and environments to reduce their costs across borders.

A world *coup d'etat*, one might say, has occurred, and still unfolds without social populations yet awakened to it. This is what we will analyse in the next chapter as an immune disorder at the social level of life-organization. Its full implications are not yet recognized even by those who see its political nature. The new system can be defined simply in the first instance. International money capital seeking to become maximally more has been accorded well-defined and overriding transnational rights to rule the world's production and distribution, uncontrolled by any limit of social, individual or environmental life-host. Tens of thousands of pages of secretly negotiated regulations bind societies and legislatures to a transnational order making illegal whatever life claim 'does not honour trade obligations'. Few people have any idea of what has been signed. Fewer still have read a page of them.[33]

There are three unexposed assumptions of this transnational regime which underlie all of its codes and articles, and they together reveal an abnormal pattern of reproductive sequence and growth.

The first is that its corporate agents assume the unconditional right to enter and access other societies' markets across regional and national boundaries cost-free, with no prior or minimum obligation to pay any of the direct or indirect costs of building, maintaining or developing any of the conditions of these markets' existence. All that is required is that corporate agents agree among themselves through mechanisms of inter-government co-ordination to a system of self-protective rules called 'free trade agreements' not infringing *each others'* rights to this access.

Since market access to what is owned and exchanged in another society has in fact enormous costs for that society which are borne by its citizens' past, present and future taxes and government deficits, this assumption is basic. The benefits of these tax-supported goods are to be received cost-free as entering corporations buy and sell whatever they choose in other societies' markets without having to pay for their use of the market infra-structures themselves. Their commodities are, furthermore, produced elsewhere, replace jobs in the host societies, and are obliged to provide no jobs in the markets to which they sell. The home society provides armed-force and police protection across its territory, developed laws to protect its agents and goods, publicly paid-for roads, subsidized utilities, sewage systems, water supplies, and many other domestically financed and highly expensive protections and infrastructure. To these expenses are added still further major public costs of protecting foreign-owned corporations' patents (for example, in medicines) and enforcing intellectual property rights (for example, over farmers' seeds and authors' texts, even against their own growers and writers in the host societies).

Since foreign corporations and domestic corporations seek to lower taxes towards zero, and simultaneously seek subsidies and incentives to make themselves net tax recipients, their pattern of behaviour symptomizes an underlying programme which rejects any obligation to pay the costs of the publicly financed supports and services they use, and demands more from their social hosts as far as can be extracted. Current trade regimes grant this free-rider status to all non-domestic corporations within the international territories covered by them, and increasingly to domestic corporations as well by reductions, exemptions and subsidies to keep them, in turn, from investing elsewhere under the same terms.

All private corporations are served by this free-rider status, but no social host is. All corporations are served as well by competitively falling tax-rates, but no social host is. This is why there is unanimous support by transnational and other corporate bodies for these transnational trade terms. As free-riders on public purses and deficits, it is in their monetary self-interest to institute these regimes everywhere. To pay for this underlying programme of competitive subsidization of corporations, societies must correspondingly reduce their social spending for public needs. In this way a spiral of bankrupting public sectors to subsidize private corporations is set into systemic motion with no limit to its further advance.

Since private corporations are the first to insist that there is 'no free lunch' for others, their assumption of the right to ever more public subsidization of their own operations – including the public funding of negotiation and implementation of these overriding trade regimes themselves – disguises an unexamined parasitic relation to host societies, which is then projected onto the poor to abolish social assistance to them as bleeding society with their demands.

The second hidden assumption of transnational corporations in the global system is that damages and losses to them are to be contrived, recognized and regulated in detail by international trade regulations, but damages and losses to workers, governments, publicly owned resources, environments, communities and any other economic sectors are not to be recognized or regulated at all.

There are two levels of incoherence at work here. The first is that private corporate interests are to be protected in every respect by transnational regulation, but no *other* interest is to be so safeguarded. The second is less obvious. It is that the public interest which governments are constructed to represent is 'too costly'. In contrast, the private interests governments are intended to regulate, but not subsidize, are not selected for cost reduction.

The third and most pernicious assumption of the transnational programme is that the damages and losses inflicted by corporate bodies on their social and environmental life-hosts are not to be paid for by the corporate agents who inflict them. They are to be borne by their victims and host societies as 'hard adjustments to the global market'. Corporate persons individually and collectively thereby assume immunity from and non-liability for the harms they do to others by the operations of their mutually protective agreements. They thereby assume in corollary that only those who are not responsible for these costs and damages are to bear and to pay for them, however this may further depredate their financial capacities to survive or develop as social or individual life-forms. [34]

In any other context, we would call this set of assumptions psychopathic. Nonetheless they are now assumed as givens within the global system as its transnational corporate vehicles occupy one civil and ecological life-fabric after another. Environmental resources tens-of-millions of years old may be polluted, degraded and exhausted by private corporate exploitation across the globe with no requirement at all to pay for the damages *or* their prevention. Working people and communities across the globe may be deprived of their livelihoods, security and ancestral homes by rootless corporations entering their societies, extracting what is required for further money-sequence growth, and then abandoning them for another site of the same money-sequence growth. None of this process is recognized as a problem by the global market paradigm, or by governments which exhort their populations to 'compete harder'. It is in this way a different sort of order than witnessed before. It is *structured* with nodal assistance by governments to exploit, depredate and leave life-hosts across all national borders so as to turn what is appropriated into more money returns for non-living growth cycles.

The world's multiplying Free Trade Zones (for example, the Maquiladora zones on the border of Mexico and the US) are demonstration sites for the pure expression of this system's 'freedom'. Such zones grant the transnational corporate bodies they host the freedom not to pay taxes, not to re-invest capital, not to allow workers unions, not to be subject to national pollution laws, not to pay minimum wages, not to have maximum work days or weeks, not to obey established health occupational safety laws and not, in general, to be bound by any rule to contribute to their social hosts, however much they receive in public infrastructure and services or the hard work of host citizens. At the same time, hosted corporations are protected by the limited liability terms of corporate law and trade regime regulations from being held responsible for the environmental, health and social damages which they bring to the human and ecological life-systems they enter and exit.

A final assumption then follows easily in train. It is that there is no way to prevent the 'harsh' consequences of these harms because they are 'inevitable', and their costs to publics, workers and environments are 'necessary adjustments' to the 'tough new reality of investor value'.

Manufacturing the Debt Crisis to Eliminate the Civil Commons

The puzzle may remain how developed societies with evolved social infra-structures could allow this conversion of their peoples and environments into dispensable means for transnational corporate investors. Even the armed might of invading war-machines could not manage such a takeover without a prolonged fight. In part, it is precisely because the invasion has not been armed or visible that it has infiltrated so effectively. As it has been famously attributed to John Foster Dulles: 'There are two ways of taking over a society's economy. One is by armed force, and the other is by financial means.' Masked throughout by popular slogans and abetted by domestic agents in the corporate, financial, media and academic sectors, the colonization succeeded by the internal means of operant conditioning by corporate chain communication systems and active assistance by public-sector collaborators.

But there was a deeper preparation that succeeded in achieving the essential groundwork. First, citizens had to be convinced that the popular and long-evolved social sectors and life-security systems their forbears had struggled for were no longer feasible. Ideally, they had also to believe that abandoning them flowed from their obligations as citizens. Since neither of these contingencies seemed in the least likely, it came to be a truism of social scientists that big change to 'the welfare state' could not be won without a crisis within.

There was no doubt that the welfare state was deplored by the corporate sector for many reasons. First of all, it provided unpriced goods by public means to citizens. This is the antithesis of the corporate market model, and rules out profit-making wherever it is allowed to penetrate. The vast financial-security and insurance industries, for example, which have exploded in growth in global market conditions, are cut off at the knees by a fully developed social-security system.

Second and more generally, the welfare state makes work in the employment of corporate hierarchies not serving any life good less attractive, and less necessary. People can increasingly 'live off the government' by working in the social sector for a public good like education or other social service, or by living impecuniously on unemployment and welfare allowances. This undermines the disciplinary apparatus of the labour market which it has depended on since its inception in the fifteenth century.

Third, a welfare state generates regulations to protect life in the workplace, in the environment and natural-resource sector, and almost everywhere else business looks to cut costs of production. It is thus 'too costly' in another way, and 'a regulatory stranglehold on business'.

Finally and most dangerously, an activist social state propels a growing tendency of government supported by electorates to manage revenues from publicly owned natural resources, to develop public ownership in strategic areas, to build new sectors of employment and service to life needs, to employ youth, and even to replace banks in creating and loaning money. All of these initiatives grew with the welfare state, and the pattern was global. Such developments constituted 'the threat of socialism' or 'communism' to the standpoint of the market fundamentalism that was to be expressed in the global market restructuring to come. They had to be brought to heel, and at best eradicated.

The adversary within was called 'Big Government', just as it was in the 1930s when Roosevelt's New Deal was inaugurated. Big Government had to be turned back before it 'enslaved' the US people inside their own borders. This may seem a disordered assertion, but even a Canadian law professor could declare in this vein that the Christian community 'should turn to face the true enemy of all people of faith, the secular socialist state in Canada and its fellow travelers'.[35]

The strategic difficulty was that in the societies of the world where social spending had provided public health care, free education, income security for the old and the unemployed, occupational health and safety regulations, public broadcasting and transit, conservation areas and environmental protections, and selective public ownership of universally-used enterprises, these public goods were very popular with electorates. Somehow, they had to be prevailed against by 'the private sector'.

Big Government was not what one might think. It was not the gargantually wasteful and destructive military-industrial complex which was to spend almost a billion dollars a day during the Reagan administration, attacking or threatening with massive armed force any alternative economic order on the horizon. Nor was it ever more police and prisons for non-white and impoverished US citizens. Nor was it even the commanding ranks of the federal bureaucracy, the rudeness of officialdom to ordinary citizens, or policies of documented US state terrorism across the world. Against all intuitions about the meaning of terms, 'Big Government' meant assistance to the poor, the sick and the old, and protection of the workers and the environment against corporate toxins and pollutants. It meant 'binge spending on social programmes' like pensions and medicare, 'suffocating regulations' on industrial effluents and hazardous working conditions, and the 'culture of dependency' of destitute families and children on 'government handouts'.

The underlying logic of the market's abhorrence of these public expenditures was never mentioned, and hardly recognized by anyone. But what made these public life goods abhorrent to the corporate market mind-set at a pre-conscious level was that they *had no market value, and yet they cost money.* Society must therefore undergo 'the second American revolution', as a Republican Congress later termed it, and sweep the world clean of all such entitlements to life goods not mediated by corporate enterprise.

Of course, the public justifications never disclosed their origins, even if they were recognized. The reasons given for this reversion were, in fact, quite endless. The entire apparatus of the social security system was a 'total failure'. The 'environmental bureaucracy' was 'a terrorist organization'. 'Politicians were spending the country to death.' 'Liberals' were 'destroying the moral fabric of America'. Above all, government spending on social programmes was 'a disincentive to work', 'a destruction of the family', 'an assault on business', a 'distorting influence on the market', 'an unbearable taxload', a 'discouragement of private investment', 'big brother telling people how they had to spend their money', 'an attack on individual initiative', 'the undermining of freedom', 'forced helplessness and dependency', 'a campaign to discredit traditional values', and 'an assault on citizens' faith in God'. These social expenditures 'raised the costs of production', 'restricted the movement of private capital', and '*coercively redistributed wealth*'. They were, it was implied, tantamount to a declaration of war on the round of real value, money being invested for more.

So a war had to be declared back. But nothing could be done about this 'insidious welfare state', this 'greed for entitlements', this 'insane spending spiral' if 'misled electorates' kept supporting it. The civil commons developing outside the control of the private corporate system was 'a disaster', but public consciousness of its benefits to people's needs was not convinced. Thus a plan to 'curb the excess' had to be formed from the commanding heights of the Oval Office itself to 'clean up the mess' and 'make America great again'.

A strategic conjuncture of *government debt and inability to pay it* was then constructed to change the course of history. Before it was played out, it had reversed almost every gain of the electorally responsible public sector of universal social programmes and entitlements which had developed across the societies of the globe since the Great Depression and the Second World War, and before.

Two large-scale operations did the trick. They were quietly put into motion with the Reagan presidency which was militant in its programme to 'turn back the tide of state dictatorship' within as well as without US borders. 'State dictatorship', though few knew this at first, had a domestic referent as well as a foreign one. It meant social security programmes to protect and enable citizens' lives.

Military programmes to threaten and destroy life outside the US became more sancrosanct than ever. But social programmes to serve life *within* were the internal enemy to be vanquished – universal entitlements to health, education, income assistance, old-age pensions, environmental protection, public broadcasting, the arts – the list was as long as what could be enjoyed without a money price. This was the underlying determinant of the rage against social programmes which grew in outspokenness as the process of resteering society in mutant directions unfolded.

In both cases, the ultimate weapon that was used was not visible, and not the nuclear or armed-force terror that life defenders had their eyes on. In the case of the Soviet Union and its allies, the armaments race was *the means* to achieve the unmarked objective – *bankrupt the enemy state*. The strategy succeeded. But it was not until years later that the strategy was publicly acknowledged by Republican insiders triumphal in their 'victory over the Soviet Union'.

In the case of the internal enemy, the method that escaped detection was in principle again *the same* – bankrupt the state, in this case the welfare state that was blocking, appropriating from and subverting every step of the competing global market model from within rather than from without.

Strategic analysis is distinguished from conspiracy theory by the fit of the analysis with the known facts and established system-deciders. In the corporate system we have observed mutate from the traditional and classical models of a free market, the system-deciding property has been the delinkage of its calculus from all parameters except money demand at every moment of its sequences. Given this paradigm frame, it is not surprising that attack upon an opposing system should be at the level of *escalating its money inputs beyond manageable levels, while reducing its revenues at the same time.* In the case of the Soviet Union, this strategic plan was managed by an arms race of escalating expenditures at one end (almost a billion dollars a day at its height by the US), and by embargo, boycott and trade-pariah status at the other end to ensure the reduced revenues of the much poorer USSR to pay for these ever rising costs.

In the case of the welfare state, such that existed in the US,[36] the underlying attack would be by the same method of bankrupting: escalating public expenditures on the armaments race to unprecedented levels and, at the other end, radically reducing revenues by tax-cuts and other transfers of public revenues to corporations and high-end taxpayers who together comprised the core of the Republican constituency. The symmetry of strategic pattern did not have to be conscious to work. A paradigm frames and selects for pathways of decision that are compatible with and express its system-deciding principles. But then again, it would be surprising if these deductive moves were not consciously made by game-theoretical analysts and financial advisers at the heart of the US strategic planning process.

Yet because this social infrastructure to serve the life of all citizens and those in need had become part of the fabric of society's life, its destruction was not a preference that could be openly sold, even in the context of a managed public discourse. This evolving civil commons had developed over decades of political response to historical demand. After the World Depression and the Second World War, social cataclysms which had almost destroyed the capitalist-market organization of Western society, a more life-respectful remake of the capitalist market had begun to occur. The 'welfare state' was the outcome of this reconstruction, beginning with Roosevelt's New Deal in 1944.[37] It was the historic target of the new market crusade. The millennial and apocalyptic movement was focused on the 'forces of evil' which stretched around the globe in a 'world-wide Communist conspiracy' turned silently inward at the same time on its own social economy.

According to David Stockman, Reagan's first Director of the Office of Management and Budget, the large-scale strategic goal of the Reagan planners for restoring the market to proper rule was to '*cap social spending by increasing government debt*'.[38]

Escalating government debt was not difficult to manage. It consisted of three simultaneous initiatives. The first was to *increase* military and armed-force spending by over $140 billion *a year*. This was an *increase* greater than many country's GNPs, and produced nothing the public could use for life. It was, therefore, certain to entail an inflationary uptake and to put pressure on government spending, ever more extreme pressure as compounding interest-charges rose, which they soon did to historic highs 'to get America on track again'. The Reagan administration loaded public spending onto private corporate armament production to unheard of levels, increasing the already mammoth military budget by just under a trillion dollars over seven years.[39] This runaway expenditure of public revenues for the purchase of products with no productive function or future value, certainly exemplified 'wasteful government spending'. It spent government money at the rate of almost $1 billion a day. It also enriched the major armaments-producing corporations (including General Electric, Reagan's former employer) which had co-operated in financing Reagan's presidential campaign. Unnoticed, it rapidly escalated US government debt to unpayable levels at the same time. The economy was being decisively steered away from public expenditures on citizens' lives towards a tidal wave of payouts to armaments to kill and injure, the transnational corporations who manufactured them, and high-interest bonds and bond-dealers producing nothing.

This rising tidal wave of government spending on military weaponries and systems occurred during the same period of new major offensives against social justice movements of the poor in Latin America and Africa. This was called 'the war against World Communism' and 'terrorism'. True to the redirection of US statecraft, the previous administration was decried as 'soft' and its emphasis on human rights was explicitly repudiated. By militarily attacking and simultaneously bankrupting states and social movements committed to economic alternatives to foreign corporate control, the US arms build-up performed two essential functions for the mutations of money sequences now emerging as dominant. It enriched transnational corporations and destroyed civilian and armed oppositions to them.

But perhaps the deepest policy pattern over the decade still went unrecognized, and remains so today. By government spending on the military at such levels, government fiscal capacities were set into an ever deeper hole. Even a decade after Reagan left office, the US defence budget annual military spending remained at $265 billion a year, *still* above pre-Reagan levels of armed-force spending, although the 'enemy threat' it was designed to repel had long ceased to exist. As Paul Volker, the President of the US Federal Reserve Board during the Reagan years frankly described the strategy of bankrupting government to get social spending in line (emphasis added): 'The novel theory [that came in with the Reagan government] was that *the way to keep spending down was not by insisting taxes be adequate to pay for it, but by scaring Congress and the American people with deficits.*'[40]

The second strategic conjuncture in the raising of government debt to levels which would leave ever less for social spending was unprecedented tax-reductions to the wealthy and to major corporations. Their effect, predictably, was to reduce government revenues by hundreds of billions of dollars, while simultaneously enriching wealthy beneficiaries and corporations (which, we may recall, bankrolled the Republicans into power). The Reagan government set legislated its giveaway of federal tax revenues within a year of entering office, handing out a budget-estimated *$540 billion* of government revenues in one tax-bill. This radical redistribution of public wealth went entirely to the richest 20 per cent of the population, and 77 per cent of that to the richest one per cent.[41] The bottom 80 per cent ended up net losers after this 'tax reduction for the American people'. This government redistribution of income upwards, it is interesting to note, accompanied a simultaneous reduction of the share of wages in national income to its lowest level since 1929.[42]

Before this $540 billion redistribution of public wealth to the market's richest players was implemented, there was conclusive evidence that the tax cut was not, in fact, going to 'reinvigorate the American economy', as the new 'supply-side economics' had predicted. On the contrary, government economists themselves warned, behind closed doors, that the tax reduction programme was certain to raise the government's deficit by huge margins. 'We're going to have huge deficits', the records show that Stockman's economic analysts at the Office of Management and Budget reported to the President's policy directors.[43] 'Huge deficits', however, were not a consequence which deterred the Reagan administration. Although it had proclaimed throughout the 1980 election that it was going to 'end the deficit', it in fact more than tripled it by the time the Republican administration left office.

The President's senior policy advisers accordingly elected not to disclose any of the facts of the experts' forecast of 'huge deficits'. The US Congress itself was kept in the dark. This decision, as Stockman was later to acknowledge, 'led inexorably to the massive deficits of the 1980's [and after]'. Nobel Prize-winning economist Paul Samuelson observed dryly that the deficit consequence was predictable by known market principles of behaviour. Predictability is the first requirement of effective strategic planning. 'Wall Street in early 1981', Samuelson observed, 'panted for the tax cuts simply for their favourable income effects. Once Wall Street got its heart's desire ... it did what came naturally. It dumped its bonds, bidding up interest rates [and government debt] in the process ... .'[44]

The second piece of the overall pattern was now in place. The pattern of 'revolutionizing government', as its heirs openly called it, could deepen its hold and spread from 1981 to the end of the century and beyond.

The third and final policy of the 'market revolution' was the most effective of all on a world-wide scale. It was the 'monetarist policy' of high-interest rates. These compounded rising government deficits to unpayable levels. These deficits, in turn, led to a full-scale campaign to reduce and eliminate social programmes. This campaign to dismantle social infra-structures 'to pay off the public debt' occurred across global market societies, beginning with the Third World, and was called 'structural reform'. As the Reagan administration was escalating military spending by $942 billion dollars of new budgetary commitments, and simultaneously transferring away another $542 billion of government tax revenues to America's wealthiest taxpayers, for a total of $1484 billion of lost revenues to the public sector to multiply over the years, it was also compounding its *interest payments* on rising deficits to unprecedented double-digit levels. The Federal Reserve's escalations of interest-rates, one after the other until there was deep recession, was set in motion in 1979, just before the Reagan administration took power. The US government's private-bank body, the Federal Reserve Bank, not only prescribes minimum interest rates on US debtors, including its federal government employer itself, but also thereby sets interest rates which affect most other countries in the world, for whom the US dollar is the peg-currency. Foreign debtor governments, in turn, must pay above US prime rates to receive loans, and must pay at US-dollar rates. Thus, this new 'monetarist policy' of the Reagan administration impacted across the globe. It put mounting pressure on virtually every public sector in the world.

Escalating minimum interest rates far above inflation predictably raised government debt in two different ways. Both pulled the plug on the public sector's capacity to pay for its social programmes. First by increasing interest-demands on debt from two to four times higher than previous levels, indebted governments were forced to pay vastly escalated interest loads compounding as they accumulated. This in itself was enough to propel the growths of public debts across the world even as social programmes were being dismantled. By the same pressures, thousands of small businesses predictably went bankrupt from the multiplied interest burdens and loss of affordable loans, while millions of workers lost their jobs from resulting layoffs in the policy-created recession.[45] This 'belt tightening' for life, but expanding for 'investment opportunities', predictably fell entirely on the life reproduction of people outside money-sequence functions. High interest rates did not reduce but expanded corporations and individuals inside these money sequences because money could now be loaned at the escalated rates, while at the same time writing off 46–70 per cent of its internal interest costs.[46]

Most importantly here to growth of the public debt, prescribed interest rates of almost 20 per cent prime inevitably deprived the federal government further of hundreds of billions of dollars of tax revenues which were no longer received from smaller bankrupt businesses or from millions of now unemployed citizens. In place of tax revenues, governments paid out ever more for police, prisons and other 'correctional' operations in the aftermath of millions of suddenly jobless and ratcheted-down workers and their families.

None of this, it is to be noted, was criticized by devotees to the market doctrine. Since it protected and increased the value of money, it was 'making the hard decisions'. At the same time, unprecedentedly high real interest rates imposed a vast and sudden new burden of compounded real interest demands on already out-of-control government debt. This 'unaffordable' load was, in turn, invariably taken out of social programmes, rather than made affordable by normal interest rates or income taxes. In this way, escalated, government-set interest rates predictably completed the pattern of runaway government debt. Recall Volker's comment: 'to *terrorize* the American people with deficits'.

In neighbouring Canada, as elsewhere across the world, this third mainspring of 'increasing government debt to cap social spending' was the most decisive determinant of escalating government deficits. In the first and pioneering analysis of this new pattern of government 'deficit crises' in North America, a 1991 Statistics Canada study was headed by an economist who was still concerned to understand the cause of the debt all were blaming on 'excessive social spending'. Hideo Mimoto discovered that, in fact, 44 per cent of the debt rise since 1979 was due to tax write-offs to corporations and rich taxpayers, and 50 per cent due to higher compounding interest rates.[47] This study was immediately, and without counter-evidence, repressed by the government of Canada's Ministry of Finance. The Conservative, bond-merchant Minister, Michael Wilson, had already launched a major political campaign with ex-branchplant president and Prime Minister, Brian Mulroney, 'to slash the deficit' by 'reducing unaffordable social spending'. A rewriting of the Statistics Canada study, already approved as accurate by over 20 government and other economists, was ordered, and Statistics Canada's budget was cut in future federal budgets.[48]

The mass media, predictably, declined to report any of these facts. They also declined to report a subsequent private-sector study which revealed that the cause of the federal government's still escalating debt was not social spending, but the interest-rate policies of the government's publicly owned Bank of Canada. The Bank's new Governor, an ex-Director of the International Monetary Fund, raised real interest rates to levels 5 per cent *higher* than the US 'to reassure the markets' and 'foreign bond holders'. At the same time, the Bank began an unpublicized process of privatizing its holdings of Government of Canada bonds, thereby transferring their interest payments to private banks. These interest payments would otherwise have reverted to the government, the Bank's sole shareholder. As we will see in more detail ahead, the publicly-owned Bank is authorized by the Bank of Canada Act to buy and sell bonds for the government to keep interest payments in public hands. The Bank of Canada was essentially violating its mandate and redistributing, in familiar pattern, public wealth to the money sequences of private financial institutions and, increasingly, foreign money-lenders. Government debt and deficits quickly increased at an exponential rate, while social programmes were rapidly dismantled as 'too costly for the Canadian taxpayer'.

The private study of the Canadian government's debt escalation from 1984 on was released to business readers in February 1995 by the Dominion Bond Rating Service, and it attributed *93 per cent* of the federal debt's spectacular rise since 1984 to compounding high interest rates, rates which were set by the Bank of Canada itself.[49] In contrast to the government's and the Bank's continuous blaming of the debt on 'unaffordable social programme spending', the Bond Agency attributed no significant deficit growth to the 'relatively modest programme expenditure deficiency'. The policy-driven government debt was clear now even to market bond-dealers. The facts, however, remained unreported in the corporate mass media where citizens might see them. Consequently, the across-the-board defunding and elimination of social programmes continued as 'hard decisions which have to be made', even though these facts were well known by the government's new multimillionaire Minister of Finance, Paul Martin. As in other jurisdictions, the corporate press continued to headline the 'deficit crisis' daily, while continuing to blame, against well-established fact, 'excessive social spending' for the debt rise.

By the end of the Reagan government's tenure, its choice-path to raise government debt so as to reduce social spending had achieved the unmanageable debt required. Public-sector debt had gone from 907.7 billion dollars in 1980 to 2.643 trillion in 1988.[50] In one-better, junior partner emulation, Canada's federal debt *more* than tripled during the same period. But with its Bank of Canada interest rates pegged another 4–5 per cent higher than historically high US rates, federal government debt kept skyrocketing: from $94 billion to $508 billion, more than *five* times its level by 1995 even as government social spending continued to be reduced from one level to the next 'to pay down the deficit'.[51]

In both Canada and the US, the 'cap' on social spending by 'increased government debt' had track-switched government from its ties to the life-functions of serving the common interest of its citizens to receiver, subsidy and marketing functions for the corporate market order. Yet an indicator of the uninhibited aggression of the new reproductive sequence coding the social order was that the axing of the society's evolved common life was attacked with still mounting demands for more 'privatization', 'tax cuts to business' and 'financial accountability' to 'the private sector'. The nature of the debt rise, meanwhile, remained for the public a social secret. Relentlessly blaming society for 'living beyond its means', attacking politicians for 'being on a spending binge', accusing the poor and the unemployed of 'dependency on the government', reviling every form of public service as a 'pork-barrel', the market crusade to abolish the civil commons went into what can only be called a feeding frenzy. Public spending on any interest other than private capital protection and advancement was pilloried as 'excessive' or 'a miserable failure'. Once sacred and untouchable social-infrastructure spending was attacked as an offence against 'fiscal responsibility'. The axe fell repeatedly on public health, on old-age pensions, on social assistance, on income security, on education, on the arts and culture, on public transportation, on environmental regulations and conservation areas, and on every other evolved fabric of the social economy outside the control and benefit of private market ownership and profit. In reflection on this meta-pattern since, we see the symptomology of a virulent code now occupying and at home in the life-host.

Wall Street Journal and *Forbes Magazine* columnist, David Frum, crying to be first in the race to declare 'where the axe should fall next', pointed to the target of the life-protective programmes.

> I would say on a single day this summer we eliminate three hundred programs, each one costing a billion dollars or less. The big programs, like welfare, Medicaid, and Medicare will take a little time to get rid of.[52]

Lest anyone might show him to be less aggressive in the feeding frenzy, fellow market crusader and famed neo-conservative, William Kristol, proclaimed:

> You cannot in practice have a federal guarantee that people won't starve.[53]

In Canada nine months later, the publisher of 'the national newspaper', the *Globe and Mail*, William Thorsell, called for another axe to lop off still more from the $400 million poorer school budgets. 'Cheer up and take out another 100 million!' he cracked.[54] Observe throughout the thrill of transgression, the triumph in the financial starvation of the public realm that stands in the way of the universal invasion and spread of the life-decoupled market programme now mutated beyond any connection with the traditional and classical market models.

In Ontario, Canada's richest province, the 'Reagan revolution' registered 15 years late on a widely disemployed and resentful rural populace as an idea whose time had come. By now, the strategic pattern had established itself in media culture as an 'inevitable social restructuring'. There was no need any longer to conceal the connection between debt growth by tax giveaways and the war on the social commons. Now called the 'Common Sense Revolution', market crusaders could declare simultaneously 'the need to cut social spending to pay down the deficit' *and* 'the necessity for a 30 per cent tax-cut' at the same time without embarrassment at the self-confutation. That the two policies contradicted one another by decreasing and increasing the government debt at the same time did not deter market 'common sense' from its task. 'Doublethink' is the learned capacity to hold logically contradictory propositions in the head at the same time without cognitive dissonance. What made the self-contradictory consistent here, however, was that *both* policies attacked what was *not* the market, the realm of universal access to unpriced goods.

As with the original 'Reagan revolution', the pattern of the market programme to redistribute wealth to the market from social expenditures on public health, education, worker safety, and environmental protection was deemed 'necessary' to 'get the economy moving again'. The incantation of 'reducing the deficit' was still necessary to recite for the credulous as the social infrastructure of health, eduction and life-protection was dismantled by mounting multi-billion dollar cuts. People on social assistance reduced to below subsistence levels, university funding almost halved from former levels, health-care and treatments privatized and defunded, conservation areas transformed into saleable municipal assets, municipalities dispossessed of transfer payments for their services, occupational safety inspectors and environmental police reduced to a fraction of their previous strength, farm workers deprived of the right of collective organization, teachers fired in the thousands 'without any cuts to the classroom' – all these were called 'the tough decisions to release present and future generations from crushing government debt'.

What had begun as a covert strategy in Republican back rooms more than 15 years ago was now a single life-disconnected demand. The value objectives of a '30 per cent tax-cut' and 'paying down the debt' could now be overtly twinned in the public realm without a sense of lesion in the programme. At a certain point, a society's defence system loses its bearings in the overwhelming, increasing assault on its common grounds of life, just as on the cellular level of life-organization an individual life-host succumbs to an invasive pathogen.

New Zealand's global market agents on the other side of the world managed the destruction of one of the world's leading public sectors in even shorter order than their North American counterparts. In unwitting symbolism, the stripping of society for private money control began in 1984, Orwell's marker for the totalitarian state. Here, as well, a financially managed strategy of war by attrition depended on creating the appearance of a runaway public debt. 'The country's debt crisis', reports a respected research institute, 'was deliberately manufactured during the 1984 election by leading an alleged plan to devalue the currency by 20 per cent. The financial moguls were thus given four weeks notice that the value of their holdings of New Zealand money would decline by that amount. So naturally they moved as much of their assets as possible out of the country. A financial panic followed, but it was not a debt crisis. It was a deliberately engineered foreign exchange crisis.'[55] Following this managed financial flight of the country's private capital to propel New Zealand's government into a revenue and borrowing crisis, a new economic leadership of government propounding market creed as the salvation deregulated financial transactions, cut taxes on business and the rich by 12–50 per cent, privatized $16 billion worth of public equity and institutions, and slashed the public sector at every level (reducing welfare income by 25 per cent, and charging fees for public schooling).[56]

All the while, 'social over-spending' was blamed for 'the debt crisis'. Observe the metastasis of a single code of invasion across the world. The New Zealand 'Labour government' attacked the public sector in the feeding frenzy on public revenues and assets since familiar elsewhere, and it was pervasively congratulated by corporate chain media across the world for performing an 'economic miracle'. As in all such cases, the 'debt crisis' was not solved by the public sector's dismantling. This was because it was not caused by it. Everywhere debt increased, as it continues to do at the end of the century. In the case of New Zealand, the federal government's annual deficit itself *more than doubled* by the 'market reforms' which had gutted the productive economy, from $12 billion to $29 billion by 1995, while its overall debt continued to climb.[57]

As we will see ahead, the inner logic of the global market system is not to solve debt crises, but to *keep* governments indebted on a permanent and rising basis, while continuing to selectively feed on and dismantle social sectors. The programme is coded for another form of reproduction and growth than what has been so far understood.

MAI Day: The Bid for Total Control

No sooner had societies across the globe been variously stripped of their evolving social infrastructures to serve the life security and development of their citizens' lives, than another major advance of the programme for transnational corporate rule was upon them. On the heels of the Maastrict Treaty for a common standard to reduce social programmes to protect the value of borderless money demand came a parallel initiative to link North America and Europe and eventually the countries of the World Trade Organization in a single transnational investment regime. Its front end was the Organization of Economic Cooperation and Development, and its secretly negotiated terms were to protect the rights of money investors as absolute across still more national borders, the 29 nations of the OECD.

The Multilateral Agreement on Investment was a fast-track initiative negotiated from 1995 on behind closed doors by corporate and bureaucrat trade lawyers and economists. The objective now was to recode the law itself of sovereign nations in the global market system. This was to be performed by blanket institution of a transnational regulatory framework of private corporate ownership and trade as a sovereign order with the supra-constitutional power to override national, regional and municipal jurisdictions and laws. It crystallized on the level of world rule the still emerging demands of the mutant market order as a design of permanent world rule.

The MAI's focus was protection of foreign investment capital. Its master principle was the unconditional right to 'national treatment' of transnational corporations in host societies. Under the agreement, foreign corporations must never be 'discriminated against' by any government on any level on any account, such as their contribution to the well-being of the home society. Serving the interests of the home society was deemed to be 'protectionist'. To accomplish the full colour of this right, a massive re-engineering of the access of foreign corporations to the wealth of all societies was required. Accordingly, the MAI wrote into its prototype articles the rights of all transnational private corporations:

- to export their commodities or services across all borders of locale or nation to other societies' markets with no conditions attached;
- to unilaterally purchase and own any built structure or productive capacity of any other signatory nation with no requirement to sustain its viability, employment-level or location in the home country;
- to own any salable natural resource of other countries and to have national right to any concession, licence or authorization to extract its oil, forest, mineral or other resources with no obligation to sustain these resources, or to use them in the interest of the host society;
- to profit from any commercial enterprise with no requirement to reinvest in the enterprise or any other enterprise in the country in which the resources have been received and the profits earned;

- to create credit and thus increase domestic money supply with no restriction on the amount of new currency demand so created in the host economy, however inflationary to the economy, or bankrupting to domestic citizens;
- to bid for and own any privatized public infrastructure, social good or cultural transmission without any limit of foreign control permitted by law;
- to access any domestic government grant, loan, tax incentive or subsidy with the same rights as any domestic firm with no means test, locale requirement or public-interest distinction permitted;
- to be free of any and all performance requirements of job creation, domestic purchase of goods, import-export reciprocation, and technology or knowledge transfer to the host society;
- to repel as illegal any national standards of human rights, labour rights or environmental protection on goods produced in and imported from other regions or nations.

Under the proposed agreement, all provision by domestic governments of goods to their citizens by public ownership or control were construed as 'monopolies'. Monopolies of knowledge by corporate copyright, in contrast, were specially excepted as non-monopolies. This double standard was significant because monopoly designation entailed special legal restrictions on pricing and distribution of goods which would be 'an interference with business freedom to transact' on private corporations. Any public non-profit 'monopoly' in health-care, education or other universally accessible life-good was, therefore, to be bound by the obligation to act 'solely in accordance with commercial considerations in the purchase or sale of its good or service'; to 'in particular' be prevented from the 'abusive use of prices' which might adversely affect the market share of foreign corporate investors; and, in general, to be liable for damages for any 'lost opportunity to profit from a planned investment' which might be incurred by public involvement in providing citizens with goods in which private foreign corporations could assert a market interest.

Worker buy-outs of enterprises, or return of their ownership to home investors, were, moreover, not to be permitted any favourable loan, tax or start-up cost by public authority, since this would constitute a 'discriminatory treatment' against foreign investors. 'Educational products' as well as any other product, except military, the one article of trade given full protectionist walls by the treaty, were also prohibited from any limit on foreign control or domination.

The regulating principle of all these blanket rights and powers to be granted carte blanche to private, transnational corporations was that no social life-host had any longer the power to protect the ownership or control of its markets, its built assets, its environmental resources or its right to provide life goods to its citizens that transgressed asserted corporate rights to profit from them.

Any requirement for long-term commitment of investment in any strategic area such as the nation's natural resources or high-employment sector were, moreover, forbidden. Any other condition which compromised the right of foreign transnationals to move their profits and assets from the home society to other jurisdictions with lower environmental, labour, corporate-tax or safety standards was likewise prohibited by MAI law. To round out the logic of instituting overriding rights to multinationals at public expense, all the costs of the new regime to privilege transnational corporations above governments and electorates – that is, the costs of its planning, negotiation, enforcement, adjudication, *and* liabilities for infraction – were under the agreement to be paid for out of the public purse.[58]

What unifies the diverse and sweeping prescriptions of this extra-Parliamentary formation of *a new transnational framework of law* is the single, final goal of releasing corporate investment from any interference or social condition set by national or local public authority. Every term of the agreement is to guarantee this free subjecthood of 'Investment' as sovereign over democratic decision to set limits on its movement, location, time-frame, objective, or volume.

'We will oppose', stated the President of the US Council For International Business in a letter to US officials on March 2, 1997, 'any and all measures to create or even imply binding obligations for governments or business related to environment and labour.'[59]

What unifies the private monetary interests driving this proposed regime, in turn, is the fact that transnationally mobile corporations in *all* of the signatory jurisdictions are freed from accountability to any other interest, government or citizen body in their access to all of the markets, resources, subsidies and assets of the 29 societies involved. What makes this appropriation of public power by for-profit transnational corporations possible to impose on peoples' historically evolved rights of self-government is, in further turn, its absolutized expression of the market programme of value which has come to be assumed to be the final prescriptive authority on how all societies must reproduce themselves.

This dispossession of citizens and communities of their collective rights to protect their lives and resources as their own is, in the end, grounded on the metaphysical principle which sustains the programme as its base-line given – namely, that unfettered money capital in its now mutant transnational corporate form has an untransgressible right to circulate freely through all social and natural life-hosts across the world, appropriating, exchanging, extracting, exploiting and restructuring its life-fabrics to maximize money returns to stockholders with no right of these life-hosts to limit or resist its 'free movement'.

This is the general framework of the global market paradigm set out in stark principle. On the level of abstraction, one cannot observe its implications in fact. But when we study the mutant money sequences that the new social sovereign of 'Investment' bears into social hosts, when we recognize that no limiting right or claim of life is anywhere admitted into its binding system of access and exploitation across cultural and national boundaries, and when we observe the strict exclusion of societies to maintain or generate any social alternative which might limit, replace or surpass its system of life-host use, we can recognize that it is in the end a prescription for total corporate world-rule.

This is how the invasion and occupation of societies proceeds – by *removing all defences* of social hosts against it. As for the effects of converting social bodies to temporary sites for transnational corporate occupation, exploitation and metastasis, we turn now to the savagery of its effects.

Systemic Effects of the Global Market Paradigm

Because the global market is opposed in nature to the free market model described by Adam Smith, it operates to produce an opposite outcome – not, in general, more material prosperity and well-being, but ever more money demand for the top-end, and ever wider and deeper deterioration of life-conditions for the bottom half of humanity and for the global biosphere and civil commons in general.

We will see the great weight of the evidence for this meta-pattern of the global market system in action as our diagnosis unfolds. But we can discern certain profiles of life decline that cannot be denied, only avoided. As the paradigm's prescriptions have been imposed on and penetrated across social and environmental hosts, the marginal value of labour has fallen for most workers; poverty and unemployment rates have increased to unprecedented post-Depression extremes; child malnourishment has escalated across both developed and less developed economies in rising absolute and relative numbers; social security, education and public health infrastructures have been systemically dismantled; and environmental degeneration of atmospheric conditions, water, soil, forests, and species diversity has advanced to various levels of planetary depletion and collapse.

But what is fatefully not recognized is that every one of these life-stripping effects increases and follows *from* the increased implementation and spread of the global market programme itself. This is the great unspeakable connection of the world crisis which impedes social immune response. Cause and effect, system-deciding principles and their consequences are ruled out by the system's closed sequences of reproduction and growth on the communicative as well as instrumental levels.

Because export and import figures show steep rises, because there are geometrical increases in financial transactions and dominant stock market indices, and because there are regional rises in gross domestic products where there are not meltdowns, no problem registers in the money-economy paradigm. But these gains in money transaction figures provide no evidence against any of the deepening patterns of life-degeneration at work underneath them. The system is structured to rule them out of its value co-ordinates and reference points. In this way, it ceases to engage with the world of life even as it it consumes and depredates it.

Climatic and atmospheric pollution unleash increasingly widespread and catastrophic effects in weather extremes and turbulences which science cannot keep up with. One-quarter of the world's people are known to be now starving. One-third of all children of the world are undernourished, and are rapidly increasing in number.[60] Despite sufficient food supply, the growing social sectors of impoverished people lack sufficient income to buy food and shelter. Thirty per cent of the world's workforce is unemployed by market demand, while most new jobs are insecure, low-paid or part-time.[61] Almost one hundred acres of the earth's rainforest is cut every minute by private corporations. Up to two hundred species become extinct every day from habitat destruction.[62] Eighty countries with 40 per cent of the world's population now suffer serious and growing water shortages. Twenty-six billion tons of topsoil are lost to soil erosion every year across 50 per cent of the world's remaining arable land.[63] Stratospheric ozone depletion by industrial pollutants is causing hundreds of thousands of human cancers a year, the destruction of amphibian species' capacity to reproduce, and systematic depletion of phytoplankton at the bottom of the planetary food chain. More than 60,000 square kilometres of land in over 100 countries becomes desert annually, hastened by global warming caused by industrial effluents which have risen 16-fold in the past 30 years.[64] Everywhere coastal waters and coral ecosystems bearing the most biologically rich life-zones of the world are being destroyed by pesticide and fertilizer run-offs from farms and plantations producing for market sale. The ocean bottoms themselves are being strip-mined of fish and aquatic life across vast tracts by factory-trawlers that drag the ocean floors for marketable fish stock whose take has increased almost more than fourfold in the last four decades.[65] The poor countries of the South pay approximately half a billion dollars *a day* in compounding interest payments to wealthy banks and financial institutions.[66]

The connected profile of these figures forms a global pattern of systemic life devastation without historical precedent. The system is incontro-vertibly out of control, but there are only more calls from its agents for more 'deregulation' mixed with denials or inaction wherever an isolated problem emerges in the corporately regulated discourse of the media and textbook chains.

Radical market reforms of the East European and Soviet economies have in the meantime demonstrated the 'miracles of market reform' on human populations in laboratory conditions. Following Russia's 'market liberation' in 1991, 80 per cent of the population who had previously lived with food security, basic housing and medical care lost so much by the restructuring and privatization of their economies and livelihoods that they now lived in 'destitute or semi-destitute' conditions.[67] The 'failure of the capitalist experiment' in the once mighty Soviet Union is not yet, however, a phrase that is speakable in the communications field of the global market.

Poland, Czechoslovakia, Romania and Bulgaria were not spared. They lost between 20 and 30 per cent of their GDPs and much of their social security infrastructure by 1992 through market reforms to liberate them.[68]

The global market restructuring experiment at the same time precipitately disemployed workers, reduced wages and variously cut back social programmes across the rest of the world. But in response to these world-wide conditions of social decline, increasingly life-insecure populations have been treated to a one-way monologue of market slogans.

Once more, we need to search for *exceptions* to this drowning out of life fact to get a sense of the underlying form of reproduction at work. There is a lock in this programme that has closed off the feedback to its growth and spread. Even the world's leading education systems are, by the description of one former British minister on the inside of the process, being reprogrammed by global market prescriptions 'invading the curriculum jurisdictions of universities and schools'.[69]

Once we recognize the blanket exclusion of effective regulation on behalf of rights other than those of corporate investment sequences, the overall design of the new global market order is revealed to us in lucid form. It institutes by its pattern of prescription and omission a more or less predictable train of long-term effects on the life-hosts whose interests it excludes from its calculus. When we observe the hard evidence of mounting social malnutritions, starvations, disemployments, ecological devastations, civil breakdowns, and dismantlings of social sectors and community property across the world, we should consider these effects as both connected and explicable, and traceable back to a systemic disorder in the master programme which selects for the determinants behind their occurrence.

3

The Social Immune System and the Cancer Stage of Capitalism

Social life-organizations survive because they evolve strategies of recognition and response to select out what endangers them. Thus from the beginnings of human society, people living in productive and reproductive exchange with one another have regulated their lives and functions so as to prevent or to expel what is perceived as dangerous to their communal health. Whether we consider ancient Jewish or Egyptian or Hindu or Melanesian societies, we find an underlying common pattern more or less universal to human cultures. What is 'unclean', 'polluted', 'malignant', 'contaminated' or 'defiled' must be cleansed and purified, or the social body will suffer a breakdown of its life-structure. The dominant rituals and organizing orders of daily life are thus everywhere concerned with preventing the spread of some contagion within the social body which may infect and destroy the structure of collective life. Individuals are living members of this social body, each with assigned functions to sustain its reproduction, and in their conception can no more survive its death than an organ can live beyond the organism it is part of.

Despite the primitive and primevally superstitious nature of the early development of social health systems, their overriding organizing principle of keeping the *clean* from the *unclean* to protect the social body from dangerous influences of all kinds had a host of actually effective, specific functions of social body defence.[1] For example, infected or toxic or dysfunctional foods and practices of all kinds were excluded from contact with or ingestion or adoption by the social body, thereby preserving its living members from infectious agents, poisons, and maladaptive mores which would otherwise have threatened the life and reproduction of the community.

Even 'taboos', which contemporary medical science wrongly supposes as by their nature harmful to social welfare,[2] were prohibitions surrounding the chief acts of life which persistently had as their underlying function life-protective value. Taboos against contact with corpses, or against physical punishment of infants, or against sexual acts outside of social boundaries, or against ingestion of specific substances all conferred crucial survival advantages and social-body defences against disease, injury and death.

The invasion and spread of contagions so feared in tribal societies was in way this an *embryonic form of immune recognition on the social level of life-organization* which it has been the great function of civilization to develop into effective competence.

Social immune practices subject to processes of test and falsification of what *actually* prevents disease and trauma to human communities, however, are a comparatively recent evolution of society. Scientific public health regimes originated in Europe in the latter half of the eighteenth century with, as Michel Foucault puts it, 'the accumulation of bodies' in large cities during the industrial capitalist expansion: an intensive concentration of propertyless humanity that introduced a host of new and deadly problems of runaway sewage, fouled water supplies, adulterated foods, contagious diseases, roaming street people, abandoned children, extreme poverty and degradation, infirm and aged people without familial supports, and so on – much as we see growing again in the unfettered 'free market' cities of today at the end of the twentieth century.

The idea of 'public health' subsumed from the outset a number of new and old social problems and solutions to human morbidity that were arising in the densely populated conditions of industrial civilization: hygiene and sanitation by systems of water supply; drainage and sewage; the siting of disease-bearing abattoirs and cemeteries and isolation of infected human beings; the development of medical societies and corps of doctors; the formation of clinics and systems of distribution of inoculations and vaccinations for common diseases; and, eventually, the evolution of modern medical hospitals for the treatment of the ill and disabled.

Subsequent to its initial development in Europe and Britain, 'public health' came to be associated with a host of further municipal, regional and national government regulations to secure the prevention of disease and the promotion of health in the social populations falling under the jurisdiction of these various state bodies – laws, statutes and rules to ensure the purity of food, milk and water supplies and handlers; the authorized extermination of animals, insects or wildlife suspected of contributing to or bearing disease; the quarantine of individuals and the inspection, disinfestation or condemnation of structures and buildings deemed to be health hazards to adjacent communities; the regulated safety of public places from dangers and hazards to the well-being of their users; the prohibition of practices like spitting and eliminating body wastes in public spaces; the construction and maintenance of community systems of waste and garbage disposal; the systematic testing, inspecting and screening of commercial pharmaceuticals and other non-food products to validate their safety for human use and consumption; the formation of administrative and liability norms to protect workers' health and safety in their places of employment; the provision of public centres, clinics and hospitals to administer tests, inoculations and curative care free of charge; and the institution of disease-identifying and preventative practices and educational campaigns embracing every kind of potentially disease-causing activity from drinking and smoking toxic substances to recreational sex and foreign travel.

To this very rich set of life-protective regulations and prescriptions we need to add another set which includes such entrants as, for example, the development of systems of law governing the use of exogenously powered vehicles, the licensing of drivers, and eventually the actions of pedestrians in public transportation flows. Here we move to life-protective regulation of social bodies which is not simply to prevent and treat pathogenic transmissions or behaviours which expose members of the community to life-attack by releasing *non*-human harm agents or hazards. This level of life-protection by society's regulatory formations targets harm-causing by *human* agents and practices that do not intend to harm others, but may nevertheless do so seriously and systemically if not exactly regulated. Traffic lights at busy intersections, for example, set pathways of permission and prohibition which apply to all and are strictly enforced to prevent continuous road slaughter by unco-ordinated human choices. Similarly strict laws against releasing toxic emissions into society's air and water by regularized decisions of corporate engineering departments and their superiors are also choices which seriously endanger societies, their members and their environmental life-host, but are not yet at a civilized stage of development.

Assault and battery, rape, murder and so on, in contrast, are recognized intentional harms to others, and are subsumed by the criminal law. The criminal law too is part of the great protective web within which individual lives are permitted to be safe and flourish in a developed human community. But it as well is part of a much more extended and varied fabric of social regulatory life protection which remains largely invisible to us by habitual presupposition. Even language itself, perhaps beginning in warning sounds and signifiers, is a deep weave and medium in this community web of mutual life-defence. Because this social life guardian is invisible in the global market, its supports are endangered by this regime's fancy that its self-regulating laws of supply and demand are adequate to provide for the survival of human societies and their members.

So unconscious have agents of this regime become of the unrecognized social guardian within whose social network of life-protection every moment of their existence is safeguarded that many expound an infantile 'libertarian' conceit that they owe nothing to the social fabric which tends them but what they choose to give to it. This is another symptom of the loss of the life-bearing induced in social consciousness by the mutations of the 'free market' paradigm since its original formation.

There is around all members of a developed twentieth century, in short, an historically evolved and intricately interrelated membrane of social construction of which few are aware and most dangerously blind: a vast panoply of life-protective regulative recommendations, procedures and penalty-backed laws to protect the health and prevent the disease of communities and their individual members by the multiplicity of harms, dangers, toxins, pathogens and army of negligent actions and practices that might endanger their survival or well-being.

As one considers in overview increasing state and public-sector mediations of every aspect of our lives by complexly articulated systems of life-protective circulation and regulation of our social intercourse and functions, one begins to recognize that – despite its continuous errors, oversights and dogmas – this historically evolved ordering and organization of civilized communities and states for the healthful survival and reproduction of their members is a *social immune system* of ever more developed complexity and importance to human survival and reproduction.

Following the model of immune systems on the cellular level, we can observe that societies which have not been stripped of their social immune capabilities by the restructurings of global market operations have highly developed immune surveillance, recognition and response systems. They have evolved, that is, socially constructed capacities for the continuous operation of a many-organed system of *surveillance* of the social life-host, reaching into every corner of the social organism's circulations and functions for detection of not-self challenges to its life-organization. They also have an intricately elaborated system of effective immune *recognition* and *response* integrated into the social body's operations at every level to select out the recognized threats and disabling diseases, injuries and assaults on the healthful functioning of the organic members of the social whole.

Societies acting in concert have even universalized on a global level specific quantitative indicators of the health or well-being of the world's social bodies, compiling and publishing comparative rates of infant mortality, disease frequencies and ratios, average life-expectancies and indices of mortality, distribution of required life-resources across social memberships, general fitness-levels of members' physical capacities, societies' distributed attainment of mental competences, and even their measures of self-regulation and distributed participation in the organizational development of social hosts as functioning wholes. To an increasing extent, these various *social indicators* of the collective health and well-being of societies have become more complex and detailed than the medical profiles and records of individual-patient organisms to which medicine proper has standardly confined its attention.

The Social Immune System

Once we adopt a wider-lensed understanding of human health than that of the individual patient and recognize that all individuals are also members of a larger, living whole in which their interdependent relations and functions constitute a higher order of life-system protecting and regulating its living members as a wider social body, we become aware of a very momentous evolutionary and historical development not yet recognized as such. Evolving for millennia behind our backs has developed a social immune system of increasingly complex capacities and competences upon whose society-wide-operation people more and more depend for their survival and well-being as individuals and as members of the social life-organizations to which they belong.

At its own *level* of life-organization, the social body has developed in degrees varying with the public resources at its disposal all the defining hall-marks of immune defence against threats to its integrity and health: *an exactly articulated and regulated system of self and not-self recognition, continuous and comprehensive processes of surveying the social life-host for sites and phenomena of disease, injury and malfunction*, and *evolved organic structures and strategies of response to recognized impairments of the social body's vital functions.*

It is not a question here of reducing the individual into a mere function and element of a social organism in which individuality does not exist as a value in itself. This is a metaphysical reduction which some organicist political systems like Plato's *The Republic*, Hegel's *Philosophy of History* and twentieth-century fascism have proposed, wrongly confusing the cellular and social levels of life-organization with disastrous effects when implemented as a political programme. Here the movement is in the opposite direction. The individual is not reduced to merely a moment of a social organism, to which it is assimilated as a contributory function that excludes the individual's value in itself, and for whose 'higher good' the individual may be sacrificed without real loss. This is a pathology of reductionism at the other extreme. Rather the middle way here is to recognize the social level of life-organization in its full life-protective evolution as *the basis and guardian of individual life from which the individual person differentiates as a unique and unrepeatable bearer of life value.*

It is a question, then, of understanding the individual as *dependent upon* this social host as a necessary condition of his or her life expression *as* an individual. The individual is not *reducible to*, but *grounded on* this social life-host for self-articulation to be possible. The individual achieves individuality by expressing this social life-ground in some way particular to personal capacity and choice – caring for or educating the next generation, speaking for the larger community that which has not been heard, helping to produce goods needed by others as a unique contributor, and in general bridging the individual-social division by service to the larger community in some form in order to *be* an individual.

What is of special interest here is that the individual articulates individuality by expressing and serving fellow members of the community in some way, at the highest 'the whole world' – the visionary audience to whom creators of all kinds speak. As we will find further in examining the nature of the 'civil commons' ahead, the disjunction between the individual and the society which protects and enables individuality is an artificial division which symptomizes a peculiar mutation of mind-set which has delinked from humanity's shared life-ground.

The more developed and competent the social immune system safeguarding all members of the social host from harm and hazard to each's vital life capacities, the more individuals can flourish with the assured conditions for self-realization as individuals. Conversely, the less developed or competent the social immune system is or becomes, the less the individual can flourish because of exposure to the harms, traumas, diseases, deprivations and impoverishments which the immuno-competent social life-organization does not prevent. The crude dichotomy between the needs of the individual and the needs of society overlooks this base-line reality of the ontology of the individual from which human development of every form advances.

If we consider carefully the consequences of the *loss* from our lives of an evolved social system of mutual life-protection – that is, a social immune system – then we will be soon made aware of how precarious and lethally exposed individual human life becomes without this systemic defence system of the social life-host – for example, against plagues, toxins and bacteria. Without an immuno-competent social life-organization, whether by retarded development or by economic deprivation, the results can be transnationally catastrophic. In fourteenth century Europe and Asia, up to three-quarters of individual humans suffered horrible individual deaths without this social immune defence system which we now take for granted. The Black Death was preceded by the weakening of the peasantry by the expropriation of their arable land to sheep pastures for global market export – an aetiology of health disaster still ignored in the expropriating processes of subsistence farmers across the world today for the same agribusiness export of mono-crops to foreign markets.[3] In the 'Spanish flu' epidemic of 1918–19, which was engendered by post-war conditions of social infrastructure loss with no public health systems, 25 million people died as the the pandemic circled the globe without publicly funded social-immune resources to respond to it.[4]

Thus a sobering fact of the pre-millennium global system needs to be registered. Our long-evolving social immune infrastructure has been increasingly deregulated, defunded and eliminated by unstinting attacks of global market restructuring on public sectors across the world. Regulatory, monitoring and preventative public agencies which have evolved over generations to protect and enable citizens' lives, workers' health and safety, and aquatic and land environments from the mounting industrial loads, dangers and pollutions of the borderless global market are, as these latter increase, being systemically dismantled at the same time. The effects of this social immune stripping are not tracked, because the social immune system is not recognized, and because the modes of tracking specific effects on social and environmental hosts are themselves defunded, cut back or axed.[5] At the same time, the global programme excludes or selects out the cause–effect relation between these social cutback prescriptions and their destructive effects on macro life systems.[6]

In these ways, the social life-host is rendered increasingly immuno-incompetent precisely as the conditions of the global market system unprecedentedly challenge its life-fabrics and members. The pattern of disease spread, the Harvard Working Group on New and Resurgent Diseases has concluded, '*has resulted not from pathogen changes, but from social and environmntal changes [of globalization] ... through multiple pathways [of] deforestation ... monoculture ... widespread malnutrition ... loss of publicly provided healthcare – resource depletion and chemical pollution ... [and] uncontrolled use of of chemical therapies*'.[7]

All of these determinants of emerging disease spread, we need to observe, are directly attributable to unregulated global corporate activities and structural adjustment programmes.

Society's Real Defence System

A disease disorder at the social level of life-organization is in principle the same as at the individual organic level. It is *expressed in a systemic reduction of the normal structure and function of life capacities*. We readily recognize disease reductions of our lives at the individual level, even with a brief cold virus. But we may not recognize underlying patterns of disease at the social level for two main reasons.

First of all, social systems of life-organization are far beyond our own individual sentient capacities in their function. We cannot normally 'feel that something is wrong' the way we can with a diminution of our own life functions. Systemic deficits of life function and development can impair the life capacities of the social body and, more so, its environmental host without our being much aware of it.

The second and still subterranean reason for our inability to recognize a disease in the social order of which we are members is that citizens of a society, and especially its privileged citizens, normally *identify with* the social value programme underlying and determining society's reproduction. They assume its decision-structure as 'necessary', and are pleased to flatter themselves that their ascendant positions within it are deserved and, in corollary, that those excluded are correspondingly undeserving.

The ideological strata of society can even idolatrize the social order which systemically disables and kills large numbers of those within its orbit, conceiving it as the ordering framework of nature or God – as the Aztec priest-bureaucracy did in the sacrifice of tens of thousands of people to make the sun rise, as the brahmins and ksatriya did in the caste exclusion from human life of at least half the population of India, as the intelligentsia did in the holding of slaves, women and children as the disposable property of ranking males across the official ancient world, and so on.

This is the way in which the pathogenic reproduction secures its hold, and advances with no social recognition or response. We have observed this condition in even this century and civilization – in the massacres of millions to express Nazi values in this century, and in the starvation, malnutrition, dispossession and death of tens of millions by the economic programmes of the global market in the last two decades.[8]

The pathogenic challenge is met at the social as well as the individual level when the systemically disabling disorder is recognized for what it is, and overcome by the immune defences of the life-host. This plane of life recognition and response is studied in scientific detail by the medical sciences at the individual organic level. But the same systematic study of *social* disease formations is not yet a conscious mode of understanding. Societies are, in fact, living bodies, that is, organized as interconnected systems of co-ordinated functions in unified structures of reproduction and growth. We know this if we are not obstructed by a market metaphysic that conceives of society in terms of an engineering physics model where societies are conceived as aggregates of self-maximizing atoms. We also *do* something about it as a citizen body if we do not imagine, as global market theology instructs us we must, that 'the invisible hand of the market' will providentially regulate societies to solve all of their problems.

At this point, it is not clear that global market thought has advanced beyond comprehending social defence systems as armed forces to annihilate peoples opposed to the global market's occupation of their societies. We need to observe the indicators of this pattern of thought. Across the world, poverty-stricken indigenous peoples have been driven off their land-bases by local oligarchies who seize the land for resource extraction or cash-crop plantations to export their takings to richer markets. Those who have sought to protect the life of their communities by organized resistance have been hunted down by death-squads, napalm-bombed or otherwise attacked by armed forces representing the invasive corporate agents – a pattern of events which is still occurring from Guatemala, Chiapas, Cameroon and Ogoniland to Indonesia, Burma, China and the Philippines.

The military-industrial establishment and the armaments business it leads have their own special global interests in this restructuring of life economies to money economies. They are the world's most powerful institutions of both organized violence and manufacture trade. Thus it is essential that they be sold as society's primary form of '*self-defence*' to preserve their continued control over vast pools of public wealth (for example, about $700 million a day of demand on the US public purse alone long after the Cold War is over).[9]

Society's *real* systems of self-defence, its public infrastructures of hazard and disease control and prevention, universal health care, public education, life-long income-security, social safeguarding and care for the old, the young and the infirm, and regulatory protection of the environmental life-host are in this way downgraded and deprived of their income support. They are seen as less important than protection of private corporate property at home and abroad. As we have seen, the social infrastructure of *life's* preservation and enablement has been rapidly dismantled. At the same time, ever more invasive assaults on life's support systems within societies – by environmental despoliation, by redistribution of wealth from the poor and middle-income classes to corporate money sequences, and by freedom of society's capital to exit overnight in haemorrhages of investment infrastructure – attack society's life-defence from another side.[10] By these relatively new and sudden changes to society's conditions of existence across the globe, we have come to confront a situation where cumulative breakdowns of socially evolved structures of life-security and health protection pose a more far-reaching threat to social and planetary well-being than social life-hosts are prepared for.

Yet at the same time, we know there is a profound collective impulse of societies towards protection of their life-fabrics once threats are recognized. We see this life-defence system go into very effective self-organization in emergencies, invasions, disease outbreaks, systemic dangers to children or wherever a danger to the social body or its members is registered. This is the social immune system in action. Our experience of it in military war, inventions of foreign threats and demagogic posturing has obscured its deeper-lying ground. At bottom, it is a *life*-protective response at the level of social life-organization. That its shared motivational structure across a nation or community has long been manipulated and misdirected should not lead us into misconstruing its underlying nature and potential.

The passion with which Canadian, Italian, German or French peoples, for example, have refused to submit to dismantling of their universal health-care, pensions or other life-protective systems, despite non-stop demands from market representatives for 'privatized tiers', 'necessary cutbacks' and so on is another expression of the social immune system at work. It admits of countless variations, dependent on the development of the society, and it articulates as the social life-organization of the species evolves.

In late nineteenth-century London, the idea of individual and public life-defence being connected in effective systems of social life protection was, in fact, the conscious logic of design of sewer lines, garbage disposal, police guardians, and the circulation of pure water to the social body's membership. The sewers were called 'the great intestines' of the society they served. When electrical networks joining society's members in communication fields became an essential infrastructure of social life later in the twentieth century, they were called 'the nervous system'.[11] This organizing conception of people linked across classes in a common life-organization is not new, but repressed by the surrounding metaphysical doctrine of society.

Underneath the atomistic ontology of the market paradigm has developed the immuno-competence of actual social life-hosts which have long survived by the unseen civil commons of interlocking sanitary systems serving all, ventilation and safety norms for workplaces and dwellings across society, and evolving epidemiological survey mechanisms and disease-preventative clinics distributed through the social body. All imply what cannot be conceived from the egoistic standpoint of competing market agents – a social life-host capable of health and disease as an individual organism is, and immuno-competent or incompetent as an individual life-host is.

Beginning with the city whose life interconnections demanded evolution of thinking beyond the atomic market self, the development of societies as macro life-systems evolved progressively more sophisticated structures of community life-defence against new and emerging dangers to their individual and collective memberships. Subsequent to its initial development in Europe and Britain, *public health* – a concept which expresses the emerging macro-life paradigm – came to be associated with a host of municipal, regional and national government regulations to secure the prevention of disease and the promotion of health in social populations across national and eventually international boundaries.

This socially constituted and publicly-funded infrastructure cannot depend on market exchange by its nature. From the beginning, it was developed by government through non-profit planning and social regulations binding all. As such, it naturally eludes the limited comprehension of the cash-nexus mind-set. *The global market paradigm can no more compute this larger body of life than it can compute the intricately evolved eco-webs of environmental life-organization.* Its model is confined to the simple, fungible inputs, throughputs and outputs of market money sequences. That is why such a mind-set says 'society does not exist' or 'environmentalists obstruct business'. It is also why governments implement policies to strip social infrastructures which protect human and environmental life. Their mutated market programme blinds them to the realities of any metabolism beyond the exchanges and growth of commodities and money sums.

But beneath the self-maximizing pursuit of price and profit in market sequences of money gain has been evolving a consciously constructed commons of social life-organization and universal goods upon which the deeper and long-term development of humanity and civilization have always depended. It embraces a vast system of social life-defence, from laws to ensure the non-contamination of food to liability norms to protect workers and citizens from industrial hazards, to public educational systems to develop cognitive capabilities essential to individuals' survival and self-expression within vast, interconnected organizations of interdependent functions constituting contemporary societies.

Knowing the Enemy

Because social immune systems have grown up beneath our consciousness of them, for millennia disguised behind atavistic taboos and armed forces of social defence, they have remained in their evolutionary adolescence, subject to irrational disorders. On the one hand, they have – until global market restructuring – evolved in the most advanced societies to collectively ensure the lives and reproduction of their members free from disease and breakdown. On the other hand, there have been barbaric *immune regressions* in times of extreme social stress.

Atavistic attacks on minority populations as 'unclean' or 'foreign elements' have been unleashed in murderous 'defences' of superstitiously conceived social bodies. Such strikings out in mass social confusion have increased beneath causal connection with the implementation of global market 're-engineerings'. As we will see with increasing depth ahead, 'structural adjustment programmes' have deprived people of their past life-security (for example, in the former federated socialist republics of Yugoslavia and in sub-Saharan Africa where subsistence farmers have been cleared from the land for agribusiness or oil extraction for global market export).[12] We can usually see in these cases something like a disordered social immune system at work – false recognition of a 'not-self agent' within globally restructured societies – and then destructive response by extinctive attack on the falsely identified enemy group. These outbreaks of savage virulence within communities where before, as in Yugoslavia, there had been constructive association, are then disconnected by global market ideology from the suddenly deprived life-grounds of the people involved, and even claimed to be 'rational' in the circumstances of group hatred which have been delinked from their common cause.[13]

These are primitive derangements of the social immune system, and themselves require civil commons recognition and cure. Civilization gradually selects out these social immune system disorders as long as there are not more general breakdowns in the health of social hosts (for example, massive impoverishment of the society's members which is a typical precursor of these social life breakdowns). In these cases, there is danger that social immune regimes will *atavize* to false identification of disease agents (for example, the impoverished themselves, or a different-looking group). Such disordered targetings of 'viruses' or 'foreign elements' in the social body are normally exploited by ruling interests which benefit from the disorder, as in the focus on anti-semitic, anti-communist, or racist social divisions which systemically distracts public attention from the actual disorders afflicting social life-organizations.

Historically, we have long observed these social immune disorders in various forms, from 'witch hunts' across the nations of Europe in the later sixteenth century to 'anti-subversive' exterminations in developing countries across the world in the Reagan era of the 1980s. We see them again in the 1990s in 'ethnic cleansing' operations in areas where populations have been stripped by 'structural adjustment programmes' and/or clearances of the land to make room for 'production for export'. We see them as well in 'social cleansing' operations by right-wing governments across the world attacking the poor, the gay, the unemployed and the left-wing in 'cultural wars' or other immune disorders.

These immune-regime pathologies in social bodies are perhaps history's most virulent plagues. But instead of recognizing the underlying roots of their deformation which these deranged movements exploit and direct onto scapegoats, we are apt to blame the community life-ground itself for these virulent deformations of it. In this way, we continue to miss the common life-base of social self-protective response which is the motivational source of all healthy social immune systems to protect all of society's members. In consequence, we remain vulnerable to the derangement because we have failed to comprehend the deep nature of its source, and thus of its perversion.

The consequence of this confusion, in turn, is that we fail to recognize or respond to the *actual* disorder selecting for the perversion, and so are not able to redirect society's highly developed immune capacities onto the deeper disease pattern itself. We can observe this immune disorder in systemic form with the International Monetary Fund's prescriptions for societies suffering from increasing and unpayable debt burdens. These debts continue to grow because of the high-rate, compounding interest demands on them placed by foreign market agents and money lenders. Instead of recognizing and responding to this disordered debt-system itself, which appropriates more and more of the sustenance of these societies with no contribution to their life functions, the IMF's decision structure is set to prescribe the reverse, becoming in this way a vector of the pathogenic programme rather than its prevention.

The IMF's 'structural adjustment programmes' prescribe the reduction or elimination of social spending on the needs of society's own members, and require instead the conversion of their agricultural and production systems to food and other exports so as to pay never-ending compound interest demands to foreign banks. These measures, in turn, deprive the host society further of the means of life its citizens are already short of. In this way, the IMF, which is supposed to restore the health of the economies it prescribes for, instead destroys their capacities to produce and distribute means of life for local citizens.

As the world's institutionalized agency for preventing '*monetary* instability', the IMF prescribes, in other words, that still more of the host society's *life*-sustenance be appropriated to feed the non-productive circuits of continuous money demands from foreign financial institutions. This disordered process of appropriating from domestic life sequences to feed foreign money sequences is, in fact, carcinogenic in its nature, or so we will diagnose its pattern of life-displacement ahead.[14] What was instituted as a social immune structure on the international plane operates in fact as a pathogenic invader of societies' capacities to reproduce their and their citizens' lives.

Until we are able to distinguish between society's pathological self-protection operations, which in fact attack it, and its healthy self-defence operations, we remain in a state of social immune incompetence. This is a particularly deep problem in the 'self-regulating' global market. Pathological social immune responses are on the rise across the world from the Balkans to the US. But immuno-competent response remains in a state of disorientation until it recognizes what has penetrated social life defences and multiplies within with no committed function to social life-hosts.

How to Tell Social Health from Social Disease

How can we tell a pathological social immune defence from a healthy one? The recognizing principle for any disease, individual or social, is *the extent to which it disables the life-host*. With the individual organism, we test for and discern disease by symptoms manifesting the disorder – impairments or interferences with normal operations of the body which are *states of morbidity to the extent that they reduce the range of bodily or mental function of the host organism*. Broken bones, dislocations, and torn muscles are easy to tell because they immediately present to the host a decisive reduction of its ability to move. Infectious diseases are less easy to tell. But they invariably manifest themselves as real health problems to the extent that their continuance manifests a loss of bodily or mental function that the healthy organism normally possesses.

In any case of health problem, we can always identify the severity of the affliction *by the reduction in the life capabilities of the host*. This life-reduction is, in turn, *calibrated by the extent of the loss of life capability*.

We can express these principles of individual or social health and disease in a simple general principle: The more the life-host is disabled, the worse the disease or the health problem is. The extent of the health problem, that is, is exactly recognized not only by the capabilities of life function lost in relation to the reference-body of the pre-diseased state, but also by the duration of this loss. At worst, the affliction approaches totality in its disablement, with the limiting point of this process of life reduction being the premature death of the life-host. We will examine this framework of life gain and loss in more depth ahead as the core of the ultimate framework of life value.

We can articulate this general criterion of distinction between health and disease to any degree of refinement and sophistication we choose to develop. With the social body, for example, we can readily discern by this principle that a society which loses/increases its former capacities to provide nutriments (for example, a drop, or gain, in calorific or protein intake of x per cent), or to ensure protection against pathogens (for example, a decline, or increase, of this or that transmissible disease or set of diseases by y per cent), or to provide literacy education for its citizen members (for example, a fall, or rise, of its adult literacy rate of z per cent), is experiencing a corresponding loss or gain of social health. The more significant the loss or gain, the more extended its duration, the worse or better the state of the social life-host. When the losses of life-enabling sustenance and protection become systemic, progressive and serious across significant sectors of the social life-organization, or all of it, then we confront a problem of social disease. This social disease, in turn, can be diagnosed for its cause or aetiology in the same way as physicians diagnose failing life-functions at the individual level of life-organization.

A society, conversely, becomes *healthier* to the extent that it becomes more enabled in these respects or others which extend the social membership's shared range of vital life-abilities and functions (for example, its members' average physical fitness, longevity, freedom from environmental pollutants and destruction, and scope and diversity of cultural activities). Whatever promotes more comprehensive ranges of a social membership's capacities to act, feel and think is the direction of its health protection and development. Whatever reduces or eliminates these vital life-ranges, conversely, is the direction of its disease, and obtains in exact proportion to the extent of these vital life functions which are lost. We can read the signs of these health and ill-health patterns in any society, taking the reference body of its previous state as our benchmark of life progress or decline.

Applied to the issue of *immuno-competence* of the social body, the same distinguishing criterion of *enabling* or *disabling* the life-range of the social membership can be applied. Clearly, the rampant destruction of members of a social body by massacres or systemic tortures is hard evidence of a serious disorder in the social host. Burnings of 'witches', 'eradication of subversives', 'ethnic cleansings' are all such disorders of societies, and are serious diseases in direct proportion to the degree and duration of their life homocidal destruction.

In the case of murderous attacks on members of a social life-host by the society's own armed forces – and all wars in the 1990s have been wars internal to social hosts, a deep indicator of internal social pathology – there are typically two conditions preceding such social immune disorders. First there is an agent of the disorder, for example, state armed forces within the society which have separated themselves off from accountability to the larger social body. The decoupled agent no longer operates on behalf of reproducing the interdependent whole of its members by protecting the society from unlawful violence from within or from without, but rather attacks and kills members of the society itself with no life function for its overall membership.

Second, there is typically a configuration of economic conditions prior to this usurping invasion of the social body which mark its impending eruption. This configuration of conditions is usually such that *the life-security of a large proportion of society's members has become insecure in their daily production and reproduction*. Whether this life-insecurity is caused by the gross seizure of its means of life and reproduction by a despotic oligarchy, or by the more subtle mechanisms of financial transactions which systematically enrich a section of the population at the expense of the life-sustenance of the rest, the attack on the health of the social body calls forth a *resistant* response from its afflicted membership.

This response may be inchoate and undeveloped in its ability to recognize and to respond to the disease invasion, or without the required resources to respond effectively. In these cases, that sector of the social body which is appropriating its life-resources at the expense of the community, starving its members and functions of their required means of life, prevents this normal social self-protective reaction from effective response to the disease challenge. It does so by *identifying this response itself as the society's 'disorder'*. It then attacks the bearers of the social body's restorative immune response as 'enemies', 'terrorists', 'subversives', or whatever the masking signifier might be.

On this basis, the rogue armed force of a society proceeds, usually with the assistance of an external major power which may be the primary disease agent, to destroy the resistant response from the society's productively committed membership. In this way, continued appropriation of society's resources for an autonomous rogue sub-body of its membership is perpetuated. This pattern of social immune disease led by national armed forces has gravely afflicted most Third-World societies over most of this century, from Latin America through the Middle East and Africa to Southeast Asia. Consider this brief description by a Canadian priest of the systematic destruction of the indigenous peoples of Guatemala after the democratically elected government was overthrown by a US-led military coup in 1954 in order to maintain control of its rich agricultural and then oil resources by US transnational corporations:

> The Guatemalans had been organizing co-operatives and protesting their terrible poverty. When their ancestral lands were turned into huge coffee

and sugar plantations [for international export and trade], they could no longer grow enough food to survive. The army responded to their resistance by killing hundreds of thousands in the 1980s, and a struggle for land grew into genocide.[15]

The Social Immune System Model

In the first instance, the conventionally accepted military system of social defence behaves very much like an intra-organic immune system. Indeed the parallels here are so striking that one might wonder whether the military mode of social self-defence is not an unconscious projection from the cellular level onto the social plane. 'Foreign' antigens 'invade' the host body. After 'recognition' of the 'invasive agent', the anti-body can neutralize the antigens by engulfment or by isolation as a mass, in both cases eventually absorbing the 'not self' into the host organism. Or it can destroy the 'foreign invader' by a process of cellular-wall perforation and blasting that uncannily resembles in principle the bullet and bomb attacks of military operations.

These concepts of 'self' and 'not-self', 'surveillance', 'recognition', 'foreign agent', 'invasion', 'response', 'defence' and 'attack', we must bear in mind, are all standard concepts of scientific medicine. On the one hand, one might argue that the idea of a 'social immune system' is only 'a metaphor', modelled on the intra-organic analyses of medical science. But if we consider the matter more deeply, we can see that the terms and designators deployed by medical science in its explanatory descriptions of the immune system's organic operations are all themselves *social categories*. The foundational concepts of the entire immune-system lexicon begin with the binary opposition of 'self' and 'not self', a reference ground which is the foundational distinction between individual persons and what they are not in the realm of human interrelations. The conceptual signifier of the immune-system model, 'immune', itself derives from the Latin root, *in-munus*, which refers to an exemption from Roman state prescription which compromised life prospects. Such prescription could in the case of gladiatorial service mean death for the person so commanded. Again here, we see that *the scientific concept of 'immune system' is modelled on social life and deploys social categories in all of its lexicon of descriptors.*

It is on the basis of this model of social life-organization that the further fundamental concepts and designators of immune-system operations are then developed and articulated as a unified system of meaning and explanation: (1) 'surveillance' of all the phenomena of organic processes to 'detect' any 'abnormality' in its functionings; (2) 'recognition' of the 'not-self' of disease or antigenic 'challenge'; and (3) 'response' of the 'host' body to the 'foreign invasion', 'opportunistic' pathogen, disease 'agent' or whatever is 'interfering with' or 'compromising' normal life function.

As we expose medical science's immune-system model to reflective examination of its standard categories of description and explanation, we see that in fact this model is pervasively conceptualized in terms of *social* life-organization. So the idea that social life-organization itself cannot be properly understood in terms of the medical model of the immune system is a conceptually naive objection. It fails to recognize that social distinctions, relations and aggressions are themselves the *prior* model of life-ordering and defence against attack upon which medical immune-system accounts are themselves systematically based. The point here is not to suggest that scientific medicine's social model of the immune system needs to be recast. For it works very well as it stands. The point is, rather, to lay bare the *organizational principles and operations in common between social and individual planes of life-organization*. Scientific medicine itself presupposes this systematic correlation. The structured similarity of social and individual self-protection systems is already a long-established basis of the medical model, and it has worked as a way of understanding and description. Our challenge is to recognize and deepen this overlooked common ground of understanding.

If we sustain our defined general distinction between *health* and *disease* on either the individual or the social level of life-organization, we have the *commensurable basis of judgement and evaluation we require to relate these levels of life-organization in a systematic way*. At the same time, we avoid a profound error which has increasingly bedevilled our comprehension of the relationship between individual and social life-organization. 'Individualism' has come to mean something very different from the affirmation of one's unique life capacities in a creative and autonomous way. Rather, it has come to mean something very different and opposed. Just as other meanings in the global market, it has mutated in its sense to refer to a radically *de-individuating* form of systemic assertion: *to acquire ever more money demand as an overriding programme of life without commitment to any life-host*.

This programme of acquisitiveness is not individual, because it is uniform in the nature of its goal and every unit of its content of acquisition. It is not self-interest in the classical sense, because there is no property of the self's life that is part of its meaning. Its expression is always, if we examine and track it, to follow the same pattern: to input money demand to become more money demand in reiterated sequences which secure their advance by self-multiplication. This self-multiplication, so far as it is left 'free' and 'self-regulating' has, in turn, no limit or required performance of life function to its growth.

To conceive of such a programme as 'individualism', and restraint or regulation of it to safeguard its life-hosts as 'impeding freedom' does not make sense as an issue of either individualism or of freedom, because it has no aspect of either form of life in its de-differentiated content and sequence. Its programme has, in fact, no relationship to life expression at all, as we will discover in more detail ahead. Its development marks a kind of reproduction and growth expressing the unrecognized mutations of the global market in uncontrolled, rogue forms not before seen.

From Marx to the Welfare State

Karl Marx was the first to see that the law of capital's process inverted all previously existing systems of social metabolism and exchange. He distinguished it from previously existing organizations of humanity's 'metabolism with nature' by the way in which its 'commodity cells' were produced and distributed as society's system of survival. What separated the capitalist organization of social bodies from all previous modes of social reproduction, Marx argued, was that it adopted as the initiating moment of its reproductive circuit *exchange-value* rather than *use-value* as its basis of social interaction. Whereas previous exchanges by the medium of money had begun with a *use-value* (for example, shoes) which was then sold to others for the money to buy another *use-value* (for example, food), the capitalist mode of producing social *use-value* was an inversion of this circuit. It began with *money* to be invested in *others'* production of *use-values* which, once-produced, were sold as commodities on the market for *more money*, which then began the production-exchange circuit of netting more money for the capitalist investor again, and so on *ad infinitum*.

This was a process of transformation of the social body's structure of reproduction which took centuries to institute in Britain and Europe before it spread across the globe. At first, merchants merely bought the goods that others produced independently, and sold these goods to others for more than they paid to extract a profit for themselves. They began with money, and ended with more money, but played no role in the process of production itself. This mercantile operation was as old as history. But the truly distinctive nature of the capitalist market system arose with the money-owners' direct control of the production process itself. It emerged as money owners moved from purchasing the use-values made by others to purchasing the *factors for producing the use-values themselves* – that is the required human workers, instruments of production and natural resources to produce the use-values in the most cost-reductive way, the original prototype operation of the modern corporation.

With human work and the means of production directly subordinated to the money-investor's ownership and control, the process of production could be rapidly reorganized, mechanized and intensified with no internal limit to the treatment of the human lives or environmental resources used as components in the system.

In the first volume of *Capital*, Marx formalized the transformation in the capitalist mode of reproducing society as follows:

Use-value or Commodity $\rightarrow$ Money $\rightarrow$ Use-value or Commodity or $C \rightarrow M \rightarrow C$ (pre-capitalist exchange)

changes to

Money $\rightarrow$ Use-value or Commodity $\rightarrow$ More Money or $M \rightarrow C \rightarrow M^1$ (capitalist exchange).

Marx proceeded to argue that there was a 'contradiction' between the requirement for reproducing and developing societies of human beings, on the one hand, *and* the requirement of ever more money extraction and accumulation by the private owners of investment capital. The primary contradiction he focused on was between the working class's need for sufficient means of life to go on producing and reproducing, *and* the systemic demand of capitalist investors for ever more surplus-value extraction and accumulation. To reduce this contradiction and others, Marx recommended a revolution of the economic and political system. He recommended, that is, the replacement of the capitalist class's rule of the social body and its specific metabolism of exchange by a working-class rule, and a new form of production and exchange which would regulate society's reproduction to fulfil the vital needs and capacities of all its members at a higher level of 'productive force development'.

One could say that Marx analysed a systemic 'disease of the social body', one that was disabling the life-range or health of its members in a multitude of ways. One far-reaching problem with Marx's account, however, was that the capitalist organization of social bodies was in fact *producing ever more material use-values for its members*. It was not only more productive in its yield of material use-values than any former organization of society's life, but it also turned out to be more efficient in producing machine-made goods than any *subsequent* non-capitalist organizations of society – albeit by continuous attacks on social alternatives by invasions of other societies, trade embargoes, training and administration of death-squads, a global propaganda war, blacklistings of suspected supporters, and various other means of extinguishing competing economic orders.

The capitalist form of social life-organization, however, was eventually compelled by the 'communist threat', workers' movements and a new electoral accountability to adopt preventive measures against its own internal disorders and pathologies. Advanced capitalist societies slowly and under great social pressures introduced social reforms to limit a multitude of hazards to workers' lives, and over time to protect environmental conditions of life as well. This process began with social legislation restricting working hours and factory-caused hazards and diseases, and eventually led to universal programmes of education, health and social security, an evolution whose reversal was analysed in the previous chapter.

In this way the destructive consequences of the modern capitalist organization of society were progressively counter-balanced by socially legislated protections of human and environmental life. This overall social immune development depended throughout on non-market public agencies recognizing and responding to the life needs of society's members as a whole and of its wider environmental host, and preventing disabling morbidities from taking hold in either system of life reproduction.

The Global Mutation of the Capitalist System:

Despite the long development of social immune systems within capitalist as well as non-capitalist societies with roots reaching back over centuries, a relatively sudden mutation of social orders emerged during and after the 'final triumph of capitalism'. Dramatic changes in social life-organization across the world by 'global market restructurings' of social systems precipitated breakdowns in evolved social immune systems on virtually every parameter of life-protection.

Although the following global survey of the general parameters of this breakdown is at the highest level of generalization, the patterns of morbidity it identifies are now more or less universally applicable to social life-hosts across the world. We will recall that these criteria of health and disease are that *disease* obtains and increases in its severity to the extent that it disables the vital life functions of its host; while *health* obtains or increases to the extent that vital life functions are maintained or increased.

Applying these general principles to life-organization at the social level, we can identify the following *general parameters of social well-being as basic general determinants of social health and disease in any social body*:

(1)   Continuity of life-sustenance to members of the social body;
(2)   Functioning contribution of members to the life-requirements of the larger life-organization to which they belong;
(3)   Maintenance of the biophysical carrying capacity of the environmental life-host.

Just as diagnosis on the individual level of life-organization, so diagnosis of a social life-system looks for *lesions of life function.* There is no laboratory test or method of biopsy and microscopic investigation to reveal the disease to us. We must examine social symptoms in another way than we are used to, as connected in a pattern of systemic loss of life powers. Here we adopt an overview of the findings we have been marshalling through this investigation, and assess them in these terms. As we will see, an underlying global profile of social and environmental life emerges which connects the most disparate data and investigative results in unmistakably pathological pattern at each level of diagnosis.

With each of the three general parameters of social well-being and disease which follow, serious loss or reduction of life function is the signal of a disease at work on the social level of life-organization, in proportion to the extent, duration and rate of the decline of the life plane in question.

(1) Social Life Income: Continuity of life sustenance to members of the social body.   Income security is the only way in which the need requirements of life which cannot be synthesized by the body itself *or* by independent production can be assured to the members of any capitalist-organized society. *A need, in turn, is a need to the extent that deprivation of it regularly results in reduction of the ability to move or to feel or to think.* For example, deprivation of air for a short time, or food, or water over a longer time, or of shelter, affection or variety of activity over differing periods of time, regularly result in morbidity or disablement of the human so deprived. Fulfilment of needs is in this way the most basic requirement of health, and failure to fulfil needs is the most basic cause of disease.

As the goods of life meeting human needs become increasingly commodified (that is, available only on payment of money for access to them) continuity of money income to exchange for the means of vital life-sustenance becomes correspondingly essential. Food, clothing and shelter are now only normally available to members of capitalist societies in commodity form. Safe drinking water, air, sunlight and other basic organic needs are increasingly dependent on commodity-purchase for access of social members to them. Even social intercourse and cultural participation have become increasingly dependent on money income. Reproduction itself has come to be a disastrous condition without sufficient revenue to purchase capitalist-produced goods.

At the same time, access to natural means of life-support has declined to near zero by this system's ever more global appropriation and destruction of the world's forests, species, oceans, coral reefs, fresh water habitats, soils and inter-tidal zones. Although continuity of sufficient money income is thus required to sustain the life and health of societies and their members across the world, 'structurally adjusted' societies in the global market have *simultaneously reduced and eliminated the social infrastructures that assure sufficient money life-income for members of social bodies.* This pattern of reducing the flow of vital life-sustenances through social bodies is revealed in part by the following macro-trends of social income distribution. Bear in mind that approximately three billion more of the world's people have been more or less suddenly reorganized into neo-capitalist market structures.

Real incomes for most of society's members and, if dependents, the real incomes of those who care for them, have declined across the world in a varying but consistent pattern of incremental reduction. As we have seen in even the US, wages and salaries overall declined radically – by 15 per cent in real terms between 1973 and 1992, and by 20 per cent during the same period for unskilled non-supervisory workers in the private sector. Subsequently, in 1995, real wages contracted by a full 3 per cent. At the same time the real income of the top 1 per cent of the society escalated by 60 per cent between 1977 and 1992. By 1993 this 1 per cent of US society possessed more marketable wealth than the bottom 90 per cent, and eight times more financial wealth than the bottom 80 per cent.[16]

Other national profiles reveal even more precipitate and sudden declines in continuity of life sustenance to society's members. In Mexico, for example, after infiltration of deregulated Maquiladora 'free trade zones' in 1980, the national wage and salary average declined by over 50 per cent in real terms, and unemployment rates more than doubled to 18 per cent. In 1994–95, after Mexico's government opened all of its social body to reorganization by the North America Free Trade Agreement, and after $70 billion invaded Mexico in speculative investment in the new unprotected order, civil war was raging in Chiapas over 'the death sentence of NAFTA', and currency speculation in the rise and fall of the Mexican peso still further decreased the life-sustenance flow to the Mexican people: in 1995 by an estimated 30 per cent drop in the value of the peso, a drop of grocery sales of 25 per cent, and an escalating rise in national unemployment to reach 30 per cent. During this period of extremely rapid decline of life-support income for members of Mexican society, the Mexican stock exchange rose 1000 per cent between 1988 and 1994, the number of billionaires almost doubled to 24, while the manufacturing sector declined from 7.3 per cent growth in 1989 to increasing negative growth since.[17] Mexico was dominantly described in the corporate chain media during most of this process as an 'economic miracle', which it certainly was in terms of the rapid redistribution of society's life-income to delinked money sequences.

In New Zealand, at the other side of the world, we have seen much of the profile already. After a leak by a government minister of an impending devaluation of New Zealand money, New Zealand money predictably fled the country. This caused an exchange crisis whose conditions provided the new marketeer government the desired opportunity to dismantle New Zealand's welfare state. Social spending and programmes for public sector employment, income security, health-care and education were radically reduced or eliminated. In the two years after cuts were introduced (1990–92), the New Zealand's national government Department of Statistics reported a 40 per cent increase in poverty, a doubling of youth suicide to the highest recorded in the world, a 50 per cent increase of violence against women, and a 40 per cent increase of violence against children (including a trebling of infanticide). Taxes on corporations and the wealthy were cut by 50 per cent, unemployment skyrocketed from near zero to 12.8 per cent, interest rates rose to up to 30 per cent and output plunged to negative growth rates. All this was 'to reduce the deficit'. But in fact the government deficit more than doubled from $22 billion to $46 billion.[18] New Zealand too was celebrated across the world by global market agents and the mass media as 'an economic miracle'.

In the former Soviet Union between North America and New Zealand, the rapid conversion of the social body to capitalist organization had the following outcomes in the continuity of vital life sustenance and security to society's members. Real incomes dropped by 30 per cent ; industrial production was cut in half; 60 million pensioners' lives were increasingly at risk (a large proportion from starvation); 40 million approached starvation conditions; prices increased in the early period of the experiment by 2600 per cent with bread in 1995 10,000 times its price in 1992; and violent crime and corruption ran progressively out of control.[19] In the former 'powerhouse of the Soviet bloc', East Germany, industrial production nose-dived to one-third its former level, and the real unemployment figure soared to between 35 and 40 per cent with resurgent Nazi eruptions by unemployed youth increasingly dominating German politics.[20]

None of this was conceived as a vast failed experiment with entire societies, despite tens of millions of people's ruined lives. Here we can see in near-laboratory conditions how an economic paradigm disconnected from life co-ordinates can advance across social hosts with the progressively depredatory pattern of a disease, but its effects not appear as a problem of the paradigm determining the changes.

In Yugoslavia, which stationed itself *between* the nations of Western capitalism and the Soviet Union, the outcomes of 'market restructuring' were more dramatically violent. But as we have observed, no linkage is recognized yet within the agents and agencies leading and reporting on this process between effects and cause. That the ethnic barbarism followed in the wake of macro-economic reforms pressed by the US government and imposed by the IMF and World Bank is a connection precluded from commercial and university press accounts. Subsequent to these tidal waves of market reforms, industrial production plunged to minus 10.6 per cent by 1990, and GDP by over 50 per cent in all the former republics except Slovenia by 1995. At the same time, a 'financial aid package' was imposed against the trans-ethnic protests of 650,000 workers in Serbia alone, requiring a national currency devaluation, a general wage freeze, a drastic reduction of social expenditures, opening of domestic markets to foreign commodities, and the abolition of publicly owned enterprises under worker self-management.

Deprived of the evolved common ground of social infrastructure and co-operative responsibility which linked the formerly hostile Balkan peoples across cultural lines, and impoverished by the massive disemployments, bankruptcies and collapse of productive enterprises which occurred simultaneously to pay foreign money-lender demands, the states of the former federation fell to the politics of ethnocide only after the stripping of their shared life supports.[21] None of this was noted by the international media and known academic pundits, least of all the underlying systemic recirculation of social wealth from the social infrastructures and productive workers to marketized circuits turning money into more money as an end in itself.

These social profiles exhibit a clear disease pattern. The allocation of resources to goods to support and enable life is rapidly reduced to deprive societies of their sustenance. These resources are instead appropriated to feed delinked, money-to-more-money circuits which move from one society to the next, invading them. The process of transmission of the disease is not by conspiracy. It is by the imposition and spreading of the prescriptions and entailments of an unexamined value programme whose inner logic is to select for money sequence growth as its determining code of reproduction.

As circulation of required income for life means and their production has been appropriated from ever more people across the globe, with correspondingly more revenues flowing to private money cycles of investment, whole societies have become ever more endangered and insecure. Unemployment rates rise at an exponential rate in relationship to the 1960s in the world's most developed economies.[22] Social sectors protecting and enabling life by health care, education and income security are 'axed' across continents from the Americas to China. At the same time, unregulated movement of money capital across boundaries for non-productive speculative seizures of social incomes accelerates in volume and velocity everywhere. Speculation in money value itself has become an epidemic overwhelming economies at 50 or more times greater a volume than the value of all trade in goods and services.[23] At over $1.2 trillion dollars a day, it is also an estimated 60 times greater than all the governments in the world could raise to resist its attacks on their currencies.[24]

With money demand increasingly in the circuits of money-to-more-money growth, the result is less and less money available in the economy to serve the lives of people. Social populations are thus deprived not only of what was formerly in the production and provision of means of life, but are also made ever more insecure about the continuance of what they have. Humans uniquely among the world's species think, feel and act in terms of *future life-means,* and so their present loss of access to these life-means is projected into the future to compound their life-insecurity.

At the same time, those without any independent income support, young members and unemployed members of society, a rising proportion of social memberships across the world, not only are endangered in their health and life functions by the declining incomes of those who support or aid them, as well as by deprivation of the social welfare and assistance upon which they variously depend for their continued existence. With increasingly diminishing job-prospects, the youth of the world approach the condition of a surplus population. For the young to become superfluous to their society is an inversion of the biological law of species living to reproduce themselves. It expresses the social disease pattern in the most basic parameter, the reproduction of humanity's vital life capacities across the next generation.

It is in this context that global statistics report that one-third of all children are malnourished or starving, a pattern of deprivation of the most basic means of life that has eaten progressively into the margins of the wealthiest First World societies themselves. Between 1981 and 1991 in Canada for example, the poverty rate for working households grew by 30 per cent , and by 57 per cent for unattached individuals, while the poverty rate of children grew by 49 per cent between 1989 and 1994 and continued to increase.[25] What is most alarming about this deepening, spreading deprivation of the basic requirements of life sustenance for dependent children and young workers under 30 is the universality, rapidity and progressiveness of its advance.

At the same time, higher education is defunded in the 'knowledge economy', and its financial support is turned over to private banks who extend long-term, compound interest loans to the next generation of students to become debt-prisoners of institutional money-lenders. On the wider field of social reproduction, by 1994 a segregated body of 358 billionaires had more net wealth than the total life-revenues of almost half the world's population, an effect for which the global market's system deciders select.[26]

In its May 1998 issue, the *British Medical Journal* carried a series of articles and letters by medical professionals identifying the causal pattern of life depredation and decline which was not yet recognized by the larger society. *Poverty*, these physicians concurred, *is the world's leading cause of medical disease and ill-health, and the main cause of increasing poverty is 'globalization'.*[27]

(2) Social Life Contribution: Functioning contribution of members of the social body to the life-requirements of the larger whole to which they belong.   A healthy life-organization not only requires sufficient flow of vital life-means to its contributing functions to reproduce free of the ravages of disease, disablement and death. Each of its elements must as well contribute in some active way to the well-being of the interrelated whole to which they belong to sustain their own functioning capacities and those of the larger bodies of which they are living members. This is a basic requirement of all life-systems. Just as wastage, atrophy or disease sets in very rapidly with non-use of any part of the individual organism, so it is at the social level of life-organization. We can verify by observation that social members who do *not* animate, exercise and develop their functioning abilities in some form of active contribution to the smaller or larger communities of which they are members usually decline in health and vigour, suffer higher rates of heart, cancer and other primary forms of organic morbidity and manifest mental disabilities of various kinds such as suicidal depression.[28]

Members of a human society can almost always contribute to the social bodies to which they belong in some way specific to their particular abilities. Extended families and tribal communities of former life economies demonstrate this in the active and various functions of the elderly, the abnormal and very young in the life functions of the community. Global market societies, however, increasingly tend towards an ever deeper and universal division between two great classes of social members – those who are instrumentalized in some way as paid employees contributing to the production, extraction or protection of the circuit of money-profit generation and accumulation, *and* those who are not so instrumentalized. Since the need for the former class of people decreases with capitalist development of methods of labour-cost reduction (that is, by machines and electronic circuits of ever greater powers of articulated production), as well as by the downsizing and dismantling of public sectors, the class of full-time employees in capitalist-organized societies has diminished with completely unprecedented rapidity in times of investment prosperity. Nearly one-third of the world's 2.2 billion workers have come to be chronically unemployed, with increasing proportions of even first-world social populations – most gravely, the younger generations – marginalized and disconnected from socially productive existence.[29] Because more and more of life's functions and fields have been subordinated to money-sequence expansion, there are progressively fewer areas left for those who are *not* paid employees of capital to contribute to as active members of their societies and communities. They are thereby rendered disposable as functioning members of global market society.

The loss of social function leads to a wide variety of pathological outcomes. 'Unemployment, and even the threat of unemployment, can have dramatic health consequences, including increased mortality due to heart disease and cancer. ... For every 1% rise in the jobless rate, there is a 2% rise in the number of cardiac deaths, a 3 to 4% rise in infant mortality, a 4 to 5% rise in suicides and homicides, a 5 to 6% jump in admissions to psychiatric hospitals ... [and] an elevated relative risk of mortality from cancer of 2.07.'[30] The recently disemployed man's probability of heart disease or cancer, in fact, doubles within five years with 40–49-year-old American men.[31] Adolescent suicide and prostitution rates escalate as future employment prospects become darker (as with the 12–19-year-old age group across first world nations since the late 1980s).[32]

Most visibly, ethnic wars, racist attacks, armed violence, urban riots, beatings of women and children and – in general – mass murders of unknown others rise in social sites where the unemployment of young men or clearances of subsistence farmers has become endemic. This pattern can be observed from the slums of North America to the cities of Indonesia, El Salvador or Brazil. The life-loss on the *psychological* plane to people separated from a committed function to perform for the community to which they belong expresses itself in physical morbidities, but is a distinct plane of the systemic life decline, the most central from the standpoint of the felt side of life. The mental torments of those who are deprived of any function or value in their society can only at this stage be guessed at as a social epidemic across all able-bodied age-groups and even entire societies (for example, indigenous peoples). Where no recognized work for a wider community is or can be performed, the member of the social body is made a superfluous being who has 'no reason to live'.

(3) The Environmental Life-Host: Maintenance of the biophysical carrying capacity and reproductive diversity of the external environment.   There has been wide recognition of the crisis of 'environmental sustainability'. I will not reiterate the specifics of this global life crisis here. What has *not* been widely recognized, however, is a foundational connection: that global market use of environmental resources determines their depletion, pollution and destruction.

It is true that the Soviet societies were at least as ecocidal as market societies in their five to seven decades of operation. But we should bear in mind that they were imitative of centuries-old practices of large-scale capitalist extraction systems, and competed to outperform them at this mode of relationship with nature's life resources. Despite these explanatory clues, the money-sequenced exploitation of the environment is systematically excluded as a determinant of species and habitat distribution and extinction by environmental biology and ecological research.[33]

We need not collude here with this profound block against recognizing the connection between cause and effect. We can from an independent surveillance of life-environments discern a general principle of correlation between industrial, private-profit use of environmental resources and their decline. This principle of correlation can, like other causal relationships, be tested. We can, that is, observe across the laboratory of the global market's implementation whether this principle is confirmed, or disconfirmed. The cause–effect relationship here asserted for test by observation is:

As global market use of the environment has advanced and advances across global life conditions and elements, these global life conditions and elements – the atmosphere, fresh waters and oceans, top soils, trees, animal habitats and species and mineral resources – have in direct proportion to its penetration degenerated in their capacities of life-carriage and yield.

An effective international regulatory regime to protect regional and global environmental life-hosts might prevent this accelerating pattern of destruction of its biophysical carrying-capacity and life-habitats. But, revealingly, the global market exploitation of the environment increases as its harms increase. One example is that five transnational Asian corporations which have largely destroyed their own region's rainforests have entered into purchase agreements with Latin American governments to exploit 20 million *more* acres of rainforest in the Amazon Basin with no limits on the destruction of life habitats to be permitted for increased money-value returns to stockholders.[34]

More revealingly from a systemic standpoint, global market exploitation of the environment seeks at the threshold of its cumulative environmental damage to avoid or to further reverse effective environmental regulation. This trend is evidenced in even the most prosperous First World societies such as Canada where environmental agencies have, as we have seen, been stripped of scientists, research programmes, police, independent monitoring requirements and recycling programmes. This effective deregulation was done in imitation of the US Republican Congress attempt in 1995 to dismantle the US Environmental Protection Agency by blanket rescindment of regulations and corporate rewriting of environmental legislation. The difference, which worked, was to disguise the assault by public relations slogans like 'resources for life'.[35]

On a world scale, volumes of exact rules of the World Trade Organization and North American Free Trade Agreement protected the unrestricted rights of private corporations to access and exploit natural resources and sell their products across boundaries. But not one of this mountain of regulations included a binding regulation protecting the world or regional environments against increasing pollution, destruction, wastes, exhaustion, homogenization, or extinction. The 1998 Kyoto pact to reduce potentially catastrophic emissions of 'global warming' gases of carbon dioxide, methane and nitrous oxide 'succeeded' by instituting a new market regime for private corporations to buy and sell rights to pollute the planet's atmosphere. Here again, we can observe the paradigm's enclosure within itself where only what fits the selector principle of money profit by commodity exchange can enter public-interest regulation itself. That chaotic disturbances of global weather patterns had already been unleashed by this model's restructuring of nature did not deter its reimposition as the solution to its disastrous effects.

The invasiveness of such a regime may be discerned by the following pathologies of its outcomes. The air may be increasingly unbreathable in the 'miracle' economies of the East and the South. No-one on the globe may be able to be in the sun without cancer danger. Ocean bottoms and coral ecosystems may become lifeless in multiplying regions across the planet. Tropical and temperate rainforests may be clear-cut at a rising 100 acres a minute. Plant and animal species may be going extinct at a recognized 1000 times the normal rate. The desertification of soils may be proceeding by country-sizes each year. The sounds of the world may be ever more dominantly the anaplastic din of motors burning non-renewable and productively precious fossil fuel. But the for-profit industrial exploitation of the global life-environment must be left free to increase its assaults on environmental life-systems to 'keep the economy going'.

The long-awaited 1992 UN Rio Declaration on Environment and Development provides another clue to the puzzle of global life disruption and decline not being related back to the system-deciders determining them. The Rio Conference failed, despite the 'environmental crisis' recognized by negotiators, to respond to the systemic and cumulative depredation of planetary life because there was a more basic programme by which its participants were still bound. Principle 2 of the Rio Declaration recognizes that 'States [read corporations using state environments as vehicles] have the *sovereign right to exploit their own resources ...*'. Principle 16 declares that 'the polluter should, in principle, bear the cost of pollution ... *without distorting international trade and investment*'.

In short, the world body responded with no effective inhibition of the accumulating destruction of the earth's biosphere, or the spreading regime of reproduction behind it because it remained within the ruling structure of thought. Five years after its 200,000-word programme of hundreds of steps to be taken by governments acting for 'sustainable development' within the framework of 'not distorting international trade and investment', the ecocidal problem it was organized to resolve with all governments in attendance had become clearly worse. The 1998 follow-up summit in New York concluded that overall trends 'are worse today than they were in 1992'.[36] But no tie-back to the infrastructural determinants of the progressive advance of the diseased state was considered, or arose in media discussion of the problem. Rather, disproportionate coverage was given to those who denied climatic changes by industrial gas emissions.

The Cancer Stage of Capitalism

At this stage of the global market system's reproduction of transnational money sequences to unheard-of volumes and velocities of transaction and growth, a systematic and irreversible destruction of planetary life-organization emerges for the first time in history. If we consider the defining principles of carcinogenic invasion and eventual destruction of a life-host, and do not avoid or deny the symptom profile in evidence, we discern a carcinogenic pattern increasingly penetrating and spreading across civil and environmental life-organization.

There are seven defining properties of a cancer invasion which medical diagnosis recognizes at the level of the individual organism. These seven properties can now be recognized for the first time at the level of global life-organization as well. And this is the pathological core of our current disease condition.

That is, there is:

(1)   an uncontrolled and unregulated reproduction and multiplication of an agent in a host body; that
(2)   is not committed to any life function of its life-host; that
(3)   aggressively and opportunistically appropriates nutriments and resources from its social and natural hosts in uninhibited growth and reproduction; that
(4)   is not effectively recognized or responded to by the immune system of its hosts; that
(5)   possesses the ability to transfer or to metastasize its growth and uncontrolled reproduction to sites across the host body; that
(6)   progressively infiltrates and invades contiguous and distant sites of its life-hosts until it obstructs, damages and/or destroys successive organs of their life-systems; and that
(7)   without effective immune-system recognition and response eventually destroys the host bodies it has invaded.

Three years after these common properties of disease affliction on global and cellular levels of life-organization were first identified,[37] a former US Undersecretary of Commerce and Dean of the Yale School of Management who was speaking for the 'globalization process', released a question which was not followed up: 'Or is there', he asked, 'a bigger cancer at the centre of the whole enterprise?'[38] What might be the cancer, and what was the vehicle of its invasion were not ready to be considered. But the question insists: If there *is* in fact a malignant cancer pattern advancing across environmental and social life-hosts, what is *the disease agent* that underlies its symptoms of invasion and assault?

One diagnosis could be from the standpoint of the global life-host itself. It might be argued that the disease-agent is the human species, a rogue form of proliferating reproduction in its industrial stage which exhibits the seven properties of a cancer specified above. But it cannot be the human species *per se* because over 99 per cent of the species' time on earth has been free of any such pervasive, systemic pattern of incremental environmental destruction. And it cannot be coherently diagnosed as human *overpopulation* as such because exponential human population growth beyond the environment's carrying capacities is itself symptomatic of more fundamental social determinants – specifically, mass poverty in the recent era of global industrialization where effective social response to or regulation of these conditions is not in place. We can test this claim by application to the relevant evidence. Contemporary societies *without* mass poverty or industrialized conditions have typically had *negative* rates of reproduction. The 'overpopulation disorder', we can reasonably infer from these general facts of its presence and absence, is a problem linked to specific social-structural conditions: namely, *mass impoverishment in industrializing societies where there has been a failure both to overcome mass poverty and to regulate the industrialized extraction or destruction of environmental resources in these regions.*

We can infer from these general facts, in turn, that breakdowns in circulation of vital life sustenance to members of social bodies *and* breakdowns in environmental carrying capacities are related determinants of the 'overpopulation crisis'. Overpopulation, we can therefore conclude, is a *symptom* of these deeper-lying conditions. These structural conditions, in further turn, correlate to an underlying common pattern of morbidity which we can analyse as follows.

The Nature of the Cancer Agent

There have been since 1980 two comparatively sudden and rapidly advancing systemic changes across the social bodies and environment of the globe. These two dramatic changes have attacked evolved systems of life-protection just as the stress and assault on their carrying-capacities by money-to-more-money circuits have become more rapid, intense and pervasive.

The most sudden of these attacks has been on the evolved 'social immune systems' of the world in the form of 'structural adjustments' and 'social service cutbacks' to 'pay down public debts'. These 'structural adjustments' are never admitted to be what prior diagnosis has shown them to be – namely *appropriations from public sectors of revenue by non-productive money sequences.* The language of 'necessary sacrifices' declares this invasionary pattern in code.

As life-serving systems of social bodies are thus cut back across national boundaries, their resources are dominantly rechannelled to the expansion of money-to-more-money circuits with no commitment to life function. The pattern is so aggressive that the signifiers of its agents do not disguise the underlying violence of the appropriation – 'axing social programmes', 'slashing public services', 'subjecting societies to shock treatments' and so on.[39]

At the same time as social infrastructures evolved over generations of social life struggle and development are 'axed', the declared purpose becomes more overt – to 'reassure lenders and investors of money', or, in its populist vein, 'to let people spend their money as they choose'. These propositions mean, decoded, to expand the global market's circuits of money demand. What has been traditionally known as capitalism has, in fact, mutated to a form no longer linked to the production of *use-values* for social memberships. It has, with no social recognition, changed to a system of growth no longer 'capital' in any traditional sense. As the former Governor of the US Federal Reserve, Paul Volker, warned without recognizing the rogue form of reproduction he obliquely flagged, 'The biggest concern [I have] today is that *there is a constituency for instability*'.[40]

What Volker meant is that volatility in the global system's money sequences allows for correspondingly more opportunities to profit from constantly changing margins between currency and stock values *which increase with instability of their values*. In other words, there is an unmarked 'constituency' or agent that lives from the instability of what societies and their members depend upon for their lives, the value of their money for their metabolisms of exchange and the value of their products for sale in exchanges with other societies. If there are vectors of societies' life-systems which grow unproductively from the instability of their life-hosts' circulatory access to means of life, we see the resemblance to a cancer on the cellular level of life-organization.

If the instability increases with a new 'free circulation' of the rogue sequences of growth which opportunistically expand as these insecurities of access to life means increase across surrounding life communities, and if they multiply faster and spectacularly with ever more free movement with no committed function to their life-hosts, while the latter suffer 'meltdowns' first here and then there each time more devastatingly, then a carcinogenic programme has established itself in fact in the afflicted hosts – whether it is recognized or not.

All that could keep such a rogue programme of uncontrolled and predatory reproduction growing at the expense of its life-hosts would be that their immune systems were unable to recognize the disease agent, or, at the social level of life-organization, collaborated with the disease invader as finance departments and central banks have done in the case of these 'free flows' of money capital predating societies' mediums of life exchange.

The 'constituency' for instability in the global market is in fact hydra-headed. Not only are there transnational currency traders and other financial speculators of multiplying kinds growing into ever new headways of money appropriation from life economies. There are also the global market's booming armaments trade, escalating financial services, diversifying violence entertainment businesses and security industries which grow rapidly from systemic instability of life conditions. We will analyse these 'constituencies for instability' in the next chapter.

With 97.5 per cent of all foreign exchange transactions devoted in 1998 to predatory appropriations of the world's money demand by currency speculators, the 'constituency' for instability of the global economic system appears, in fact, to have run out of control. Money investment which seeks to become more money without production of any life good or service has been known as long as usury, but never before as the dominant decision-structure of social life-organization. Even when the loan-capital circuit became greatly empowered in earlier centuries by the immensely profitable financing of kings' armies, investment-capital *as a whole* was still standardly invested in the production or distribution of useful goods.

Critics of capitalism from Marx through Lenin to contemporary analysts have thus argued or assumed that it is *industrial* capitalism that rules social bodies in its ever-widening 'imperialist stage'. Marx is the prototype of this understanding. His canonical model of the inner logic of capital's general process of surplus-value extraction straightforwardly asserted: 'The movements of this *money-capital* are therefore once more *merely movements of an individualized part of industrial capital engaged in the reproduction process'.*[41] Money capital that appears to go directly from money to more money is, according to this received view, only a specialized moment within larger capital circuits that go from money through good or service production and distribution to more money as the macro-circuit of capital's expansion.

Again, in Marx's words: 'A definite part of the total capital disassociates itself from the rest and stands apart in the form of money-capital, *whose capitalist function consists exclusively in performing these operations for the entire class of industrial and commercial capitalists.'* No Marxian analysis that I know of has disagreed with this account. This is a stunning oversight, since the gold standard, and therefore the dead-labour basis of money value which Marx supposed as money's stable yardstick, was eliminated in 1974.[42]

The *mutation* in money investment and profit occurs when money capital is no longer a phase within the circuit of the production or distribution of goods or services, but is exclusively committed at every stage of its growth only to the *multiplication of itself.* Instead of any productive or distributive function in the metabolism of money through the medium of use-value to more money ($M \rightarrow C \rightarrow M^1$), there is only the metabolism of money to more money *without any conversion to use-value in the circuit* $(M \rightarrow M^1 \rightarrow M^2 \rightarrow M^n)$.

For purposes of clarification and simplification, we will henceforth refer to this value sequence as:

$$\$ \rightarrow \$^1 \rightarrow \$^n$$

This capital-circuit mutation now emerges in many ways – from currency and derivatives speculations by high-roller dealers to the cash portfolios of mutual pension funds. Conglomerate mutual funds under centralized stock and bond managers multiplied, for example, by 12 times between 1984 and 1989 in North America, while hundreds of billions of investment dollars were decoupling altogether from the real economy at the same time in international currency speculation.[43] The defining principle of this investment mutation is that it is *no longer bounded by any national base or interest or regulation, or by any other direct or indirect requirement to commit itself to any productive function beyond itself.* It demands only to acquire maximally more money for money loaned or invested with no conversion into sustenance or service for any human, social or environmental life-organization in between. It is enabled to do this technically, in turn, by legal means provided principally by the Reagan-Thatcher administrations, by the electronification of money and the digital computerization of money transactions, and by the 1:10 or 1:20 ratio of cost to other stock transactions.[44]

Compounding interest demands on these life-decoupled money circuits proliferates the claims for more money to money holders at the same time. Long ago, the self-multiplying properties of the compound-interest cycle were marked by the financier, J.P. Morgan, who confided: 'I couldn't name the Seven Wonders of the World, but I can tell you what the eighth is – Compound Interest.'[45] By this magic of self-proliferation, the non-productive interest demands on lent money multiplied in total volume by almost 300 times in the United States between 1950 and 1995 – more than ten times the rise of GNP over the same period.[46] At this rate, the US was steered towards an outcome in which payment of interest on debt would demand the entire national income within 25 years.[47]

These reproductive conditions of delinked money sequences multiplying money demand with no productive function satisfy the *carcinogenic formula of* $\$ \to \$^1 \to \$^2 \to \$^n$. The omniverous cycle becomes the master of global economies by its not being responded to. In order to continue its growth, it must in some way strip societies of their powers of self-government to ensure that they do not impede or fetter the increasing appropriation of social resources it requires to go on expanding. 'The disposable income of the majority is being reduced,' observes a London School of Economics professor who approves of the trend. 'The big question of the coming decades is how to find an acceptable means of scaling back democracy.'[48]

The unregulated growth of a reproductive sequence within social bodies that attacks the life functions of its hosts is no less a disease on the social level of life-organization than it is on the individual level. A cancer pattern of disease is at work in social bodies *to the extent* that we observe the defining traits of its behaviour confirmed – and none disconfirmed – by observation. Increasingly, we observe, the global market's investment cycles have no committed function to any life-organization on the planet. An undertow process of unmediated money-to-more-money spread increasingly exhibits the classic indicators of carcinogenic invasion and metastasis because of its 'freedom' to move with increasing volumes and velocities in and out of any social or environmental life-host. At the same time, the life-bodies which are the site of this disease pattern do not recognize its competitive metabolism which converts ever more social life resources to feed its decoupled growth.

The spiralling debt and deficit circuits currently bankrupting governments and social infrastructures across the world are a primary channel of this progressively dominant sequence of reproduction. For example, the total debt of less developed countries to banks doubled from approximately $819 billion in 1982 to $1712 billion in 1993, after over $1.4 trillion had *already* been appropriated from these poorer societies by foreign banks.[49] This process continued, and was sufficient to collapse these societies into growing chaoses of malnutrition, illiteracy, morbidity and destitution.

These Third World government debts in general, in turn, were themselves largely contracted by agents within the society placed into rule by US-supported military seizures of ruling power. They were then sustained in rule by external military and financial institutions which assisted in circulating these original government debt-money loans into major foreign banks to lend back at compound interest, or to speculate in non-productive ventures.[50] No such process can continue for long without ravaging and eventually devastating the host bodies which have been invaded by it. We can observe the carcinogenic pattern across the nations of the world, in particular, in Africa and Latin America. Since at a certain stage of this invasive appropriation of life-resources, social populations become unwilling to continue, more 'structural adjustment programmes' are imposed on them to ensure that this invasive circuit continues without resistance. Presidential and military agents within the societies take on the expropriative programme as their own to access more money loans, much as in the behaviour of opportunistic, anaplastic cell growths.

The self-protective possibility of societies' repelling the invasion – by, for example, not paying any more to debt servicing as has occurred since the Athenian lawgiver Solon and the British King Henry IV – is suppressed as a social response. The global market programme which prescribes 'shock treatments' also stands ready to enforce the prescriptions on delinquents, by methods ranging from investment and trade embargo to military and low-intensity conflict to ensure 'the honouring of commitments'.

Thus unresisted, the disease agent advances against the weakened host social body, and spreads more deeply and widely into its organs. Society's regulating bodies submit. Restructurings of social life-organization to feed the invasive programme proceed faster and deeper. More and more of societies' resources are yielded up to free $\$ \rightarrow \$^1 \rightarrow \$^n$ circuits, and social immune resistance succumbs, that is, until the disease pattern attacking host societies is recognized. To forestall such possibilities from occurring, intellectual agents of the global market counsel unconditional surrender. 'Nation states have already lost their role as meaningful units of participation in the global economy of today's borderless world,' asserts the Director of Washington's International Centre For Strategic and International Studies. 'In the final analysis, what matters is how efficiently the surrender of governments to the global markets is carried out.'[51]

Here we encounter the subjective correlative of the not-self invasion expressed by a collaborator agent.

In general, the recommended surrender of public authorities to borderless and unaccountable money-to-more-money sequences exhibits an analogous pattern to a body's immune system collapsing. The occupation is not resisted, but treated as the self of the life-host. The invasive sequences of growth appropriate the host's nutriments for their own autonomous reproduction and spread, and leave a depredated life-host behind.

We would expect disease effects from such a systemic disorder, and these disease effects manifest over time. The life-means of food, water, shelter, and heat energy available to increasing numbers of society's members are sharply reduced. Unemployment rises, organized labour declines, productive functions for the society become increasingly insecure and overwhelmed by operations for money sequences with no life contribution. Poverty and below-poverty-levels significantly increase. Social disorientation and panic spreads beneath the mask of normality.

Where are these symptoms of life loss at the social level of life-organization not evident across the global market today? Here again, observation indicates that only where the invasive programme has been systematically repelled – Norway, for example – do these phenomena of progressive life depredation not appear.[52]

The Emergent Disease Pattern

Money-to-more-money circuits without productive commitment have long been a *tendency* of private money investment. As soon as the logic of value decision is to minimize contribution ('cost') and to maximize take ('returns') with no limit on reducing the contribution and maximizing the take, the regulating code is bound to become life-invasive. Taking maximally more out than what one puts in as an overriding law of life eventually conflicts with the requirements and limits of life itself. Only belief in Adam Smith's providential 'invisible hand' which is thought to convert selfish pursuit of profit to promotion of the social good could allow sane intelligence to accept such a regulating principle for society's economic life.

Adam Smith, however, set and assumed limits to this self-maximizing principle of investment which, as we saw in the previous chapter, opposed the regulating programme of the global market system. He did not envisage a condition in which self-maximizing money sequences became dominant which made no productive contribution to host societies.[53]

The usury form of money investment had a dubious record from the start for this reason. For centuries it was condemned as an offence against justice and the laws of God, and was long forbidden. Yet there were other forms of the money-to-more-money sequence of value which did away with productive contribution as a middle term of investment as well. We will examine these forms of the money sequence of value ahead. The manufacture and sale of armaments, for example, has a middle term between money-investment and money-return. But it is not a middle term which contributes a life-value like food and clothing, or a capital good to produce them. Then again, natural resources may afford materials to make life goods of all kinds as a middle term between money-investment and money-return. But they themselves are taken out of their natural state with little or no cost for their production, again skipping the middle term of productive commitment between the money-value of investment and the money-value of return. Their market value is received for nothing, or next to it, and harvested ready-made from public domains before moving onto the next ready-made natural resource somewhere else. Here too, productive contribution is in some sense skipped in the cycle of money maximization.

What distinguishes the pure, unproductive $\$ \to \$^1 \to \$^n$ circuit today is that:

(1)   There is no use-value production between the transformation of money into more money; and
(2)   This pure $\$ \to \$^1 \to \$^n$ circuit has become for the first time in history the *dominant* form of capital investment.

Even the world's leading productive-capital formations have moved to this unmediated system of decoupled money-capital growth. General Motors and General Electric, for example, both made more profits in 1994 from their financial subsidiaries lending credit-money at compound interest than they did from all of their production of automotive and electrical manufactures put together.[54] This pattern began with the Rockefeller fortune which reproduced and grew from oil to banks (for example, First National Bank, Citibank, Chase-Manhattan Bank). But it was not until recent years when the money-to-more-money sequence became autonomously self-multiplying that productively-coded enterprises switched their dominant pathways of growth to this non-contributing circuit of money-profit appropriation.

There is a conjuncture of historical conditions which have, in turn, made this increasing rule of economies by the $\$ \to \$^1 \to \$^n$ circuit possible:

• a borderless, global financial investment field created by recent international trade agreements;
• failure after 1972 to replace the gold standard and the subsequent Bretton Woods exchange regime with an international currency standard;
• new electronic information technology that transmits data and money-speculation decisions instantaneously;

- vast new pools of liquid capital in exponentially multiplying pension and mutual funds;
- unprecedented government and corporate job-sheddings, tax reductions and increased aggregate profit-takes during recessionary periods which together have redistributed society's money demand from public sectors and ordinary citizens to corporate capital accumulations;
- centralization of investment decisions under the control of major banks whose choices are structured by the $\$ \to \$^1 \to \$^n$ sequence.[55]

The conjuncture of these conditions has transformed the money-demand flows and circulations of the global market into a mutated circuit of money to more money with no limit of volume or velocity, or any requirement to serve life-needs. All that is reproduced and multiplied is money demand *on* wealth seeking to divide itself and grow again into maximally more money demand, leaving behind it increasingly dominant money amassments, and ever more income-sapped social systems.

In these ways, as we can observe, world society's investment decision-structures have been silently restructured in their money-demand flows and circulations towards a self-multiplying metabolism of money to more money. Because this now-dominant sequence requires ever more decoupled money growth to reproduce itself, it penetrates more and more life-sites of public sectors and private sectors across the world with compound-interest demands, disaggregating purchase-and-sale sequences or other channels for higher volume money returns, each cycle growing on the basis of a larger money base than before 'to stay profitable and competitive'. One of the primary symptoms of the increasing dominance of this mutant growth pattern is that almost no public life infrastructure in the world is secure from its appropriative demands.

This process of deprivation of social bodies to feed increasingly aggressive money circuits was not restricted to Third-World societies. We reported the example of 'monetarist reforms' in New Zealand earlier. Another is Canada where a similar pattern of assault on social life-organization by unproductive money sequences emerged rapidly after 1980. Income taxes on corporations fell precipitately, from a high of 50 per cent of the federal total to 7 per cent by 1996, accompanied by the stagnation and then fall of real wages, the stripping of public sectors across federal and provincial jurisdictions, the steep defunding of environmental monitoring and enforcement systems, and the roll back of work and safety regulations.[56]

Every step of the process was led by a three-pronged logic of policy and justification – 'to reduce the debt' (which in fact increased), to 'privatize for more efficiency' (which no evidence supported) and to 'attract foreign investment' (almost all of which, as we will see, went to foreign takeovers of domestic firms). What unified these policies and justifications was that each and all appropriated means of existence from public sectors, workers and host-societies, and rechannelled their life-revenues to transnational banks, bond-holders and corporations.

Spiralling interest demands on federal government debt, in fact, accounted for over 50 per cent of its growth.[57] At the same time, sharp, incremental reductions of income support for the poor and the unemployed and reduction towards zero of federal higher education and public health financial transfers to provinces paid for the tax reductions to corporations and the compound interest payments on the debt. Simultaneously, firings of 100,000 federal public servants overall, cut-backs in environmental surveillance and protection systems, and privatization or abandonment of evolved public transport, communication and cultural infrastructures released further public funds to feed ever more demanding money sequences.

This destruction of the civil commons by attack on its public income bases was darkly accompanied by a government-subsidized explosion of armaments sales to the Third World, up almost 600 per cent from 1990 to 1994.[58] To round off the pattern of appropriating from life sequences to feed money sequences, sharp escalations of child poverty, increasing systemic youth unemployment and dead-end jobs, and over a million citizens in foodbank lines disclosed symptoms of a systemic disorder. The federal debt in the meantime *rose*, 50 per cent from compounding and increased interest payments to foreign and domestic money lenders, and 44 per cent from tax-subsidies to capital-owning agents. The government deficit from these payouts was serviced by eliminating life-protective social programmes, while the debt itself drew off this 'saved' money to pay more interest on *it*. In 1997, after all the sacrifices seemed over and the *annual deficit* was nearing zero, the *overall debt* drawing all the compound interest had continued to rise in accordance with the unseen programme, by almost *50 per cent* from 1990 to 1997.[59]

In causal background to this rapid disaggregation of the social fabric to reloop its life revenues to money sequences, the federal government secretly deregulated bank reserves in 1991 to zero, so that the large private banks who had lost billions from speculative loans to bankrupted billionaire developers and foreign speculations could lend money at compounding interest to the government without money stocks to back them up. Since 95 per cent of all money demand is created by private financial institutions creating interest-demanding debt, the banks were, with finance ministry assistance, extending their right to mint money to the outer limit.[60]

The government and the Bank of Canada simultaneously continued to privatize the public debt by redirecting tens of billions of dollars of high-interest loans to private banks and off-shore money-lenders. This privatized debt and its compounding interest loans, in consequence, had to be paid to these banks and transnational bond merchants instead of to the Bank of Canada, whose sole shareholder was the Government of

Canada itself.[61] In this way, underneath pervasive market declarations that society was 'living beyond its means', the social infrastructure of the country was progressively liquidated to feed the rapidly expanding food-cycles of banks and other money-sequence agents. The private banks themselves made mounting record profits year after year still rising in 1998, while coming to control more and more of the economy's money circulation and demand for further gains in foreign speculations, stockmarket derivatives and other rounds of non-productive money sequences growth.

The pattern may seem surreal, but it follows from the system-deciders of the global market programme. It may seem specific to one victim society, but it is not, as we have seen. The account above is a detailed tracking in situ. The transnational rationale for the overall process of depriving the social body of money for productive *life* functions is always, wherever it occurs, 'to fight inflation', which means decoded, *to preserve the value of money-demand.* Thus in Canada and the US, for example, the US Federal Reserve System and the Bank of Canada in the 1980s increased the money-for-more-money rate of interest for all credit from lending institutions to historically unprecedented rates above inflation, up to 21.5 per cent prime 'to wrestle inflation to the ground'. This policy selector systematically bankrupted productive companies, disemployed citizens by the hundreds of thousands, and reduced national productivity by $140 billion for each point drop in the money inflation rate.[62]

We examined this planned recession from a strategic standpoint in the last chapter. Here we are interested in the logic of the ingressing paradigm of reproduction. We can observe from these figures of trade-off of citizens' livelihoods and social productivity *for* an increase in the value of money the same underlying pattern which we have been following throughout – the displacement of the preservation of the well-being of society as the organizing principle of government by another principle, the preservation of the value of money as its ruling aim.

In the 'New Labour' government of Tony Blair in Britain, submission to such banking policies was conceded as the new administration's first major act of government on ascension to power. As if by prior agreement with London's financial district, Blair immediately transferred to the Bank of England the constitutional right of elected government to manage the central levers of public authority, control over money-creation, interest-rate policies and currency-exchange rates.[63] The rationale was the same as propounded by the ruling bank and financial lobbies across the ocean – 'to protect the value of money against inflation'.

What was kept unspeakable as in all global market societies was a profound home truth that does not emerge in even public whispers. The money sequence itself is *maximally inflationary because its every money gain is secured with no productive input to society – the very recipe for inflation.* The reason inflation does not occur is because the revenues going to workers' wages and to life-protective social sectors are simultaneously cut back to ensure that more money does not chase the goods available. Again we can observe the carcinogenic pattern of money sequences of growth appropriating from society's life infrastructure. But a paradigm without life co-ordinates does not respond to that.

In the rest of the European Union meanwhile, the Maastricht Treaty provided for the surrender of even more of governments' constitutional monetary and fiscal powers to the banks – in this case, the European Central Bank and a European System of Central Banks. Under the Maastricht Treaty, bankers were, in effect, handed control over the flows of money revenue through Europe's social bodies – money supply, interest rates, exchange rates and public financing under bankers' formulae with no accountability to the European Parliament or national parliaments and assemblies, or any elected body at all. The bankers' unprecedented new powers included rules to *keep* them unaccountable by strict exclusion of any attempt of elected bodies to influence them.[64]

The already skyrocketed unemployment of Europe – multiplied by a factor of eight since 1961 and still growing – and fierce downward pressure on social programmes were thereby coded to continue or intensify. The Maastricht Treaty's financial terms of a deficit-to-GDP ratio of 3:100 had already led to systemic attacks on social programmes by the governments of France and Italy, before aroused populations fought back. Still, the underlying programme remained in place across continents – to protect money sequences and their continued advance against the claims of life.

Under the regulation of such a system, life-deprivation is certain to follow. Thus depletion of social hosts' capacities of life-sustenance have occurred from the most undeveloped to the most advanced societies of the world since the post-1980 deregulation and transnational trade treaties began. In the case of Canada, for example, infant mortality rates, the quintessential indicator of social health, rose an astonishing 43 per cent soon after the federal government's surrender of its social-sector revenues to banks and corporate investors, the first recorded rise in over 31 years.[65] But like other consequences of the global system programme, it was not noted as significant. At the other end of the world's social bodies, in Africa, an estimated 500,000 *more* children died from the imposed 'restructuring' of their countries' economies to ensure increased flows of money to external banks, while spending on health care declined by 50 per cent, and on education by 25 per cent since the 'structural adjustment programmes' of the global system began.[66]

As the $\$ \rightarrow \$^1 \rightarrow \$^n$ circuit advances through societies, it also diverts the *private economy*'s revenues for production to its own decoupled growth and self-multiplication. The pathogenic growth pattern reaches across divisions of private and public sectors. New modes of mutating the metabolisms of exchange for use-value to the autonomous proliferation of money-demand are many and aberrant in form: turning bankrupt governments into social debt-collectors enforcing money lenders' terms on progressively poorer public sectors; demanding ever more unconditional tax-breaks for foreign investment and debt over equity; massive diversion of bank credit to non-productive speculations instead of job-creating enterprises; globe-roaming attacks on national currencies by speculative buying and selling in multi-billion-dollar-profit accumulations which create no use-value and which cripple social and economic orders overnight; disaggregation of productive enterprises into broker-and-lawyer-dismantled assets-for-sale by leveraged buy-outs which pay for themselves by unproductive appropriation of the liquid capital of the bought firms; government deregulation of high-interest savings-and-loan banks so that their principals can expropriate up to $500 billion from taxpayers to pay for their speculative money-into-more-money diversions; reloading of the tax-obligations of banking and financial institutions and their investment customers onto the backs of productive members of society with less aggregate income to extract; rechannelling of citizens' savings in major banks to continuous billion-dollar mergers and buy-outs with no productive gain; round-the-clock arbitrages and speculations on derivative market and currency values disconnected from any life or productive function; and steering of vast mutual and pension funds that now bear the privatized old-age security of the First World's middle class into socially delinked money and stock speculation transactions.

Everywhere the channels of money investment are redirected to uncommitted metabolisms of money-to-more-money in place of differentiated commitment to life functions. The hallmark properties of carcinogenic disorder are evident, but they are masked by pervasive declarations of 'new prosperity', 'market opportunities', and 'economic growth' on the one hand, and demands to 'compete harder' for them on the other.

Business journals in the first half of the 1990s estimated that the US monthly electronic trade in currencies, futures derivative instruments, stocks and bonds, operating beyond effective government regulation exceeded the entire annual GNP of the US. In 1998, it was estimated the money volume turnover of currency trading exceeded the entire gross domestic product of the US every three days.[67] Of these currencies churned over every day which melt down economies overnight, less than one of 70 dollars of effective demand goes for trade in goods or services. At the same time, the financial sector's annual volume of trading was inflated by 1994 to at least 35 times greater than the dollar turnover of all production and distribution of goods and services.[68] As these indicators disclose, the money-for-more-money circuits with no commitment to social hosts have overwhelmed them. This is perceived from the standpoint of the paradigm to be 'a fantastic bull market', and the life resources raked off to feed it are reaffirmed as a 'necessary process'.

The effects of this transnational decoupling of 'the free flow of capital' is not only blocked out of view by global market agents. They demand that governments withdraw from *any* attempt to regulate their penetration across the world's borders. 'In the face of myopic trade policies, or efforts to regulate or control capital flows,' warns the US investment giant Goldman Sachs to the US Senate Committee on Banking, '*the marketplace will treat harshly even the largest nations.*'[69] The right of mutant money sequences to override all attempts by sovereign governments to regulate them is overtly proclaimed. 'We are like the supranational government of the world', declares a major New York money manager to a national radio audience. 'Where we see that politicians are doing things that are inappropriate, we hold their feet to the fire. And the way we do that is by moving a lot of money. Politicians [society's elected representatives] are *irrelevant to the process.*'[70] Again, the axial framework of sovereign government itself is repudiated as without right by the anaplastic money growth sequences.

'The growing consensus among the G-7 members [the governments of the US, Japan, Germany, France, Britain, Italy and Canada]', reports the *Washington Post*, 'is that *the G-7 cannot influence events much anyways.* Immense flows of private capital have intimidated the G-7 officials from any efforts to counter them.'[71]

Here the succumbing of society at the highest levels to the rogue code invading social life-hosts is observed at the epicentre of the process without recognition of or response to its deep meaning.

The Social and Environmental Life-Response

If we consider in historical overview the inherent and defining structure of money-capital from its inception as first usury and then merchant loan, we can see that through its various stages of development, it has always been governed by an *internally* determining law: *to maximize by any vehicle, method, or channel open to its entry the ratio of its owners' money-demand increases to money-demand inputs.* As technology has rapidly developed, the velocity and volume of this money sequence has correspondingly intensified and expanded. With the new dominance of the $\$ - \$^1 - \$^n$ circuit, it has surpassed all previous bounds and limits of life to its self-multiplication and expansion.

Because there was never an *internal* limit to traditional capital which would inhibit this pathogenic sequence of growth, we might say that the *potential* of carcinogenic mutation and invasion of social hosts has existed from the beginning. For centuries, however, a horizonless stretch of cultures, habitats and natural elements, national boundaries and regulations of trade, society-wide movements to protect working people's capacities and their local environments, a global spread of liberation movements against colonization and expropriation of resources, the growth of public sectors and welfare systems out of world depression and war crises over the last century, and the institutionalization of alternative forms of socialist organization together hedged in the uncontrolled growth of money sequences.

But the regulating code of this growth sequence – to seek ever greater volumes and velocities of multiplication of itself – has always had pathological effects on life-hosts. The enslavement and genocide of entire societies in Africa and the Americas, the cumulative destruction of environmental hosts across the world, and arms races to produce sufficient weapons of mass-destruction to obliterate the globe many times over are historical inscriptions of its career path.

The long-term discounting of the destruction of other life by money sequences under the label of *'externalities'* – a canonical concept in the economist's and businessman's lexicon – is, if we examine it from a clinical perspective, a self-disclosure of the carcinogenic tendency from the inside of it. It reveals its pathogenic programme of reproduction by its displayed marker of not-self. *What destroys the host life-body, its agents acknowledge, is 'external' to its own growth.* As long as this logic was constrained by social regulation and democratic accountability as well as the abundance of the world of life beyond its control, it could continue without threatening its social and environmental life-hosts – although two world wars and depression almost collapsed these social hosts as well.

What enabled the industrial market system to reproduce beyond these profound crises of breakdown were progressively instituted and systemic limits of life accountability – the development of mass democracy, the growth of countervailing industrial workers' unions, and the advance of social legislation that protected people's and workers' lives against 16-hour days, mass disemployments, hazardous work conditions, enslavement of children, destruction of the health, old-age security and life-quality of its living factors of production, and reckless looting, pollution and depredation of the natural environment.

We must bear in mind that not one of these limits on the industrial corporate market system was generated by the logic of profit-maximization, and all were and still are fiercely resisted as undesirable and unaffordable by the agents of the global market programme. The hard truth is that, underneath the faith in the invisible hand, the ruling goal of this system and the requirements of human and ecological life have nothing in common. The one can only be made more consistent with the other when it is regulated to be so.

Efficiency in the mass production of machine-made goods is the historic competence of the traditional capitalist system which can serve life. It is a competence upon which the species has learned to depend, and it can be regulated so that it does not overrun life. But it is precisely this regulation by the common life interest which has been stripped away in this stage of the corporate market system: precisely at the same time it has mutated so that life-useful commodities between its inputs and outputs of money-profit are no longer its dominant pathway of growth.

Transnational corporate bodies and money syndicates are not living forms. They bear a different form of invasive power than any yet experienced by social life-hosts. They are not recognized as invasive by governments of social hosts, even though they may appropriate, consume, depredate and abandon the wealth of societies as devastatingly as an occupying army (as oil corporations and currency speculating syndicates have done). They are not human in nature, although they are masked as persons under law – a key to the immune disorder of social hosts. Perhaps most importantly, because they are not living beings, they do not die or conceive of a better world, but are propelled by a single and exclusive imperative of reproduction and growth – to turn money-demand inputs into more money outputs, ad infinitum, with each cycle of growth of money demand maximally larger than the last as the condition of continued reproduction. Their legal charters are now permitted to prescribe this as their sole fiduciary function, while the 'Limited' which is placed in apposition to every corporation's name means that the liability of all stockholders is 'limited' or null for the life-destructive consequences of its activities. Since these non-living vehicles of money-demand growth are recognized as 'persons' under law, their operations are also afforded the full protection of rights of living individuals, with overwhelmingly more resources of financing and legal departments to protect their operations against the claims of life.

When, in addition, the most dominant corporations and money syndicates have grown larger in revenue command than most nations, and are permitted the 'freedom of trade' to sell in, buy, take over or abandon any society's markets, resources and built infrastructures with no conditions of access, ownership or resource-exploitation allowed, then social hosts are effectively exposed to not-self appropriation, depletion and civil depredation for sequences of growth that have no obligation to them or to any life-function.

When, finally, the global system requires as the first principle of its freedom the non-accountability of its transnational agents to any social host, then we are able to see that the disorder has grown beyond politics or party. It has mutated into an increasingly aggressive and opportunistic sequence growth appropriation and self-multiplication which feeds on every level of life-organization it can penetrate. Collaborating humans are the mediating agents of its invasion.

The consequences of this disease phenomenon are not yet fulfilled. But there is an unmistakable pattern of depredations of planetary and social life-hosts, in part what medical terminology would describe as marantic. The synergistic effects of cumulative destruction of the planet's basic conditions of life (air, sunlight, water, soil and biodiversity), of stripping and appropriation of social funds for infrastructures of life sustenance and circulation, of corporate intolerance of bearing the costs of protecting and maintaining civil and environmental life capacities, and of escalating, delinked self-multiplication of appropriative demand on life not subordinated to any more general life requirement, together exhibit the classic pattern of cancer mutation and spread.

On the level of social life-organization, the host of the carcinogenic pattern differs as much from the individual host as societies do from particular organisms. But principles and patterns hold across levels of life-organization. Laws of physics and chemistry, or patterns of evolutionary and pathological development are not confined to one kind of life form.

The essential problem of any serious disease pattern is that the *immune system of the host body does not effectively recognize or respond to the pathogenic challenge and advance*. Malignant cancer is the extreme of this pattern. On the level of global and social life-organization, failure of social immune systems to recognize and respond to the disease agent is understandable once we realize that the surveillance and communication organs of host social bodies across the world are structured to rule out recognition of social disease determinants. Corporate media and information systems, that is, *select for reproduction only those messages which do not contradict the money-sequence organization of social bodies*. Consequently, whatever exposes the systemic disorder of this structure of social organization is normally refused transmission through its media of communication. In this way, social immune systems have been rendered incompetent by transnational conglomerate control of most recorded information produced and exchanged across the world – by the mass media, by corporately produced textbooks, and by academic funding systems.

Because of this increasing subordination of social systems of surveillance, recognition and response, whatever *does* recognize or respond to the determinants of the current disease-pattern is normally suppressed by the very structure of organizing social life whose mutated codes and circuits have reproduced the carcinogenic pattern. The immune suppression is now global – over 90 per cent of all foreign news output, for example, is controlled by five US and European multinational news agencies – and this monopoly of public communications by a handful of firms grows more pervasive and top-heavy with the advances of the system to larger and larger scales of technological and ownership integration.[72] Cancer takeovers of life-systems prevail by not being recognized by their hosts. This is our predicament today.

Life-bodies recover when their immune system recognizes and responds to the disease-agent reproducing and growing within them. At this stage of capital's mutation and invasion, manifestations of the disease occupation are increasingly evident. There are also partial recognitions of biosphere and social-structural breakdowns and money-capital circuits decoupled from productive life functions. These phenomena, however, are not yet linked. As on any level of complex life-organization, the social host must recognize the disease-agent and its pathways of reproduction before it can effectively respond to it by curative intervention. If the recognition of its invasive code is clear and systemic, then effective response can proceed. This could be a transformation of the world's now failing political and economic systems which nothing but a global cancer could effectively elicit.

The Life Code versus the Money Code: The Paradigm Shift

The techniques which induce a paradigm change may well be described as therapeutic, if only because, when they succeed, one learns one had been sick before.

Thomas Kuhn

The Engineering Model of the Market

Global social and environmental life-organization are now pervasively invaded by a money-to-more-money sequence which reproduces and grows money-demand for transnational corporations as an end in itself, with no commitment of these corporations or their regulating code to the life-hosts which bear them. We have analysed this pattern of aggressive and uninhibited multiplication of non-life cycles of appropriation and growth as carcinogenic in character, and systemically destructive of social and environmental hosts in effect.

We now confront the problem of how to find our life-ground and its resources of response to this pathogenic pattern. Before proceeding further, we need to clarify the distinction between the *genetic programme* of a cellular life-organization and the *value programme* of a social life-organization. In cases of a carcinogenic disorder, *both* genetic and value codes are programmed to a sequence of uncontrolled multiplication of an agent which overruns the host body with demands of growth which have no committed function to the life-host, and whose decoupled appropriation of its nutriments deprives the life-host of what it requires to sustain its vital functions. But there is a profound distinction between the two forms of pathogenic sequence. *The genetically-coded sequence of a cellular cancer cannot normally be altered by the life-host's decision. The value-coded sequence of a social cancer can always be modified or reset.* Both, if not effectively recognized and responded to, can destroy the life-host they have invaded. But the value code invading a society can, if it is recognized, be consciously limited and redirected by social decision, policy formation, and regulatory intervention. Humans collectively as well as individually have choice in their sequences of decision and action. At the cellular level, so far as we know, cancerous invasions cannot be redirected except by the destruction of the disease-bearing cells themselves.

With life-organization at the social level, then, a higher form of evolutionary possibility always exists – adaptation and development of life-hosts' structures of reproduction into new orders and sequences of life-form without the long, unconscious and accidental changes of genetic code required to enable the transformation. This is called 'cultural evolution' or the like, and it is specific to the human species. No other species alters its way of life within a generation or so on a recurrent basis. Along with this capacity there exists a related alternative pathway of change out of a pathogenic condition. Society's immune response to disease invasions can operate in a non-lethal, constructive way which does not entail the killing of the disease-agents. Instead of obliterating the pathogen bearers, a society's conscious self-understanding and instruments of policy implementation can reorder the pathogenic sequence itself without destroying its human vectors. For at the social level of life-organization, it is a modifiable value code not an inalterable genetic code which is the problem.

It is true that a value programme such as the money-to-more-money sequence determining every decision of transnational corporations' operations may as well *be* genetic the way its bearers behave. Its system imperatives are conceived to be as inalterable as laws of physics. Its values are presupposed as regulating structures given by the nature of the world whose operations are necessary, universal and inevitable. Deviation from the prescription set is assumed impossible, dangerous and abhorrent at the same time. Non-conforming societies are marked for isolation, embargo, destabilization and armed attack. This is the instituted mind-lock of the system.

But in fact, there is not a single moment of the entire global corporate system which is not governed by a socially constructed value-set of programmed preferences which are no more determined by physical laws than caste-orders or colonizing regimes of the past, whose coercive prescriptions were just as dogmatically assumed as laws of nature or the cosmos. It is certainly now supposed that societies have 'no alternative' but 'to adjust' to 'global market competition' and its master value prescription of 'maximizing returns to stockholders' – that is, reducing money costs and increasing money revenues for artificial corporate constructions. It is now also assumed that every decision and variable of this sequence of 'value adding' is propelled by a single, overriding imperative, money-demand. But such a metaphysic of value, however pervasively automaticized, is no less a metaphysic of value. It is an unexamined and reified preference set. This preference set is, in turn, expressed in an elaborated structure of values and effects which is from start to finish socially manufactured, socially sustained and socially enforced to hold through every moment of its determination. It is no more like the laws of motion of physics to which its conventions have been assimilated by economists than the etiquette regimes of feudal China which were regarded with the same awe. But since this value system has been reproduced with such habitualized regularity and token-fetishization across the world, it has come to be seen by its human functions as imposed by external laws rooted in the order of the universe.

This metaphysic of value has, in turn, given rise to a corresponding theology of a ruling invisible hand, inviolable economic laws, heretical doctrines and sects, subversive unbelievers, punishments for disobedience, and – to ensure compliance with the doctrine's commands – never-ending sacrifices of the unwealthy to ensure society's accession to some future but never realized heavenly state. But however this system's prescriptions are hypostacized or deified, however much its money tokens are absolutized as final worth, however much its coercive conventions are imagined as nature- or god-given laws, and however much alternatives to it have been globally liquidated as enemies of the cosmic order, the fact remains that it is a social construction which, like all social constructions, implements principles of value it expresses, and is open to change by its social life-hosts.

More to the point in the current condition, the value programme can be recognized as increasingly destructive to social and environmental life-hosts, and can, accordingly, be consciously regulated and limited so as to comply with human and ecological requirements. The problem is that these requirements, incredible as this deep fact may seem, *have no place whatever in the paradigm of the global system*. The needs of life itself are a null value in its entire metric. But in restoring this model of economic organization to some accountability to life itself, society can respond to what attacks its structure of vital functions in a different way than the cellular immune system – not by physically attacking the human agents which have succumbed to and aggressively bear the disease-pattern, but by *regulating and limiting the non-living corporate forms within which they are temporary contrivers and functions.*

In the end, it is these non-living vehicles of the mutant growth pattern that must be redirected. This life realignment is not technically inaccessible once the pathogenic pattern and its corporate bearers are socially recognized. Already available instruments of social sovereignty, domestic and international law, and democratic accountability are adequate to the task of restoring life function, as we will see ahead in analysing the evolving civil commons and its social immune competences which underlie all of these advanced forms of social organization. The issue is not one of obliterating mutant genes which invade the social body's life, however much human vectors of the pathogenic pattern may come to operate as if they were mutantly programmed. It is the deeper-lying issue of recognizing and re-regulating the locked, mutant value sequences of transnational corporate vehicles which organize humans.

From Ricardo on, the prescriptive regimen of the industrial market system has been conceived as invariant as iron, long the favoured term to describe the external 'laws' believed to run it. As with the predetermined operations of the machines this system advances by and conceives itself as, the notion of values or social choices was alien to the industrial market paradigm. Although in every respect the elaboration of an unexamined value theory, which the system originated and sustained as the referent of every judgement it quantified, the functionaries and describers of its coercive programme came to think of it as above values. They even came to think of it as 'value-free', although every moment of its regulation without exception presupposed a value judgement. Like the machine-structure this system imitated, the issue of what is good and bad was not permitted to interfere in its operations. But unlike the machine, 'economic science' could read the laws of what ruled it. It thus observed verifiable regularities which were construed as analogous to the laws of *mechanics*. For example, people deprived of their land tenure and commons and without means to live, people hungry and with families who would otherwise starve, could be observed in verifiable and predictable ways to sell themselves for the best price they could get, while masters who selected or did not select them for employment would, with even more iron predictability, never pay more for their labour factor of production than the market rate. Rational self-maximizers both, they provably conformed to invariant laws of supply and demand which ensured that the lowest-cost factors of production which could be bought would be bought, and labour or other factors in oversupply would not be bought. This cost-efficient succession of minimal money inputs, maximal revenues that all could get, and the output of competitively priced goods and profits for stockholders all proved the iron necessity of the laws by which the system was ruled.

That people were made in this manner to be enslaved to a mega-machine was not conceived as a problem by economic science. It appeared as an observable system of regularities which verified the laws. The operant conditioning of allowing just enough life means to remain enslaved and no more, the ultimate iron law of starvation was thus thought to be the work of the invisible hand by Adam Smith, and the law of human gravity by David Ricardo.[1] There was, after Smith, no question of values or morality to be intruded here, but merely the findings of objective science uncovering the immutable laws of economics. The system ran like a machine, used machines, and was increasingly conceived in every respect *as* a machine. Accordingly, it was known to be only scientifically comprehensible by physics-like laws, which were, in turn, dominantly modelled on nineteenth-century mechanics. That the entire system in its operation and its self-conception was conceptualized and structured in terms of *non-living matter* never occurred as a problem to the paradigm.

First the mechanics were those of Deism, with the human face of more wealth of nations to approve it, the economics of Adam Smith. Then there was just the machine as God without a face, Ricardo and after.

Science without values was the only way to read this immanent order of the world. Its conception as a machine structure was never admitted or even noticed by economic scientists and advisers to governments because the paradigm of mechanics cannot reach beyond the operations of mechanics to understand them. Moreover, it flattered the self-importance of the economists that their mechanistic metaphysics was so eagerly gobbled up by political rulers and their rich patrons, and paid them more than other disciplines. On the level of the paradigm itself, the presuppositions which went with the coercive metaphysic underlying them predictably expelled all properties of life from their mechanics. The established paradigm came simply to presuppose predictable, invariant and homogenously consistent atoms of self-maximizing consumers and producers within a model whose operations quantified and converted outputs and inputs into mathematical formulae without ever considering any aspect of life in their calculations. The production and consumption for human life for which the system was once assumed to be intended was no longer connected to life requirement at any level. Eventually the symbols substituting for the realities became autonomous in endless strings of econometric equations which never touched the life-ground even by the reference terms of mechanics.[2] The system decoupled from the life-host in method and in practice simultaneously, with no consciousness of adherents to the paradigm that this posed a problem.

But the world still seemed to afford hypnotic evidence to the senses of this mechanical model at work regulating real life. The clear rises and falls of the prices, the re-engineering of every life form that existed to serve or be destroyed by it, the movements of exact parts into assembly and reassembly, the throughput of all existence to money-measured outputs – everything that was permitted to exist, or to be seen to exist, operated just like the mega-machine which was presupposed as the model regulating and describing it. The human condition itself was submerged in the value programme of the money-sequencing machine, with nothing but the machine as signifier or signified. As for the science of economics, all but heretics knew the right way to understand what was going on – to track the routes and returns of the machine by its laws of motion and effects, with the life substance or its needs never entering the picture.

The industrial market model and the engineering paradigm by which its structure, functions and sequences were comprehended and, in turn, reproduced, was in this way instituted as the system-deciding framework within which the economy was understood. That this conception ruled out of view the very life requirements an economy is supposed to serve was a contradiction at the core of the programme which never registered. The paradigm was not questioned, but presupposed and further imposed on societies 'to adapt to'. Even Marx proclaimed its massive life-reorganizing operations 'the laws of motion of modern society', deploying the Newtonian nomenclature of mechanics to decipher the great machine. Interestingly, the leading social revolutionary of the epoch was certain in the same vein of engineering mechanics that the great machine would 'discipline, unite and organize by the very mechanism of capitalist production' its own slaves to overthrow it, having to derive even revolution from the inevitable lock-steps of its supreme rule.[3]

Subsequently, the language of mechanics grew so pervasive in the social lexicon that in the global corporate system of today, hardly an economic thought is communicated that does not stay strictly within the conceptual boundaries of engineering mechanics and the operations of inanimate matter. The unifying principle is that every human property or life need is expelled from calculation and from the mind. The life-ground itself is covered over and lost, and none of its vital claims now remains in the system's calculus. The categories and correspondences are all of mechanical functions. 'Inputs' and 'outputs' begin and end the process of making what is, in fact, the means of human life. 'The economy is overheated' or 'cooled down' for what is, in fact, a life-and-death matter of having or losing a livelihood for millions of persons who will be employed or disemployed by the interest-rate falls or rises prescribed by central banks. 'Structural adjustment programmes are in place' for what is, in fact, the coerced deprivation of entire societies of their people's ensured access to food, health-care, basic literacy, and means of life when starving. 'Pump-prime methods', now presumed an unacceptable interference with the great machine, 'are being considered' when what is, in fact, at stake is the investment, or non-investment, of society in productive livelihoods for countless millions of citizens who are out of work by the machine's investment cycles. 'Free circulation of goods and capital are essential' for what is, in fact, the demand of a blanket, unconditional right of foreign transnational corporations to access and appropriate other societies' markets, natural resources and built infrastructures, with reciprocal requirements for the life of host-societies prohibited by law. Finally in the repertoire of what Karl Polanyi long ago called 'the Great Automaton', there is the global recourse which Polanyi never saw of 're-engineering' societies by 'shock treatments' which strip them of their still organic infrastructures of life support and force them at gun-point to serve the world machine's ever more insatiable demands for more resources to feed it.[4]

Every lock-step of the system is assumed by its believers to be 'necessary', 'inevitable' and 'with no alternative'. This is as one would expect from a paradigm which is modelled on the laws of mechanics, and which has expelled the properties and requirements of life from its calculus.

What is true in the macrocosm is true of the microcosm. The humans inside the machine's throughputs are not conceived of as human, but as purchased contents of the 'labour factor of production', and are accordingly stripped of all vital properties which do not fit into the mechanical paradigm. All that matters of human productive life which is employed – if it is not employed, its only function is to reduce the price of labour – is its service to the regulating mechanism of money-value-adding production which, in turn, is a subsidiary element of a corporate system which is set to reproduce and grow in money-demand worth as its single operational programme. In the analysis of all processes of production and exchange into their constituent phases of use for the machine, human life necessarily disappears. In the methods of scientific management, the face, the body's needs, the urge for diversity and fresh air, the love of life's exhilarating ranges of thought, feeling and self-movement are all barriers to the programming of precise and detailed motions and operations to be performed for the money-into-more-money mechanism without wasted motion or time.

Since a machine is more suited to such machinal functions than a human life, once it is cheaper to substitute one, then the human worker is 'shed', with concerns for the fate of his or her family and existence irrelevant to 'the necessary operation'. That is why 40 million workers in the US itself could lose their livelihoods in 'restructuring operations for globalization', and corporate spokesmen and economists not comprehend what 'the political fuss' was about.[5] The terms used were 'discontinued', 'displaced', 'excessed', 'downsized', 'severed', 'reallocated', 'rightsized', 'deselected' – all in accordance with the underlying regulating model of mechanics which now substituted for, ruled out and force-fitted life to its ultimate programme. As for people who were reduced to no means of or contribution to life itself, they would 'just have to *adjust*'. The system they were to 'adjust to' was not human or alive. Nor was it instrumental to any form of life, including the social life-hosts it moved in and out of with no required commitment to their survival. It was what ruled, and all that lived was required to adjust to it, whether as instruments or refuse. All that remained of value in the system was the sequence of multiplying money-demand for non-living corporate stock-sets.

Not even the most quintessentially human virtuosities are now outside the mechanism's dictates. Surgeons are programmed to a time-costed set of reactions and prescribed medicaments by 'health maintenance organizations' which have a single overriding function, to increase the money-value of stocks held. That 80,000 people a year die from the malpractices of this system in the world's most profitable market is not an issue that enters its calculus, any more than the fact that it fails to treat 38 million people in the same society.[6] The paradigm does not subsume these life-and-death facts because it does not factor life into its accounts. At the same time, the professoriate which bears the higher learning of society is itself being radically 'restructured' into the industrial schema of Taylorist discrete functions, automated information machines, and administered operations within digitalized training mills.[7] In short, there is no life form left at even the most distinctively advanced levels of human life expression and service which is not being rapidly transformed into detail functions of the money-demand mechanism. In such a condition, the 'necessity' of every move flows not from history or life need or social choice, since all of these are null quantities in the system's equations. It follows from a prescriptively instituted economic paradigm which selects solely for more money-demand for corporate vehicles. Since the paradigm regulating the mutation cannot discern anything as other than as it should be in this process, but only what follows from its principles of decision and calculation, these consequences are perceived as 'inevitable', and rapidly 'adapted to' by society 'in order to survive'.

The fuel of the global machine from a human motivation standpoint may seem a touch back to life – the desires of consumers for goods, and of stockholders for profits. But in the paradigm, these are merely homogenously propelling dispositions of the global machine's selection and exclusion operations and do not complicate the model's rigorous mechanics with any life quality. Human motivations too are made to fit the engineering mechanics framework by presupposing that they are uniform in unit, quantifiable, additive within and across individuals, and with a single mechanical direction of propulsion – always and everywhere towards maximally more, whether outputs of money or inputs of consumables. The 'motivation factor' is an atomic propulsion that is as invariant and predictably ordered as the moving parts of a machine.

Needless to say, reality is less simple, even within the compulsory regimes of the global automaton which select for those who fit, and against those who do not. But even within this enforced mechanism of existence, human life resists, chooses, relates, projects and evolves past any such programme in ways its apparatus cannot begin to understand. This is one reason why economic forecasts and predictions are almost invariably wrong. But this does not detain the armies of followers of the model. For it only provides more demand for economic formulae, while the engineering model continues to perform its deeper, hidden function – which is to rule out life's properties and requirements from interference in the reproduction and growth of money-demand for corporations. This is the defining closure of the system and its regulating paradigm, and is what allows its money circuits of growth to mutate, decouple from and attack social and environmental life-hosts themselves with no problem registering in its calculus.

The metaphysic underlying this literally monstrous preference-system does not disquiet the paradigm's adherents because there is no room within it for reference to life on the basis of which concern about life's destruction can be recognized or aroused. It rules life out of its concerns a priori. To speak of the 'cruel heartlessness' of this system's decision-operatives misses the deeper lying disorder of which they are active symptoms. The paradigm for comprehending society's production and distribution of goods, what economics is about, has incredibly delinked from the requirements of life at every level.

'If people are not living up to their potential,' declared Joseph Stiglitz to the American public in his post as the Chair of the Council of Economic Advisers to the President, and now the World Bank's Chief Economist, 'then the economy cannot live up to its potential.'[8] Deconstructed, Stiglitz's exhortation meant that society's sovereign is 'the economy' (that is, money-valued growth of the market), while the means of its fulfilling '*its* potential' is society's people. They must become what serves it, thereby reaching their potential as instrumental to the economy reaching its. All that remains of human life in this system, in the end, is what it can form itself into to serve the world machine of money-to-more-money circuits for money investors, to which all societies 'must adapt or not survive'.

Thus we confront a new law of global selection – a world structure of survival, suffering and death which favours only what makes money for those with more money than they need for life; or, more strictly, more money for money sequences borne by non-living corporate accounts. Life has no theoretical place in this regulating logic of selection and exclusion, and so life in practice is, perfectly consistent with its paradigm, everywhere ignored, violated or destroyed in accordance with what can be extracted from it to feed and multiply these money-demand sequences. At a certain point, these sequences go their own way, appropriating the vital functions and conditions of their life-hosts themselves with no inhibition or barrier to restrain them. This is the predicament we diagnose.

What is clear from the character of the master paradigm that regulates and propels this disorder is that having expelled life and all its needs from its categories of understanding and prescription, it follows unavoidably that whenever this system's effects begin to attack its life-hosts themselves, those remaining within its programme cannot fathom that anything has gone wrong as long as they remain within its standpoint. Indeed, the cumulative propensity of the mind-set is to rule out from view whatever resists or recognizes that anything has or *can* go wrong with this system. Such thoughts are conceived as 'subversive', and dealt with accordingly.

What also follows from the life-expelling structure of this economic model is that any property of human life that might be construed as of value in itself – such as natural beauty without price, knowledge that does not add money value, social relations that do not attract investors, history that cannot be sold, even fresh air, non-carcinogenic sunlight and foods – does not and cannot compute to the system as of value. Any non-priced value is repelled as a nullity. Unless life fits into a money sequence, it is disaggregated and reaggregated to do so, or ruled out as valueless – for example as 'useless education', 'unaffordable health-care', or 'natural resources not put to work'. This is not seen as reason to reject the paradigm, but as an imperative for all that exists to be mutated into service to it to be recognized as of value. Such a programme is, however, not a fixed structure of the world, or a law of motion of physics. It is the value-set determinant of a gravely systemic social disease.

Distinguishing Necessity and Choice

Values are specific to beings who can recognize and act on conscious alternatives by their nature. With the value code of the global market system, there has been much confusion within the doctrine's followers and advocates about whether or not the economic order they prescribe to all societies *is* a value system. On the one hand, it seems to be understood as constituted by the commands of an immanent God whose 'laws' and 'invisible hand' cannot be disobeyed without severe 'punishments' and 'sacrifices' to the disobedient. Here we are told we have *no choice about what the values we live according to are*, but only the choice of complying with, or violating, what is known to be right and good. This is the global doctrine as a theological creed. The values of the market are prescribed from on high. This view is to be distinguished from the co-existing belief of the paradigm's followers, which is that the laws and necessities of the system are purely secular, laws of science and the structure of production and distribution to which all societies must conform if they are not to suffer a collapse in their economies – just as people fall down and hurt themselves if they do not mind the laws of gravitation. These distinct strands of the global market doctrine are continually conflated, which is another symptom of the doctrine's inner confusions. But what is common to all market metaphysics is that the choice of how we are to live is in effect denied. Yet at the same time, there remains an *implied choice*. For both scientistic and theological versions tell us that if we do not do what is necessary, the consequences are 'certain to be punished by the market'. This entails that there is an option – an option which admits of countless alternatives.

However much the value code of the global market might be prescribed to us all as 'necessary', then, its rules of how people in society must live remain a matter of choice even to doctrinaires. As such, these rules are not programmed like genetic sequences. A doctrine which proclaims 'freedom' and 'freedom of choice' as its supreme value, while simultaneously proclaiming just as certainly that we have 'no choice' and 'no alternative', contradicts itself. This absurdity is critically revealing, because it exposes the depth of the disorder we are dealing with. It is an ideological symptom of a deep-structural conflictedness.

In fact, no economic or social system, including the global corporate market, can run for one minute without countless millions of decisions and actions made simultaneously in accordance with its assumed value-structure to reproduce it to the next minute intact. These decisions and actions become robotized by coercion and habit, it is true, and in this form appear to be constrained by a necessity as iron as natural laws. But all these conforming decisions and actions are nevertheless 'made', and together constitute a social construction, however much like a cosmic machine to which we must all adjust it is made to appear in the dominant paradigm.

A social manufacture can always be structured otherwise. Indeed this is what those who bear the market value code are themselves doing to previously existing decision-frameworks of societies. They are '*re*-structuring' them. Behind these countless simultaneous decisions and actions now called the 'global market *revolution*' – a concept which implies the property seizure which is taking place – is a social value programme which is implemented increasingly from minute to minute, and year to year. It is the elaboration of a generalized social preference sequence which, in the end, reduces itself to a single master formula: to *transform money into more money for corporate money investors, lenders and option holders with no social or political barriers to this process*.

Most people perceive no choice in these matters of what is popularly recognized as 'The System'. They obey orders, dress as they are told, seek the money rewards of performance in accordance with the imperatives of the system, and avoid detection of any failure to serve their employers' commands in every observed word or deed, accepting the dos and don'ts as obediently as in the most exacting feudal regime. But there is not one of these sequences of behaviour which could not be otherwise. We tend, it cannot be denied, to presuppose these elements of social value codes as given and even 'natural' or 'necessary'. We do not normally give them much thought. But no-one except the mechanical determinist would deny that we *could* do otherwise, and that we have, however unthinkingly, *chosen to do what we do* individually and collectively – usually '*in order to survive*'. But survival itself is one basis of value decision, and one we can understand in very different and opposed ways. The purpose of this analysis is to show that in fact our assumed goal of life survival is being undermined systematically while we think we are providing for it, most of all on the collective and planetary level.

The normative decision structures or value codes we live by are not 'laws of motion'. They are sets of rules or principles distinguishing between what is desirable or of value, and what is *not* desirable or of value. They designate what is 'good', and rule out what is 'bad'. In the market system, the value code that underlies people's normal decisions and actions is always, from the very beginnings of this normative order, one which *affirms more money revenues and consumer satisfactions for oneself, and rejects less money revenues and consumer satisfactions for oneself* – however little or much may be at stake here. These are a priori principles of value and disvalue in this value system applying to all within it, and have over time come to be conceived as prescribed by 'rationality' itself. We have analysed already the market's underlying moral system disguised as scientific law. But the essence of what we are left with in this value-code is the sequencing of people as moments of predetermined circuits of money-demand seeking to become more.

The global corporate market and the pursuit of money profit are thus no longer what the free market was for Adam Smith, in a deeper way than we have considered. Adam Smith understood the market as a *means* to achieve the 'wealth of nations'. In the corporate system, in contrast, nations, people and environments are understood as the means for the pursuit of stockholders' profit. Whereas Adam Smith construed the market and its rule of monetary self-interest as instrumental goods promoting greater and cheaper quantities of human consumables for social well-being, his instrumentalist ethic has now been stood on its head. Today in the market doctrine, all that exists, including human society itself, is conceived to be of value only so far as it secures corporate money profit. Societies are now understood to succeed or fail *as* societies in accordance with how well or badly they serve this usurpacious goal. One cannot read a daily paper without finding, if one looks beneath the particular shadows on the wall, this underlying social absolutism at work on every page, disguising itself as the mechanics of engineering realism at the same time to keep the claims of life and choice expelled from social consideration. In this global market system, it is the success of private, borderless corporations and their ruling programme of 'value adding to the inputs of capital investment' which is, in one form or another, the categorical imperative binding all life.

Life in this way becomes a corporate instrument to fuel and feed its money-demand growths, rather than becoming more vital life with corporations as its means. No common interest of life is recognized in the paradigm. The common interest is everywhere assumed to be the serving of corporate money sequences, or as it is now put, 'competing in the global marketplace' and 'attracting investors'. The distinction between what serves the social life-host and what occupies and strips it thus collapses, and the social immune system lets the invasion of an alien system of reproduction and growth in through every public-decision node. Every step of the succumbing is led by the declaration of 'necessity', and every imagined reward is by the contradictory promise of 'more freedom'. What alone is 'more free' in this global mechanism is the sequence of money-demand itself becoming more money-demand with no barrier or obstruction of life to its advances and occupations.

The Systemic Effects of the Mechanical Market Paradigm

Because the global market is opposed in nature to the classical market model of national wealth production described by Adam Smith, it operates to produce an opposite outcome – not, in general, more material prosperity and well-being for a nation or its citizens, but ever more money demand for the top end, and ever wider and deeper deterioration of life-conditions for the bottom half of humanity and for the global biosphere in general. We see the great weight of the evidence for this meta-pattern all around us, but it is never publicly linked back to the economic paradigm from which it follows, because this relationship is beyond the model's capacity to discern. These life-destructive effects are not seen because life itself has no place in the mechanics of the model. Yet they flow predictably from a code and sequence of value which everywhere treats human life as a means, does not compute life or reduction of life in its metric, and requires the disaggregation of life as its medium of development.

Thus as the global market mechanism has penetrated ever more widely, the marginal value of labour has fallen for most workers; poverty and unemployment rates have increased to unprecedented post-Depression extremes; child malnourishment has escalated across both developed and less developed economies in rising absolute and relative numbers; social security, education and public health infrastructures have been systematically dismantled; and environmental degeneration of atmospheric conditions, water, soil, forests, and species diversity has advanced to various levels of planetary collapse. The evidence is in for all of these life-reductive patterns. It is just not connected, nor tracked back to its systemic cause. For all of these life reductions and destructions are perfectly consistent with the paradigm's principles, and increasing quantities of its exchanges and returns. What the followers of the model see instead of the world-wide life degeneration and further impoverishment of the poor is increased trade, stock-market, profit and other aggregate money-sequence figures. Therefore they cannot accept the criticisms of the system that may peek through because they can see very well from the standpoint of the paradigm that the global market system is doing spectacularly well.

Celebrated American CEO Albert Dunlap, who is renowned in the global market for raising the stock price of Scott Paper Corporation over 230 per cent by firing 11,000 workers, has this to say about the problem of mass unemployment: 'The responsibility of the CEO is to deliver shareholder value. *Period.*'[9] He adds, 'Yes I made a lot of money [from stock options]. But I *created* six-and-a-half billion dollars' (emphases added). Dunlap exemplifies the closure of this programme to all life reality beyond corporate money accounts. But it would be a mistake to blame the symptom rather than the underlying paradigm of value regulating and propelling it. George Gilder, economist author of the 'bible of the Reagan revolution', *Wealth and Poverty*, is more glowing in tribute to the market programme's money multiplications and advances, but no less morbidly narrowed in lens. In reply to rising concern that the 'market revolution' had resulted in vast destruction of peoples' lives and livelihoods, he refers triumphally to the code's statistics of gain: '*42,621 merger and acquisition deals worth 3.1 trillion, 899 billion in shareholder gains, the doubling of stockmarket value in real terms, and [the increase of average] per capita income by a third* [as average US wages dropped to their lowest real level since 1929]'.[10]

Gilder here follows the dominant paradigm perfectly. The mechanics of money-sequence value are all that register or compute to the mind. Life gains or losses are not denied or affirmed. They are simply expelled from the calculus and the discourse, even as they are raised as an issue. This is the hallmark closure of a paradigm no longer capable of coping with the actual world. Because the numbers Gilder cites refer only to the exponential gains of corporate money sequences and aggregates – even the average-income increase is derived from these gains – he manages to block out the world of life entirely. This is the character of the model. That such figures do not relate to life well-being at any level, and are fully consistent with spreading life catastrophe, does not remotely dawn on Gilder nor, remarkably, does it occur to his fellow discussants. This is the hold of a closed paradigm across individuals, in even a questioning venue.[11]

Although mounting export and import figures may show geometrical rises in financial transactions, these rises may occur at the same time as the natural resources and ecosystems of societies are stripped, the productive lives and living wages of millions are eliminated or drastically reduced, and social life-support systems are dismantled. There is nothing to import and export rises which would entail otherwise, and massive evidence that in fact all of these assaults on life-fabrics have occurred as global trade has increased.[12] Although double-digit or significant rises in GDPs may also register on a diminishing basis in some regions like China and Chile, all that such GDP figures measure is *total registered money transactions*. The goods and services which are bought and sold to yield these numbers have no relation to the increase or loss of life. GDPs rise with every increase in medical costs to treat more diseases and traumas, with every new repair and legal bill for automobile crashes and injuries, for all transformations of forest habitats into clearcuts for throwaway paper, and from every weapon produced to kill and maim people. The GDP or GNP as measure of a society's well-being are perhaps the clearest marker of this paradigm's underlying value disease. It registers mutilations and destructions of life, so long as they fetch a price, as 'goods'. As we will see, the destruction of life to increase money sequences is the major pattern of this corporate global system.

Nonetheless, these monetary rises are tirelessly recited by market analysts and corporate agents because these are their only value reference points. The doctrine in this way ceases to engage with the world of *life* fact. On the contrary, its adherents prefer the certitude of repeated slogans and quantities of the mechanism's exchanges and returns, and attack in the media all 'protectionists' and those who 'fail to adjust to the new reality'. If the problems of the actually existing life-world persist because doctrinal incantations of the engineering model do not in the end resolve crises of life deprivation and ecological collapse, they cannot register in the model's calculus. From the standpoint of the model, therefore, it only makes sense to ignore them.

Yet the life-ground is what all that lives depends on for every moment, and its conditions are everywhere. People have 150-billion-neuron brains with a minimum of 100 axons each, which provides the abilities to see and understand the meaning of these facts, and the pervasive threat to their air, their sunlight, their children's future, their food, their water, the life habitat itself. They can perhaps feel the sun burning lesions into them, the air harder to breathe, the water and food chemically laced with carcinogens, the loss of biodiversity and rise of scavengers, the trash that clogs the channels of the life flow across boundaries. Many more feel the invasion depredating and polluting life than the vector's media begin to acknowledge. This is in 'fiduciary trust to stockholders'. Thus the bearings of life gain and life loss are nowhere explained or connected in the public realm.

The system's set-point is, in fact, no longer consistent with the vital reproduction of the life-hosts it invades. On the level of the global life-host, three-quarters of all bird species are in decline, one of every four mammals is endangered, and one-third of plant species is extinct or threatened with extinction. Water supplies are depleted and polluted so that the United Nations estimates that two-thirds of the world will be short by 2025.[13] But past constraints of wilderness, national boundaries, protected cultural differences, regulatory impediments, rising social economies and governmental activism are discredited. The system is clearly out of control. But there are only more calls for more 'deregulation'. This pattern is not 'caused by us all', as new-age analysis would internalize the problem. It is a system of predictable effects of a ruling social value programme presided over by a few hundred transnational corporations. They are not alone as sustainers of the disorder. But they wield unheard of directive power over the world's money-investment sequences. The largest 300 transnational corporations, for example, control 98 per cent of all direct foreign investment, while the largest 600 control 80–90 per cent of all trade among industrial countries, and 60 per cent of all land cultivated for export.[14] As these transnational corporations dominate investment, trade and agriculture across the globe, they employ in their 'job creating' enterprises just 3 per cent of the industrial nations' workforce.[15] Now over 60 per cent of new jobs offered in North America and Britain are part-time, and unprotected wages are subject to 'unprecedented violent, downward swings'; security of employment is no longer assured; and minimum wages are being inexorably reduced (falling, for example, by 40 per cent since between 1981 and 1995 in the US).[16] Poverty levels among the unemployed as well as the employed are rising universally, with 60 million Latin Americans, for example, driven beneath the poverty line by 'free market reforms' which are declared 'unavoidable' to 'get the fundamentals right'.[17] The 'fundamentals' here refer to what is required to sustain and increase money gains for investors, not what is required to reproduce and develop human life.

Non-supervisory, private-sector workers in the world's most dynamic market economy have watched their wages fall over 20 per cent in real terms since the 1970s, while social-security and environmental protection systems have been cut by hundreds of billions of dollars of funding.[18] In Western Europe, the most regulated of capitalist economies, policies of corporate 'labour-shedding' have still expelled human labour at a rate rising seven-fold in 30 years – from a 1.5 per cent average unemployment rate in the 1960s to an average of 11 per cent in 1993.[19]

Radical market reforms of the East European and Soviet economies have demonstrated the 'miracles of market reform' in more dramatic ways. Following its 'rescue from communism' by 'deep market reforms' between 1990 and 1993, Russia's GDP fell by 17 per cent in 1990–91, by 19 per cent in 1991–92, and by 11 per cent in 1992–93.[20] By 1996, swiftly 'privatized' industries' free-fall in production had reached 50 per cent, and nearly 40 million people no longer had enough food to eat.[21] It has not recovered since. 'Market transformed' Poland, meanwhile, lost over 21 per cent of its GDP between 1988 and 1992, Czechoslovakia almost 20 per cent, and Romania and Bulgaria 30 per cent or more during the same period.[22]

The pattern of social life degeneration could hardly be clearer, but as long as aggregate money-demand rises, no problem can be perceived by the market value paradigm. It is set to relate to money gains, and life losses do not compute. Thus 'market reforms' are seen as successful, and effects are not related to cause. Those positioned in the money cycle do well in this life-stripping game. In 'the newly liberated Russia', 'privatization' sales of public assets benefitted an estimated 5–7 per cent of the population, but 'market reforms in general halved industrial production in three years, and reduced 80 per cent of the population to 'destitute or semi-destitute' conditions.[23] Murder rates have, in the meantime, doubled while male life spans have fallen precipitously to 57 years of age and are predicted to continue to fall further.[24] Yet global market doctrine remains no less triumphal and certain of its prescriptions for the world. There is a systemic disorder here which is not seen.

As with the individual psychopath, delusions of grandeur magnify as disasters multiply. But the trumpeted successes do not stand up to the scrutiny of sanity. In no national society in the world have market reforms and restructurings reduced rates of poverty or child malnutrition and starvation. In no country where they have been imposed have they increased public access to health and educational resources, provided workers with more job-security or benefits, or protected the air, water, and soil quality of the planet more effectively. They have, in fact, done the opposite in every society, even in the vaunted 'economic miracles' of Chile, China and the 'tigers' of Southeast Asia (to which we will return ahead). Go over this summary of basic *life-value regressions* in even the world's 'market miracle' societies again. Can you find any society in the world in which these measures of life security and health have not declined?

Where increases in gross money values of national products and exports have occurred, the record of life-values continues to slide. Everywhere market 'restructurings' and 'adjustments' have escalated social inequalities, consistently increased real unemployment rates and part-time jobs without benefits, eliminated or reduced minimum wages, and reduced the lifelines of funding to every public form of social security, learning, health-care, culture, and transportation which societies had achieved over half a century or more of social development. Again, is there any exception in the world to this pattern of social disintegration by what is openly called the 'global market revolution'?

What of opposition to this systemic decline of social fabrics and planetary ecosystems? In every society upon which 'market reforms' have been imposed, popular opposition to this process of 'deregulation', 'privatization', and destruction of the shared grounds of life has been overridden, or ignored, as 'fearful of change' or 'unwillingness to adapt'. Political voices representing the interests of the civil commons, independent citizen and worker organizations and memberships, and citizen majorities increasingly terrorized by economic insecurity and the job decline for their children have, in Orwellian style, been treated to a one-way catechism of market slogans. Once more, we need to search for *exceptions* to this drowning out of oppositional voice to get a sense of the underlying pattern at work here. There is a lock in this social programme of value that has closed life-feedback off from its reproductions.

Consider, for example, the following example exposed by Victoria Brittain. We can see in it the long arc between the programme and its consequences in a pattern that news reports do not track. Observe the principles of this competitive re-ordering of the world at work in pure form. Ask where the global market doctrine of value rules any one of them out.

Unita's primitive fascism [which has killed over 1,000,000 civilians over 15 years of civil war] holds Angola in thrall. It is one legacy of the Reagan doctrine. For years, the United States withheld recognition from Angola's MPLA government because it was socialist and had Cuban troops to defend it from the apartheid regime of South Africa. At the same time, Washington transformed the army of the leader, Jonas Savimbi, into a formidable military machine because he was billed as a democrat. The doctrine distorted the society, destroyed the infrastructure and impoverished people beyond imagination ... No amount of US dynamism and optimism can now knit together the catastrophic unravelling of this society ... People wash in sewers and puddles ... A nurse will let a child with meningitis die, keeping the prescribed drug to sell in the market ... Government salaries for [public sector] nurses, doctors, teachers, professors and top civil servants are so absurdly low that no-one can live by these jobs ... Oil earns $10 million a day ... going straight into foreign bank accounts ... Fortunes are made buying [the local kwanza currency] at one rate and selling at another. The ostentatious luxury of the cars, houses, foreign health-care and education ... has never been so evident ... Leaflets denouncing the government's inability to provide a living wage, water, electricity, education or health care ... are denounced on the radio ... and the media are saturated with appeals for belt tightening ... Aside from the Unita-controlled areas, other commercial interests linked to powers in the government are mining diamonds legally at a furious rate.[25]

The 15-year pattern here reveals another paradigm illustration of the market value programme in its unfettered imposition and elaboration. In market ideology, such cases have been celebrated as victories of 'the free world' over 'communism'. We hear of no exceptions. The crown of the triumph is the former Soviet Union, where every vital life indicator except contesting voices is dramatically down. Here too, the civil commons has been stripped in the name of 'restructuring'. But the facts of civil collapse are never connected back to the market 'restructuring' which preceded them. Rather, the collapse is pronounced to be the fault of the non-market order within which it never occurred.

The 'Reagan doctrine' of the free market which prevailed in Angola also 'defeated communism' and 'restored free enterprise' in Guatemala, El Salvador, Grenada, Nicaragua, Mozambique and Vietnam. Here too malnutrition, poverty, unemployment, and street crime are higher than ever after death-squad intervention on behalf of the global market's system of freedom. But the doctrine perceives no problem because money counts are now increasing – GDPs, commodity exports and profit-margins. The US government presses hard again for the same 'victory of market forces' in neighbouring Cuba. If the non-white infant mortality rate in Cuba is far lower than the US, and literacy, nutrition levels and health care are at incomparably higher levels than those countries 'saved by the US from communism', such facts do not compute to the market value system. This is because its parameters of competitive ranking are not in terms of life gain or loss, but in gross terms of rises and falls of money aggregates. We observe here, in short, a peculiar concept of '*competition*' and '*victory*' at work. It means, in reality, something deeper than we yet imagine.

If we comprehend this pattern of competition and victory in terms of what it effects for or against life's survival and development, we find a correlation. The more that the money sequence advances across the world in regulation of social life and posting of gross quantitative gains, the more that social and natural life-organization is diminished in the measures of vital life. Thus wherever we observe the 'victory of global market forces', we observe also the reduction of environmental habitat, of social health, of nourishment, of education, of productive employment rate, and of freedom from destitution. Are there any exceptions?

With the pattern of 'global market competition' now leading the countries of the world into ever more 'deregulated' economic orders, we find a wide spectrum of variations on an unseen global theme. This hidden theme is *the downsizing of life to upsize the sequences of money.* The law-like pattern of the 'global competitiveness' we have learned to presuppose as the final goal of world societies is the subjugation and transformation of global life *itself* into functions and refuse of transnational money transactions: dismantling of the civil commons, worker-shedding, and increased life-resource depletion, on the one hand, and on the other hand, the market's money-sequences borderlessly penetrating and widening their conversion of human, civil and environmental life into temporary moments of their growth. This pattern of displacement of the life-ground is the underlying meta-pattern of the global market programme. What appears to be nations competing against one another to sell to each other is, underneath, *the market's money sequence of value competing against the natural and civil life-fabrics of the world.* This transnational process of defeating the claims of human labour, environments and social sectors to continued life in any other form but transient functions of expanding money sequences is the pathological pattern. It does not proceed without strong resistance. But whatever blocks or resists this regime of selection and exclusion for global market appropriation is declared 'non-competitive'. If it resists with force of arms, it is 'terrorist'.

Understanding the Life-Ground

The Regulating Principle of a Life-Sequence Economy

Let us now seek our deeper bearings in the logic of the life-system itself so that we can understand more exactly what an economy must be in accord with if it is not, as now, to strip social and environmental life-hosts to serve decoupled circuits of money growth. We have seen how the market model has mutated to a form which attacks its life-hosts rather than serving them. We will now specify the positive nature and requirements of the life-ground which is the ultimate reference body of any economic organization which produces and distributes for its human members' continued and improved existence, rather than against it.

The *life sequence of value* can be formulated in its most basic axiom form as the sequence of development:

$$Life \rightarrow Means\ of\ Life \rightarrow More\ Life\ (\ L \rightarrow MofL \rightarrow L^1)$$

In this formula, *life* refers specifically to sentient life. Sentient life, in turn, is life which can *move, feel* and – in the case of humans – *think* in concepts as well as images. These three planes of being – (1) organic movement, (2) sensation and feeling, (3) conceptual and image thought – are the ground of *all* life value, however we might order them. That is, there is no value of life that exists which is not such in virtue of bearing or contributing to one or more, at best all, of these planes of life participation and enjoyment.

This is a comprehensive general claim. It is also at the most basic level of comprehending the bearings of what is of worth in world existence. No principle could be more important for humanity to be clear about. Since such basic and universal common grounds of value are today lost in an anchorless relativism reflecting the disorientation of our condition, there is automatized skepticism about all such unifying principles of value binding us. But this value ground can be tested in thought experiment to see if there is even *one* exception, even one value of the great panoply of values we know of which falls outside this triune parametric. Even the *otherworldly* religions end up conceiving their God as the absolute form of these three fields of life value – the Being which can do all, know all and experience all. Even the principle of multiplying difference which repudiates all unifying values for irreducible polyversity of views ends up *by* this very commitment holding to these underlying fields of value as the ground of what is differentiated. No matter how far we go with testing of the common life ground, there is, in truth, no value that exists which does not derive all of its value from bearing and expressing one or more of these fields of being.

This may seem a foundationally self-evident ground from which to build, but its recognition is unsurpassably important to recognize. In the current world in particular, there has been a pervasive loss of value bearings. Post-modern and relativist denials that there is any unifying value ground humans share have complemented the global market's expulsion from public discourse of any value ground but its own. This is how ideologies work to maintain underlying value programmes. To restore the life value ground as our reference body of worth is the base-line break from the delinked money code of value which is unravelling our civil and ecological life-fabrics. It is the first, necessary step to recognition of what endangers the actual life-ground upon which, in fact, every breath drawn in the world depends. It is the initial moment of the recovery process from the mutant value regime which regulates society towards another, life-invasive system of growth.

The life sequence of value is not a fixed state, but a permanently moving process. It admits of countless ranges of possiblity, all decreasing or increasing the *range* of life enjoyed in the previous moment or time-span. Our range of organic movement or thought capacity, for example, goes measurably down with the loss of sufficient oxygen, or protein, or potable water, or clean and secure surroundings of life. The longer these are deprived, the more seriously life is reduced, to the extremes of permanent impairment and death. Overall, each of the three parameters of life and value always admits of *ranges of function*. These ranges of function or capability, in turn, grow or diminish with the nature of the economic conditions within which they live. They diminish when these conditions deprive the life concerned of what is required for it to be healthy (as the vital capabilities of the malnourished child of an impoverished family are diminished). Or they grow when these conditions afford these means of vital life to the life or lives in question (as with the opening horizons of movement, felt being and cognition of the same child in a family with daily access to nutritious food).[26]

Means of life refers to *whatever enables life to be preserved, or to extend its vital range on these planes of being alive.* Breathable air, nutritious food, clean water, adequate shelter, affective interaction, variety and space of environmental surroundings, health care when sick, and accessible learning conditions are *basic* 'means of life'. They are called *basic* because without any one of them, human life is known to be reduced in its range of vital capabilities by precise *degrees* of loss which the practices of the health sciences, educators and social scientists variously investigate and report. Disease, impairment or death over time are the consequences of their continued deprivation, for individuals or what individuals constitute, societies. A person collapses and dies in minutes without oxygen or in very polluted conditions, in days or less without water, in not much longer without food, and so on. All this is more or less exactly known. Whatever the disputes, they are about degrees of life reduction and loss, not about the truth of the life-destruction.

In Niger, 'over 500,000 children are slated to die before 2000 on the basis of payments to the IMF,' reports Oxfam International, calculating from the *deprivations* of basic means of life the *deaths* which will predictably follow.[27]

It is typically asserted or assumed that *need* cannot be defined, that what is one's need is another's desire, that individual differences and preferences differ too widely, that need is an inherently normative concept, that if one defines need one is prescribing to others what they must have or not have, and so on. This repudiation of life bearings is what one would expect in a global condition where another system of value has become dominant and occupies life-hosts. In economics in particular, the concept of need has been banished from every text, class and boardroom as effectively heretical. The term occurs nowhere in any recognized school or model and, as we have seen, the global market paradigm for a century has universally excluded life requirements from its calculus.

Welfare economics, a normative branch of economics, may seem an exception. For it employs value judgements of what *ought* to be produced, how production should be organized, and the way income and wealth ought to be distributed. But welfare economics itself never touches down to the life-ground in its dominant schools. Pareto optimums, cost-benefit ratios, compensation principles, efficiency gains and losses from social interventions, income-distribution consequences of public policies, social welfare functions, aggregated preference orders of communities, and contingent valuation methods to quantify willingness to pay of social populations have given rise to much debate and arcane proofs and disproofs. But human need or life requirement as such never enters any equation. The closest economics gets to life is to subjective reactions to priced goods and real or posited money-demand conditions. What one never finds is connection to more basic ground and what life actually needs from the economy to go on living: either in the microcosm of individuals or in the macrocosm of social and environmental life-hosts. The issue of *life's* reproduction or growth, or deficit and destruction, is unspeakable in the paradigm. Its benchmarks of life never go deeper than consumer preferences, which as we know can be operantly conditioned in circumstances of controlled information to prefer state arms races to public education and health, and carcinogenic junk commodities to continued life itself.[28]

After the paradigm shift which regrounds economics in the life system its programme now assaults and destroys, economists will relate to what is required for life from the economy – not merely what can be extracted from life to increase commodities sold and money flows to investors. The needs of life are not difficult to identify. They are only said to be impossible to define across individual preferences because we have lost our life bearings within a global condition whose regulating paradigm and system excludes life requirements from its premises and inferences of judgement. *A need for something exists if and only if, and to the extent that, deprivation of it regularly results in an absolute reduction of its owner's life-range capability.* We can prove what is or what is not needed by the simple device of observing what happens to a human life *without* it. What is needed for individuals before all else are the basic means of human life specified above. And the same goes for individuals taken together as societies. Breathable air whose ingestion does not reduce the capacities of the lungs to inhale and exhale or induce other organic disfunction is such a foundational need, both for individuals as such and for the communities of human life they together compose. But everywhere in growing urban market sites and beyond, the quality of air deteriorates, to the point that in most of the cities of the world the air systemically produces bronchial and other diseases at epidemic levels, from Calcutta to Toronto. We can walk through the list of basic means of existence and find a cascade down of capacity to carry healthy life. With even food, an apparent exception in still increasing absolute carrying capacity, the combination of population increase driven by mass impoverishment, exhausted and depleting soilcovers from intensive monoculture farming and pollution-induced climate change, increasing reliance on genetically altered and homogenizing plant and animal varieties more vulnerable to disease mutations, and the increasing inaccessiblity of the poor to either land or food commodities together indicate a more precarious and declining life condition. With health-care and education, though less deadly in their absence than other basic needs, there is also a downward slide of their carrying capacity and accessibility to both absolute *and* proportionate numbers of the world's people. In Africa, for example, literacy and health-care systems collapse as governments are now forced by international market institutions to spend four times more on compounding interest payments to foreign money lenders than on all public health and education combined (endless payments for debts that were incurred and accumulated for the most part by elites allied with transnational market forces and depositing flight capital in transnational market banks).[29] The life sequences of human as well as environmental bodies are in these ways globally degenerating while trade and export figures within the money economy are celebrated. We have not considered the means of life of affective interaction because it may seem least affected by global market trends. But here too the decline of this basic means of life would seem difficult to deny since the sites for it are radically reduced by commodified socialization by mass television which cannot interact, and by pervasively insecure employment conditions which, as we have seen, are known to select against healthy social relations. The point here is that an economic paradigm which does not relate to human needs as a factor or determinant of its calculations is bound not to be aligned with them in its recommendations and implementa-tions, and the facts everywhere demonstrate this consequence to have in fact followed systematically as this model's effects.

The Institute for Innovation in Social Policy at Fordham University seeks to track social indicators of well-being in the US, which puts it at the marginalized forefront of the economic sciences by actually relating to life co-ordinates in economic investigation. The Institute's methods do not penetrate to the life-ground itself, and the vital means of existence which are directly required to sustain the human life sequence in a healthy condition. But it follows such indicators as infant mortality, child abuse, teenage suicide, health insurance coverage, drug abuse, alcohol-related traffic deaths, homocides, and poverty among children and the aged. With each of these markers, we can see that an increase in quantity – or, in the case of one, a decrease – correlates with a reduction or destruction of human lives. A non-deranged economic model would relate to such life parameters, not preclude them in principle. But these figures would become more exact in a life-sequence model by going beyond, say, the 'lack of health insurance coverage' to the *loss in range of vital life function* by those without the insurance. This is the only measure that ultimately counts in the life-sequence analysis, and it keeps understanding grounded in what counts. For it could be and may be the case that people in general are better off without corporate medical care which, as we have seen, kills more people in the US by malpractice than all traffic accidents and shootings put together. Or for further contrast between this 'social indicators' approach and life-sequence analysis, statistics of 'drug abuse' give a meaningless category and figure of life gain or loss unless we know how much life is normally reduced or destroyed by the 'abuse' – that is, by life's consuming a harmful substance as a middle term between its significant moments. Even the economic avant garde of the Fordham Institute can easily end up measuring what is, in fact, not a matter of harming life at all, but of transgressing legal or social mores. Grounded life-sequence analysis, in contrast, *keeps its eyes on life and its capabilities to think, feel or do, observing whether there is maintenance, growth or decline in these vital fields of being alive*. Its method goes underneath statistics of the above kinds which do not or may not yield this information, and looks for life substance as such – whether it and its vital means are tending downwards or upwards in direction, and in what respects this is so.

The figures of the Institute for Innovation in Social Policy are not fully life-grounded in this way, but they are well-being indicators at a remove or two from the actual life sequence. Their 'well-being index' has been kept since 1970, and it confirms the downward trend of life indicators which this diagnosis has documented in other ways. Indeed, the Fordham Institute's figures show a very dramatic profile of decline since 1973 – from a peak of 77.5 to a low of 38.1 in 1991, a drop of over 50 per cent.[30]

When we consider downwards or upwards trends from the life-sequence standpoint, we work from a general parametric of understanding and judgement that is straightforward in principle. To *reproduce* life is to maintain its achieved ranges of capability on the planes of thought, feeling and movement. To *increase* life is to widen or deepen achieved ranges of one or other of these planes to more comprehensive compasses of ability. To *reduce* life is to diminish or to extinguish any vector of these vital domains of being alive. These greater or lesser ranges of life capability are what we will call the defining parameters of *life value*.[31] They apply in microcosm to individuals, and in macrocosm to societies.

A society, for example, might be rising or falling with respect to its literacy rates (conceptual thought), visual art facilities and streetscapes (image thought), physical fitness (organic movement), and family-solidarity or depression indices (felt being). Disease incidence could be rising or falling in any area, and with it all three fields of life could be gaining or losing, since disease typically reduces capabilities of thinking, feeling and movement all at once. That is why a disease-free and disease-preventative social condition is so complex and important an achievement, being the heart of what we have called the 'social immune system'. The examples could go on indefinitely, and as they are considered, we will see that all which we might regard as of value in a society falls within the triune parametric of life value. At best, social goods enhance all planes of vital life at once, as do breathable air, nourishing foods, clean water, and all of the basic means of life so far identified. Conversely, their deterioration or absence has the opposite effect, and – as under the system-deciding money sequences of the global market – may destroy people's lives and their environments systematically by stripping or polluting or defunding or otherwise depredating life's vital means at every level. For the money-sequence system of the global market, all of these life means are 'unaffordable' as a public interest, or require at the least 'trade-offs' which reduce them. This is because from the standpoint of the money code of value, the market needs these resources to 'be competitive in the global market', 'to attract and keep investors', 'to pay down public debts' and so on.

Life-sequence analysis must, of course, go beyond the directly vital means of human life if it is to understand the wider life-ground of which human individuals and societies are a part, and upon which they all ultimately depend. The dominant conception shared by Marxist as well as bourgeois thinkers, however, is that non-human nature is of value only so far as it can be used instrumentally for human purposes, not as a value in its own right. From the life-sequence standpoint, this means that all of non-human life can be of worth as a *means* between human life and more human life, but none can have value as such independent of human purposes or enjoyment. This conception eventually became ecocidal in its effect as the economic model regulating the use of environmental resources, the model of engineering mechanics, became so empowered by fuel-driven machineries of extraction, effluent and pollution that it was capable of destroying ecosystems in minutes and of despoiling the world's forest covers, fresh and saltwater habitats, soil mantles, aquifers, and air and atmospheric conditions for life over decades. In the calculus of this model, we have observed, life claims do not even appear to be denied. They are simply blocked out of the system's decision matrices.

Marx recognized the need to steward the earth's resources, but only for human use – although there is some argument over this. Orthodox economics has never seen the issue, only responding if at all to external pressures, and then doing so by extending its life-blind model to new terrains – declaring that only open markets in pollution credits, or privatization of public resources, or other market remedy can work. In this way, the paradigm's adherents exhibit again their incapacity to think of a reality beyond the paradigm. When problems it cannot apprehend are forced home, the response is never that the paradigm lacks resources to see the most basic facts of life. Rather the response is that if these very basic facts of life are to be considered at all, then they must be made to fit the paradigm. Otherwise all attempts at resolution will be 'impractical', 'impossible' or 'dangerous'. Since the paradigm's expulsion of life needs is inherent in its logic, this closure should perhaps not surprise us. But where working-class movements and civil constituencies may succeed in forcing some attention to *their* life claims, the larger mute environment has had no such recourse to protect and enable its life sequencing.

Yet a general fact is beginning to dawn. The general fact is that human and environmental life sequences are linked so that *people's health depends on the health of their environments.* In the words of the World Health Organization, it is now recognized that 'poor environmental quality is responsible for around 25% of all preventible ill health in the world today'.[32] A life-sequence economy requires that human and environmental processes be comprehended as intimately interrelated. The needs of the environmental life-host as an overall life-organization are, at the same time, the needs of society and the human species. For if the former are disrupted, then the latter are endangered derivatively. It is not so much an issue of becoming non-anthropocentric in order to save the environment, the standard environmental position. It is an issue of regrounding in the life-sequence at all levels in order to save it at each. For the life-ground is at risk as a whole, and with it the human species.

The ways in which the destruction of the environmental life-host is at the same time destroying human means of life is a many-layered story, as intricate and connected across all conditions as the vast global ecoweb itself. But from the grossest view, we can see that, say, the rupturing of the ozone layer by commercially marketed toxins not only endangers other forms of life going extinct by it, such as amphibians like frogs, but humans too, both directly by exposure to cancer-causing and immune system weakening ultra-violet rays, and indirectly by the loss of what depends on frogs, such as various fish and waterfowl populations, and insect control by what they eat. Since phytoplankton too and numberless other species also are damaged by ozone-layer holes, this single strand of the life-ground destruction effected by corporate market processes could be elaborated across the planetary life-host with ever-widening circles of destructive consequences implicate in the pathway of a single money sequence left to self-regulate.

As we know, *this* particular money sequence whose consequence is to to turn sunlight into carcinogenic rays, deploys chlorofluorocarbons in its priced commodity for sale which eat the ozone layer. But this market cause of the problem has, unprecedentedly, been in some part externally regulated by international regulation, the 1991 Montreal Protocol. This protocol went beyond the market paradigm for its guidance, and set a limit on what the corporate market could continue to manufacture, buy and sell. Protection of global life from a systemic mortal danger was in this case a *life* need which managed to register and be responded to outside of the market's self-regulating mechanisms. Although much less effective than is desirable, such an international protocol discloses the *life-sequence economy* in embryo. Systematic deepening and generalizing of its regulatory principle is required to restrain the many carcinogenic circuits of the global market juggernaut. We will return to this issue in discussing the civil commons, human society's conscious defender of the life-ground whose resources include international life-protective law as a keystone structure.

If we think of the life-ground in an interrelated way that corresponds to its *actual* interrelationships and the interdependency of all its conditions, then we can see in principle that there is unlikely to be *any* systemic destruction of the non-human environment which will not at the same time reduce human life directly or indirectly in the longer term. This is on the one hand a truism, but on the other hand a life-and-death principle to which the global market system is inherently blind.

If we consider this regime's most general assaults on the non-human environment, we can quickly understand the pervasive interlinkage of human and environmental health and well-being. Persistent organic pollution, for example, not only destroys and degrades other life-forms and habitats, but by doing so harms humans directly and indirectly – poisoning and despoiling the common life conditions and life properties we share with other creatures, like eyes, ears, skins, lungs and need for water, but also by doing this to them, simultaneously polluting the food or other resource they embody for vital human use. This pattern of life assault by corporately produced pollutants on *both* human and non-human life could be spelled out at great length, ranging from the perhaps polluted meat on the table to urban smog that insults our organs while acidifying forest and aquatic habitats, to the agribusiness chemicals destroying coral reefs and underground aquifers. To separate the human and the non-human reductions and destructions of life here is artificial. It impacts the entire life-ground by polluting any process of it. The destruction of life habitats by global market operations also advances by other means – clearcutting forests the size of England and Wales every year, scraping ocean bottoms with miles-long dragnets of factory ships so no fish stocks are left, blacktopping countrysides and wetlands for urban developers as fast as the forests are felled – we have seen the facts. The point here, again, is that what assaults, reduces and destroys non-human being also attacks the conditions of human life both directly and indirectly. 'We cannot', say the indigenous peoples, 'harm any part of the earth without harming ourselves.'

The reduction of biodiversity is another themal consequence of the 'free' corporate market. The systematic extinction of the species at hundreds of times the natural rate will also continue as long as this system is not regulated by the ordering requirements of a life-sequence economy. As long as this system is left to self-regulation by the non-life principle of multiplying money-demand for money investors, it will continue to eliminate the costs of life-protection which have no place in its calculus. But just as the reduction of other species and of biodiversity itself are calamitous for other life-forms, they are also by ecological transitivity disastrous in the long term for the still increasing human species which remains. We know that most life-protective medicinal substances come from other species, and that only a small fraction of these species, which are going extinct at the rate of over 100 species a day, are yet known to health science.[33] Only one effect of the destruction of biodiversity, then, is humanity's loss of its fount of medical and pharmacological cures and antidotes.

But the effects for humanity of the reduction and destruction of non-human species are far deeper and wider in reach than this. The presence of other species in one's environment is a vital need which people's universal demand for plants and pets, excitement at seeing wild creatures, birdfeeding, and animal sights in film, tourist or other forms variously expresses. Then as well there is the original people's dependency on other creatures for their most basic means of life. A place without other species is in fact tomb-like, and every species humans want or need near to them to be more alive as humans is dependent for its life, in turn, on many other species down the food chain. Here again the life sequence of humanity radiates out to the larger life sequence of the environmental host and all of its sub-sequences in order to reproduce and grow as human. The more we consider the matter whole, in other words, the more we recognize that the life sequence of humanity in the microcosm and the macrocosm has implicate in its middle term of 'means of life' the rest of the planetary host.

A thought experiment here illuminates the point. Try to identify any species, or any continuous condition of the world at all, *whose loss would not reduce humanity's means of life.* The loss, we find, of even the most presupposed or distant condition of the planetary web qualifies here. This is because the nature of the life condition is, as the Buddha long ago recognized in his First Sermon, that 'everything depends in its origination on everything else at once and in unison'.

The second part of the thought experiment is more disquieting. Try to identify a single species or continuous condition that is *not at risk* from the advancing operations of the self-regulating corporate global system. Even the weather, we now discover, is increasingly destabilized by this system's still spreading industrial effects – with threats and precipitations of infectious diseases, droughts and food production crises, temperature extremes and natural disasters of flooding, storms and hurricanes, and rises in sea-level endangering coastal communities and intertidal ecosystems across the continents. The consequences of an industrial engineering model with a self-maximizing money-to-more-money sequence as its drive-wheel is cumulatively disastrous for the life-ground on every level. This is not an apocalyptic vision, but a scientifically documented causal mechanism whose connections have been blocked out. The more technically empowered this system becomes, the more pervasively it takes over economies across the world without life-sequence regulation, the more its automatized programme invades and destroys life-organization.

Within the strictures of this omniverous mechanical model, another general fact remains blinkered out which its value calculus cannot see – the interlocking relationships and connections between environmental health and human health. The pardigm block here is remarkably pervasive in effect. The 1992 Rio Conference on the environment, for example, with thousands of participants, conference articles and declarations from 160 countries did not once make the connection between the well-being of the two intertwined life-systems. The Rio Conference was not alone in this disconnection. It is a systemic block of market culture. In consequence, environmental agencies employ few health professionals, medical schools and universities do not generally research or instruct on the relationship, and public communications systems and journalists do not investigate it. But there could hardly be a more important relationship to global life, or to the recognition and response of social immune systems to the pathological pattern invading social and planetary life-hosts.

We might in this light broaden the regulating principle of the life sequence beyond humanity to the environmental life-host with whose health or stable reproduction humanity's vital well-being is interdependent. We have represented the human life sequence as Life $\rightarrow$ Means of Life $\rightarrow$ More Life. We might then write the same life sequence large as Global Life $\rightarrow$ Means of Life $\rightarrow$ More Global Life, or simply as $L \rightarrow MofL \rightarrow L^1$ to be understood at the highest level of generality. But this would obscure a distinction which needs to be made. For what is different about the environmental life-host, global or bioregional, is that its means of life are perpetually provided by its own spontaneous cycles with no requirement of productive plan to *make* these means of life by artifice, as post-hunter-and-gatherer humans have long done. This distinction is at the heart of much indigenous and spiritual wisdom, and is articulated perhaps most subtly by Lao Tzu's timeless *Tao-te Ching*. As human engineering technologies have become ever more destructive in their powers of disaggregating natural life systems, this difference in means of life production has become decisive in the life-organization of the planet. Humanity in the programmed form of the mutating global market system has, unlike any other species or culture in time, come to threaten the planetary eco-web itself by rogue money sequences taking over human economies and their environmental life-hosts at an exponential rate.

The way in which humans can sustain their environmental life-host, then, is not by providing for *its* means of life, for this is not required or possible. The only way in which 'sustainability' of the environmental life-sequence can be achieved is by humans *not systemically depleting, polluting, or destroying* it. It takes care of its own life-sequence in the macrocosm and of an infinitude of sub-sequences at the same time with no interference needed. This is 'the great harmony ' as this miracle has been called across periods and cultures until the global market system. What is needed, simply, is that the invading corporate mechanism now dismantling and poisoning it across boundaries is externally restrained. The one-way programme of turning nature into parts for commodities and the rest into a bottomless sink for industrial effluents is ecologically insane.

Environmental stability and biodiversity are also what humanity needs to reproduce itself intact and in health. This interdependency of human life with its environmental host, once considered, may seem as obvious as the weather. But it is a grounding reality which cannot be recognized from within the global market paradigm. Even the most progressive presupposers of this model who seek to go beyond it to consider the endangered life system, such as the members of the Brundtland Commission, still imagine that the current scale of money-sequenced growth can multiply by a factor of 5 to 10, with 'sustainability' still possible.[34] They are symptoms of the deeper problem.

The Brundtland Report never penetrates to the money-sequence programme underlying and driving this unsustainable 'growth', nor does Herman Daly, who recognizes that such growth cannot be sustained. But Daly aptly defines the conditions which must be established for economic growth of *any* kind to be environmentally sustainable:

> Renewable resources should be exploited in a manner such that: (1) harvesting rates do not exceed regeneration rates and (2) waste emissions do not exceed the renewable assimilative capacity of the local environment.[35]

Daly also points out to us what is deducible from the current market paradigm's expulsion of the life factor from its calculus: 'The concept of an optimal scale of the aggregate economy relative to the ecosystem is *totally absent* from current macroeconomic theory.' But we might observe a shortcoming of Daly's revolutionary inclusion of the requirements of the ecosystem in macro-economic thinking. His two conditions of sustainability to correct the blindness of the received paradigm are precisely appropriate to a life-sequence economy. The problem is that they themselves remain blind to the requirement of *species biodiversity* which is at the heart of a life-regulated economy. For it is possible to harvest resources, such as trees or fish, at a rate that does not exceed regeneration rates, but still thereby lose biodiverse habitats by replacing them with resource plantations. The harvested trees, for example, are replanted, but only the types that are useful for reharvesting, and by methods of planting which make them uniform in age and distributed in rows. The living forest is thus destroyed. Only the current commercial resource is reproduced. The harvesting rate of trees does not exceed the regeneration rate, in accordance with Daly's formula. But biodiverse habitat and species are obliterated.

The same problem attends *any* 'resource regeneration' that is not regulated by a principle of biodiversity preservation. To overlook this core requirement of a life economy is, in implication, ecocidal. For it follows from the mere reproduction of a *fungible resource* that the life system from which it is extracted is dispensable. This blinkered thinking characterizes the positions of even the most avant-garde economists, who remain stuck in the engineering model of uniform-block throughputs even as they expose the long-term unsustainability of the current paradigm's methods. But this blind-spot can be corrected in principle by adding a third principle of a life-sequence economy to Daly's first two:

(3) *biodiversity of reproduction and distribution of species is not reduced.*

We know that the life factor must be reintroduced on every plane to prevent the global market system from stripping and degrading the life-ground to ever more reduced carrying capacities for life. And we know that the principle of life's process is to reproduce and grow through means of life as its middle term, achieving more comprehensive ranges of vital capability as it evolves: whether within the species by extensions and deepenings of thought, felt being and organic movement of individual and social life, or among the species by evolving biodiversity and niche habitats.

There is a unifying principle of life regulation and development at work here on all planes of vital existence. Economies and their organizing models must be regulated to comply with the life code this principle expresses, or they become to that extent pathogenically invasive.

An economy, we might conclude, succeeds in reality rather than in claim to the extent that life's ranges of vital being are maintained and/or increased for its members, by both internal provisions of the vital means of life, and by non-destruction of their environmental life-host. An economy fails to the extent that the opposite occurs, and the life of its members and their environmental life-host declines on these planes of life growth and participation.

These parameters of the life code of value are not mysterious or opaque. On the level of the individual. even very small reductions of the vital range of breath, feeling, organ or limb are normally experienced as '*something wrong*'. Our lives revolve around the enjoyment of these fields of life as givens, and we quickly seek to restore by any means available to us their reduction or loss. But such contractions of vital life range cannot in principle *register* in the priced transactions of the market paradigm's metric, even if they were to strike every economic agent at once and fatally in the long run.

The *measure* of life value is not only with us every moment beneath conscious or theoretical recognition. It is in fact the ultimate ground of motivation behind every market commodity we want or purchase, which we are conditioned to believe these priced commodities will deliver. Every market advertisement appeals in some way to this life-ground, while at the same time decoupling us from what actually will serve it – for example, by posing images of beautiful natural habitats and human forms, while simultaneously stimulating by association with them a desire to buy commodities which harm life, such as cigarettes or automobiles. This is the delinkage from life needs which is the global market's inner logic, all the while promising us greater range of vital life by buying and consuming its priced goods. We re-enter the real world when we look to what *in fact* enables our vital ranges of mind, sentience and action to flourish and grow, and attend to ensuring our access to these actual life goods. This is what an economy is by its nature required to do – to ensure the production and distribution of what is not in abundant supply for its members.

The underlying measure of life value which any sane economy is regulated to serve is not imprecise. Life value is exactly calibratable in its gains and losses, in an individual or across individuals in a society, or in the reproduction and distribution of species across an environment. The entire corpus of scientific medicine is testimony to the long and painstaking development of ways and means of assessing and responding to precisely defined deficits of normal human life ranges – mainly, by diagnosing disease and prescribing treatment for the known deficits of life range which it brings about. The entire practice of formal education as well can be decoded as the process of judging and enabling more comprehensive levels of thinking across defined breadths and depths of cognition. Yet again, environmental protection can be understood as the body of practices which effectively defend the evolved scopes of life of the species and ecosystems around us. All of these general life co-ordinates of value are basic indicators of a society's economic success in conditions of scarcity of life-means, and increasingly so as such means of life become scarcer. From the standpoint of a life-sequence economy, the more of life's breadths and depths are reproduced and extended by its provisions and distributions, the better is the economy's and the society's objective condition. Conversely, the more of these life domains are reduced or lost, the worse is the economy's and the society's real condition. The predicament that the global corporate economy poses to us is that *public health, educational and environmental expenditures to realize a life-sequence economy are 'cut back' or 'axed' across the world in accordance with the demands of a closed paradigm of value which judges these expenditures to be 'unnecessary' or 'unaffordable'.*

The propelling drive-wheel of this system's overwhelming of the life-ground itself is, as we have seen, 'the money sequence of value'. Its limitless and exponential demands, we have also observed, increasingly imperil the conditions of social and environmental life-organization. The next step of diagnosis is to track exactly the rogue and uncontrolled pathways by which this mutating money sequence invades its life-hosts.

Tracking the Rogue Pathways of the Money Sequence of Value

The money sequence of value is often confused in its outcomes with the maximimization of utility. Although it can certainly have this serendipitous effect, its regulating objective is to maximize money returns over money inputs by whatever means is perceived to best achieve this outcome. Its structure of reproduction, called 'profitable investment', can be represented by the formula:

$$\$ \rightarrow Commodity \rightarrow More \$$$

or

$$\$ \rightarrow C \rightarrow \$^1$$

With the pre-capitalist use of money, money does not begin and end the exchange sequence in this way. On the contrary, life begins and ends the exchange sequence, and money is only a *medium of exchange*. The baker or the shoemaker makes shoes or bread, and then exchanges them for money, in order to buy other life-goods with the money received. Here the money received and spent stands in as equivalent to means of life, because its reproduction is solely to exchange means of *life*. Most people normally use money in this way – not for money gain, but for life gain. Money in this form is not a curse or inverter of value, as Marx's and others' critiques of money may imply. Money in its form as a *universal medium of exchange for life-goods* is one of the great institutions and inventions of history. We might therefore add an intermediate formula here to represent this still life-affirming value sequence:

$$Life \rightarrow Money \rightarrow Means\ of\ Life \rightarrow More\ Life$$

or

$$L \rightarrow \$ - MofL \rightarrow L^1$$

In this specific form, the sequence is *not* the money sequence of value, but the life sequence of value. It is not invested as money to have more *money*, but to have more *life*.

The money sequence of value, in contrast, begins with money and ends with money in its reproductive cycle. Means of life are what *money*, in the person of its agent, uses as a middle term to become *more money*. More money, not more life, is the regulating objective of thought and action throughout this value cycle: which is normally reiterated in compounding sequences to ever greater accumulations of money value. This is the prime money sequence, so brilliantly exposed and critiqued by Marx in *Capital.*

Value judgment within the money sequence does not calculate whether *life* gains or loses by its transactions. The objective is to net more money for money investors. Indeed, it is famously held that any other objective is 'a betrayal of fiduciary trust to stockholders'. It follows from this value calculus that wars, ongoing car crashes or endemic diseases can be occasions of momentous 'value adding' and 'economic prosperity', so long as they promote increased profits for shareholders, or – with GDP – increased volume of priced transactions in the aggregate.

Since those programmed by the money sequence of value always assume that more real money demand expresses more value, they conclude in one of the most fateful non-sequiturs of history that *more real money demand is always better for the individual or for society.* This value metric has become socially institutionalized in such standard measures of social well-being as the Gross National Product (that is, the total money value of the goods and services sold in and by a national economy, which registers no life debits in people killed by it or environments degraded by its activities). Such a value system, unfortunately, *suppresses the distinction between life and death itself.* In failing to distinguish between life-wealth and money demand *on* life-wealth, it systemizes a deadly confusion. If money demand on the wealth of life keeps increasing, but the wealth of life keeps decreasing by its demands, then the market or money calculus cannot recognize the problem. According to its value metric, all is well and prosperity and development are being won. This value confusion can lead, if its logic is not seen through, to the stripping of the life-world by money demand until the life fabric can no longer hold.[36]

On the face of it, the money sequence produces at the most competitive cost possible a good which people are willing to pay for in preference to other such goods on the market. In the beginning, these goods or commodities were what people in fact needed for their lives – food, clothing, and so on. Cloth was the first major commodity of the capitalist market, and food was a byproduct of the sheep that provided the wool for the cloth. Unnecessary commodities or destructive commodities came later on, although the money sequences within which they were sold for more money than invested was never distinguished from the original money sequence of producing goods that served life. We will analyse these mutations of the money sequence ahead.

Yet even the original money sequence produced effects that were not taken account of in its calculus. All that was seen was the provision of the goods it produced at a lower price per unit than other producers could achieve. In fact, the same narrowed view is still declared as axiomatic in the global market today, and it is patiently explained to students and readers of the business media as an argument of infallible authority and deductive precision.

> The goal is to earn a profit in the face of vigorous competition. Where consumers have choices, profits in a given industry are driven down to the minimum level that might still attract capital from alternative investments of comparable riskiness. In such conditions, profit is not only defensible, it is a social obligation. It is the difference between the value society derives from the product – measured by the price consumers are prepared to pay for it at the margin – and what it costs to society to produce, measured by the price of the labour, capital and other inputs that went into producing it.
>
> I stress society. The means of production may be privately owned in a capitalist economy but they are still, in a sense, social: They are scarce resources to be allocated among competing users in a way that best serves society. It happens that competition and prices are better instruments to this purpose than central planning, but it is no less social a process for being conducted through private markets. Profit, likewise, may be privately earned, but it is a calculator of a social return. Those that do not produce for the collective good in this way are dispatched with a ruthlessness that would do any Maoist proud: They are driven out of business.[37]

This justification of the primary money sequence is of hallmark quality in its clarity and accuracy. It identifies in language accessible to all the precise principles and argument at the moral core of the global market doctrine. The explanation also provides that signature of market rebuttal, a smirking aside on communism – in this case, the hero of all critics of capitalism, the Emperor Mao. There is, however, a problem. Everything which this model explanation prescribes as the way we ought to live to 'create value', to fulfil 'social obligation', and to 'best serve society' is perfectly consistent with destroying the lives of people employed by it, or the environments used by it. Such life-destructive effects, however, are ruled out of view by the paradigm as 'externalities', and so do not pose a problem to its adherents. For those who regard life as of value, in contrast, these effects are of the first importance in understanding the real world.

Consider, for example, Claudia Molina. She works for a subsidiary of the transnational corporation, Fruit of the Loom, making a clothing good needed in modern life at a cost-competitive price. So far, so good for the model. In one of the 'newly democratic societies of Central America', as these conditions are expressed to us, she works with other young women from 14 years old up, 'at the best price for their labour factor of production as they can command in the market'. Still the paradigm presents to us a well-ordered moral universe of free contractual exchange and social obligation at work by the operation of the money sequence of value.

But there is a catch that is not computed by the paradigm. Claudia and her young women peers work 15 hours a day from Monday to Friday, and then work a 22-hour shift for the weekend. A *97-hour week* at life-deadening labour. They are paid 38 cents an hour, or a few cents more for dexterity.[38] The finished product they produce for their employer thus generates vast *'value-added' creation* – the 'difference between the value society derives from the product, the price consumers are prepared to pay for it at the margin' *and* 'what this product costs society to produce, measured by the price of the labour, capital and other inputs'.

Thus, it follows from the moral equation of the money sequence in its most productive form that this super-exploitation of young female workers is maximally fulfilling a 'social obligation' and a 'collective good'. For it is 'best serving society' by working young people 97 hours a week at life-deadening labour at 38 cents an hour, thereby expanding the difference between the cost of the product and the price paid for it – an immense 'value-added' contribution to society. Mind you, the 'value added' in this ethical system is, in fact, private money-profit that goes to the dividends or equity of owners and stockholders of another society who, in turn, will in all likelihood contribute none of this 'value added' to the society or people producing the object after they have paid their labour costs. They will invest it in more 'high value-added' production here or elsewhere, thereby 'creating jobs by investment', and compounding their 'service to the collective good'. In this way, the principle of maximizing profits to promote the social good is realized, and the 'social obligation' to do so is fulfilled.

In such ways, even the primary money sequence of value, which produces goods for the life of consumers who can pay, at the same time depredates the lives of those producing the goods. This consequence is never factored in as a cost by the market paradigm. Rather, it is a *cost reduction*, because the only costs considered are monetary costs to money investors and consumers, not costs to life. At the same time as well, the Maquiladora factory site and its surroundings where Claudia and her fellow labourers work have been cleared of all life habitat, while also fouling and poisoning the immediate and wider environments by industrial and waste effluents on a continuous basis.[39] In this way, 'value adding' and the 'service to the collective good' produce what is, in fact, 'a living hell'.[40] But again none of these systemic life reductions and destructions factor in the paradigm as a cost, but rather *as cost savings*, because it excludes costs to life a priori.

To recognize these systemic costs of life excluded from the bare money sequence given in formula above, we can let 'C+' stand for the means of life produced (as distinguished from 'C-' which produces a commodity that is *not* a means of life), and let '(-)' stand for the external costs to life it incurs. Thus the formula is revised to represent the specific type of money sequence described above as:

$$\$ \rightarrow C+(-) \rightarrow \$^{1}$$

These life-depredations of the *productive* money sequence may seem enough to condemn it as deranged before we consider the rogue money sequence which produces no good of life at all. This was the conclusion of Marx. But the problematic is not fully fathomed. The money value programme undergoes fundamental *mutations* in its sequence over time. In its classical capitalist form, it invests in buying factors of production (labour, instruments of labour and natural resources), and organizes them to produce means of life (for example, clothes, foods, homes). Then, to complete the investment sequence, these commodities are converted back into money again, with the 'value added' of profit by sale to buyers in the market. But the money-into-more-money sequence *mutates* insofar as its middle term is no longer means of life, but what are *not* means of life. This is a logical space left open in the commodity phase of the money sequence which has two further general variations, each also ignored by the market paradigm:

(1) Artificial, adulterated or otherwise *debased substitutes for means of life.*

This form of commodity ranges over a vast and increasing range of goods, from almost all bread sold, once 'the staff of life', to – recently – genetically-altered foodstuffs of every kind which have no testing for their long-term effects, and which have trade prohibitions on labelling them.[41] The term used for most of these ersatz foodstuffs has long been 'junk food'. But the *non*-junk foods of meat, fruits and vegetables have also been increasingly invaded by the same process of life-degraded substitutions without conceptual recognition. We might call this wider class of life-inferior substitutes *counterfeit foods* to designate its full set.

Foodstuffs are only one area of this money-sequence pattern of replacing means of life with inferior substitutes ('*inferior*' being defined as what does not enable life as well as what it is inferior to, in proportion to the shortfall). There is, in general, *no* area of vital life good which has not been significantly replaced by inferior counterfeits by money-sequenced production. If we consider overall the basic need areas of life, we can see that money-sequenced production of the means of life has directly or indirectly led to markedly and sometimes dangerously inferior life goods in a number of the most vital areas – the air we breathe and hear, the water we can find and drink, the free environmental space and biodiversity we can access, the affective interactions with others in our vicinity, the cultural participations of our free time, as well as the safe and nourishing food available around us.

But the point here is not to broadbrush all money-sequenced production as a regression. For the matter is mixed, and few of us reading this book would find life more vital and alive in an economy without money-sequenced production which has excelled in machine-made goods. The point is, rather, to note the tendency for this form of economic organization, if it is not regulated by the life sequence, *to override vital life requirements and needs at every level insofar as it becomes more monetarily efficient to do so, with no internal limit to this life-destructive propensity.* This pattern mutates more dangerously as it finds pathways of 'value adding' to money inputs other than producing for life wants. But we need to observe that it attacks life barriers even *within* this circuit, and does so with increasing delinkage from organic life. This is the aetiological disposition which eventually finds fully carcinogenic pathways of growth.

(2) Objects of wants which serve no life need of their buyers, but have been *operantly conditioned* by a classical stimulus-response schedule of reinforcements to induce a predictable vector of the target population into a behavioural willingness to pay for the commodity so advertised.

This class of commodities is not a substitute for a means of life which is needed, as the preceding class of commodities is. Desire to buy it is created by a process called 'demand stimulation' by economists. There are any number of such commodities on the global market, and they increase in variation and number as a necessary condition of the continuous process of market creation which must be propelled by its mechanisms to reproduce and grow. This is why the paradigm assumes that there is 'unlimited demand for priced goods and services in any market economy', an 'unlimited demand' posited by the model which is continually fuelled by market conditioning schedules. In matters of the psyche too, the engineer's model of input (conditioning signals) and output (predictable behaviours of specific commodity purchase) underlies the operation. The money sequence can only continue if money investment is converted into money-added returns by the middle term of a commodity that is purchased by consumers. The *differentia specifica* here is that the commodity is not a means of life, nor an inferior substitute for a means of life, but an object of a want that has been conditioned into existence.

Walmart stores, the world's greatest oligopolist retailer, conditions its customers into buying what they do not need, for example, by constructing an environment in its warehouse-block stores that 'augments an individual's predisposition to feel overwhelmed and anxious, compelling unplanned buying'.[42] In general, the typical transnational corporation now spends more on advertising its commodities than on production itself, and even research-intensive pharmaceutical firms spend twice as much on 'demand stimulation' as they do on researching their pharmaceutical remedies – figures which reveal from the measures of corporate accounts themselves the extent to which creating and managing wants overrides production as a regulating objective of corporate business.[43]

If we were to try to list the commodities which are not needed by their purchasers, but whose sale is an outcome of operant conditioning, we might well end up identifying most of the commodities sold in the global market today. The realm of television is an apt site for such investigation of the various levels on which what is not needed for people's *life* reproduction or growth is marketed, instead, for the reproduction and growth of money returns to corporate investors. Here the want-creating process operates pervasively through both the ads and the programming itself so that people are thereby systematically constructed as desirers and buyers of corporate commodities which do not provide them with means of life, but rather the opposite.

That is, consumers in this money sequence do not access a means of life such as an object of aesthetic experience on the television screen, or information on an object for sale that they need, but on the contrary the life capabilities they bear are *debased* by the commodity they consume. This is true in two ways. First, the middle term of the commodity on view or for sale does not enable life's vital well-being or growth, but retards it in passive consumption. People are not made to think, feel or do more vitally than they would without the consumption, but have their thinking, feeling and doing done for them. Secondly, the regulating principle of the advertisements they see is to condition them into the view that their *life is lacking or in a state of deficit unless they purchase the commodity for sale*. The result of such blanket conditioning is predictable in the aggregate. Most people, who watch an average of four or more hours of television each day, will be conditioned into believing that their lives are lacking in general, and require more commodities to be adequate or successful. So this commodity circuit of the money sequence not only does not enable life by its nature, but it disables people's lives by continuously representing them as lacking what they are made to want.

There are also the opportunity costs of allocating resources to such non-enabling commodities *in place of* life-enabling commodities. Here the opportunity costs include not only the labour, natural resources and other factors of production expended on unnecessary and debilitating products instead of life goods, but also the loss of non-renewable resources and the additional loads of effluents and waste-products entering the environment. These costs to life, again, do not compute to the model. To distinguish these two variations of the money sequence of commodity production from the first sequence which produces means of life, we write 'C-' to stand for the commodity, because it is not a means of life, and '(-)' beside it to represent its negative external effects:

$$\$ \to C\text{-}(\text{-}) \to \$^1$$

From the standpoint of the life sequence, then, we find that the first three variations of money sequence have variously invasive, disabling effects on life which are not recognized by the received paradigm. Even when the commodity produced is a genuine means of life, as distinguished from a counterfeit means of life or the object of an artificially induced want, money-sequenced production results in systemic life-reductions screened out by the market model. Even Marx's formulae of capitalist circuits do not register these mutations of the original life-means commodity.

But the mutations of commodity circuits become still more life-invasive and dangerous as corporate money sequences seek new channels and pathways of maximizing money-value added beyond commodity production to serve life needs. The next variation of the money sequence makes a qualitative departure, and after 1945 becomes increasingly dominant without notice of its radically mutant form. Its distinguishing feature is *a directly life-destructive middle term.* The commodity whereby money increases itself is in this case *a commodity that is known to maim and kill life.*

Life-killing Commodities as the Middle Term of the Money Sequence

Here we move to a directly and intentionally life-destructive commodity which marks this type of money sequence as pathogenic on its face. This too is a mutation in the investment sequence which is not registered in market theory or practice, even when it becomes the leading commodity of manufacture and international sale. By not being recognized, it deepens and spreads as a circuit through the social life-host's reproduction process. The need to inhibit its growth does not register in the life system's feedback loops.

There are two principal forms of this life-destructive mutation of the money sequence's middle term. The primary form is to invest in producing and selling lethal weapons. These are researched, designed and produced so as to destroy human life and its infrastructural supports with the maximal efficiency which the physical, biological and engineering sciences can achieve.[44] Most public research money in the world's richest nation is assigned to this form of research, which is then appropriated by private corporations to produce, sell and export increasingly expensive and deadly weapons for profit.[45]

The weapons commodity began its truly modern history with the study of falling objects and projected missiles by Galileo. Its simultaneously scientific and commercial development has since consisted in ever more lethal instruments to obliterate people and settlements against all possibility of life defence, with a frenetic escalation of this process after the Russian Revolution of 1917 to rule out any alternative to a money-sequence economy. In the life-blind calculi of the money sequence, however, the systematic assault on both host and external life-organizations by the life-killing commodity – through vast resource diversion as well as direct devastation – is not factored into the market calculus. Since the debits of life do not enter, no costs can be perceived as long as money returns increase. The armaments commodity can become, as it has, the most profitable manufacture of global trade. But the problem remains beyond the reach of the paradigm's theoretical resources. What kills and deprives human life is *for its calculus the same* in value as what serves and enhances life. The distinction between life and death itself does not register.

The pathological equivalence of life and death within the money-sequence economy can only be seen as pathological by a paradigm of economic value which incorporates the distinction into its metric. Because a life-sequence economy calculates with life gain or loss as the regulating yardstick of all its decisions, the military commodity could never become a dominant moment of its reproduction and growth. In contrast, a money-sequenced economy selects *for* weapons commodities as highly advantageous: with ten times more money spent on promoting arms sales than on civil exports by the government of Britain, for example, long after the Cold War is over.[46] The capital-intensive market systematically favours armaments commodities for production because of:

(1) their uniquely high value-added price, whether sold as an overall weapons system or as an individual component, accessory, replacement, or part (for example $26 billion for the first five years of research and development of the US 'Star Wars' programme, or $7417 spent by the US government to General Electric for two one-cent pins);[47]

(2) their specially rapid rate of obsolescence and turnover, which follows from both arms-race market conditions and from rapid destruction of these commodities by their use;

(3) the monopoly or semi-monopoly position of armaments manufacturers which flows from: (a) the designation of military production designs and methods as state secrets; (b) the high capital costs of armaments technology and manufacture; and (c) the privileged linkages of established military producers with government defence and procurement agencies;

(4) the large-scale and secure capital financing of military research, production, and cost-additions; a funding which is ensured by coercive state mechanisms of public taxation, resource allocation, and national-debt imposition, and which is available to no other system of commodity production.

It is these special advantages in principle of the weapons commodity that continue to favour it for production and sale in a mutated money-sequence economy. Economic advantage is conferred as long as the effective demand for them is selectively available from public revenues, which draw upon the future tax receipts of societies as well as current revenues by long-term debt financing. Here again, we see the intimate connection between the parasitic money sequence which produces nothing but compound-interest debt charges, and the money sequence whose middle term is means of life destruction. Neither serves any life requirement, and each propels the other by its increases. International money lenders thrive on armaments competitions which can only continue by increased debt, and weapons commodities complementarily provide ever more instruments of terror and destruction as a last resort to compel indebted nations to pay multiplying debt loads (for example, by enforcing a trade sanction). It may be no accident that Japan with no international projection of mass-destructive military power has hundreds of billions of non-performing foreign loans, while the US does not.[48]

These underlying properties and circumstances favouring the military commodity in the global market explain that the apparent 'madness of the arms race' and 'the insanity of the military institution', while surely true from a standpoint that values life, are in fact perfectly rational from the standpoint of neo-classical economics. But this deep-structural determination of market product selection is not recognized by even the most concerned critics of its virulent *effects*. The causal mechanisms remain concealed. That is why peace-movement understanding continues at a loss as to how weapons of mass destruction can continue to be so dominant long after any justification of national self-defence has been removed. It is also how stories of humanity's natural aggression, love of war or other dark species properties can continue to be believed in as long as the underlying systemic cause of the disorder remains blocked from view. And so the weapons commodity continues to flourish in the global market even if the declared enemy has disappeared, even if no armed conflict at the end of the 1990s is between state militaries, and even if societies have been largely stripped of their social infrastructures to continue expending more on weapons.

We will see ahead that high-tech weapons also have other functions in the global market. Yet while they stimulate, expand and open ever new *markets* for the money-sequence economy, they have no contemporary function for *life* reproduction and development. The US 'precision bombing' and militarily-enforced embargo of Iraq after the Iraqi invasion of Kuwait in 1991 may seem to be a counterexample, apparently protecting human populations from rogue aggressions. Here the Leviathan armed forces of the US military equipped with the most deadly weapon commodities may appear to fulfil a life function. But even if we ignore the fact that the invaded territory, Kuwait, was originally part of pre-colonial Iraq and is a colonially constructed client oil state with over 95 per cent of the population excluded from voting, the deeper fact remains that the 'precision bombing' and subsequent military embargo of Iraq did not dislodge the regime responsible for the aggression. On the contrary, the regime's leadership remained more powerful than before, in large part because the military commodity solution killed an estimated 1,211,285 people, mostly children, and stunted and wasted over 40 per cent of those children remaining, essentially by the bomb damage to clean water and sewage pipes across Baghdad, which could not be replaced because of the subsequent, militarily-enforced embargo.[49]

Life destruction by the money sequence's development and use of military commodities also continues in peacetime. It is estimated that the single greatest source of environmental pollution in the US is the military-industrial complex, and that one-quarter of the public monies which are expended on weapons commodities across the world 'would eradicate poverty, homelessness, and illiteracy, as well as pay for the clean-up of all our major environmental pollution' at the same time.[50] Whether the funds now devoted to life-destroying commodities would achieve all of this or not, it is clear that this deadly mutation of the money sequence has appropriated public treasuries for its growth, and systemically attacks and depletes life and life resources both directly and indirectly.

While this mutation of the corporate money sequence is clearly pathological to a view grounded in life, its pathways of appropriation are selected for further reproduction and growth because they serve the money sequence of value precisely and systematically. Since the dominant paradigm blocks out the problem by its confinement to a money-value metric, and since the military-industrial sequence of value-adding is so central to the growth and development of the corporate state, the madness continues in the absence of any remotely credible threat to nation-state borders. In order to understand why a money-sequenced economy can systemically select for what attacks and deprives the lives of social and environmental hosts, we need to bear in mind that the production of the military commodity functions to promote the global market system in three underlying ways:

(1) It operates as the ideal commodity by its special market conditions of supply and demand identified above;
(2) It appropriates funds from or depredates natural and community life-goods, and thereby correspondingly opens up markets for priced commodities in their place;
3) It enables the clearance of indigenous and unarmed peoples from their lands and resources to ensure money-sequence restructuring of social life-organization;[51] and
(4) Its highly developed life-destructive resources are visibly available to terrorize or attack opposition life movements against the mutating global market regime.[52]

To better comprehend the life-depleting advance of this mutant money sequence, we might consider its normalized spread within the social life-fabric of the world's most powerful market society. In the US, during the 1980s there was a real increase of *46 per cent* in government military spending, while federal public funding for life goods was radically reduced to pay for it – public housing by 77 per cent, educational funding by 70 per cent, employment training by 48 per cent, mass transit by 33 per cent, and child nutrition by 19 per cent.[53] This was not to meet a real threat from external enemies, but systematically served the money sequence of value in the ways specified above. Note the basic life spheres thereby deprived – housing, education, child nutrition and pollutionless train transit.

Public-sector funding for corporate production of armaments came in this way to be $26 billion *higher* in real dollars than it was in 1980, when the designated World Enemy to justify all of these expenditures, the Soviet Union, still existed.[54] The evident derangement of expending over $700 million a day on weaponed forces to obliterate an enemy that no longer existed, while attacking the life-spheres of the public sector for money 'savings' at the same time, was *not* insanity from the standpoint of the money sequence paradigm. It was maximally rational, and further ensured scarcity of life goods to favour its continued global market selection for production and sale.

This is an underlying point which needs emphasis, because we are apt to think that the outcomes of such a programme of value are so obviously opposed to the common interest that they must be recognized. It is true that people who value in terms of life and life gains recognize that these patterns of choice and judgement are deranged once they are exposed to attention. Yet if they precipitate no unfavourable effect in the market's sequences of value, but on the contrary appreciate profit and provide dynamic new spheres for investment in market commodities to replace what is lost from nature and the community, then there is no restraining mechanism within this system to recognize it as a disorder. Rather, its money-to-more-money circuits are reinforced and extended by the very life reductions and systemic losses they effect. The system thus feeds on the life destructions it causes.

The weapons commodity, however, is only one of several life-killing commodities which currently propel the global market system.[55] Other forms are increasingly manufactured and sold as the middle term of the money sequence as well, even though their content is known to cause disease to and kill human beings in predictable millions. The contemporary cigarette commodity, for example, bears an estimated 4000–5000 chemicals into its consumer, a number long known to be highly toxic and deadly. But unlike the weapon commodity, its life-assaultive properties have traditionally been denied rather than asserted by manufacturers. The feeling its consumption produces of enhanced being is, in fact, the response of the body's immune system to deadly toxins entering the life-system. International epidemiologist Richard Peto of Oxford University estimates that smoking is responsible for 3 million deaths per year world-wide, which will likely reach 10 million in three decades. In China alone, Peto estimates that 50 million people will eventually die from smoking-induced diseases. Former US Surgeon-General, C. Everett Koop, observes: 'I think one of the most shameful things my country ever did was to export disease, disability and death by selling our cigarettes to the world.' Clayton Yeutter, the US Trade Representative, who adopts the money sequence as his guide, however, has an opposed view. He celebrates the increased trade figures and US cigarette exports to the global market (my emphasis): 'I just saw the figures on tobacco exports a few days ago and, my, have they turned out to be *a marvelous success story.*'[56]

Here we see in clear expression what we can call the global market's death sequence affirmed as an optimum good. Yeutter does not see the implication of his position, of course. He sees export figures of a leading American commodity rising dramatically, and trade blocks against it by other societies falling after a World Trade Organization ruling in the US's favour. As other political and market leaders, he comprehends the economic situation here from the received market paradigm of value. His affirmation of what is, in effect, the suffering and death of millions of people is not wicked by his design. He merely remains within the global market's metric of value. He is, in other words, an active symptom of a deeper disorder of a regulating economic logic.

That other nations were, in fact, forced to import US cigarettes that would addict their youth and kill their citizens by the tens of thousands was not an issue. This was a matter of 'free trade'. Countries such as Thailand and Japan which sought to curtail the deadly effects of addictive poisons on teen-age smokers by tariff and non-tariff barriers were, therefore, dismissed as 'protectionist' (a revealing term). Young girls and women who were low-rate smokers and had not yet been exposed to the demand stimulations of saturation ads of smoking women were congratulated with billboard plaudits that 'you have come a long way baby'. They were market-researched 'consumers coming to participate in globalizing trade and investment'. The consequences flowed inevitably from the 'free trade' paradigm's self-regulating implementation. What had changed since Adam Smith was, of course, that commodities designed in such a way as to cause disease and kill were now a middle term of the money sequence.[57] But this difference was not one that the model could register within its calculus. That slow and painful premature death would predictably follow on the level of the life sequence for ever more millions of people was not an issue that could by its nature enter its accounts.

Whether by the middle term of weapons or cigarettes or some other commodity that is constructed so that it causes death to humans, we may represent this directly deadly form of the money sequence as follows:

$$Money \rightarrow Commodity\ Destroying\ Human\ Life \rightarrow More\ Money$$
$$(\ \$ \rightarrow DC \rightarrow \$^1\ )$$

Means of life destruction as a whole have become, without the current economic paradigm recognizing the pattern of the sea-shift, a more dynamic middle term of the money sequence than means of life. But there are two species of this commodity which require further distinction – commodities which are produced and sold for assault on and destruction of life, such as weapons, and commodities which are produced and sold to *represent* assault on and destruction of life, such as mass-produced visual images. The two are connected, but the latter is far more pervasive. The global production and marketing of images, films, games and other portrayals of terrorizing, wounding and murdering people increases in both sites and vehicles each year. As a leading edge of the 'entertainment industry', a major growth sector in the global market, the representation of terror, harm and death has ever more branches of manufacture and sale. Although its portrayals and images often have as their referents real injury or killing (as in mass-marketed violence in 'sports' and 'news'), this commodity form is still *re-presentational*, not real in its assaults on living structures. With the screens of the media watched up to an average of five hours a day across the world, thousands of killings, shootings, acts of terror, fatal disasters, tortures and, in general, irreversibly violent insults and deaths to human bodies in single or mass numbers are daily portrayed and consumed to 'attract viewers'. The regulating principle of their manufacture is that they advance money-sequence gains. Thus all are contrived, selected and marketed in accordance with this final criterion of worth.

In sum, whether real *or* representational, the $\$ \to DC \to \$^1$ sequence has always the *destruction of life as its logic of money gain*. We might properly call this second form of the money sequence, therefore, *the death sequence of value*.

Means of destruction of life are also at work in other monetary sequences of value – principally, in the use of *non*-human life as raw materials for this or that commodity in the ceaseless transformation of money inputs into increased money outputs. The levelling of forest ecosystems to raise domestic animals for killing for meat, for example, also erodes and depletes topsoils, water supplies and natural ecosystems. This commodity production alone, it is estimated, slaughters 6 million animals a year in the US, has resulted in the destruction of 260 million acres of its forests, appropriates half of all the country's water supplies and, by deforestation, extinguishes an estimated 1000 species a year across the world.[58] But none of these *life* costs enters the ledgers of the global market calculus as losses.

One might say that the mechanized conversion of the organic into the inorganic to maximize the returns of the money sequence is the meta-value theme of our era. Its systems of expression include, more generally, the world-wide industrial extraction of natural resources which leave behind them extinguished ecosystems above and below the earth and the water, and which pervasively contaminate the life-systems remaining with the poisonous effluents of their processes of production and sale.[59] Strictly speaking, however, the death sequence of value is confined to investment circuits in which means of life-destruction are the *commodity* which is manufactured and sold.

The death commodity is also especially prominent in the manufacture of ever more efficient machineries to directly tear natural life-fabrics apart – rainforests, ocean bottoms and earth strata – in order to extract their marketable elements. Large-scale factories of slaughter on land and sea also transform myriad domestic and aquatic animals into dead meat. These highly articulated machines to dismantle and to slaughter life-systems and animals develop scientifically alongside armament commodities for killing human beings. Similarily efficient in their technical capacities, they rip up soil communities, demolish forest worlds and strip aquatic ecosystems in minutes so as to ensure the maximum velocity and volume of competitive money-sequence gains. They cage, kill and process animals at the rate of millions an hour with the biological sciences as their servant.[60]

But, again, none of these advancing forms of the money sequence which reproduces itself by commodities that kill or represent the killing of human life is perceived as a problem. In truth, the mutation of commodity production and distribution is not seen, least of all as a deepening economic pattern invading life fabrics and psyches. In this way, the disorder eludes the life defence systems of social hosts, and spreads in the mask of 'economic growth' even as it destroys life at the rate of 5000 civilians a day every day,[61] and deprives societies of many times more resources than are spent on social programmes to protect their children from malnourishment and disease. Combined with the next major mutation of the money sequence, with which it works in symbiosis, we see the complete loss of orientation to the life-host's needs of reproduction and differentiation, and all the hallmarks of progressive carcinogenesis on the social level of life-organization.

The Money Sequence Decoupled from Production

As discussed in Chapter 3, the money sequence which produces and distributes *no commodity at all* between its money investment and its returns-plus-profits is the most significant mutation of the money sequence in the global market system both because it has become the primary 'restructuring' agent of societies with no commitment to their life needs, and because its invasive and depleting consequences for life-hosts are not yet publicly recognized as a systemic disorder. Unlike the weapons commodity of the military-industrial complexes, there is not even yet a socially organized force to recognize, resist and turn back its growth by the equivalent of arms control.

In this form of the money sequence, the investment circuit transforms money into more money in a self-multiplying circuit which is decoupled from the middle term of production altogether. This exponentially escalating money sequence now commands a conservatively estimated 40 times more money value daily than all expenditures on goods and services put together. As we have found, its pattern of money-begetting-money can be recognized by the carcinogenic marker:

$$\text{Money} \rightarrow \text{More Money} \rightarrow \text{More Money}$$
$$(\$ \rightarrow \$^1 \rightarrow \$^2 \rightarrow \$^3 \rightarrow \$^n)$$

This money-into-more-money cycle is reproduced and expanded in many forms – currency and derivatives speculation, arbitrages, leveraged buyouts to strip assets for sale, and, most systematically traditionally, compound-interest demands. The forms of its multiplication increase as it is left unregulated by governments, with derivative financial instruments alone (which depend on the prices of *other* 'securities' or things than themselves) increasing by an average of 50 per cent every 12 months. The money sequence here produces no good for society, or anything at all, but can like currency speculation or compounding high interest or the proliferating avenues of this sequence in general propel huge sums of leveraged money demand into motion and appropriation of resources with no contribution or relation to real productivity or life requirement of any kind. Its unregulated tidal flows have destabilized, massively devalued and 'melted down' economy after economy from Mexico and Peru to the 'miracle economies' of Asia themselves. No social life-organization, save Japan, has not been adversely affected by compounding-interest demands pressuring for and stripping down social infrastructures which protect human and environmental life so as to feed its omnivorous demands.

In the case of Japan, this money sequence's damages have moved across its social body by the conversion of profit revenues from planned productive enterprises towards speculative money-sequence ventures – first internally to real estate speculation (which drove up real estate prices, before the crash in 1991–92, to a higher worth in Tokyo alone than all the land of the US), and then externally to tidal flows of hundreds of billions into other societies in loans and non-productive buy-outs. In both cases, the speculative bubbles of non-productive money sequencing collapsed, while good money has been thrown after bad by continuous multi-billion dollar bail-outs of private banks, the top five being once the richest in the world.[62] Japan as the rest of the global market, but in its own way, rapidly declined as it lost its bearings in the real economy, and flooded its value-added money wealth into government-subsidized money sequences that produced nothing and eventually undermined the world's most prosperous economy, along with the life-support systems of their Asian cousins who 'caught the Asian flu'.

But the paradigm of 'free capital flows' whose freedom is always for non-life forms, is not inhibited by these catastrophic effects. On the contrary, its agents call for ever more of it to cure the disasters it causes, repelling any counter-claim for social life preservation as 'out of touch with the new reality'. With the most established of the non-productive money sequences, compound-interest debt, the bleeding of societies dry by debt-charges is pronounced permanent like the seasons. A CitiBank official explains to us why societies must be permanently in debt, and forever pay compound interest to money sequences that contribute no productive function to society (emphasis added):

> Let's be clear. *Nobody's debts are going to be paid.* ... Paying back isn't really the issue. The issue is the borrower remaining creditworthy and able to carry the debt, but not repay it.[63]

If we parse the meaning of this paradigmatic position of the global market (where all transnational corporations are also major money lenders by interest-bearing credit), we can see that the principle is in perfect accord with a carcinogenic money sequence which keeps increasing its appropriation of public resources or people's incomes with no committed function to the host which it feeds off in perpetuity. Since this parasitic appropriation has rapidly grown in the last two decades – personal and government debts are now at higher levels world-wide than since 1929 – and since there is a progressive depletion and redirection of life-sustaining public and personal revenues towards feeding these life-decoupled circuits, the parasitic pattern turns invasive. As its demands mount, and accumulate with unpayable debts and compound-interest loads increasing current deficits in a vicious spiral of money-sequence extraction, social life-organizations founder and buckle under the demands for ever more interest on compounding accumulating debts. We have seen many of the clear indicators of this pattern in Chapter 3. They include the death of over 500,000 children a year from interest demands on their governments which end social programmes for health and bread, the rise of interest payments at ten times faster a rate than wages, the multiplication of real money paid by poorer countries to foreign usurers by 16 times their 1975–79 rate between 1980 and 1994, and the escalation of world interest payments at a rate of growth 25 times greater than on global food itself.[64]

The figures give a clear profile. Ever rising payments to the global money sequence at the expence of the life sequence are a systemic, advancing depletion of sustenance flows to life-hosts, approaching the exponential rise of a carcinogenic disorder. But if governments do not reroute all of this life-support revenue to pay interest loads on time, their societies are then subjected to 'Structural Adjustment programmes' (SAPs). These further strip their social infrastructures of health, education and local investment resources to pay the further loaned interest payments, while still carrying the debt at higher, compounded levels. The International Monetary Fund and World Bank who represent the corporate money lenders in these demands, the 'International Financial Institutions' (IFIs), never 'bail out' Third World governments as they are represented as doing. In fact, they only lend them money on 'structural adjustment' terms to pay all the interest charges to IFIs which then rise further because of the loans and the higher rates charged for downgraded debtors. It would be difficult to find an equal of such extortionate tribute in history.

If the debts, as in Vietnam, were contracted by the wartime enemy of the government, or as across the Third World were offered by the IFIs to corrupt dictators, who then put the loaned funds back into their banks as private fortunes, this makes no difference to the demands to pay all of the debts and their compounding interest charges. Any failure to 'fulfil debt obligations', whatever its ground or life-emergency base, is viewed as a 'moral hazard', the revealing language of this value system in maintaining the money sequence's continuous and rising appropriations of public revenues from societies whose people lack sufficient money to buy food to eat. That no productive or life function is served by these predatory extractions is not an issue that is ever publicly raised, or is tolerated if it is. From beginning to end, the money-sequence paradigm excludes the tie-back to life function as out of bounds.

This design of the model has further implications which are imposed by the world-wide SAPs. These ensure that social life-organizations adjust to their re-engineering at every level of input and output. Underneath all the claims and counter-claims, justifications and accusations about the World Bank, the IMF and SAPs, the following underlying principles regulate their operation across the world:

(1) The debts are not to be repaid, but the compound-interest payments are to be ensured in orderly increase;

(2) Devaluation of currencies is typically prescribed, with the consequence that wages and salaries are reduced in real terms and people work longer and harder for enough to survive;

(3) Food or other commodities for export are demanded to ensure the hard currency is paid to international money lenders;

(4) Local investment by government or the maintenance of self-employed co-operatives to provide means of life for domestic populations are dismantled, thereby requiring local dependency on imported commodities and export of unprocessed products to First World markets to pay for the imports and to provide hard currency to pay debt charges;

(5) All unpriced or government subsidized goods of food, shelter, education, public health-care or other life-goods are converted to market mechanisms of price and profit;

(6) Financial assistance for 'safety nets' is consumed by foreign financial advisers and temporary assistance to volunteer-run schools and clinics without stable public funding;

(7) Environmental resources and other exploitable local economic sectors are opened to unobstructed access, ownership and control by transnational corporations so as to ensure foreign currency for interest payments, reduced cost inputs, and unprotected markets for transnational commodities and capital;

(8) All of the above must be agreed to by local governments to ensure against international financial blacklisting.[65]

These are the underlying principles which regulate SAPs, across the world. If there is resistance to any prescription of the overall global market programme, as with the Mayans of Chiapas who resisted the 'death sentence of NAFTA' prior to the 'structural adjustment programme' for the country which soon followed, the financial community calls for eliminative order to ensure stability for the money sequence's high value-added returns. The following words are from a press release by the Chase Manhattan Bank, a Rockefeller corporation which knows the connections between the money sequences of oil, weapons and compound interest. Death is promised for those who fight back:

> While Chiapas, in our opinion, does not pose a fundamental threat to Mexican political stability, it is perceived to do so by many in the investment community. The government will need to eliminate the Zapatistas ...[66]

We can note that life and life needs have no place in this instituted decision structure. They are not a factor of any equation *until* they obstruct the advance of the money sequence by local co-operatives, free education or inoculations against disease for children, government investment in local food security, above-starvation wage costs when less can be paid, self-sufficiency or non-priced goods, or resisting human bodies fighting for their lives. Then life barriers to the smooth operation of the money sequence's progressive extractions and invasions of life fabric will be selectively restructured, defunded, and lethally attacked if resistance persists.

Here is what happened to Peru to ensure the money sequence's progressive appropriations of public wealth and poor people's wages to 'carry debt loads'. A series of SAPs from 1975 on ensured permanently rising compound-interest payments from that impoverished society, more than halved wages by devaluation, reduced food consumption by an estimated 25 per cent, raised bread and bean prices by over 1000 per cent, slashed wages by two-thirds in the public sector prior to a cholera epidemic in 1991, increased infant mortality and population malnourishment to new levels, and generally depredated the life of the vast majority to ever reduced levels of health and vital function.[67] These are the 'shock treatments', as they are called, to ensure that social life-bodies pay enough and on time to the non-productive money sequence invading them.

Understandably, life resists. In the case of Peru, armed movements of the poor were denounced, attacked, imprisoned and massacred as 'terrorists' in a prolonged dirty war consummated by the Fujimori government which was heralded in the corporate media as a heroic success story, while screening out all the causes of the fightback, including the sentencing of hundreds of people by hooded judges to prison without legal process.[68] When the Japanese Embassy was occupied on December 17, 1996 to reverse the now constitutional state terror, no mass media reported the reasons in weeks of saturation coverage. They attended instead to the high-tech military operation which spent weeks to kill the mostly teenaged occupiers with their hands up.

In such cases, the blocking out of life parameters is extended from the economic engineering model to the media marketing sites producing news stories on the life resistance to it. No connection to life co-ordinates remains.

The epistemic problem is that the dominant economic paradigm of understanding does not and cannot recognize the fatal inner logic at work here. As it leads a process of unravelling life fabrics in accordance with its bottom line of money valuated gains, it drives the wheels of increasingly catastrophic effects. As with other lethal value programmes in other places and other times, the pathological pattern is not seen because its motivational structure is presupposed as 'normal', and its harshest consequences as the 'necessary' workings of invisible fatelines which cannot be meddled with by social intervention or ameliorative plan.

In the macrocosm, the destructive and the parasitic as well as the still productive money sequences are masked as normality under the single general concept of 'capitalism': although the meaning of 'capital' as wealth that is used to produce more wealth has shifted from production for life to appropriation *from* life as the ruling pattern. As this mutant pattern advances and spreads, global market 'value adding' comes into ever sharper contradiction with the life sequence and its internal requirements for maintenance and growth. The longer it continues as a self-regulating system, the more deeply the life sequence on both social and environmental levels is systemically depleted and degraded in even 'normal' orders. In the end, an emergent crisis poses a social choice: Either civil society defends the life code of value against these life-blind circuits, or human and planetary life will be increasingly stripped by their cumulative money-to-more-money demands.

In general, we find that the macro-outcome patterns of this system disclose an *inverse* relation between the growth and development of life and the growth and development of money investment, as opposed to *correspondence* which the current paradigm assumes. Thus, for example, while 100 or more species are made extinct every day from the impact of global market activities,[69] and while the number of all of the world's children who are malnourished increases past one in three,[70] the money value of shares in the broad US market skyrockets to six times total value, while bank assets in money value is created beyond legal-tender reserves at a ratio of almost 300 to 1.[71] The assumed correlation between aggregate real dollar value increases in the world economy and increases in the world's well-being is in such ways found to be the reverse of the facts.

On the micro level again, the restructuring of societies by the global market programme operates in two themal ways – by 'free trade' and its prescriptions of 'open borders and comparative advantage of production', and by 'structural adjustment programmes' which re-engineer societies both to accomodate unregulated trade and to pay unmanageable debt charges to foreign lenders at the same time. Always the money sequences combine to disable their social life-hosts' own self-regulation. To conclude with another paradigm illustration of the failure of this model in fact to produce and distribute scarce goods to social populations, and its systemic tendency to dismantle societies' very evolved life capacities to survive, we consider now the case of Rwanda. Before 1990, Rwanda's food production was protected by public subsidies to the 70 per cent of the rural population who grew it, and by restrictions of foreign imports. But when coffee prices predictably plummeted due to overloading of tropical commodity markets with comparative advantage exports, Rwanda's export earnings dropped 50 per cent. A structural adjustment to sustain the succubus real-interest monies to foreign money-lending corporations was therefore imposed. The Bretton Woods institutions prescribed a 50 per cent devaluation of the currency, six weeks after a Tutsi-led rebel army from Uganda entered the country. The collapse of real earnings triggered steep price increases in basic foodstuffs and fuel, public services collapsed from lack of revenues, malaria and child malnutrition rapidly spread, famine struck the south of the country, and farming families desperately chopped down 300,000 coffee trees to return to the non-export farming by which they had traditionally lived.

A second devaluation was then ordered by the International Monetary Fund, at the height of civil war in 1992, privatizations of gas and telecom-munications followed, and public investment projects were halved in such life-serving projects as inland swamp reclamation to meet the country's increasingly severe shortage of arable land. The money disbursed to the government from the new loans on the basis of the ordered devaluation and 'cost savings' so as to pay debt charges was, however, diverted to purchase Milan and Apila missiles and a Falcon jet from

France along with other killing commodities, as well as to increase the army by eight-fold with mostly unemployed youths.[72] It was then that the massacre of hundreds of thousands of people began.

Again, all was reported in the corporate media with no connection back to the life circumstances which had engendered it, or to their prior devastation by global market forces and restructuring reforms. 'How the global market experiment failed' is not yet a thought.

We can discern from these operations and consequences of the global money sequence of compound-interest debt how 'the borrower remaining creditworthy and able to carry the debt' can destroy the life-fabrics of societies. These are malignant tumour cases, and like those at the cellular level of life-organization, are accumulations of rogue sequences of reproduction and growth that do not remit, but grow worse as they progress. The money sequence linked to the death sequence is the way in which the cancer expresses itself as visible tumour.

In more 'normal' societies of the restructuring global market, the money sequences of $\$ \to C(-) \to \$^1$, $\$ \to C\text{-}(-) \to \$$, $DC \to \$^1$, and, most prominently, $\$ \to \$^1 \to \$^2 \to \$^n$ advance incrementally beneath the recognition of social hosts with the full nodal assistance of government departments of finance and central banks. But they cannot be recognized in their life-invasive effects because the global market paradigm which is presupposed is not structured to identify or to respond to life threat or loss, however systemic. In even the most stable First World societies, structural adjustments dismantling life-protective social programmes combine with bull rushes of stockmarkets whose money-demand value has no base in increased productivity or real wealth. Corporate mergers, acquisitions and money-account managements combine with the disconnection of millions of employees from their livelihoods to gain higher next-quarter profits. Management option rises, financial fees and privatization of public pensions and student loans enrich a non-productive sector, but strip older and younger generations of their security of future. Currency speculation roams randomly around the world destabilizing societies, contributing no function to wealth creation and redistributing money-demand in haemorrhages of hundreds of billions of dollars out of societies that require it, and into the hot-money circuits of money dealers. Redistribution from life that needs it to money functions that are not alive metastasizes as a pattern across continents, leaving depredated social populations and environments behind from Latin America to the Indonesian archipelago.

These phenomena all express and follow from the money sequence of growth that produces nothing, has no commitment to social hosts, and seeks only to become maximally more of itself. Beneath all the emerging facts that emerge in glimpses – 1 per cent of US households owning more than 90 per cent, under 500 billionaires with more money demand than half of the world's total population, one US corporate stockholder with more wealth than 100 million fellow citizens, speculators and money lenders controlling public policy across the globe – there is a single propelling programme, to restructure global life-organization to the money sequence's autonomous growth. Because all of the variations of this $\$ \to \$^1 \to \$^2 \to \$^n$ sequence select for money increases for money leveragers and against any contribution of life good, they continuously require, if inflation is not to occur, off-setting revenues from the processes of production and distribution of society's *real* means of life – from, for example, the wages of workers or the budgets of social infrastructures to make compound-interest payments to banks or for the devaluation of home currencies. By thus appropriating revenues devoted to producing or distributing life goods to feed financial circuits which produce nothing but more money demand, the decoupled money sequence reroutes former expenditures on life needs such as public health, education, social welfare and pensions to payments to progressively expanding $\$ \to \$^1 \to \$^2 \to \$^3 \to \$^n$ rounds.[73] As societies go ever deeper into long-term debt, chronic high unemployment, falling real wages, and horizonless economic doldrums or meltdowns, their problems are never linked back to the system-deciding money sequences behind them, but are attributed to 'failure to adapt'. In this new structure of evolutionary selection, no society is favoured for vital reproduction.

Can the alternative economics of Marxism help us here? One would think that Marxian theory would have the methodological resources to identify this decoupled circuit of accumulating money gains without the production of any use-value. But, in fact, Marx never witnessed this money sequence in the mutant forms it assumes at the end of the twentieth century, nor its dominance over the productive economy which is historically unprecedented in the capitalist epoch. He presupposed a gold standard for money that ruled for centuries as a real basis of money demand, a basis that was only ended by the Nixon presidency when it refused to redeem US dollars for gold between 1971 and 1973 – apparently to evade dollar-denominated debts contracted through the Vietnam War. Note again the connections between the decoupled money sequence and public spending for commodities of destruction. We must bear in mind here that the US military superpower, then and now, has and exercises the effective and post-Marx right to reduce its world debt as it decides to by devaluating its currency – against gold bullion then, or against US-dollar-denominated debts now.[74]

Another major historical economic change has occurred since Marx's day in the value base of money capital. The fractional reserve system whereby banklenders store gold, or since Marx legal tender to back up their interest-bearing loans, has been essentially eliminated. Reserves to back loaned money with cash now stand at 3 per cent in the US and elsewhere, like Canada, have been eliminated altogether. This permits banks to lend compound-interest-bearing cheque-money with no reserves underpinning it, thus creating the equivalent of money at a rate 25 times or more beyond legal tender – most of leveraged 'capital flows' across borders and currencies.[75] At the same time, large corporate financial departments lend by credit, also interest-bearing, which adds ever more volumes of capital and consumer money demand into local and global market circulation, with no underlying value of gold standard or legal tender as its base. The long-established, labour-calculable source of all currency and credit which Marx knew has been abolished, and private 'capitalist' banking corporations and operations mint over 96 per cent of circulating money and capital flows with no foundation in gold or any other equivalent of sunk labour.

So, in short, money which stands at the base of the entire global market system is not at all the expression of real economic value as it was in Marx's day. *Money's value is what other money's demand on it says it is.* Money and the international capital flows which bear its demand in GDP-size aggregates have delinked from the real economy, from an equivalent in sunk labour, from gold, from cash reserves, from government control of currency and credit creation, from every base that might keep its demands and growth sequence oriented to economic reality.

Thus it is not surprising that Marx did not think that the money sequence could become an unproductive ruler of nations, or become as we have seen carcinogenic in the properties of its relationship to its social life-hosts. Marx understandably, therefore, rules out any such possibility when he argues in *Capital* that '*movements of money capital are therefore once more merely movements of an individualized part of industrial capital engaged in the reproduction process*'.[76] In this view, money that does not produce commodities as its middle term of gain is only a forwarding phase of money that does. This assumption has since been made foundationally false by the money sequence's historical mutation. No Marxian analysis has since revised Marxian theory to accord with this transformative fact of the real world economy. Economic models, left and right, can become locked in their established programmes so that the tectonic-plate shifts of reality underneath and contradicting their categorial schemas are blocked out. Here the very nature of 'capital' itself has fundamentally altered. It is no longer linked to productive force development, no longer profits and advances across the world by superior productive efficiency, and so no longer 'disciplines, organizes and unites' direct producers into a productively integrated army marching to a wider productive design. Capital's delinkage as accumulated money demand becoming ever more capital demand with no middle term of commodity production at all, or with destructive and waste commodities as its middle terms have together hollowed out the capital-production drivewheel itself. What is now the dominant system-decider is tidal flows of borderless and uncommitted 'capital' demand backed by weapon commodities of mass destruction dismantling and consuming social and environmental life-hosts.

Capital in these forms, then, is no longer capital, in even the Marxian sense. Its mutant money sequences have, as the anaplasiac cells of a cancer on the individual level of life-organization, lost orientation to the axial framework of the host body, lost differentiation of function related to the life-host's requirements, lost co-ordination with other forms of itself, and ceased to have any productive function for social life-organization at any level. This is a regressive, mutant form of reproduction which seeks only to multiply itself.

Within the still-standing shell of classical and neo-classical economic theory, this profound transformation in economic reality has not been registered. Because economic orthodoxy has evolved into ever more self-referential equations that block out any reality that confronts it, it does not recognize the destructive mutations. All that it can relate to are money inputs, throughputs and outputs relocating around the world to minimize costs and maximize revenues, and the countless constitutive equations this sequence can be represented as in disconnected moments and phases. That this money-demand movement is in the end based on no grounding real value underneath it, but restructures what produces real value and the reproductive and growth capacities of life-organization itself, is not an issue to which this self-enclosed system connects. But the effects of this theoretical disorientation on the real world it prescribes to eventually intrude; economies which have been held up for years as models for the rest of the globe to emulate melt down overnight. As now even the global market's most complaisant voice, *The Economist*, acknowledges (emphasis added): 'Among economists, support for the free movement of capital is *an article of faith.*' Citing the academy's bastion of this faith, Harvard University and a leading professor of trade, it reports the dawning realization: '*We have no evidence it [free movement of capital] will solve any of our problems, and ... it may make them worse.*'[77]

When an economic paradigm is based on an article of faith, and the evidence mounts ever more graphically that under its guidance social and environmental life-organizations increasingly decline and collapse, the paradigm is refuted by hard fact, whether this is recognized or not. Indeed, even the claim that it is *capitalism* at work here becomes more than dubious since this system ever more preponderantly produces nothing at all in its most enriching circuits, while at the same time 'attacking', the term of preference, the mediums of exchange whereby people live. The continuing assumption that this is 'capital growth' is clearly false when the real capital bases of societies lose their value overnight with no relationship to their productive performances or capacity to produce real wealth. This is a fact now obliquely admitted by the government of Japan itself. 'The root cause [of the Asian meltdown],' says Japan's Deputy Minister of Finance, Euiseke Sakakibara, 'has been the huge inflow of capital into Malaysia, Thailand, Korea and China. And all of a sudden ... all of it has fled from those countries. ... This is not an Asia crisis. It is a crisis of capitalism.'[78]

The meaning of capital through all its historical phases – cattle, chattel and capital – is 'wealth that can be used to produce more wealth'. The meaning no longer applies here. If the meaning of a concept no longer applies to its referent, the referent is something else. A conclusion follows. The crisis is not truly of capitalism, but a non-functioning deformation of it. Like all cancers, the mutant forms of uncontrolled, disoriented self-multiplication have no committed function to their life-host.

The money sequence paradigm has in this way been superannuated by reality. Three months *before* the economies of Asia collapsed, in what should have been a wake-up from the long sleep of dogma, the IMF, the structural adjuster of world economies, celebrated Korea and Thailand as having 'the fundamentals right'.[79] The fact is that neither the IMF nor the transnational financial institutions it represents, are competent to understand the economic breakdowns they have led, one after another, across the world.

At this point, the principles of a life-sequence economy, which in some way have been recognized by all surviving social life-organizations through history, are required to restore the bearings of globalizing societies. The problem at the nub is that orientation to the life-ground and recognition of the progressive threat to its social and environmental life fabrics has been lost. Let us now turn to the underlying, deep bearer of the life-sequence economy which has been, beneath the pervasive hysteria of global market ideology, with us all along.

5

The Great Vehicle of the Civil Commons

The meta-problem confronting global society is that dominant and expanding money sequences have come into ever sharper and more destructive contradiction with social and environmental life-organization. As the mutant sequences grow, the life-ground on both social and environmental levels is systemically depleted and degraded. In the end, the emergent crisis poses a social choice: Either civil society defends its life-organization against this uncontrolled non-life reproduction, or human and planetary life-webs will be increasingly restructured into homogenous moments of its growth.

The epistemic problem is that the dominant economic paradigm of understanding does not and cannot recognize the fatal inner logic that has developed within its abstractions. As its prescriptions lead a process of unravelling life fabrics into conformity with mechanistic sequences of money-valuated gains, its programme drives the wheels of increasingly catastrophic effects. As with other closed programmes in other places and other times, the pathological pattern is not seen because the motivational structure it demands is presupposed as 'normal' or 'natural'. As with the 'natural' structures of slavery, private property in women, caste subjugation, or the conception of non-human life as unalive, the most murderous consequences are accepted as the 'necessary' workings of invisible fatelines which cannot be meddled with by social intervention or ameliorative plan.

But in fact, the *symptoms* of systemic disorder have already been recognized by countless non-governmental agencies, groups, and still-thinking individuals across the world who are aware that the system has gone gravely awry. On the other hand, this emerging recognition and response of social immune systems is confronted and overwhelmed in the corporate media of public communication by armies of the global money sequence invasion – tabloid columnists, chambers of commerce, bankers, editorial boards, corporate think-tanks, financed politicians, policy servants, conglomerate boardrooms, stock and bond sales forces, speculators, developers, economists, and academics and administrators in the public sector itself who bear the money-code as the determining programme of their preference and decision systems. These are the disease-agents. They are not genetically sequenced to the life-invasive spread and growth they bear, but operate by the locked mind-set of a paradigm that no longer relates to the requirements of life-organization on any level.

Finding the Common Life-Ground

The key to carcinogenic advance in any life-host is that it *masks* its pathological code of reproduction so that the afflicted body does not recognize or respond to its threat. The only resolving response to it is to identify its genetic-code marker or, in a social system, its value-code marker as a 'not-self' aggressor. We are in the throes of this process now. The immune problem is that even the elected governments of advanced industrial societies which have been progressively stripped in their life protective capacities by the unregulated and mutant money sequences are supine in response. As we have seen, they do not recognize the systemic attacks on society's life-organization. Governments have become, instead, the equivalent of invaded lymph nodes, no longer selecting out the carcinogenic sequences of reproduction and growth, but abetting them.

Social immune recognition and response is evolving instead on the level of social memberships themselves. The turning point on a visible political level may have occurred in France in 1995. Amidst a steeply escalated unemployment rate of 14 per cent, a social-protest movement seemed to arise out of nowhere from a civil service strike against the loss of pensions and social security by the global market's preferred instrument of invading developed social life-fabrics – the 'national austerity budget'. Joined by more and more citizens beyond the affected workers, the protest swept across the country and continued with little notice from the world's corporate media for an astonishing and unreported six months. It was reduced to 'December strikes', just as mass city strikes and protests later across the ocean were reduced by media counts to small fractions of their actual turnouts.[1] The mass social movement of the French people, eventually reported a British educational weekly (emphasis added), 'focussed increasingly on the question of whether a future determined by transnational economic forces is the only perspective, or whether the future of French society can still be determined *according to other parameters*'.

Note that the framework of 'no alternative' is here first presupposed as the given ground of society's reality. But then the protest of a world-historical people over six months demands the recognition of the possibility of 'other parameters'. The loss of bearings is so advanced that there is no explicit conception that these other bearings might be the vital reproduction and growth of society's membership itself. That 'transnational economic forces' could be those of a life-sequence economy rather than the maximization of money returns to non-living corporate vehicles has not yet arisen as an option.

Confronted by this undeniable fact of a people struggling for its social life, the eminent French daily *Le Monde*, in turn, was internally ambivalent on the nature of its meaning. The uprising against the programme of 'no alternative' is first conceived as the option of a past already gone, 'the cultivation of a nostalgia'. Then, as if deeper recognition stirs underneath the programme, the uprising begins to be understood as against the stripping of *society's shared life-ground.*

> Striking railway workers and non strikers alike cultivate a nostalgia for a way of life that is under threat. However modest that way of life may be, it is made up of a well-established social order, a source of better health, more leisure and well-being. That is the nub of the crisis, because this world is crumbling, and order is collapsing.[2]

A few months later, on March 20, 1996, the Government of France issued a wake-up Memorandum to its European Economic Community partners. It called for 'emergency initiatives' on resolving Europe's unprecedented post-1945 unemployment rise, over seven times its rate in the 1960s. At the same time, it sought discussion on Europe's formerly high minimum workplace standards which were falling precipitately as the continent's over-supply of labour climbed. 'When 18 million people are out of work', the Memorandum read, 'and more than 50 million are threatened by social exclusion, the European Union's duty is to respond.'[3] But the government of Britain opposed any response at all. It declared intervention as an 'interference in the market' and 'an abandonment of national autonomy'.[4] Observe here that it is the market's money sequence of value which is conceived as the bearer of 'national autonomy'. But the 'social exclusion of 50 million people' does not register as a problem of national self-direction. Here once more we see the lives of tens of millions of people repelled as external to the market model's programme. Just as 'freedom' attaches only to the subject of transnational money capital, so 'national autonomy' means only the autonomous right of this decoupled money capital to exclude 50 million people from their livelihoods.

This underlying struggle between the evolving social immune system of European life and the uncontrolled transnational money sequence was also at the heart of the European Union's struggle to ensure its Social Chapter was accepted by a continuously recalcitrant British government which was the political face of the transnational money sequencers of London's financial district.

But there was no successful headway of social immune response for almost two years to these problems of collapsing social life-organizations.

The France-wide demonstrations finally ended, and the neo-liberal programme of the English Tories held sway. When I first wrote the above paragraphs in 1995, there seemed little hope of remission. The prognosis seemed to become hopeless when in April of 1997, the President of France, Jacques Chirac, overtly backtracked from earlier concern about the unemployed and socially excluded, and proclaimed the value of money as society's ultimate yardstick of social worth. 'The French people', he declared, 'must express themselves clearly on the scale and speed of change over the next five years *if we want to affirm ourselves as a great economic and political power equal to the dollar and the yen.*'[5]

Aroused by the deadly marker Chirac now exposed as the regulating sequence of his national leadership, I wrote the following text which was published in the *Guardian Weekly* – much as a macrophage cell of an alerted immune system seizes the genetic marker of a cancerous reproduction to display to the surrounding cell community on the social level of life-organization. This is the way of the individual within the social immune system, in one way or other across populations to survey, to recognize, to decode the marker of the pathogenic invasion as it occurs and to exhibit it to the surrounding global community.

What is the tune to which all parties and politicians now dance? It is to turn money into more money for money lenders and investors.

What is the way to ensure that all of Europe stays in step? It is to have a single money-regime whose terms dictate that all nations strip down their social sectors to better serve corporate stockholders.

What is a people and a country when all that exists is to serve the sequence of money becoming more money for those with money?

France's President Jacques Chirac declares the new destiny of nations in a stirring annunciation of the new order. 'The French people', he proclaims, 'must express themselves clearly on the scale and speed of change over the next five years if we want to affirm ourselves as a great economic and political power equal to the dollar and the yen.'

When a leading cultural centre of the world announces its final purpose as an increased power of its money, we know that a moral insanity has invaded the heart of civilization.[6]

The outcome of the French people's and the European Union's struggles was, within two years, a completely unexpected victory of the Socialist Party in the national elections of France in June of 1997, and the support of the Social Chapter by Britain after another national election returned the 'New Labour' Party of Britain to office. These may seem small advances, in particular when the 'New Labour' government leader, Tony Blair, dealt with the press monopolist Rupert Murdoch to hold off monopoly legislation in return for press support in the election, gave London money-sequencers their demand to hand over the monetary policy of the British government to the financiers' representative, the Bank of England, and then came down with a first budget that favoured corporations over low-income earners.[7] Still, that the protection of people's lives was entered into the regulatory regime of the European free trade zone and now included the population of Britain was a major step in the codification of the social immune system of the world's most developed social region.

Perhaps more significantly, the government of France under the newly elected Prime Minister Lionel Jospin committed itself to a 35-hour week to relieve unemployment and provide workers more free time, a legislative initiative regulated by the parameters of a life-sequence economy rather than the corporate money sequence. In such ways, the social immune system evolves its instituted regulation of economic reproduction, pushing back the carcinogenic sequence from continuing to eat away the livelihoods and life prospects of tens of millions of people. The corporate sector declares ruin and open war against the moves, which follows predictably from its programme. But just as battles are fought continuously on the cellular level of a life-host that is invaded by a system of reproduction with no committed function to it, so too on the social level of life-organization. This is the real 'competitive reality' that has been so far harnessed by the global corporate order to its invasion and subjugation reduction of social life-hosts. This is the geostrategic track-switch of the invasion – to trigger societies themselves into following the banner of 'increased competitiveness' of the transnational forces which are occupying them.

Far more surprisingly than France and Britain, the war between life and money sequences began to enter into the public statements of the World Bank, which has been so long without the bearings of the life-ground that it cannot discern the destruction by World Bank policies themselves. We have seen how the World Bank has led the assault of global 'restructuring', prescribing to all countries alike the new global imperative of 're-engineering' environments and 'unfettering' money capital to become more money capital with no obstruction by standards of life-protection of labour, people's villages, indigenous peoples or ancient ecosystems. 'The World Bank firmly rejects', for example, 'the principle of linking free trade and investment agreements between wealthy nations and newly industrializing countries to compliance with workers' rights.'[8] It also demands 'wage flexibility' so that workers can be employed for below subsistence wages, and further declares against 'non-wage benefits' which 'distort market competition'.[9] All of these positions follow from the global market programme. All are distinguished by their imperatives of overriding life needs to regulate societies by money sequences.

But at the same time, the World Bank conversely claims, without recognizing the internal contradiction, that structural reforms '*will only be sustainable if they reduce poverty and the distribution of income is made more equitable*'. 'Governments must', it continues, 'construct a framework for labour policy that ... *supports collective bargaining* in the formal sector, [and] *provides safeguards for the vulnerable.*'[10] As if schizophrenically divided between the contradictory demands of opposing programmes of value, and unconsciously seeking some resolution in the face of the accumulating global facts of unemployment and immiserization, the World Bank looks to find its ground in the life-value bearings it has until now ruled out of its calculus. As the italicized terms indicate, life's preservation and growth, not money investment's, are the stated parameters of concern. Even if the World Bank's statement is only rhetoric – which seems likely [11] – the fact that the inchoate parameters of a life-sequence economy entered into its public declarations at all is significant. It indicates a social-life fightback that must be deferred to. It contradicts the sole focus on money capital's autonomy and rule of economic organization. One could say it represents a break from the mutant money code to the life code at the macro-level. But was it then and since only a *mask* for the World Bank's continued operations on behalf of the corporate money sequence's occupation of the globe?

In human affairs unlike cellular, there are internal conflicts as well as external. The same body can be split between regulating codes within itself. The World Bank went further in the direction of this conflict. It announced in the face of mounting public criticism of its long record of life disasters by market-driven policies and mega-projects, *a new value calculus* beyond money transactions. Its researchers proposed *another form* of social wealth calculation: '*a new system that measures the wealth of the world's nations by integrating economic, social and environmental factors ... [including] the economic value of land, water, timber, sub-soil assets, ... water systems ... education, nutrition and health care*'.[12]

On which side, the question arises, does the World Bank and the international constituency of nation-states it represents, really stand? The conflicts of life and money value codes are expressed in its statements, but not recognized as conflicts. The World Bank has entered the throes of a deep-structural value war it does not consciously comprehend.

In its first test application of the environmental sector of social wealth calculation, the World Bank's new dedication to finding lost bearings in a life economy collapsed in the face of corporate money sequence opposition. It declined to confront Chilean timber corporations who declared any deviation from money-sequence rule 'a threat to national sovereignty', which we know is code for the freedom of corporations to operate across borders with no accountability, while hiding behind the flags of their social hosts. When the very lucrative business of converting old-growth forests owned by the public into rubble and private money profits as fast as possible was briefly surveyed in the relatively small economy of Chile to establish 'an environmental accounting unit', war was declared by Chile's extractive industries against the accounting protocol as a 'foreign invasion'. That all of Chile's ancient forest resources and ecosystems would be rubble and brush in under 50 years at their current rate of extraction was not seen as an 'invasion' by the exporting timber corporations. Even the World Bank's modest initiative to calculate the *economic value* of these forests, and nothing else, was ferociously denounced by the occupying corporations. They attacked the study of the forest's sustainability as 'defective', 'blown out of proportion', a case of 'meddling', and a 'threat to Chile's economy'.[13] The World Bank's team-leader was removed from his post, and the 'environmental accounting unit' was suspended. In its first halting step toward representing the value of life in its programmes, the World Bank quickly retreated back into its boardrooms.

We see here the nature of the war. The submerged struggle of life and money sequences within public institutions is at work on many levels. Whether they will continue to succumb to their occupation by the pathogenic money sequence, or become regulated for the protection of life, is not decided. There is recognition and response emerging, but it is as yet only partially conscious, as it must be at the level of social life-organization. But it can emerge in the most unexpected places. Even within the US Republican Party – whose legislation to dismantle the country's Environmental Protection Agency was itself turned back by an aroused public in 1995–96 – there was in early 1996 an extraordinary uprising from within. The Party's most resonant speech-writer and a presidential candidate began to lead an unheard of series of attacks on the very bearers of the money sequence who financed its political representatives. With Americans being fired from secure jobs at the rate of two to three million every year, and profit and stock markets soaring to ever higher record levels of capital gains during the same period, the need to recognize and respond to the threat to fellow members of US society's life was briefly sensed.

The right-wing fundamentalist, Patrick Buchanan, said the unbelievable to national television and to assembled party members: '*A cancer is eating away at the economy.*'[14] Quite as astonishingly he analysed American society as in a state of impending internal war: 'All the knights and barons will be riding into the castle and pulling up the drawbridge, because they're coming. All the peasants are coming with pitchforks after them.'[15]

As if the mask had been stripped for a moment from the value-programme draining the life of its social life-host, aspiring president Bob Dole recognized the same pattern in glimpses: 'Corporate profits are setting records', he said, 'and so are corporate layoffs. ... Big corporations are getting tax-breaks they can't justify.'[16] Buchanan had flagged the erupting division between the reproductive sequence of ever more money for money investments and ever less livelihood for society and its people. 'The interests of the corporate chieftains ... and Wall Street profits', he declared before the media withdrew their spotlight, '*no longer coincide with America's.*'[17]

We know in advance that any such emergence of immune recognition within the political party representing the disease-pattern must be repressed to sustain the money sequence's advancing occupation of the social host. And we know that the cancer pattern he briefly recognized, like the Dean of the Business Faculty of Yale two years later,[18] will not be discussed in the corporate media or academy, any more than it was discussed when it was first advanced in a special public health issue of one of America's leading public affairs journals in 1995.[19] These predictions follow from the fact that the means of public discourse are owned and financed by the very corporate bodies which lead the money-sequence invasion of their social hosts. The rule of reproduction of these corporate media is, as elsewhere, *to rule out whatever exposes or invalidates the global market programme.* Only by doing so can the advance of this programme's occupation of societies continue. None of this needs to be conscious, but all of it is testable by observation. It is entailed by the requirements of the programme itself, whose system-deciding sequences flow from unexamined assumptions. Any view that criticizes the money beneficiaries of the programme or calls on people to resist is in this system excluded a priori.

And so it happened. Buchanan was pilloried for weeks in the corporate media as anti-semitic, as crypto-fascist, as dangerous and irresponsible – properties that had never before been applied to him by these media organs, although the words and actions they described had been on the record long before his speech at the Republican convention. What he actually *said* at the convention, however, was not repeated. Nor was the content of what he said considered. Most of all, the problems to which they referred were no more discussed than they were before he spoke. This is how the immune disorder of society continues. The channels of public communication are closed to whatever reveals the occupation.

But the deeper question arises in the aftermath. What was Buchanan *motivated by* when, as a very experienced political and media operative, he declared these unspeakable confrontations of the money-sequence disorder to its party representatives? One could say it was political demagoguery to attract votes. But this would naively overlook both the wealth of the delegates he was speaking to, with over a million dollar average annual income, and the further knowledge he would have of the acute hostility of corporate press barons and advertisers to his message. That the recognition should arise with such outspoken militance in such a site of US society's life-organization is an indicator of an immanent war even within the human vector bearing the pathogenic pattern.

The answer need not be mystified. Underneath the money programme lies a deeper code, an identification with the members of one's society and the common life-ground they share. Not even a corporate ad can succeed without appealing to this underlying life-ground, before it repressively desublimates its identification into a conditioned demand for a commodity. It propels even a Republican on the right into jeopardizing his career to express it. It is the basis of what we have analysed as the life-ground and sequence, the experience of life's needs and capacities on the macro-level of community. It is what sometimes makes people sacrifice their lives, typically without understanding its wider meaning.

The wall against recognizing the systemic nature of the disorder afflicting the life-ground problem is this. The underlying pattern which unifies the symptoms and exposes them as a systemic disorder remains kept out of view. Where the subjugation of human society and its environmental life-host to the money sequence of value *is* made visible, it is normalized as 'a necessary price that must be paid'. Even the sharply increased malnutrition and death of infants or suicides of teenagers across the world does not detain this life invasion's demands. They are 'harsh realities' to which 'society must adapt'. Such a pattern of 'sacrifices' of people's life-interests to 'reassure investors' and promote 'the growth of the economy', that is, the increase of money-sums at the end of each money sequence, eventually reaches limits of people's submission. The life-devastations it results in provoke outrage. But the nature of the value system behind the 'greedy' and the 'ignorant' who enact it is not yet clear. The cell community does not recognize that it is a mutant economic paradigm at work in precisely sequenced outcomes, and that it is not the symptoms of it that need correction. The problem is a system-deciding social programme of value which rules out all alternatives.

A few weeks after Patrick Buchanan's flagging of 'the cancer eating away at the economy' at the 1996 Republican convention, the Harvard economist and Secretary of Labor, Robert Reich, declared an underlying war between life and money value systems long before his colleagues in the Clinton Presidency. We may recall here that Secretary Reich was a conflicted expressor of the global market value programme from the beginning. After he understood the new order in terms of slogans of 'needing to compete' and to 'become knowledge workers', he awoke to the ongoing reality of disemploying the American working class in millions every year. 'The majority of Americans are losing out in global competition,' he earlier declared, 'but it is inevitable and irreversible in the new economic order.'[20] Having observed a continuous fall of wages in times of record profits and stock market gains, and the loss of two to three million US workers' jobs annually since his embrace of the new order, Reich seemed to be discovering his life bearings. He bravely chastised the large corporations for waging '*a war*' of unemployment and declining wages on workers. But, predictably, he was all but ignored by the corporately owned media, even though it was the US Secretary of Labor who was speaking. It is an error to imagine that the media 'love conflict in high places'. This conflict was repressed.

But in the *New York Times*, another telling exception emerged. In a series on US unemployment in March 1996, one more step towards recognition of the systemic disorder was made. The continuous stripping of the US wage- and salary-earning citizens for the escalating profits of US money-investors was now seen as a *structural problem*, not only a problem of 'knights and barons'. Reich made what amounted to a call for the assertion of society's life-interests over the money-programme attacking it, and urged society to 'recognize' the system that was dispossessing its citizens (emphasis added):

> As corporations have focussed more and more intensely on increasing shareholders' returns and less and less on improving the standards of living of their workers, it should be no surprise that the stock market has soared while pink slips have proliferated and the paychecks of most employees have gone nowhere. Do not blame corporations and their executives. If we want them to put greater emphasis on the interests of their workers and communities, *societies must reorganize them to do so.*[21]

Consider Reich's last two sentences. We are not to blame corporations or their executives. We 'must *reorganize them*'. There are two very important issues Reich raises here which we need to unpack. The first is that corporations and their executives do not exercise personal choice in their continuous assaults on workers' lives and on communities to maximize money profits. That is why, Reich implies, it is not appropriate to attack them *as* responsible. They are, in the terms of this analysis, programmed by the money sequence of money-profit maximization to decide and act as they do. 'There is', in the words of the now universal invocation of the doctrine, 'no alternative'. Behind the corporate CEOs dismantling social and environmental life-fabrics, there is a determining structure of preference which requires them to choose this rather than that, from moment to moment, day in and day out, and this embedded value programme, with all the elaborations of its prescriptions, is what regulates and orders them as mere functions of its system. They re-engineer all life-organization to its demands as determined elements of a machinal order. As the genetic code and sequence of a cancer is to the individual organism, so is this ruling programme to its social life-hosts. Reich's recognition of a structural disorder that must be reoriented to society does not go so far, but it penetrates to the systemic nature of the problem.

Reich's implied denial of choice and responsibility here, however, remains within the mechanism of the paradigm. Its metaphysic does not admit of choice *out* of it by the programmed. This is the paralysis of choice within which the epoch remains held. If the individual bearers of the value programme cannot choose beyond enacting it as moments of its money gains, how can others who are regulated by the same programme at other levels steer them? In this way, the responsibility for choosing out of the social programme is relegated to hopes or fantasies of revolution. As we will see, the steps for reordering the mutant money sequence of value into compliance with social and planetary life-requirements are already in place, but the responsibility of recognizing them is evaded.

Given the mind-lock of the corporate decision-structure which looks only to money gains and not life gains in its calculations, Reich concludes: society '*must reorganize*' [corporations and their executives] to put greater emphasis on the interests of working people and their communities'. 'Reorganize' is a strong term. It means structural change in the system it refers to. Here the structural change which the US Secretary of Labor thinks is necessary is a change which requires the interests of working people and their communities to be built into the corporations' decision-programme, whether they accept it or not. '*Society*' must prescribe what is required for the life-interests of workers and the people as a whole against the money value-code which prescribes on behalf of private capital profits alone. Reich does not state all that his words imply, for his recognition of and response to the problem is still at an emerging state. But the war between the life of society and the money sequences of corporations which he publicly signals is an unprecedented act of recognition by an in-office, US cabinet member: an economist minister of the central government of the world's most powerful economy, advising the society he represents that they must restructure the corporate economic programme which he identifies as the problem.

Again we need to ask, what is the agent, in this case Robert Reich, moved *by* in this act, and to *what* does he appeal in others he speaks to – in this case, the mostly privileged readers of the *New York Times*? What he says confronts the ruling programme and its bearers in the centre of the nation that leads its imposition on the world, and it does so in the most prestigious press organ of the programme's propagation. It quickly ends his political career. It puts him at odds with the very global market hegemony he had so successfully represented in the past. That it happens at all is the phenomenon to be explained. One cannot plausibly claim it maximized his monetary, or political or even academic interests. It clearly did the opposite with at least the first two. The only reasonable explanation is that he identified with the wider, common life-interest of his country's people, and spoke out for it. Recall that it was the unemployed or the insecurely employed – people who could never pay back or reward him – that his words spoke for most of all. In the paradigm of the market where all that is done is done for self-interest, and for the narrow interest of money gain at that, Reich's action cannot begin to be understood. From the standpoint of the life-ground where it is the shared concern for life and its defence and growth that rules, Reich's action is an emergent expression from the deep.

Reich resigned from his office several months after his unsung act, penning a book from the freer life space he was now in fittingly entitled *Locked in the Cabinet*.[22]

Such emerging expression of the life-ground and its macro-imperative of protecting the life of its membership as a whole, what we might call the social immune impulse, is even at work within the bearers of the decoupled money sequence itself. Human beings are never only a programme, though they may remain imprisoned within one. We have already observed the uninhibited aggressiveness of transnational currency speculators who claim to rule as the 'supra-national government of the world', and publicly threaten politicians with having 'their feet held to the fire' if they do not conform to their dictates.[23] We have also read the extraordinary report from *The Washington Post* that the 'growing consensus' among government officials representing the most developed market nation of the world is that 'the group [the G-7 states] cannot influence events [of the international financial markets] anyway'.[24] These are clear markers of the invasionary code, and its agents could hardly be more bereft of the wider life commitment we see arising elsewhere.

George Soros is one of them, and at the top of the takers from life. He is the world's leading currency speculator, famous for appropriating $10 billion in money-demand over ten days of buying and selling money with no productive contribution to any form of life. He is thus an exemplar of the global market disorder. Yet Soros, like Reich, sees beyond the demands of the money programme to other requirements of social life-organization. Soros writes (emphasis added):

> Commercial banks ... seek to maximize their profits within the framework of existing regulations and they *cannot afford to pay too much attention to the systemic effects*. Even if a bank decided to abstain, there are many others anxious to take its place. Thus even those who realized the international lending boom was unsound found themselves *obliged to participate or lose their places*. There is an important lesson to be learned: *participants are not in a position to prevent a bust* ... the lesson to be learned here is that *financial markets need to be supervised. Only some kind of intervention ... can prevent boom/bust sequences from getting out of hand*.[25]

With currency speculation now expending 30 to 70 times as much money demand per day as investment in the production of goods and services across international stock markets, the estimates vary, the 'busts' can be disastrous for entire societies. We have seen, for example, how Mexico's social fabric was drained overnight leaving the majority of the society increasingly destitute; and how, on the other side of the world, the meltdown of Asian miracle economies has stripped populations of up to 80 per cent of the value of their wages with no co-ordinate of life need entering any step of the process, or of the global market response to it. Across the world, the same out-of-control metastases of money capital invasion and exit break societies' evolved economic capacities to feed their citizens. There is, as Soros a major profiteer from this very process recognizes, no reason to think that a *system so unregulated by any interest or consideration but private money seeking to be maximally more money 24-hours-around-the-clock can have any other consequence over time.* Only a programmed blindness to the disorder could sustain it. But while the global market system is normalized to exclude all life interests beyond itself, the resistance of the underlying life value ground arises in even the money-speculator Soros.

Two years later, Soros went further. He publicly declared in an *Atlantic* article in 1997 that: 'I now fear that the untrammelled intensification of laissez-faire capitalism and the spread of market values into all areas of life is endangering our open and democratic society. *The main enemy of the open society, I believe, is no longer the communist but the capitalist threat.*'[26]

Again we ask, what could be the underlying concern motivating the currency speculator Soros? What is the ground of value from which he challenges 'capitalism' itself, from whose forms he himself has derived his entire fortune? The fundamentalist Republican Buchanan spoke from the shared life-ground of his wider community, 'America's interests' – not understood in the usual way as US transnational corporations' rights to enter and own the markets, natural resources, enterprises and cheaper labour of other societies with no limits, but understood as the right of ordinary people within the US to jobs and wages that would sustain their lives. The neo-liberal academic and cabinet minister, Robert Reich, also spoke from the same underlying common life-ground when he proposed the 'reorganizing' of corporations and their executives to protect the 'standards of living' of US workers. Both elite members of the system recognized its decision-structures as in serious and worsening conflict with the lives of the American people themselves. Both implied a systemically pathological alien order invading the larger community, the unaccountable extraction of money profit from the producing members of the social life-host. Both responded with strong proposals of fight-back and reorganization of the out-of-control exploitation and oppression by the life-attacking new regime. All of this is implicit in what they say. But the underlying common life-ground and its articulation here is not yet explicit. They are, in the conceptualization of this diagnosis, agents of the social immune system in formation, agents of the life-ground which it expresses and defends – speakers for the conscious organization of this shared life base, which in its overall configuration is the civil commons.

Soros is another variation on the theme. It is, in fact, the social substructure of history and has evolved beneath our conscious recognition. Even symptoms of the disorder that attack it see the disorder. The civil commons they bear in this recognition is the life-ground becoming conscious in them as a larger form of life-organization than the ego, or the class or the party. In its protective capacity, it is the social immune system at work at the individual level. They all assert from this underlying connective base, but they do so with different and still vaguely conceptualized ideas of the macro life sequence they affirm.

In the case of Buchanan and Reich, it is American workers' livelihoods in general that they identify with against the system that attacks these livelihoods. In the case of Soros, it is first the regulation of banks and bankers to prevent 'boom and bust cycles' of the economy as a whole that he recognizes as necessary to defend social hosts against what threatens them with 'systemic effects' of harm. In the second instance, Soros recognizes the totalitarian closure of market ideology, which rules out any alternative but itself. If we penetrate underneath the Popperian argument he advocates, the life need and capacity he is grounding in is that for self-determination and range of life voice. In resonance with the deeper civil commons movement he expresses, Soros *also* refers to 'income redistribution' and 'social institutions' to safeguard 'common interests on the global level such as preservation of the environment and the prevention of war.'[27] 'Society has lost its anchor', he says. In fact, this anchor is found in the underlying requirements of the life-ground which all his concerns imply a commitment to defend. In short, with all these diverse emergences of protest, whether from the demonstrators in Parisian streets or the multi-billionaire Soros, we find an unseen, unifying logic to their various expressions, and an emerging clarity about the uncontrolled global market mechanisms which endanger social and environmental life-hosts they speak out for. In the end, the assertions of all of these people are ultimately affirmations of the life sequence of value at the *macro*-level of social life-organization, and the call for its defence against the growing systemic threat to it.

If we connect across the fields of emerging global consciousness of 'something wrong' at the macro-level of social life, we see that beneath the daily normalization of the abnormal in the dream constructions of the corporate media, social immune responses are rapidly evolving. We have observed them erupting within the European Economic Community, within the World Bank, within the mainstream parties and government of the United States, and even within the mind and life of the world's most successful currency speculator. On the one hand, there are the vital requirements of social and environmental life-organization made self-conscious in the voices and programmes of countless thousands of grass-roots campaigners and groups and simultaneously in awaking agents of the disease invasion itself. On the other hand, there is the fixed repertoire of unregulated money sequences seeking to multiply across the world's civil societies and planetary life-webs as a 'new global reality' of borderless money capital with life as its substance of consumption.

The Hidden World of the Civil Commons

The civil commons is *human agency in personal, collective or institutional form which protects and enables the access of all members of a community to basic life goods.* We have seen its emerging expressions in immune recognition and response to the attacks of corporate money sequences on the working peoples of America and Europe, on civil life variety and stability, and on environmental life-hosts.

The civil commons has countless *forms* from the beginnings of human evolution, and across the most disparate cultures. It is what our lives depend on wherever we may be, for it is the conscious organization of humanity *as* human in relationship to the life-ground which is its base. But astonishingly the civil commons is not recognized, lacking even a name by which to call it. It has been lost in the velocities and volumes of money demand which have isolated and overwhelmed societies across the planet, like a body losing its memory.

Let us look at a simple form of the civil commons at a cultural distance to see its shape concretely in a society that bridges us from its ancient past to the present. This form of the civil commons is braced round with the pikes of social immune defence, not like other forms of the civil commons such as language, which can be accessed without limit of supply. I quote from a text by George Monbiot of Oxford:

> During the long dry seasons in the far north west of Kenya, the people of the Turkwel River keep themselves alive by feeding their goats on the pods of the acacia trees growing on its banks. Every clump of trees is controlled by a committee of elders, who decide who should be allowed to use them and for how long.
>
> Anyone coming into the area who wants to feed his goats on the pods has to negotiate with the elders. Depending on the size of the pod crop they will allow him in or tell him to move on. If anyone overexploits the pods or tries to browse his animals without negotiating with the elders first he will be driven off with sticks: if he does it repeatedly he may be killed. The acacia woods are a common: a resource owned by many families. Like all the commons of the Turkana people, they are controlled with fierce determination.[28]

In the last 30 years, the civil commons of the Turkwei has been destroyed. I say *civil* commons to mark a distinction between 'the commons' as nature-given land or resource which is *not* regulated by human agency to serve life, and such natural or human-made goods of life which *are* so regulated. In the case of the Turkwei commons, enemy tribes, the Kenyan government, UN agencies and minds like Garrett Hardin, author of the famous *Tragedy of the Commons*, could not discern the civil commons at work protecting and enabling the reproduction of a shared life resource of the community for the continued access of all members to live from. The pattern was at bottom much the same as 30 years later in the 1990s, anticipating the growth of the closed market mind-set which now threatens the larger world.

Since the underlying civil commons could not be seen, 'the commons' was perceived as an unmediated natural resource which it would be better to privatize in the hands of a market owner who would most effectively harvest and sustain its resources in his own interest. This happened across Africa and elsewhere. The resources were rapidly used up to market for as high a price as could be got. In every case, there was soon no more common for the community to live from. It is in such ways that a programme of thought blinkers out reality to reproduce itself, while setting the conditions for private exploiters to become richer by consuming the community-stewarded natural resource at low cost, and then moving onto the next. This is, in fact, the macro-sequence of transnational money capital whose food cycle of consuming the common resources of life has ever increasing velocity and scale.[29]

Thus it is important to distinguish between 'the commons' as nature-given land or resource and 'the civil commons' which effectively protects it, and ensures access of all members of the community to its continuing means of existence. In fact, the traditional village commons of England – before they were enclosed by early agribusiness capitalism – were regulated like the Kenyan acacia trees of the Turkwel River. That is, there were strict village rules or customs to ensure both that the natural resources were preserved, and that there was continued access of all members of the community to their life wealth (for example, the rule that a commoner could only turn out as many head of livestock to the shared pasture as were kept in the household corral over the winter). This is the nature of the civil commons in its earlier forms as 'the commons'. It is 'civil' insofar as the common life-good it embodies is protected by conscious and co-operative human agency.[30]

We can see from this base-line distinction that what was once the 'commons' of nature *becomes* 'civil commons' as it is preserved by conscious human acts and social constructions (for example, effective laws against environmental pollutants that destroy the 'global commons' of the atmosphere or oceans). It is not difficult to follow the next step of what is, in fact, the argument of human evolution and history. The civil commons is humanity's long-buried, but still-evolving ground of solution to the planetary crisis which increasingly engulfs social and environmental life-organization.

At this point, we might pose a question which touches many of the diverse bases and expressions of the civil commons across history and cultures. What unifies the so far alienated meanings of the following phenomena?

the nature of language
universal health plans
the world wide web
common sewers
international outrage over Vietnam or Ogoniland
sidewalks and footpaths
the Chinese concept of *jen*
the Jubilee of Leviticus
public streetscapes
water fountains
Robin Hood of Sherwood Forest
the air we breathe
effective pollution controls
indigenous music
Buddha's principle of interdependent origination
old age pensions
universal education
Sweden's common forests
government regulations on toxins
the buffalo of the old west prairies of Canada
red deer in the Scottish highlands
a city plan
the second commandment of Yeshua
the watersheds of Haiti
family values
the world's oceans
the principles of the Nuremberg Charter
the grasslands of Mongolia
unemployment insurance
the global atmosphere
life-protective building codes
maximum work hours and minimum wages
social assistance
the Hindu *atman* or the Christian soul
the rule of law
child and women shelters
parks
public broadcasting
clean water
anti-smog legislation
the UN Declaration of Human Rights
occupational health and safety standards
village and city squares
the Brazilian rainforests

inoculation programmes
indigenous story-telling
the Ozone Protocol
the Tao
the peace movement
death rituals
animal rights agencies
community fish-habitats
food and drug legislation
garbage collection
the ancient village commons before enclosures

What is in common among these diverse weaves and regions of social life across historical periods, cultures and social purpose is that *all one way or another have as the conscious social goal regulating their diverse functions the universal access of community members to basic life goods.*

What is conversely in common among them is that *the global market system threatens each and all in their universally life-enabling ideals and functions.* That is, each and all are either in conflict in principle with this market system's imperatives, or are suffering or have suffered stripping or degradation by its global operations. Since these means and sources of life are in many dimensions of extent what humanity requires to live and grow, we can see from another side that what reduces or endangers them is a systemic threat to the larger body of life.

Let us briefly explain these aspects of the civil commons understood across time and place, each in this light of their life-protective and enabling functions. Let us also consider whether even one can be provided by the global market, or is safe from the current corporate market's occupying invasion.

Let us begin at the human ground of the civil commons with its model, its prime medium, and its universal organizer of projective imagination and understanding. *Language* is all of these, and is the deepest layer of the civil commons. We do not know its origin in fact, but it is certain that it has in all its emergences been the primary survival trait of all societies and the species as a whole. By the ability to communicate by universal names the relevant referents of the life-ground and the world's creatures, plants and minerals – food to eat, water and game sources, places to go or not, names of individual members, and so on – language has been humanity's most important distinguishing tool and the communicative field of its evolving ideas, projects and creations. It has lifted humanity onto another ontological plane by its second-order world of signs and concepts within which, indeed, we may by self-referential discourse live disconnected from the space-occupying world beneath.

What is most important about the nature of language for us here, however, is something we are apt not to register. *Its terms and grammars do not occupy space, and so cannot be lost to others by others' appropriation of them for use.* The wealth of language is in this way open by its nature to an infinite sharing without deficit or exhaustion. In truth, language becomes richer and more useful to anyone for communication in any direction the more others share it. The most important general sense in which this is true is that all of the planes of life enjoyed by any individual human being – felt being and action as well as thought – become richer without known bound the more that the language of others and the self is shared to signify aspects of any of these fields of life body which has not yet been comprehended or experienced.

Consider, for example, what any of us would know, experience or do *without* language. If not 'the blooming, buzzing confusion' of William James, it would be a life reduced to the body's particular sentient experiences of itself.

Language is thus a moving margin of life-range, deepening and broadening the more people have and use it in common. Without its shared use, it becomes a 'dead' language. Privatized in its ownership, as in the global market, the process of language dying is relatively infinitesimal, but incremental. Confined to a class or priest caste in its written form, as it has been through history, it loses its powers to communicate in direct proportion to the narrowness of its confinement. Language, in short, becomes greater in its life value the more universally it is accessed, both in oral presence and in writing. As an inherently shared source of all fields of life's value – of the mind, of sentience and emotion, and of the possibilities of action – it is the quintessence of the civil commons.

Education is its formation into orders and sequences which are worth reproducing and developing as such forms. *Universal education* is the civil commons of language in all of these advancing forms of understanding.

As the quintessence of the civil commons, language is a model of the overall civil commons in two ways. First, it bears the principle of the civil commons in pure form, with none of the difficulties of distribution among different persons or groups which we know well with space-occupying goods in proportion to their scarcity. The civil commons, we know, is *that which protects and enables the access of all members of a community to the vital goods of life*. Language does this in the comprehensive ways we have seen, and it does so on all the planes of life the more effectively and broadly its wealth is open to all's use and enjoyment. The more radically individual their comprehension and communication of it, the more life's vital ranges are enabled to differentiate and extend.

The other primary sense in which language is the model of the civil commons is in its concealment *as* an inherently and universally shared good. Language is a community-based structure, and the more it is so the greater its powers are for the individuals of a community. This is *not*, however, a property of language that is observed in the mountains of works written on language. This concealment of language's underlying nature as communal and the basis of individuality at the same time is typical of all the life goods of the civil commons. Their wealth for individuals *as* common property conflicts with the narrow metaphysic of global market doctrine because the latter's inherent logic is to privatize all that it can privatize as priced goods for corporate shareholder profit, which is then proclaimed as the necessary ground of 'individualism'.

Language is a model of the civil commons, then, in the revealing sense that its nature as a shared life good promoting individuation is systemically repressed. What should be self-evident to the most everyday sensibility requires a dis-covery to reveal it. If you doubt this, identify a single place where this property of language is observed. This is one reason why the civil commons has been so effectively invaded and occupied by the global market and its programme of unbounded privatization. As with language, *we do not see the civil commons underneath us that our lives stand on*. That is why the most deeply excavating step of our condition and of the social immune competence to correct is on the level of language's common ground – the primary shared capacity for human resistance to the disaggregating forces of the global market. But as every kind of expression and denotation of language itself becomes the 'intellectual property' of transnational corporations, we are slow to awake to this enclosure of the civil commons at its most foundational level of all. As even those who live from language in the realm of higher education watch their words and constructions privately appropriated by corporately owned journals who pay nothing to universities or authors for them, and still rejoice in their 'academic publication', we can see how the occupation proceeds with the collaboration of the occupied. This is the invasion of humanity's consciously constructed life-ground at the level of the mind itself.

On the other hand, how far can this enclosure of the civil commons of language proceed if its very concepts of *masking* the invasion – 'freedom', 'free market', 'capital', 'cost efficient', 'terrorism', 'competitiveness', and 'globalization' – are *understood* by the community of language users to mean the opposite of their corporate assertion? How effectively can 'the glue of ideology' work if its every word is recognized as absurd, and as an attack on the common basis of humanity, its shared speech and meaning? Language moored in an awakened civil commons conscious of itself provides a site of battle over every word this carcinogenic system must disguise itself in to advance a step. It is not 'words only' at stake, but the underlying deciding medium of society's struggle for its shared life.

An extension of the civil commons of language that moves it across the globe in seconds is the international electronic network that we now know as the Internet. Its technology began and continues as a civil commons formation, as well, and is known as 'shareware'. Although grounded in civil commons technology, and used as a civil commons medium open to all who choose to participate, it is represented in the global market as a triumph *of* the global market, invented by its military-funded corporate researchers, and the next major medium of marketing in the world. All this is predictable from the occupying forces of this system which claims everything as properly market created, manufactured and sold for a profit. But, in reality, military contractors only pursued an already existing communications infrastructure developed by scientists and universities – ARPANET. The advanced technology itself arose from the civil commons. The 'shareware', as it is still now designated among its non-commercial users, was structured as a civil commons resource – that is, for the universal access of all members of the community who sought its communicative life-good. As a civil commons invention, 'shareware' like most else of human-constructed value was created, regulated and used without profit-driven money prices of the global market selecting as users only those who pay costs plus margin to private corporations. As Douglas Rushkoff puts it, 'the fact remains that every single major development in online technology and communication came as shareware. Since big business took the wheel, we haven't seen anything significant ... .'[31]

The machines used to convey the universally accessible messages are now priced, of course. Machine-made goods have long been the master domain of private corporations, the one important area in which the global market seems competent in its productions and control – if we leave out the 'external' effects of this market production on workers, communities and environments by unhealthy working conditions, industrial pollutants and unrecycled waste, which only effective regulation by public authority – another civil commons formation – can control. But even here, even with the machine medium of the universally accessible goods of shareware, the global market 'creates all sorts of compatibility problems as corporations fight for dominance in the marketplace. It's harder to send attached files to multiple recipients or create a Web site than it was five years ago. ... While *shareware developers create problems to address universal needs, businesses develop programmes in order to create needs.*'[32] This latter principle of distinction is italicized because it can be generalized to explain the defining difference between the civil commons in general and the global market, between a life-sequence economy and the money-sequence economy. The former provides means of life to all for the protection and gain of their lives. The latter contrives conditions where prices must be paid by those with money to private corporations to access these means.

At this point, we might note ancient philosophical declarations of the civil commons in code form in the context of its repression in the historical past. The principles of the classical Chinese notions of *jen*, the second commandment of Jesus, the Tao, the Hindu *atman* and Buddha's 'law of dependent origination' are, for example, all variations on the civil commons *insofar as they instruct an opening of the mind towards the universal view which excludes no life condition from its recognition and response. Jen* is that 'which cannot bear the suffering of another'. 'Love thy neighbour as thyself' requires the identification of the other as the self so that the care of the self's life is universalized. The Tao is all that exists as body or space, in a harmony of 10,000 functions which the human function is to understand and be. The *atman* is the boundless thought within, from which all manifests and connects as the divine dance of God's cosmic body. The law of interdependent origination holds that there is no condition that exists that is not all, that does not depend on all other conditions for it to come into and be sustained in being.

These are deep waters of philosophical conception, but they have a shared implication. The master principle of the civil commons, to protect and enable access to life goods, follows from each and every one of these first principles of the world's great inspirational philosophies.

What is different about the civil commons is that its ideal to be realized has, in fact, been socially actualized in the bodies of societies' social immune systems and common life resources. It is *the goal to be realized* – universal access to life goods of all members of the community, a community which may in principle include all of the planetary ecosystem. But at the same time and in social reality, it *both falls short of and is already far advanced in the direction of the ideal's achievement*. Universal education, for example, is plainly an ideal not yet realized. But it is an ideal that admits of *degrees* of realization, and the achievement of the civil commons is to have taken it as far as it has – for example, to the point that all members of the community can read and write at some level, or learn to as a civil commons entitlement without corporate price. While the level may be low, and many still remain outside the circle of literacy, this condition needs to be compared to a situation not so long ago when hardly any members of any society could read or write at all.

Here we are put in mind again of the *degrees of life range* of social or individual life-hosts. These vital life ranges can advance or regress in any life parameter, and a sound judgement of good or bad, better or worse follows from the evidence of each respectively. It is in this quite precisely identifiable progression, or regression, towards or away from the realization of the civil commons that we find what might be called social development, or its opposite. Far from the civil commons principle being a rather foggy matter, as with the great religions and philosophies of the past, here the realization is already built into societies, and is identifiable to a reasonably exact degree of achievement. Every society but a collapsing one has always had *some* civil commons of universally accessible life goods made or kept that way by social construction – for example at the most basic level, funeral customs to ensure against pathogenic spread from the corpse to any member of the community, ways in which children can learn to speak and to follow hygiene practices, inhibiting provisions against battery of fellow members, paths that all can walk on or public places to sit, or community water sources for all to drink from.

Every one of these universal accesses to life goods which the civil commons normally achieves for its members can, conversely, be reduced, cut back, obstructed and neglected in countless ways we see in the sites of impoverishment around us. Wherever this happens in any respect, it is a decline of life at the most ground level, and recognized as such by social members who have not internalized or been been conditioned to a rogue value programme.

In this way, the progression or decline of the civil commons is the most fundamental social fact there is, though like the sea to the fish not recognized. Unlike the question of whether you 'love your neighbour', or follow the Tao, or are enlightened to the principle of dependent origination, *the question of whether a society's civil commons is intact, falling or gaining in the life goods all its members have access to, is a real-world issue and of life-and-death reality for all on a practical level.*

This may be why this infrastructure of human evolution and history is now hidden from view. Once we adopt its vital, shared life parameters, there is no masking. It is the solid compass of value by which 'society which has lost its anchor' finds its life bearings, and resists what depletes and invades it.

If we look over the expressions of civil commons phenomena we began with, we will observe that the unifying principle of all is not only that they provide some universal life good to all society's members by human design. Almost all of the contemporary constructions of the civil commons – universal health care, health and occupational safety standards, public education, city streetscapes, parks, pollution regulations, consumer law protections, sanitation infrastructures, old-age pensions, city plans, unemployment insurance, social assistance, environmental regulations and the rule of life-protective law in general – are social institutions requiring money revenues to be reproduced and developed in the contemporary world. *It is these universal life goods which divert revenues from money sequences* which the mutant global market, therefore, reduces and axes as 'unaffordable', as 'creating dependencies', as 'unnecessary', and so on. These are the phrases of the global market 'restructuring' which lead the invasion into the civil commons at every level, and all have a unifying antigenic direction: to convert social life functions into severed money sequences which have no commitment to the life-host.

Thus across the globe, effective regulatory controls on what is dumped into, assaulted by or extracted from the air we breathe, the water bodies around us, the atmosphere our climatic temperature, rainfall and winds issue from, the forests which hold the earth together and provide habitat and carbon dioxide consumption, the ecosystem processes which recycle life remains to life again, the retreating soil covers our food is grown from, the marine habitats that bear the food of entire continents and ageless ecologies of diverse life, in short, the life-ground of humanity and all species are ruled out, or stripped back as 'too costly' or 'unnecessary' under the global market programme.

Effective regulatory regimes, the civil commons in its social immune function, are required to preserve every one of these conditions of life from further depredation and destruction. But not one of these carrying capacities and conditions of life is not declining rapidly from global market assault, in circumstances of correspondingly falling environmental protections. The civil commons is society's long-evolving system of conscious human protection of the larger life-host humanity lives from. We saw it in early form in the commons of Kenya and English villages before their destruction. Its modern form which alone ensures impartially monitored, inspected, policed and enforced defence of the community's life-host is *a well-funded public authority.*

In this connection, consider what *else* but government authority has, or ever could, provide effective life protection against large-scale industrial effluents and extractions. As masking phrases and hallucinations of 'voluntary compliance of corporate stakeholders', 'pollution credit exchange systems', 'an alternative to the state' and so on are relentlessly prescribed to public authorities, we see how the pathogenic pattern penetrates social immune defences. As an antidote to this masking, we might ask whether we would ever accept such forms of preventing violations of human life by those with major vested interests in doing so – say, voluntary compliance or violence credits for trade among known batterers and rapists.

Here is where the evolution of the civil commons finds its form in the tax-supported, institutional form of *government agency.* Without its effective structures and operations to defend all of these basic conditions of human and other life, both nationally and transnationally, social bodies are denuded of their social immune system – *that aspect of the contemporary civil commons whose function is to survey the social and environmental life-hosts continuously, recognize the not-self entrants or internal mutations which have no committed function to the sustainment of the life-host, and respond with effective means of selecting out the harmful substances or practices which endanger the life web of its members.*

The civil commons is already highly developed to perform these functions with respect to violent assaults or poisonings of human beings or dumping personal wastes into the streets. It does so effectively through ongoing, government-instituted means of detection and consistent enforcement as well as, over time, that internalization of life-protective sensibility and habit that is the hallmark of the civil commons in its maturest forms. This same principle of the social immune system to protect all alike in the community from life harm only needs consistent extension to the environmental life-host upon which human life depends for its sun, air, water, soil, and so on. That there has not been such extension of life-protective regulation in a lawless condition where the environment becomes more dangerous or depleted than any criminal gang could ever make it – with over 90 per cent of cancers, for example, caused by market-made products and wastes – is an indicator of our seriously pathogenic condition. Both the problem's causation and its solution are clear in the light of our deeper civil commons bearings and what has evolved to this point as its public agencies. The problem is the loss of our bearings.

The deep levels of the civil commons respond to this systemic attack in ways ranging from environmental activism on the ground to international protocols to protect the ozone layer and emerging initiatives for environmental standards in international trade treaties.[33] On the level of *human* life protection, the civil commons which seeks by its nature to protect and enable all life it identifies in its community, moves its margin of community outwards as it develops – from fellow villagers in the primitive commons to all human life in the potential 'global village' of today.[34] This is the countervailing, progressive human dimension of our condition today which is reconstituting the civil commons as ever more effectively universal.

Its global binding has evolved most dramatically since the end of the Second World War with the Principles of the Nuremberg Charter, the Universal Declaration of Human Rights, and other declared norms of universal life protection which themselves have been under mounting attack by defunding and exclusion by the invasive corporate money code.[35] But the civil commons has also evolved *as a way of seeing and judging* that now links across human domains of all societies. What, for example, made the whole world of humanity speak out in large numbers, expose themselves to injury or suspicion, and even become imprisoned in their commitment to remove invading US armed forces from Vietnam after 1967? However one sees this war, as armed invasion or not, what needs explanation is the *identification* with the loss of Vietnamese life of millions of people of other races, cultures, histories and kinship genes, with no self-interest of money, position or power to be normally gained in the struggle, but perhaps lost, carrying on as if *their* lives were at least partly at stake. Certainly the now dominant explanatory schemas of monetary or genetic self-maximization do not work here.

Or again, why is there still global indignation and rage at the frame-up hanging of Ken Sara-Wiwa and seven others in Nigeria after they led over 300,000 of a total community of 500,000 in peaceful demonstrations in 1995 against Shell Oil's and the military dictatorship's pollution and depredation of their lands? Here again we see the phenomenon earlier diagnosed. Such responses cross classes, cultures, races and genders, and are grounded in *a civil commons identification which admits of any degree of development or breadth of range.* If people observe or know of the destruction or brutal reduction of vital life ranges where no compensating gain in or security of others' life can explain it, they rebel from within as if there was an acquired structure of thought which put them 'in common' with the lost life, and the life that remains. This is *the civil commons within*, and is not a spiritual conceit. It is a general fact that is so self-evident underneath acknowledgement that murderous state and corporate agents will go to any lengths to provide cover-ups, rationalizations, silencing of witnesses, and full-page ads to keep people from this civil commons connection across all boundaries.

Because the received theories of motivation cannot compute such bonding across divisions, however basic, recognition of the underlying shared life-ground at work here becomes another revolutionary act of recovering what is already there. It is in fact as evident a structure of thought as we will find in social consciousness. That is, if we see that life has been truly maimed or killed with no other life secured by it, and to the extent of life so destroyed, a correspondingly strong reaction against it is normally aroused among the life-sensible. This is probably not a natural response, because there seems much historical evidence of indifference or even stimulation by such assaults in lower cultures and persons.

Where there is an evolved civil commons sensibility, its concerns for fellow members of the community extend wider as it develops, past the family or the region to the nation and outwards to the civil commons of the world as it might be. The civil commons is an open possibility. Peace, environmental and transcultural movements of all kinds are an expression of this movement outwards. Perhaps its first written form of recognition was the Jubilee Year marked in Leviticus which freed all slaves and bonded servants, returned lost land, and forgave everyone's debts (Chapter 25). '*Family values*' are in one sense regressively narrow, but in another sense carry the civil commons principle of universal access to life goods for members independent of their capacity to pay in its most basic form. When they are hungry without food, sick without means, old or unemployed without support, family values of the life sequence ensure they have the means of life they lack. When society reaches a certain level of civil commons development, the whole community provides these means of life in the form of social assistance, universal health care, old-age pensions and on through the entire developed infrastructure of socially constituted means to protect and enable the lives of all of society's members, their environmental life-host, and also fellow creatures of every type. These mark the level of civilization of the society in question. But these evolved means of the macro life sequence of social bodies are also continuously attacked, defunded and by many carcinogenic channels redirected from the civil commons life sequence to the market's money sequences. The masking language of 'big and inefficient government', 'dependency', 'debt crisis' and so on lead these carcinogenic invasions into the life-fabric of the social host. But tracking the money metabolisms of the social host always reveals the underlying pathogenic pattern of means of life appropriated from the social host and consumed by increased money sequences of growth.

The issue remains of comprehending the resources of the evolved civil commons and its social immune capabilities. These are in fact available.

But the civil commons as the body of the macro life sequence of society protecting and enabling all its members' needs is to be explicitly distinguished from the government waste, costly dependency and bureaucratic deformations which still obscure its underlying, evolving form.

Saving the Civil Commons from Government Waste, Costly Dependency and Bureaucratic Deformations

Life's shared requirements can only be consistently recognized and protected by what consciously selects for their fulfilment, and against what violates them. The social bearer of this vocation is what we have designated the civil commons. It replaces the market superstition of a providential invisible hand that looks after everyone by the device of their market self-seeking alone. But the civil commons can only perform its vocation insofar as it is funded to be *able* to perform it in its long-evolving historic stewardship of the life commons out of which it grows. This is the *infra-human function* of the civil commons. It has been at work in some form since first peoples evolved to understand that 'the earth is our body'. It has been at work again in the ancient village commons whose customs forbade privatization and overloading of commons resources. Today this protection of the environmental life-host takes the form of such governmental bodies as environmental ministries and agencies and – at a germinal stage – effectively enforced laws at national and international levels. The global market system can be seen to be *carcinogenic* in its pattern to the extent that it strips, as it does now, the evolving civil commons of its effective means of environmental protection.

In regard to human life, the civil commons has a highly evolved system of both protecting and enabling civilization's achieved ranges of vital existence. We have designated the *protective* functions of the civil commons as a 'social immune system' whose benefits are accessible to the entire social body. This is the hallmark characteristic of the civil commons on both its preventative and nourishing functions – universality of life service. Just as it is a violation of the civil commons' logic of value to have, say, one safe sun to shine or one clean air to breathe for those possessing money demand, and another hazardous sun or air for others in accordance to their ability to pay to the money sequence, so it is a violation of the civil commons' logic of value to have educational opportunity, health-care or old-age security for one class of society, and less or none for the rest. Here too there is far more to the civil commons than meets the eye. There is a world of shared goods which protect and enable human life which the value system of the market rules out of view or discriminates against by its money-sequence calculus. Not only do we share in common the filtered or unfiltered rays of the sun, the earth beneath our feet and the stars above, but we have in even the most market-shrunk civil commons of the world socially owned and universally accessible life goods which could be privatized with enormous increases in the market's money-sequence revenues – sidewalks, for example, and public education.

The civil commons in all its forms is at work if and only if it functions in some way to enable life to hold or extend its vital range of capacity and expression by means which are *universally accessible* to all of society's members. Since universal entitlement is the opposite of market right, and therefore attacked as unaffordable wherever its good can be transformed to a priced commodity, we define the concept to rule out misconception. 'Universally accessible' means *available without market price or other exclusionary fence to it, where need and choice concur with the common life interest served.* That is, a citizen is not forced to have any good if it is not chosen, or entitled to it if it does not serve life's maintenance or growth (as, say, right to access to higher education for one without the competence to read does not oblige or entitle that person to enter university). Access to the life good entails that it advances the life sequence, or is a means whereby life becomes more vital or comprehensive than without it.

The law of selection of the civil commons differs from most government as we know it, but not its core mandate, by selecting for what serves the life sequence, and ruling out what does not. The first general sense in which it selects for the life sequence is that it evolves a framework of law and *regulatory protection* for human and environmental life. To the extent that it develops, it safeguards life not only from the pollutions, depletions and destructions of the environment, but from the violations of human life by those actions and processes which effective human, civil and labour rights prevent. This is the 'preventative function' of the civil commons, prohibiting what harms human or environmental life.

The second general sense in which the civil commons selects for the life sequence is through the provision of goods to directly *enable* human or environmental life to grow. This is its positive life function. Thus, those who cannot read or write are educated so that they can read and write, and have universal access to ever more advanced levels of education as they develop. Those who are unwell have access to medical care, and before that to the preventative functions of the civil commons to protect against illness. The unpaid without money are provided with civil commons work, the elderly are guaranteed pension funds, and the citizenry in general enjoy the society's clean water, untoxic air, and undiseased public places, green parks and city centres, public communications and arts facilities, safe sidewalks and treed streetscapes, libraries, information centres, play areas and wilderness parks.

Each and all of these shared public goods of both the 'preventative' and the 'progressive' kind respectively protect or enable life. Each and all serve the life sequence of value. None, in contrast, is available to all citizens by means of the market, and all follow from the *logos* of the civil commons. To say that 'the welfare state does not work' or 'these provisions develop dependencies', or 'the state has too much power already' is to refer to other structures of non-life expenditure examined ahead.

In consequence of its enactment of the life sequence of value rather than the money sequence of the market, the investment circuit of the civil commons *nets more comprehensive life rather than more money income at the end of each reproduction of its circuit.* Money here returns to its proper value function – being the means to the fulfilment of the life value sequence, and not the means to advance what attacks or harms life. By distinguishing these functions of money, and returning its exchange-value to the civil commons, we begin the nodal selecting out of the carcinogenic sequence.

Two consequences follow from selection for the life sequence by the civil commons. Whatever is *required* for the civil commons to serve life is a legitimate function for public financing and support, whether by government or other organization acting for the community as a whole. But this commitment has an austere converse. Whatever is *not* necessary to fulfil a common life-interest is *not* a legitimate function of government, nor of any community-financed body. Thus, all subsidies and tax-benefits of any kind to for-profit corporations, or bureaucratic regulatory apparatuses which do not protect or enable the life of society's members are *ruled out* by this criterion of selection. By the application of this single principle of civil commons integrity alone, vast revenues would be released from illicit government expenditures on private money-sequence interests and bureaucratic over-regulation which usually serves those interests – perhaps most of current state expenditures.

These implications follow clearly from the principles of the civil commons and its mooring in the life-ground. Governments across the new 'global market order', however, are systematically biased against the funding and support of these common life interests of society. They are, that is, programmed to serve the requirements of the global market money sequence *as* 'the common interest'. *This collapse of distinction between the common interest of society and what the global market demands* is at the heart of the current crisis of government revenues. It is an equivalent on the social level of life-organization to the spread of a carcinogenic sequence to the lymph nodes. Its processes do not select out decoupled money sequences of growth, but fund them at the expense of life goods for the social body. This inner logic of the global market system is at work everywhere – from ubiquitous tax write-offs to money sequences with no committed function to society, to defunding social services so as to pay compound interest to foreign money lenders instead of to national public banks.

This systemic depletion of the nutriment flows of the social body to feed decoupled money sequences is a predictable consequence of the global market programme. But even critics of the consequences focus on the downstream effects of dismantled social infrastructures rather than exposing the regulating paradigm *behind* them which systematically biases public policy and expenditures to life-destructive effects. This deepening bias of elected governments is demonstrated by the following transnational patterns of state expenditure whose phenomena we have observed throughout this diagnosis:

(i)   *public budgets and subsidies for armed forces, weapons manufacture and armaments exports whose expenditures typically exceed the total federal monies spent on education, health and social assistance, and whose dominant usage is to serve the interests of private money-sequence assets, operations, entitlements and expansions;*

(ii) *continuous major subsidies, tax-reductions and special exemptions to private corporations, investors and banking operations advancing and extending money sequences of value with no accountability back to the societies paying for them;*

(iii) *licensed giveaways of publicly-owned natural resources and broadcast airwaves to private industrial and media oligopolies to use in whatever manner maximizes their private profits with few or no requirements to protect or to enable the environmental or cultural lives of society's members;*

(iv) *privatizations of public debts at high compounding interest rates at the cost of the taxpaying public, and transfer of government control over the creation of money to private banks and financial institutions to extract further money from the public at rising rates of individual and government indebtedness;*

(v)   *continuous expenditures on special-interest infrastructures to serve the transportation, sale and consumption of market commodities which increasingly endanger human life and depredate the environment (for example, ever-widening roads, highways and water thoroughfares for high-powered, fossil-fuel engines); and*

(vi) *in general, ever more intensive representation and deployment of government finances, ministries, departments, agencies and public sectors to the servicing of large-scale private corporations and money-lenders as their public debt collector, armed-force protector, contract supplier, subsidizer, employee trainer, foreign advertiser and agent, and insurer against liability and loss.*

In these ways, governments have mutated in their function to become more and more dominantly coercive debt collectors on behalf of banks and foreign bond-holders from citizens who have received little or no benefit from the debts, and international trade agents and deal-makers for transnational corporations against the most basic interests of domestic workers and businesses, using the armed force of the state to enforce the society-stripping invasion.[36] These underlying patterns disclose their symptoms on a continuous, daily basis, but the design of their service to global money sequences of value and deprivation of life sequences everywhere is not recognized. Rather, the public's resources still devoted to the life sequence of value are blamed for governments' debts, and defunded further to pay more to compound usury circuits, corporate subsidizations, and mechanisms of state violence and coercion.

As long as there remain major government expenditures on serving the special interests of the market's money sequence, then there *are*, in fact, sufficient public funds available to fund the civil commons which serves the common life interest. The problem is not one of 'unaffordable social expenditures'. The problem is the systematic bias of government revenues away from their common-interest mandate to the private interests of the market's ruling programme of value.

It is not only 'government waste' which is projected back from money-sequence service to life-sequence functions of the civil commons. Another masking operation of the global market programme is the media-pervading message across social bodies that people should not 'rely on the government to do things for them' and that 'a culture of dependency' is bred by governments' social services. It is then concluded from this premise that privatization and social-service cutbacks will release society from this 'culture of dependency', and at the same time develop people's autonomous capabilities. We have seen the unstated implication of this argument – that only those who can pay the market price will then be entitled to such life-goods. But prior to this argument's implications, there is a more fundamental disorder. This programme of value transforms facts of its *own* disorders into failings of what it attacks. This is an operation of *projection* which we have observed above with the problem of 'government waste'. It achieves its apogee on the issue of 'independence' and 'self-reliance'. It is important to recognize the mechanism of misrepresentation here because it is the normative drive-wheel of the ideological assault on the civil commons to clear the way for corporate market appropriation of its revenues.

The attribution to the beneficiaries of the civil commons of 'dependency' or 'lack of self-reliance' is disordered in two ways. The premise is false because the life-serving functions of the civil commons in fact *enable* citizens to do autonomously what they could not do if deprived of these universally accessible life-goods. For example, the civil commons' goods of health care, or pollution control, or recycling waste disposal, or a clean water supply, or artistically designed public spaces, all enable citizens in the short or long range to access more vital ranges of life *as* independent individuals. Their autonomy is not therefore reduced. On the contrary, citizens are secured in their life base and widened in their independence by not being subjected to distractive and deteriorating conditions of squalid surroundings, ill-health and environmental hazards. It is a mark of the invasive hold of the market programme that its slogans can invert this inherent property of a vital public sector into its opposite in appearance.

The civil commons' processes of public education, for example, *demand* autonomy of learning, decision and performance as a necessary condition of access to its facilities. Otherwise, one is cheating. It is perfectly well known that depending on others' work in place of one's own can expel one from the educational sphere of the civil commons. Yet it is just as well known that purchase of others' performance in the market is the very axis of its transaction system. Far from diminishing self-capability here, the civil commons demands it. In contrast, the market requires the purchase of others' performance at every step of its money sequences.

It follows from these opposed logics of freedom, one of human agents, the other of the purchasing power of money, that the assertion that the 'competitive market better develops people's independence' is perfectly false. Money is, by its nature, *demand on others' work*. In the money sequence of value, it is the propeller of all the system's moments. But no independent capability is required to have and use money demand. It is preponderantly inherited, gained by investment in what others do, appreciated in value by resources or land that already exist, and in its non-wage-or-salary forms is '*unearned* income'. Once money-demand *is* possessed, even less is required to buy what its owner wants. The sole condition for purchase is that one has enough money to pay the price. The owner and payer of money does not, therefore, require any self reliance to pay the price of any product or service in the market. In this way, the money sequence promotes a 'culture of dependency' as its condition of advance. The reality is the opposite of what is asserted.

Money here individuates by the quantities of its demand. One *is* what one can buy. The individual who has no money to buy 'is nothing'. Autonomy or independent capability is in this way discriminated against. Only those who are willing to sell what they have, or to buy what others have, can transact. Persons therefore are dependent on money, not character or intrinsic worth, to go on living. This is not independence. It is dependency with no limit.

Once a good or service is sold, its purchaser does not then 'stand on his own two feet'. No autonomous capability is required. The consumer consumes, the dealer deals what has been made by others who, in turn, are told by others what to produce – all for money sequences which have no requirement of independence at any moment of their circuits. This is a circle of dependency and servitude where the autonomy of human life is, in truth, ruled out.

As the global market demands everyone to sell what they can do at whatever price they can get to produce more ready-made commodities and services for others to consume, it reduces people to dependent functions of money capital prescriptions. They become labour factors and consumer functions within the regulating money sequence, and live within determined roles of its system of demands – making or selling junk, spreading pollutant effects, sequencing money in destructive and self-multiplying rounds.

This is a wheel of Ixion on which two commands are written, 'Obey and consume'. People's loss of their capacities to do, think and feel for themselves is registered in the logic of the market's own language. 'You must sell yourself' so that you can buy. And 'you must buy this' to be. That you lack what you must buy is the first premise of what commercials tell people round the clock. That you must sell what you are is the law of the body's survival. And so machines move increasingly instead of people, mass-produced images substitute for thought, and environmental life-hosts are increasingly tranformed into temporary commodities and long-term waste. But all depend on continuing the sequences to survive.

In contrast to this drive-wheel of dependency, obedience and natural destruction, the civil commons provides its long-evolved alternative, sells nothing, and needs nothing to sell. It develops and grows the more that people's health, learning, leisure and environment are enabled to realize their intrinsic life capacities. That is why the measure of a public health programme's success is how free from treatment for disease people become; of educational attainment how much people are able to demonstrate autonomous learning; and of public art how far the artist can count on the self-reliant thinking and judgement of the public. The unifying principle here is to maximize the life capabilities of society's members in every life-sphere. We know what *is* and is *not* the civil commons by this criterion. If it protects and enables life to grow autonomously with universal access to its life good, it is the civil commons. If it makes people dependent on and obedient to external demands, it is the opposite – a sphere of special-interest control. The profoundest value of the civil commons, and in the end its greatest threat to the global market value programme, is just this. It enables people to be free of the money sequence's relations of dependency and command, and to enjoy and serve life as a value in itself. This is the meaning of 'citizen' in its unalienated form; and it is the opposite of 'dependency' which the market doctrine projects onto it.

With the a-historical understanding that has characterized the global market party from its historical beginnings, its doctrine conceives of any social life function as its limit, and therefore 'socialist'. In this way, the civil commons is miscomprehended by another masking invalidation which selects it out as a target to attack.

In historical reality, the public institutions to enable the life preservation and growth of all of society's members have existed as long as common sources of water, food and meeting places to talk. Universally accessible earth, water and forests, community health-care, educational and cultural resources for all, shelter for every member, a public communications system, conservation rules and practices, free recreational spaces, social care for the children and the aged, integration of the handicapped and the shamanistic into daily life, historical and environmental monitoring and record keeping of past events, public arts, centres and places of life reverence, and heritage preservation as the shared life of the community are not recent inventions. They are the life-substance of society which precedes the epoch of the global market by millennia.

But the state which proclaims the 'common interest' as its defining function, and is the source of the regulating laws and tax revenues whereby the common interest can in fact be served, has deforming internal bureaucratic structures which select *against* this common interest being served. Instead of the civil commons, we find administrative rank systems serving themselves, corresponding to the corporate market's law of self-multiplying command.

There are, that is, management layers, perquisites, support staffs and costs *within* public sectors which are not, in fact, necessary to the performance of functions on behalf of the common life interest (for example, education and health bureaucracies which are unaccountable to, segregated from and in budgetary control of the primary teaching and health-care functions of these public-sector institutions). These bureaucratic strata are not inherent in public-sector formations, nor expressions of any law of nature or 'iron law of oligarchy'. They are cost-inefficient administrative decouplings of public revenues and resources into self-multiplying bureaucratic offices and salaries. In truth, 'bureaucratic waste and empire building' in the public sector imitates the logic of market management, and is eliminable by release from the market model.[37] The public bureaucracy assimilates itself to market management, without the discipline of market competition, in the following ways:

(i)   *exclusive control over and access to budgets, facilities and personnel files;*
(ii) *proprietary right to command subordinates in a hierarchical chain of command; and*
(iii) *entitlement to special privileges, offices, services and margins of money not available to those performing directly productive functions.*

Not one of these powers or prerogatives belongs to a public-sector office by private property right. Not one of them belongs to any management level by public mandate or life-service function. And not one is a requirement of performing any life service given the appropriate qualifications of the public servants concerned (for example, teachers, doctors, scientists, career civil servants). Insofar as each and all of these proprietary powers and privileges are without legal or functional requirement, they can be ruled out by the principles of civil commons self-determination, and are as government is winnowed into its legitimate civil commons functions. They have been presupposed as 'rights of management' in unexamined subjugation to the corporate paradigm of authority. As such, they are alien superstructures on the body of the civil commons which are a carcinogenic growth of their own kind. Yet, ironically, it is just this market-imitative disorder which is claimed to be correctible by 'market methods'. Here again we note the supplementary disorders of denial and projection so systemic in market ideology.

The legitimate and sovereign authority of the civil commons is straight-forward: the common life interests of society and its environmental host. These common life interests are, in fact, *already* sufficiently articulated in civil commons law and constitutional objective. These binding life requirements, not the dictates of individuals occupying roles of hierarchical office, are what all who are employed in the public sector are obliged to serve and obey as the condition of their continued function and financial support – the teacher to teach subject-matters, the doctor and nurse to enable health-care, the environmental steward to ensure the application of protective life-principle and law. Thus whatever office, staff, salary, perquisite or regulatory mechanism does *not* serve these life-protecting and enabling functions directly, or as a necessary condition, does not qualify as a legitimate expenditure within the civil commons.[38]

The Africans in bureaucratic social sectors in Africa call the appropriators of these non-productive offices and expenditures 'the committee men'. Trotskyites and others have called their system of reproduction 'the Stalinist bureaucracy' in pre-1989 East Europe and the former Soviet Union. In Asian societies like Pakistan, the organization of public-sector expenditures is so manipulated to serve the privileged office holders within it that even the education system itself has collapsed in sinecures and waste. Sufferers of self-perpetuating structures of official privilege and control in state bureaucracies in North America totemize such deformed public sectors as immutable 'Administration' or 'City Hall'. But, in truth, these non-contributory growths on the civil commons' life functions do not have any legal title to any liquid or physical capital as their own; do not derive any right to command or special privilege and emolument from any such basis, or from any constitutionally mandated function of the public institutions hosting them; and are not, as the market managements they imitate, accountable to the money sequence. They are parasitic, often destructive structures which the evolution of the civil commons is obliged to shed to serve its life-enabling vocation. This principle of civil commons integrity, in fact, brings us to the core of the money sequence occupation of governments whose finance and trade bureaucrats have become effectively traitorous to the common interest they are employed to represent.[39]

The distinction between *administrative functions* which are necessary to serve the life interests of the civil commons and *bureaucratic hierarchy* which is dysfunctional, is exactly discovered by recognizing the two legitimate functions of civil commons management:

(i)   *to regulate financial accounting and disbursement in strict accordance with a legislatively determined grant system to fulfil such mandated life functions of the civil commons; and*

(ii) *to provide a centrally established credentials and appraisals board at the level of the funding government to ensure that minimum performance standards are being achieved by all recipients of public-sector expenditures.*

Any *other* expenditure which does not directly perform a life function of the civil commons – from teaching or medical care to waste-management service – does not qualify as a legitimate expense. It follows, therefore, that it be defunded. Such expenditures are not yet distinguished out in public budgets, and thus sap the civil commons of its resources of life function. This is the cancer state of the disoriented patient at the level of social life-organization.

Expenditures on offices or office occupants, salary margins, assistants, privileges or usurpacious powers not serving life-protecting and enabling functions of the civil commons are, then, another kind of carcinogenic growth. But there is no need of revolution or radical dispossession to restore civil commons' expenditures to their legitimate function. Occupants of such unnecessary positions can be redirected to needed social life services and protection, or their offices retired as they fall vacant.

These principles of management of the civil commons follow in every step from the life sequence of value which is its regulating principle. If they appear 'radical', they are only so in the sense of returning to the life value-ground of the civil commons which has guided its development from before history began. In current industrialized countries with a highly educated generation of youth increasingly without a life function to serve, strictly life-serving functions in the public sector can both realize this new generation's capacities as humans, and uplift the lives of those they are able to serve.

Three responses are required, in summary, to steer the civil commons towards fulfilment of its historic vocation:

(i)   to identify any office or expenditure *not* qualifying as strictly necessary to the performance of the civil commons' and government's legitimate vocation of providing life-protecting and enabling goods accessible to all;

(ii) to reduce or eliminate any such life-superfluous office, salary and other expenditures before any reduction of direct life-service by withholding public funds in accordance with this criterion; and

(iii) to redirect by specific financial allocation all government or non-government funding of the civil commons to positions directly serving society's life functions (for example, to those who care for, teach or heal); and, conversely, away from all other offices, staffs and perquisites in public-sector organizations (for example, bureaucratic supervision, co-ordinators, advisors, and rank offices and officers in general who do not enable life to become more comprehensive life as their functions).

In this way, the civil commons can both develop its capacities for disinterested life service as a value in itself not subordinated to careerist rank and salary self-seeking, and, at the same time, release its resources to enable the vital life functions of society's members by regenerated younger generations across the world now wasting in demoralizing unemployment and sales of unneeded or harmful commodities. As with regulation of the global market, so with regulation of government, the principles of the life-ground and its sequence of value clearly guide judgement through the current social-organizational crisis. As on the individual level, so on the social, the host of a disease-invasion can only recover by all its endogenous life-powers and immune defence capabilities rising to the pathogenic challenge.

Implementing the Civil Commons by International Law

The carcinogenic sequences of the global market can only advance across very differently constituted societies if the life-defending borders of these different social life-organizations are in some way overrun to permit the penetration of the rogue sequences. As we saw earlier, John Foster Dulles succinctly identified the avenues of penetrating nations' borders some decades ago: 'There are two ways of taking over a nation's economy. One is by armed force, and the other is by financial means.' The method used in the last decade has been transnational trade and investment treaties imposed by corporately financed governments. We examined the inner logic of these secretly negotiated and barely known agreements in our deconstruction of the Multilateral Agreement on Investment, the most recent and totalitarian of these instruments for subjugating societies across the world to the life-consuming programme of the global market's money sequences.[40]

The MAI was an incubus of the World Trade Organization, itself a mutation of the GATT, which prescribed from December 1993 on that no society could refuse any commodity across its borders on grounds of its 'process' of production or potential harm to social memberships. Thus it became illegal to prevent the mass influx and marketing of deliberately addictive and lethal US chemical concoctions called 'tobacco products' into one's society to target children and women, prohibited to pass laws marking foreign imports of dolphin-laced tuna, unlawful to label genetically engineered soya as genetically altered, a prosecutable crime for peasants to plant without royalty payments seeds of their own crops and regions that had been patented by transnational corporations, and a violation of trade obligations for local government to refuse to buy oil extracted by forced labour in Burma under the SLORC military dictatorship. These were merely phenomena of an underlying principle now instituted as world law with no society voting on or aware of the new rule of nations – *the overriding right of transnational corporate commodities to be exported into other societies' markets, however internationally criminal in origin or harmful to home societies' healthy survival they might be.*

The MAI went further. It sought to prescribe for the 29 leading economies of the OECD, without the prior leverage of debt required, the blanket right of foreign corporations to all of this *and* the further invasionary title to own or access without condition any natural resource, built infrastructure, government investment, or anything of any home society that could be bought or sold.

Throughout governments kept the negotiations secret, and assured populations that all was normal.

The emerging civil commons of the world formed itself against this further metastasis of the transnational occupation of societies. Through the new civil commons avenue of the Internet, through street demonstrations across the globe, and through in general a growing social immune recognition across borders, the MAI was stopped in the Spring of 1998. Remission was won for the time. In the uprising of social life against this latest advance of the life-eating circuits of 'the global market', the European Parliament voted overwhelmingly against the treaty as 'leaving populations unprotected', and without any regulatory commitment to 'sustainable economic growth, employment, healthy social relations, protection of the environment ... and cultural policies'.[41]

We may recall the words of the President of the US Council for International Business here. He declared the life-excluding nature of the MAI as unconditional, in perfect accord with the global market paradigm. 'We will oppose', he proclaimed, 'any and all measures to create or even imply binding obligations for governments or business related to the environment or labor.'[42] Despite the international immune resistance to this position and the European Parliament vote since, the MAI's government representatives remained within the paradigm's presumption of corporate money sequences as absolute with no right to be accorded to life. The Dutch State Secretary Van Dok replied, 'The European Parliament has nothing to say about it.'[43] That is, since the matter was not the jurisdiction of the Parliament, its view was not worth discussing – an 'externality' in the logic of the doctrine. The Secretary-General of the OECD, Donald Johnston, said all concerns for people and the environment raised by the MAI were 'nonsense'.[44] This is the transnational reflex to any life concern raised against the paradigm, a predictable equivalent of a word processor's incapacity to compute.

What we can observe here is a frontal conflict between the civil commons which is forming across borders and the money-sequence occupants of transnational trade institutions. The latter has all the world's major money-sequencing corporations and occupied government offices on its side. But it is confronted by the powers of an aroused social immune system and civil commons that now link across borders and grow by the day. The Chiapas uprising against NAFTA from January 1994 that has made Mexico ungovernable, the mass strikes of the French people against austerity market budgets seeking to remove pension rights and a completely unexpected change of national government within two years, indigenous and oil-worker alliances in Ecuador and Nigeria that expelled two of the world's most powerful corporations, Texaco and Shell, from their lands, the 1997 general strike against structural adjustment programmes in Korea that unseated the government and preceded the Asian meltdown, the refusal of Indian women and farmer peasants to accept the ownership of their seeds by WTO fiat, the fall of the Indian Congress government and the arrest of its leader for corruption who had tried to impose it – all of these are uprisings from the civil commons against the global market programme.

US President Bill Clinton, in June of 1998, spoke to the World Trade Organization. He said that it must 'open its doors to scrutiny and public participation'. He also recognized for the first time by any head of state 'the race to the bottom' of transnational corporate cost cutting that was depredating societies and environments. He even said the unspeakable for captured governments, that there should be 'environmental protections' and 'labor standards'. 'We should be levelling up,' he said to the WTO, 'not levelling down.' Predictably, Clinton's statement was greeted 'with a resounding silence'.[45] The standpoint of life requirements is repelled automatically by the money-sequence paradigm and its agents.

Yet a deep general fact holds beneath the surface, and even the awakening social immune recognition. Most of the universal standards required to protect human and environmental life are already in place. The greatest normative achievement of the civil commons on the international level was won by 1950. Universal laws to regulate the conduct of nations across borders began in earnest on the sacrificial pyre of tens of millions of people after the Second World War. These norms of conduct were agreed to by governments, signed as solemn covenants, contested in their normative content by no state on the public record, and in principle protect all citizens and citizen bodies without exception. They are, again, the elements of the evolved substructure of the civil commons and its social immune resources that have not yet emerged to social life-hosts as their shared life-compass and codified regulatory system to recognize and turn back the money sequences occupying societies. Disoriented governments and electorates have not yet recognized that not only is the global market system decoupled from its life-hosts' requirements of vital existence. It is also a lawless regime which daily ignores, violates and overrides the entire body of established life-protective international law developed to inhibit deadly forces of transnational aggression.

Up until 1998, the safety and protection of human and environmental life have been completely excluded from all transnational trade agreements except the European Union's Social Chapter. Tens of thousands of regulations of the WTO, the NAFTA, the MAI and hundreds of bilateral trade structures prescribe rights in exact detail, but attend only to the guarantee of the rights of transnational capital and commodities *against* regulation by public authority. Investment and commodity claims to legal protection in this money-sequence universe are absolute and universal. Human or environmental life's claim to value or right is not binding in one subsection.

Until the NAFTA, the term 'environment' was not mentioned in any international 'free trade' regime, even in rhetoric. It is not once mentioned in the many volumes of the GATT/WTO. Now the key concept 'protection of human animal or plant life or health' occurs in certain NAFTA articles (that is, Articles 709–24, 902–13), with no protection in fact *required*. This seems, at best, an ambivalent advance – an advance of words with no substance. This is the global market's way. Words and images substitute for reality where reality demands a response. But more remarkable and disturbing is the fact that the NAFTA which does *mention* the issue of 'life protection', identifies only international *environmental* agreements which can prevail over private trade right. It says nothing of *human* rights laws or obligations at all. Yet solemn, universal covenants of human rights – such as the very central Universal Declaration of Human Rights – were ratified and signed by governments across the world half a century ago. How could such cornerstone international law be blanket-excluded when these trade agreements themselves are strictly enforced as internationally binding?

On the one hand, we could conclude that this arrangement is lawless, and expresses a final usurpation of human civilization by a barbarian value programme. On the other hand, one can also seek to build on what is there as an unprecedented *advance in international law itself*, despite the absolutist bias deforming its current expression. As we well know, international law has been to this point more or less impossible to enforce. Either its covenants and articles have been treated as mere paper, or its exceptional enforcement has been driven by the geostrategic demands of the transnational corporations' central host, the United States government. What these trade agreements have shown, despite their pathology of money-sequence invasion, is that there *can in fact be enforceable international law*. Articles have been codified in the finest detail, international dispute-resolution mechanisms have been instituted, and multilateral rulings have been prescribed and complied with across borders of formerly alien social systems. Despite its so far deranged imbalance and blindness to the requirements of planetary and human life, transnational trade regimes have achieved an effective international co-ordination, regulation and enforcement that has not before been approached.

It is this characteristic, which has made every major international head of state believe that 'the global market' and 'world trade' are all for a higher good, the '*multilateral*' reorganization of the world, beyond the narrowness and divisiveness of 'national self-interest' and 'protectionism'. Trade of commodities and circulation of investment capital, in this immuno-incompetent view, replaces military conquest and destruction as 'the way of nations' competing on the global stage'.

There is an important core of truth to what has so far been a mask for carcinogenic money-sequence invasion. 'Free trade' regimes have been effective forms of transnational regulation of money-sequence competition. Is this a great step forward, or the final institutionalization of global market occupation? Is it the framework of global society's maturation beyond military nationalism, as it pretends, or the borderless metastasis of a carcinogenic code borne and spread by the disease-vector of a corporate plutocracy?

Given the difficulty of reversing this tidal shift, and given the common framework of relations at the economic base of life that has been instituted, we are confronted with an historic dilemma. Either we seek to turn the tide back by national abrogation of these disordered regimes which are now accountable to no interests of human or environmental life-requirement. Or – for societies for whom it is too late to turn back – we seek to '*harmonize upwards*' instead of downwards, and turn the enforceable frameworks of international and world trade law into a balanced regulatory structure made effectively accountable to norms of life-protection.

If we bear in mind the previous century of developing national and international standards for the protection of human, social and environmental life against programmes of virulent totalist rule which have attacked societies in the past, we can put this new phenomenon in a wider-lensed perspective. The world has in place 'solemnly pledged' laws for protecting human life, all signed by the world's governments over a century. This has been the codified response of the civil commons over decades of struggle to militant fanaticisms of special interest claiming a right to rule the world. This emergent normative order of life protection has been cast in known law to regulate across states and classes. Its achievement is unprecedented in history. It has been paid for in the blood of tens of millions. The societies of the world have the Nuremburg Charter, the Universal Declaration of Human Rights, the International Covenant on Civil and Political Rights, the International Covenant on Economic, Social and Cultural Rights, the Conventions for Prevention of Torture, the Prevention and Punishment of the Crime of Genocide, the Elimination of all Forms of Racism, and the Political Rights of Women as a body of codified international law. Most significantly, it has the 1974 Charter of Economic Rights and Duties of States which declares the 'inalienable right' of governments 'to regulate and supervise the activities of transnational corporations'.

All of these norms of law are unified by a single, underlying principle – *to safeguard human life from harm by forces of ascendant power*. The great majority of the globe's nations are already signatories to these world covenants and conventions, and are obliged by their contractual agreement to comply with their life-protective terms.

The problem is that none of these global norms is yet applied. They have no framework of effective authority to ensure compliance with their life-protective norms. But this problem can be straightforwardly resolved. It does not require 'world armies' or 'interference in the internal affairs of other nations'. Effective application *requires only the binding recognition of these life-protective laws in international trade agreements.* Just as, say, the Montreal Protocol on Substances that Deplete the Ozone Layer or other international environmental agreements and conventions have recently been allowed to prevail over NAFTA obligations, so other codified international agreements to protect human and environmental life can be recognized by a more precise device. If transnational trade agreements were to be lawful rather than lawless, international covenants on human rights and environmental protection could be made normatively effective by non-military means.

We know why codified international agreements to protect human and planetary life are *not* now recognized by international trade agreements. The obligation to comply with international law is repudiated because the global market programme does not relate to any interest beyond its own money sequences. Its prescriptive sequences of multiplying money for those investing money rules out all life needs and requirements a priori. All that counts in its value metric is sale, profit, and price. The existing body of life-protective international law could become enforceable within international trade agreements *by the conscious instrumentation of this monetary self-maximization itself.* That is, the signatory states from which transnational corporations exported their products would have to comply with these norms of codified international law *as a condition of the free entry of their products into other societies' markets.* Otherwise, the sale of these foreign products in other societies would be subject to tariff or non-tariff barriers for the exporting party's violation of international law.

Under a rule of law, international trade agreements would simply specify that existing international law protecting human rights shall prevail in trade disputes without violation of trade agreement. Without such recognition of law, these trade treaties are clearly lawless in design. It is symptomatic of our condition that such a basic fact has not yet arisen as an issue of public discussion. Transition to a rule of existing law would not be difficult. Just as NAFTA has been obliged to admit such a condition into its Article 104 with respect to specified environmental conventions, so established international law on human rights can be so recognized.

This seems a minimal concession to moral sanity. Importing societies would then be able to at least block entry of commodities into their markets whose manufacture or extraction in foreign nations violated recognized international law.

There would be no question here of 'interfering with the internal affairs of other nations', the standard pretext for impunity in violating the most basic human rights to produce market goods at 'competitive prices'. Nations which seek free access to the markets of other countries to sell their goods would be obliged, on the contrary, to *exercise* their national sovereignty by complying with basic international law, in particular law which they have solemnly pledged to uphold. Importing societies would no longer be compelled, as now, to keep their domestic markets open to foreign commodities which have been manufactured or extracted in outlaw nations which are known to be guilty of gross and systematic violations of human rights, including by mass murder and genocide. If the norms of 'national sovereignty' and 'internal affairs' are to be appealed to, it is surely the importing country which has the prior right to determine whether its citizens will aid and abet international crime by purchasing its effects.

International law and national law which duly recognize it in matters of the most heinous international crimes – war crimes, crimes against humanity, genocide, mass murder, systematic torture and slave labour – are now completely excluded from the terms of current transnational trade treaties. Not only are these most primary laws of civilization excluded. Current transnational trade regimes implicitly require, as we have seen, that all such international law is *overridden*. For their articles of trade prohibit all 'tariff or other barriers' to incoming products, even if they are manufactured in death camps. No society has a right to 'discriminate' on 'extra-jurisdictional grounds'. Therefore there is under these new trade arrangements no jurisdiction from which to resist even genocidal commodities being exported into one's country. Under the emergent regime of transnational trade, nations must accept such products 'to honour trade obligations'.

Since no government is permitted to 'discriminate against' commodities entering its society for sale even if made in human blood, the implication is clear. These trade regimes provide secure trade protection and abetment to any crime against humanity which is committed by signatory nations. No other country may 'discriminate' against their exported products, even if they are proven to be manufactured from the raw materials of a genocidal clearance. The work of slave or child labour, or the 80-hour weeks of a militarily terrorized people with no rights to speak, to organize or to live free from torture are shielded by trade impunity. The offending corporations are protected, that is, against any trade barrier to the sale of their products at 'more competitive prices' in other societies' markets, with all right to refuse their entry abolished by international trade law. This is how a programme of value can become an inhuman monster. These implications in principle have already been systematically carried out in fact.

The GATT/WTO and the NAFTA explicitly prohibit 'extra-jurisdictional' considerations as a ground for tariff or other barrier to foreign commodities. The Multilateral Agreement on Investment among the 29 nations of the OECD specifies the same prohibition. Societies cannot discriminate in trade against international crimes, even the most heinous violations of international law, unless these crimes occur 'within their territories'. This is to 'avoid trade disputes', and to ensure there are 'no barriers to the free flow of capital and goods'. The whole catechism of the money-code of value is proclaimed in defence of *keeping out* 'disputes about human rights' from international trade arrangements.

But there is, in truth, more than the mere issue of avoiding trade disputes at stake here. There is the issue of compliance with existing international law. We are referring here to the very norms of civilization over which the Second World War was allegedly fought, as well as wars since, and upon whose regulatory civil commons base any global order is required to be founded to be lawful. The issue here goes to the heart of human civilization. Yet transnational trade regimes now make it *illegal to comply with these laws* by the entailment of their terms. This is the primary marker of their pathogenic nature.[46]

These problems have not gone unremarked by corporate executives who are still grounded in life reality. A former director of the Shell Group asks: 'Will companies buy the products of forced or prison labour? Will they use the army or the police to defend their installations? Will they buy arms without adopting international norms in their use? All these things have happened ... Companies have a clear choice: to use what influence they have, or to do nothing.'[47]

The CEO of Reebok International adds: 'Now the interesting thing about being aware is that you're stripped of everyone's favourite excuse, the excuse of ignorance ... Yet how can we disclaim responsibility? ... 100 million to 200 million kids are at work, many, many chained to a kiln or a loom, sold as bonded labourers at as young as three years of age, many tortured indiscriminately ... With Nike's leadership in market share and Reebok's leadership in human rights [contractual standards of human and labour rights], I believe the collaboration could be awesome.' Nike Inc. declined to respond to the invitation.[48]

To 'aid and abet' a crime means, under law, any 'act which facilitates the commission of the offence'. Purchasing a commodity which is produced by a criminal action clearly 'facilitates' the continuance of that action. It delivers money and profit to the perpetrator of the offence. By doing so, it also sustains the criminal intent and action of the perpetrator, who is encouraged by this profitable outcome to persist. The complicit party too is rewarded by access to the perpetrator's home markets and resources in reciprocity. It follows, therefore, that this facilitation, encouragement and profit from international crimes of the gravest kind under law – genocide, murder, torture, slave labour, gross and indiscriminate violation of human rights – constitutes a *joint* violation of law. Both the perpetrating party and its aiders and abettors benefit from the violation by mutual profit.

Precisely such relationships among perpetrators and abettors of international crimes are ongoing and increasing within the global market system. Not only are they ongoing, but WTO and other trade regimes specifically *prohibit* any trade action against international criminal acts. *The sole generalizable and peaceful recourse available to law-abiding nations, refusal to trade, is thereby ruled out.* In consequence, entire nations of citizens are compelled to be party to these crimes by the requirement that their countries must admit the products of criminal processes of extraction or manufacture into their domestic markets for profitable sale. It is in this sense that these transnational trade agreements *themselves* are criminal under international law by ruling out compliance with the most basic laws of the community of nations.

The issue here is not recognized. But it is an issue which societies claim to go to war about. How then can it be that nations who purport to respect international law continue to increase their financial support and collaboration with trading partners incontestably guilty of the most heinous violations of international law by war crimes, crimes against humanity, genocide, mass murder, enslavement, and systematic torture? China, for example, is demonstrably guilty of all these crimes in Tibet, and so is Indonesia in East Timor and, in the past, in Bali and Java. The same is true of the state of Nigeria and its partner, Shell Oil, in their plunder of the Ogoni people in oil-rich Ogoniland. All these crimes have also been perpetrated in the highlands of Guatemala, and elsewhere against indigenous peoples in oil or resource-rich regions. The State Law and Order Council in Burma also clears its lands of people for foreign investment in oil and tourism. All of this is done with the *prescribed* complicity and abetment of other nations under transnational trade conspiracy.

Where justification is thought necessary, it argues that this profitable complicity with criminal violators is in fact good. This is predictable from the programme. Whatever promotes 'the free circulation of capital and commodities' realizes with the summum bonum of the doctrine. It is even argued that this is beneficial to the victims because it will 'bring freedom and democracy' to the afflicted societies. These justifications are the subjective correlative of the cancer sequence. They are repeated as mantras whenever the issue of human rights arises. The case of Burma is vivid. The Nobel Laureate and elected leader of her people, Aung San Suu Kyi, has specifically addressed the issue. Told of the British Foreign Minister's tirelessly recited claim that 'through commercial contracts with democratic nations such as Britain, the Burmese people will gain experience of democratic principles', she replied as follows (emphases added): 'Not in the least bit, *because the so-called market economy is only open to some. Investors will only help a small elite to get richer and richer. This works against the very idea of democracy.'*[49] The Dalai Lama has also seen through this mask of the invasive disorder. In October of 1992 in a long personal audience, he said to me: 'The Chinese government is destroying my country, killing my people, and still Western countries make only greater trade relations with China.'

The problem here is not 'human nature' or 'Asiatic authoritarianism'. It is, at bottom, a problem of the lawlessness of transnational trade regimes. Once transnational trade agreements are made compliant with international law, then offending corporations and captive governments will have an interest in restraining their systemic complicity with atrocities. Otherwise their failure to honour their commitments will expose their exports and entries into other societies' markets to lawful trade barrier. As with domestic law, citizens would have to have legal standing to pursue legal remedy and register complaints – as they are now excluded from doing in any matter under these regimes.

In considering the rule of law so far overridden by the global corporate usurpation, it is worthwhile having before us the definition of a 'crime against humanity' as this is now specified in criminal codes, and as it is already applied within societies to parties which have committed these crimes 'extra-jurisdictionally':

> 'Crime against humanity' means murder, extermination, enslavement, deportation, persecution or any other inhumane act or omission that is committed against any civilian population or any identifiable group of persons, whether or not it constitutes a contravention of the law in force at the time and in the place of its commission, and at that time and in that place, constitutes a contravention of customary international law or is criminal according to the general principles of law recognized by the community of nations.[50]

Once international law is included in now rogue trade regimes, there are also long-recognized international labour norms to be complied with. Underlying all of these norms too is the single, unifying principle of life-defence which regulates the social immune infrastructure of society in general, and which is here protective of all members of society so far as they work rather than money-sequence for a living. Since committed function for the social life body is what any society or civil commons is borne by, and since its labour functions are its materially constructive life functions, labour's life is to be protected and enabled as the very substance of any life economy. Workers themselves in the collective agency of workers' movements and unions have over generations achieved a system of life protection in advanced jurisdictions such as Europe, and thereby for all of society – leading the building of the modern civil commons in such areas as universal health-care, education, pensions, unemployment income security and minimum wages. But in the mutant money sequences of the global market which have decoupled from the life-ground of society itself, there is no regulation to protect or enable life, *including the lives of the global market's most numerous market agents.*

This is not because universal and recognized norms of worker life defence have not been developed and agreed to across national boundaries and continents. In fact, there is an evolved, codified and transnational structure of life-sequence norms to cover workers as a 'factor of production' in market economies which the International Labor Organization of the United Nations administers – for example, comprehensive standards of life security, the employment of children, migrant workers, and workplace safety. Included in rather than excluded from transnational trade regimes, these requirements of life protection would block money sequences from consuming the lives of workers across the globe. They would do so by ruling out *as a condition of access to other societies' markets* such tumorous effects of the global corporate system as hundreds of millions of child labourers working around the clock, systematic persecution of union organizers, and employers demanding 80-hour work weeks in disease-causing conditions.

We have seen that internationally codified rules *can* rigorously prescribe a round-the-world protection by thousands of articles and subsections. No distance is too far, no enforcement too rigid to ensure safety of transborder movement for the rights of the money sequence to royalty payments from peasants, prosecution of governments for policies to provide subsidies to local food to eat, or continuous monitoring of 130 nations' economies to ensure compliance with unconditional transnational corporate rights to their home markets. But if the global market agent owns only her own life and limb to sell, then this mutant global system denies all rights of protection. In fact, *not a single right of the seller of labour is mentioned in thousands of pages of articles of trade regulation, even if labour is the vast majority of people's only commodity of sale in the global market.* 'Bills of rights for corporations' does not adequately capture the structuring of rights here. They are 'bills of *no* rights to workers' or, more accurately, since workers with rights before have no rights here, 'bills to abolish the rights of workers'.

Thus, these trade regimes rule out no violation of human life. The disorder here can be formulated in a simple categorical principle which is the system decider of the entire regime: *All rights to money demand on life, no rights to life itself.* Thus, exposure of workers to poisonous air and lethally hazardous substances, 17-hour days and disease-producing conditions, life-endangering demands, child and forced labour and threat of death for union organizing – all these devour the lives of workers with no regulatory inhibition. It is in such ways that the wage share and real incomes for workers have fallen across the world for two decades in the global market and for over 50 per cent are below absolute poverty levels, that undernourishment, malnourishment and starvation afflict 1.8 billion people, that independent unions are illegal, attacked or diminishing across boundaries, and that 100 corporations compete to sell instruments of torture in the global market to sustain the repression.[51]

It may be objected that the European Union has evaded the claw-hold into living labour's body that this system has instituted across the rest of the globe as 'a self-regulating market of free circulation of capital and commodities'. After all, it has a social chapter to protect life in its trade agreement that includes 'the right to work', 'the right to medical assistance', 'the right to social security', 'the right to protection against poverty', and so on. But because the selector law of global market money sequences is to reduce life input costs to a minimum towards zero, all such protections of life are computed as 'excessively costly'. The predictable result is mass unemployment in Europe – over 50 million workers without jobs and 2 million more thrown into long-term unemployment every year as delinked money sequences haemorrhage out from social hosts with life-protective regulations towards those with fewer or none.[52] This is perceived as the 'market discipline' of the system, namely, in effect, to reduce life to increase non-life growth. Thus one in six Europeans drops below the poverty line, children are hungrier by the millions, youth thuggery explodes in Germany and elsewhere as youth unemployment goes over 20 per cent, and the pattern of life depletion and destruction continues as predictably as a disease whose determinants are not controlled.[53]

Because it reduces the employer's costs of labour to work people as long as possible for as little as possible in the least costly conditions 'to compete in the global market', this system can only get worse as the supply of labour increasingly outpaces the global market's demand. This is a predictable decline for the lives of the two-thirds of the world's workers who are employed, and worse still for the third who are not. This systemic decline of life for the great majority of humanity in accordance with the self-regulating mechanisms of the global market has already occurred, in fact, and will progressively advance – the hallmark sign of a life-threatening disease – the longer global market money sequences are permitted to invade societies with no strict regulation by life-protective norms. The fact that the social immune system has already evolved and is in place to ward off the pathogenic invasion is the signal of an immune breakdown at the social level of life-organization. The missing link is consciousness *of* this breakdown itself to redirect the money sequences back into regulation by life-coded selectors.

The solution is time-tested. There have been developing laws prescribing and enforcing norms to protect the lives of worker members of the market economy for well over a century. It is only with the Great Reversion of the deregulated global market that the disease disorder of world life has worked its way into developed societies themselves so that nowhere is even the most secure workforce safe from the pathogenic life-stripping. This is because impelling every step of the global market's money sequences is its inherent drive to reduce costs and maximize appropriation for non-living corporate bodies as the overriding law of economic growth – the eventual formula of cancer for social hosts. Such a model is pathogenic by its nature. Not only does it require the life-protective norms of the civil commons to regulate it to defend all life-organization from its depredation. Money sequences themselves must be strictly limited to their domain of useful function, machine production, and made accountable in every life-damaging step to the evolved overseeing authority of the civil commons.

Selecting Against the Cancer: Regulating Money Sequences by the Established Civil Commons

Corporate taxation is one instrument of public authority to bring corporate entities into some committed function to social life-hosts *within* the movement of the money sequence itself. Taxation is imposed on the *output* side of the money sequence. It can be prescribed to receive back a reasonable share of the revenues required to sustain the public infrastructure and services that business depends on for every step of its transactions. Or it can be to recover costs and deter the negative externalities to social and environmental life-systems by natural resource severances, pollutions, wastes and other harms not paid for by corporate agents.

As earlier documentation has made clear, transnational corporations pay less and less in taxes for the infrastructure and services they receive from societies, and still less to pay back the immense costs of the damages they cause and the public resources they degrade or consume. The current transnational system not only favourably selects life-depredating corporations which move to investment sites with few or no environmental regulations, labour standards and human rights protections. It also selects for comparative advantage those corporate money sequences which evade tax obligations to social life-hosts. In these ways, the self-regulating global market promotes money sequences which exploit and loot social and environmental life-organizations. We have observed how the various money sequences have so mutated in this direction that their original middle term of means of life has been progressively displaced, at the same time as their negative externalities to human and ecological life have become more devastating. Government taxation is one of the systemic inhibitors which can resist the disease invasion.

But taxation is what global market rationality repels by its nature. Indeed, cost-cutting businesses gravitate by the laws of the market to those societies or regions which not only exempt them from taxes, but provide them well with cash-equivalent *subsidies* of great variety so that they become 'net tax recipients'. This food cycle of corporate money sequences consuming public revenues they contribute less and less to is called 'incentives to invest': which means, in effect, redistribution of public wealth to corporate money sequences. The global market competition to avoid taxation has by this process advanced to the stage that resists any taxation at all.

As public revenues are redistributed to uncommitted money sequences, there are further demands for 'more efficient government' to subsidize them with special supports (that is, more truck-gauge roads, cheap power-supplies, tougher prisons and police, more international export-oriented government, market training and product research in place of education, privatization of profitable public sectors and facilities, and increased access to publicly owned natural resources at nominal or no cost).

All of this global pattern combines further with compound-interest-rate exhaustion of societies by banks and money lenders. The net result is debt-imprisoned governments operating as servants and resource-suppliers to private corporations on the backs of working citizens paying ever more in regressive tax loads. The first line of resistance to this bleeding of social hosts by corporate tax evasion is a *minimum and transnational rate of corporation tax*.

The same arguments as applied to other minimum transnational standards apply here. Without common minimum standards, there will be no floor to the corporate competition to strip life costs towards zero. Common standards of corporate taxation or other minimum standards do not, as is often claimed, 'diminish competitiveness'. On the contrary, they elevate it towards 'the level playing field' of equal rules claimed as desirable by global market agents. But here the equal rules serve life, not money sequences.

The motivation to comply with a minimum tax standard is, as with all such standards of an international market, access to other societies' internal markets. The condition for access is compliance with the standard, or no access. This is the principle of current trade regimes, but the standards protect only transnational corporations. To require such standards is not 'interference in other nations' sovereign affairs', another upside-down mask behind which transnational corporations hide. It is an exchange of rights and obligations so far usurped by transnational traders.

On the micro-level, tax evasion by individuals is just as systemic as by corporations in the sociopathic global market. One-third of all financial assets deposited by individuals were in off-shore financial hideaways by 1997.[54] It requires the same transnational regulation to defend social bodies. Most fundamentally, a minimum standard transnational tax on speculative and unproductive financial transactions is required if social hosts are to resist the money-sequence cancer spreading through their life-support systems.

Throughout, the logic of the civil commons of life-protective standards remains the same. Select against what attacks and depletes social life-organization rather than for to turn the tide of the cancer's advance. In particular, an international tax at source on all 'spot conversions' of one currency into another is required to stem the massive outflows of life-sustaining resources from societies. Spot conversions are the moving edge of the carcinogenesis, transforming the mediums of metabolism of social bodies into predatory sites of money-to-more-money feeding.

If the currency attacks continued, their taxation would return sufficient revenues to societies for shared risk insurance against them. But the margins are so small in these large-volume exchanges that a fraction of one per cent of taxation would probably render them unviable as money sequences. In 1998, there were $2 trillion of such international transactions every day, 97.5 per cent of all foreign exchange transactions (compared to under 20 per cent in 1975).[55] All such transactions are *tax-exempt* in the global market, as opposed to life goods which are taxed across populations. Here again we see the pathological selection for money sequences. It is compounded by interest and capital gain write-offs to favour them further, even where they attack society's life-fabric.

A minimal tax on all such speculative currency transactions is, in fact, a very conservative social immune response. But the closer one gets to the predatory circuits of the global market, the more aggressive and incoherent their culture becomes. Any obligation beyond the freedom of money-demand to become more money-demand in uncontrolled self-multiplication is repudiated by captive governments themselves. Finance Ministers repudiate any tax at all, even a quarter of one per cent, as 'unenforceable'. Central bankers react with the absurd response that a tax on international money speculations is 'counterproductive'. The nations of the European Union itself peg to a single currency with loss of their control over social spending as well as exchange and interest rates in order to escape the beast attacking them.[56]

We see here the global market derangement in its purest form. The life-stripping code of money-for-more-money displays its carcinogenic marker in full flag. The absolute refusal to commit an iota of tax-obligation of hundreds of billions of dollars of money-demand on societies to the social life-hosts being predated is a cancer growth without inhibition. As it moves across all borders of restraint past succumbing governments we can observe it in metastasis. The collapse in months of the world's model market economies in Asia by unregulated money sequences with no commitment or function to their social hosts could hardly have exposed the systemic breakdown in clearer light.[57]

To recognize the depth of the immune disorder here, recognized as 'a problem' even by its agents from their standpoint as citizens, we need to bear in mind that a minimum tax for financial transactions or currency speculations is easier to impose than most terms of existing trade treaties. It was originally the concept of an economist specializing in transnational financial transactions, the Nobel laureate James Tobin, and has since become immediately viable by great advances of capacities of transnational electronic monitoring within a unified global trade regime. Digital tracking of money transactions can be achieved by far more direct and convenient device than the processing of a simple sales tax. Collection of the tax can be a very popular condition of membership in the GATT, or any other trade regime. The right to deal in the world's G-7 financial centres, where over 80 per cent of international currency speculations take place, can be contingent on consistent compliance with the regulation. Governments can co-operate in a financial tax's application across borders, and prosecute its violation as in any other crime, but with immeasurably greater ease of detection. The very small number of agents involved is far more easily regulatable than the hundreds of millions of people bound by other laws. Three-quarters of global spot transactions are inter-dealer exchanges, and focused in large trading institutions. Conversion to securities other than money to evade the tax are costly, risky and less liquid.[58] In short, nothing prevents an international standard tax on currency speculations, or financial transactions in general except *the refusal to apply it*. Once again, we see how the global market's carcinogenic programme has occupied social hosts, with the finance and banking sectors of government the vectors of the disease within societies' regulatory organizations themselves.

As money-to-more-money circuits become increasingly autonomous, social consciousness more than ever fetishizes money demand as the sovereign authority of the world issuing imperatives that must be obeyed. The lifeblood of societies' civil commons and citizens' livelihoods is circulated away to 'pay off deficits as a national emergency,' 'reduce social costs to attract investors,' 'cool down the employment rate to ward off currency devaluation', 'deregulate the labour and resource markets economy for greater efficiencies', and so on. The litany for expropriation is recited every week, and it is everywhere the disguise for the underlying advance of money-sequence invasions reducing the sustenance of life sequences to feed on.

What is not acknowledged is the unseen seat of the disease invasion – *that money sequences are overloaded far beyond the capacity of social and environmental capacities to carry them,* and *increasingly attack life-serving functions to continue their decoupled growth.* Insofar as they are without productive outcome of any kind, more and more generate wealth to the economically parasitic, deprive the civil commons and the poor, and progressively demand ever more revenue extraction from social hosts, their reproduction is incompatible with societies' survival and development.

This overloading and pathologization of money sequences is, in fact, behind every crisis people face in the global market – behind the stressing and breaking of the planetary environment's carrying capacities, behind government debt and deficit loads and crises across the world, behind the ceaseless mergers, acquisitions and job-sheddings by corporate finance departments, behind the speed-ups of every process of work and resource extraction, behind the privatization and enclosure of evolved civil commons heritages in every culture, behind at this historical juncture the Asian meltdown and the great slump of Japan itself.

We need not summarize all the symptoms. But consider some figures of money-demand aggregates increasing exponentially on life systems at every level, every new unit of the escalating load requiring 'more competitive performance' or 'more competitive cost cutting' from individual, social and environmental life-hosts, with no limit set to the breakdown of their vital capacities which will be demanded. Bear in mind that every one of these demand inputs advances by compounding increase as long as the global market system continues its life-attacking growth. Bear in mind as well that the meaning of 'discounted cash flow' which is the moving line and reference body of global market value, means that what is today $100 in real terms is *the same as* $100 + compound interest in one year ($110), two years ($121), or 20 years from now as the *starting base* from which 'worthwhile enterprise' is calculated. The system is by its inner logic a horizonlessly expanding money-demand machine engineering all that lives *to extract more money value from it, to reduce the costs of continuing its existence, or to extinguish it as of no money worth.* If the victim societies melt under the 'free circulation' of the hot money flows, then this is because they did not 'adapt effectively'. The processes of natural and cultural selection here confront their systemic re-ordering to carcinogenic money sequences as 'the new reality'.

For example, the global market calculus assumes that to an input of $10,614 in 1955 an output of at least compound interest multiplication will be set into motion as new money demand ever after and, in stock funds, $5,309,000 in 1998 (that is, an over 500-times increase in 43 years).[59] This 500-times increase is what goes to 'the investor' who performs no function in the increase, nor in the productive economy to receive this increase, nor in serving the life of any life-organization to be entitled to all further exponential multiplications.

In 1998, the combined money-demand value of US pension and mutual funds to whom this multiplication is promised was $9 trillion, or 30 times the net money worth of the US's 60 richest market agents, with more new money-demand going into these funds every quarter than all the US superrich own together.[60] These were predicted to grow at the rate of at least the rate of the past, perhaps much faster. At the same time, both British and Canadian national pension funds planned to redistribute all of their public funds into the global market of transnational money sequences as well, instead of as in the past lending to governments, investing in jobs for the young, or committing to any defence or growth of life at all. Meanwhile the poverty of children, dead-end youth prospects and the slips in environmental carrying capacity in both societies continued to climb.[61]

During this collapse of life-system bearings and money-sequence metastasis, the once mighty machine-shop of the contemporary world, Japan, came to the end of the line. It reached the *surplus money wall* in the early 1990s, performing as a harbinger of the disorder no-one saw. When the speculatively driven prices of real estate and Nikkei stocks plunged, and the richest banks in the world could not find productive enterprises to invest in and steward as their successful automobile and electronic industries had done since 1950 by long-term, careful financial ministry planning, Japan's money sequences had no way out. When the hundreds of billions of uncommitted money-demand first invaded and then exited Asian stocks and currencies in 1997–98, leaving societies there on average halved in their money access to means of existence, Japan was left with hundreds of billions of debt that could not be paid by the lenders, and no outlets in place for money-sequence advances behind the armed force of land clearances and forced market openings favoured by its US corporate competition. Its own economy was shrinking in money-rated output, unemployment was still relatively low at under 5 per cent, interest rates were near zero at 1.5 per cent, and it controlled *$12 trillion* in loose money with no connected function to any real economy. Japan's predicament was perceived as its sin of 'declining growth'. But with its unmoored banks loaded with a secretive trillion in bad loans and in danger of imploding, Japan's government pumped over $200 billion of still more, public funds into new capital and back-ups. Robotically lock-stepping to the global market paradigm, the IMF and the US government demanded still *more* borderless financial deregulation, just as they had prescribed for all the economies of Asia that had already been melted down by such borderless financial deregulation.[62] Japan's government, not recognizing the gallows wit and still locked in the paradigm themselves, promised 'a big bang' of more deregulation in Japanese financial markets.

When a long dominant paradigm fails in its prescriptions, it calls for more of its failed prescriptions to solve its failures. Its circularity becomes terminal. What is not recognized is the underlying principle of the escalating failures: that *financial crises always follow from money-value delinked from real value,* which has many names but no understanding of the principle at its deepest levels. In the case of Japan and the Asian economies, every phenomenon of their crises follows from self-multiplying, uncontrolled money-demand leveraged into ever more money-demand seeking only what can make it still more with no connection back to real value or the requirements of life itself. As long as Japan stuck to planning and financing within the means available to it, the construction of efficient light automobiles or electronic commodities by long-term planning, it led the world for decades. Then it lost its bearings of both productive and national priorities in the floods of super-leveraged, borderless and decoupled money circuits. The rest has been history.

In fact, this is another variation on the inner story of the global market paradigm which has eaten away social bodies across the world – first, the Vietnam War on borrowed money that produced no life-goods but destroyed them, then the rushes of loose oil money after the price hikes into Third World societies in compound-interest loans with no integrated linkage to their life economies, all along the arms race of the US and the USSR bankrolled by ever more credit money with no base for products which did not serve but sapped the life economy, backgrounded by the debt-led boom of junk commodities and services with no life-enabling function that leaves an ever more polluted and wasted world behind. These are all phenomena of the money sequences of $\$ \rightarrow C(-) \rightarrow \$^1$, $\$ \rightarrow C\text{-}(-) \rightarrow \$^1$, and $\$ \rightarrow D \rightarrow \$^1$ which were formalized in the last chapter.

But the disorder only began to strip economies of their social infra-structures, hollow out their job and livelihood bases and melt them down overnight when the money sequence of $\$ \rightarrow \$^1 \rightarrow \$^2 \rightarrow \$^n$ was deregulated altogether to become maximally more anywhere at anytime, at any velocity or volume, with no social conditions attached. Recall that between 1947 and 1973 before the money sequences decisively mutated into socially decoupled self-multiplication, the real GNP of Europe rose as much as in the previous two centuries put together.[63] The rapidly evolving social economies and falling profit takes that accompanied this growth were a provocation. Within a few years, the world entered the hot circuits of the cancer stage of capitalism, called 'freedom' in the global market, where no committed function of any kind to any life-organization inhibited aggregate money-demand multiplying as an end in itself.[64]

None of this is necessary. Unlike cancer at the cellular level of life-organization, all of it is preventible. The missing base from a financial standpoint is that the currency of the cancer circuits, money itself, is not printed or controlled by public authorities as constitutions require. Currency and coinage, issue of paper money, bills of exchange and promissory notes, interest charges and legal tender – in short, all forms of money – have been in principle under sovereign governments' legal control from the beginning of the market epoch. But with the creeping takeover by the global market regime, these traditional government powers have been secretly wrested away or abdicated beneath the notice of electorates. Money-demand itself, what people assume they must earn, is daily manufactured by private finanical institutions in ever newer forms of M-2, M-2+, M-2++, M-3, M-3+, L, and so on. Monetary dogma cannot admit that money has broken free of its anchor, and so leave it multiplying in its mutant forms while squeezing only government money and social expenditures. The private demand multiplication itself is driven at the base by continuously creating and issuing debt at compound interest with no legal-tender reserves to ground it. What counts as 'capital requirements' in place of reserves is itself massively asset-inflated (as Japanese banks learned when their real-estate and stock market holdings were suddenly halved in value). It is this privately fabricated money-demand multiplication that drives the carcinogenic circuits.

A direct solution to this problem was long ago proposed by an unlikely source, the arch monetarist, Milton Friedman himself. He advocated that private banks and financial institutions should be kept out of the money-creating business altogether by a government requirement of *100 per cent reserves on all loans they issue*. 'The chief function of the monetary authorities [of the federal government would be] the creation of money,' counselled Friedman. This was an opinion shared with others, including Friedman's more consistent mentor at the University of Chicago, William Simon. The government '*would leave as the chief monetary function of the banking system the provision of depository facilities, facilities for check clearance, and the like*'.[65]

Such a policy, perfectly in accord with long-existing law, would deprive the money-sequence cancer of its growth sustenance overnight. It can only establish itself and invade on the basis of demand it leverages far beyond its possession and in contradiction to its hosts' life needs. Applied to historical trends, this means that there is no invasion of military war, compound-interest public debt, unneeded megaproject, currency speculation, foreign takeover, unwanted merger, pollutive technology, or any other systemic invasion of life in the transnational market which does not depend on this unseen pathway of invading its life-hosts. *The cancer-set goes only so far as the money-demand the money sequence creates for itself. No further. This is the inner law of its growth and spread, and of its gatekeeping by public authority.*

None of this is meant to deny the need for credit beyond legal tender. Confining money creation to the limits of gold-based legal tender is a prescription for depression, the other extreme. The original American revolution was fought, according to Benjamin Franklin, not so much over a tea tax as over the removal from the Colonies of their right to create money – 'colonial scrip'. This publicly created money was 'issued in proper proportions to the demands of trade and industry', and it brought them continuous prosperity until it was prescriptively replaced at the behest of the private Bank of England by gold-and-silver coinage which dried up the money supply and brought 'streets full of the unemployed'.[66] History repeats itself, the second time not as farce but as the pathological disorder of a paradigm that has seceded from reality.

The Great Depression, more famously, was also sustained by restriction of money supply and credit. But *credit permission beyond legal tender is a system-deciding policy* which self-serving financial parties cannot be allowed to control and extend with no internal limit but their own private gain, as statesmen have understood over centuries.[67] Otherwise society develops a money cancer. Thus it has been in the global market. Public-sector Keynesianism has been replaced by privatized debt whose rapid-growth deficits show up in society's life rather than public accounts. Private money-demand multiplies itself beyond legal tender with no connection back to any productive standard, with no limit of leveraging ratio, with no relationship to the carrying capacity of the environment, and with no reference whatever to the life needs of societies and their members. This is the determinant set of the social carcinogenesis. It is either regulated back into consistency with the social and environmental life-ground it depletes and consumes, or its life-hosts will be progressively depredated by its uncontrolled self-multiplication.

If such a reclamation of constitutional authority over society's creation of money were to proceed, societies would quickly relieve themselves of the claw-hold debts and interest demands on their governments which have unravelled environmental and social life-fabrics across the global market. In fact, *public control of money creation and credit has long been a successful mode of robustly democratic market governments to sustain full employment, to pay back large debts and to grow their social infrastructures at the same time.* Instead of being bled by foreign money lenders on a permanent basis and sacrificing their civil commons to do it, they have lent the money and paid back the interest to themselves with elected governments as their civil commons in financial form.[68]

The practicality and liberative success of this method is the best kept secret in the global market. Canada since the 1930s has had a Bank of Canada Act which permits all of this up to 35 per cent of total federal debt, and with specific reference to its powers under government direction to 'regulate currency and credit in the best interests of the economic life of the nation', to 'mitigate by its influence fluctuations in ... unemployment', and 'to promote the economic and financial welfare of the nation'. This legislation was used on and off to achieve all of the above objectives until the mid-1970s. Then the linkage with the life economy of employment, social security and health-care, and freedom of the citizenry from foreign debt was severed by escalating foreign loans, privatizing the debt, increasing interest rates to 22.5 per cent prime to compound the drain on the treasury to emergency levels, abolishing all cash-reserve requirements, and seeking to change the Bank of Canada Act to make the preservation of the value of money the sole term of reference.[69]

In the European Union's Maastricht Treaty, completed in 1996, a similar logic of detaching central banks and the future European Central Bank itself from all ties to the life economy was engineered – by requiring that deficits be reduced to 3 per cent of GDP, thereby entailing raids on social programmes to conform; by abolishing the powers of member nations to increase or decrease money supply in place of commercial banks; and by removing all right of governments to control their country's interest rates to serve the common life interests of their people instead of solely to preserve the value of money. So far had the delinkage of banks from the life economy and electoral accountability been taken that the Treaty required of the European Central Bank only to 'maintain price stability' and 'remove all restrictions on the movement of capital' with, under Article 107, the explicit prohibition of 'any Member State' or 'other Community body or institution ... seek[ing] to influence' the ECB.[70]

Again, these mutations of public institutions into servitude to corporate money sequences has no ground in constitutional or other law, and indeed requires the overriding of both, as the Treaty itself implicitly acknowledges in Section 6:61, 'Legal Basis'. As elsewhere across the world, mutant institutions follow mutant money sequences in delinking monetary instruments from any accountability they have in law to the common life-interests of peoples, or from any accountability to any life-interest at all. The European Union, the most well-ordered economic organization in the world, had at this stage of its development succumbed to the carcinogenic programme, even though its advance had already resulted in the highest unemployment and poverty rates in the heart of Europe since the Great Depression, and ever lower ratios of investment in the real economy.[71]

Poland's planned entry into the Union was indicative of priorities. Eight million people on two million family farms were slated in 1998 for dislocation and removal by 'restructuring' plans. The secretary of the committee for EU integration commented, 'We will need to redeploy country dwellers.'[72] Even in the home of a social dimension to the global market system, the life economy was not affordable if lower costs for money sequences could be achieved by forcing eight million people from their homes and livelihoods, and turning the pastoral countryside into agribusiness farms and corporate monoculture. But here as well, there were codified bases for containment of the carcinogenic programme. The Maastricht Treaty still bore the commitment to 'a high level of employment and of social protection' in its Article 2. Social democrat governments were replacing financial parties in government power across the Union, France and Italy were intransigently opposed to the social programme reductions and sought more life economy initiatives, and Norway out of the Maastricht strait-jacket had near-full employment, no reductions of social security and increasing connection of oil revenues and employment to society's standards of life. As always with social life-organization, the carcinogenic sequences remained subject to curative intervention by the vehicle of the civil commons with all its evolving resources anchored in the life-ground. At the marrow of the matter, regulation of money supply and growth and its calibration of flows by interest rates to serve the life economy was to be the axis of life recovery.

In the pure-type situation, all money-creating powers revert to public authority, are tied to the rate of real economic growth so as to avoid inflation, and are lent to enterprises producing goods serving the life economy. While on the one hand, the European Central Bank was a monster of the corporate money sequence writ large, it could also be bound by its member governments and the Community constitutional base itself to be the instrument of decisively subordinating corporate money sequences to the life requirements of social and environmental hosts with no more intervention required in the economy than was already permitted by constitutions.

Private banks and financial institutions would in such a condition be returned to the normal rights of private market agents. They could continue to lend their money stocks as their stockholders chose, but on the basis of 100 per cent reserves rather than on the private creation of money for multiplying money sequences. Should this direct and constitutional reclamation of public authority over society's money creation and interest charges be achieved, there would be an end of the matter. Outside the circle of government debt, micro-credit agencies and statutorily recognized regional credit unions with functions tied to the life economy could provide monitored everyday credit for such purposes as local employment, small business loans, environmentally responsible extractions of resources, and all the life-serving functions now expelled from the global market. In the Third World subsistence economies and in the larger non-monetary economies in general across the world, peoples and societies can stick to the life economies of sustenance farming and mutual provision for each others' needs, and be infinitely better off without any relationship to foreign money lenders or export-crop schemes driven by leveraged money sequences expelling them from their lands, homogenizing their food crops for foreign markets, and debt-enslaving them.

This is a meta-story in itself. The emerging liberative agent in the Third World is the unwaged force of women who are not yet disconnected from the life economy by their work. They serve life, not commodity production. They are the hidden underpinnings of the world economy, and the wage equivalent of their life-serving work is estimated at $16 trillion.[73] But their enemy and the enemy of the life-ground is not yet clearly flagged. It has a simple core to its rogue programme, which leads the life-destructive invasions of this realm of the life economy as well – money-demand multiplying beyond cash reserves to become more money-demand subjugating life-hosts with no accountability to their survival.

Putting a stop to the *first determinant of this money-sequence invasion by 100 per cent reserves* for all international banks and financial institutions, and to the *second determinant by tying all interest-created money-demand to fulfilment of specified life requirements* is the pure-type way to arrest and reverse the carcinogenic advance in its tracks. Whether or not the life-appropriate resolution is possible in the circumstances of market-coded public bureaucracies and governments, it recognizes the concealed aetiology of the social anaplasia, the nature of its pathogenic invasion, and the social immune response to prevent its further metastasis. Every step of resistance to the cancer field can find its axial framework in the logic of this resolution.

In this light, we can observe such a course of treatment *admits of degrees.* Because all banks and financial institutions are ultimately the privileged creatures of government's discretionary entitlements, they are not in a position to claim the unconditional right of 'private property' so absolutized by other bearers of the market money code: a code which represses the distinction between money-multiplying sequences and productive property as the basis of its masking ideology. Banks, in fact, are perfectly unproductive institutions which have appropriated ever more monopolist control of people's money stocks and, in general, society's money creation and compound-interest returns. Because their self-regulation prescribes for delinked money-sequence multiplications alone, banks *select against* life-serving uses. The predictable consequences of this system is to dispossess shared life resources to increase corporate money-demand. Banks are the paragon of this pattern. Their loans and investments go ever more preponderantly to non-productive and life-destructive uses – asset-stripping buyouts, disemploying mergers, destabilizing speculations in currencies, gambling on stock-market derivatives, predatory repossessions, financing blanket takeovers of local firms by foreign multinationals, privatizing compound-interest loans which bleed public sectors dry, funding ecologically devastating mega-projects with no environmental or social criteria, co-financing lethal armaments manufacture for international sale, and selecting for ever more disease-causing transnational corporate processes and commodities as long as they maximize money returns. *All of these loans and investments are made on the basis of leveraging high ratios of demand to legal tender, which escalates the volume and velocity of the depredatory effects.*

It is clear, once exposed, that sociopathic loans and investments which raid and dispossess the very home societies which charter, provide money-stocks, insure and protect the private banks financing them is a systemic disorder. But this assault on social life bodies and their citizens is not an anomaly. It follows predictably from the system-deciders of the global market paradigm. Along with their partner financial institutions – the stock markets, the insurance corporations, and the financial arms of corporations which all conform to the same delinked money sequences in every decision – these predatory operations of big banks are *selected* for reproduction and growth by the system.

Socially destructive loans and investments which depend on domestic savers' money and societies' grants of bank charters can be controlled everywhere they occur *by means of the conditions they depend on.* The solution need not be society's revolutionary expropriation of the principal capital owners of society, and reconstruction of the economic structure into state ownership of the means of production. Such a solution does not take into account the long-evolved codification of law and existing public institutions of social life-organization which are torn apart by attempts to reconstruct society anew. This is the logic of the industrial engineering model of the global market which supposes that societies can be disaggregated and reaggregated to fit prescriptive mega-projects.

The long evolved codified fabric of society which protects and enables its members' universal access to life-goods – from individual rights to free speech and security of person to universal health-care, education and public spaces – is the civil commons bridge between society's past and its future which provides *already settled common ground* from which to grow. The demands of the global market system or other despotism advances by overthrow of this underlying civil fabric. Note how everywhere the self-regulating global market now extends, it restructures constitutions, established employment security, civil practices and age-old indigenous and village rights. 'Revolutionary changes' are a very old bourgeois shuffle. Successful social change is effected in the long term by building on what is life protective and enabling and already instituted in a social body. This is the life-code of the civil commons which develops across generations.[74]

As with life on the individual organic level, so with life on the level of social organization, only exact interventions have salutary effects. The inner logic of the cure is known. It is to make now uncontrolled money sequences and multiplications *accountable to known requirements of the life economy*. This normative restoration of the health of society's life is realized to the extent that *money-demand flows are calibrated to society's known life-requirements from the source of money creation and interest charges themselves – market society's economic marrow.*

If, for plain example, a market society clearly needs more money-demand to be directed towards creating more jobs to resolve its high rate of unemployment, which a self-regulating global market can never do, then it follows from the logic of a life economy that interest rates should be very low and long-term to domestic enterprises which create and maintain secure jobs. The requirement here is so obvious that only a paradigm severed from the life-requirements of its social hosts could systematically block it from view. This arrangement in some form has, in fact, already been long implemented in the form of social capital formation, special development banks and public infrastructure in the most competitively productive economies since the last century.

Such conditions for bank money lending could by well-articulated policy ensure not only higher employment, but thereby a more productive society, more diversified business activities, and a wider tax-base to fund society's public goods. Small businesses, which now create upwards of 90 per cent of new jobs in the world's economies, could be given lower rather than higher interest rates in proportion to jobs created, instead of being consistently under-credited and under-financed by banks whose decision-structure *selects* against these life functions. Enterprises qualifying for selection by not only their creation and maintenance of secure jobs, but also by jobs which served the life economy in new ways not attended to in the global market – for example, reclaiming socially excluded life for contributory functions – could not only be given low- or no-interest loans, but be financed with grants from specific money-supply pathways for life-sequence advances in the civil commons.

In short, a logic of interest and money creation *selecting for life growth rather than for corporate money growth* flows from a life economy paradigm. Micro-credit systems from Latin America to the Indian subcontinent, still on the backs of volunteer labour which is preferred by the World Bank to ensure containment, are proto-forms of life economy financing.[75] By the same principle of linkage of society's domestic money supply to society's most pressing life-requirements, interest rates of a life economy are calibrated proportionately *higher* for economic activities which create no life-good, and inaccessibly high for the lowest-ranked loans on a life-service scale (for example, currency speculation or armaments manufacture, which are now favoured because of their money-sequence scale). That there are now no interest-rate distinctions recognized by banks except as they serve the Mammon of aggregate money-sequence growth, and that in fact society's interest rates *rise* whenever livelihood gains by increased employment are registered, is another clinical sign of the social morbidity of this choice-structure.

Relating rates of interest to society's most basic life-requirements by distinction between enterprises which are productive for the life economy and enterprises which are not would by itself enable domestic economies to fulfil the actual common interest of societies. It would do so without a single intervention in private property rights.

Deployments of society's money-supply and interest-charge instruments for serving the common interest have a wide range of options. For example, there is a lethal lesion in the market's ability to provide financing for the research, development and production of life-protective products rather than life-destructive ones. Here too, a percentage of the overall loan and investment accounts of private banks, or of the tidal flow portfolios of *tax-deductible* pension funds, could be required as a condition for renewal of bank charters or for pension-fund deductibility.[76] Grounded in the life sequence, we can readily recognize that waste-and-pollution-reducing product substitutes and pollution-abatement technologies are required at an emergency level for the preservation of both local and planetary environments which are now degrading, losing biodiversity and collapsing at rates unprecedented in geographical time. The answer always given by corporate agents is that none of these product substitutes or technologies are possible until they become cost-competitive in the market. This is true, and why the global market paradigm is unequal to the global challenges which humanity faces.

In contrast, the life economy's system-deciders select for life's vital reproduction and growth. They select for economic responses to the emergency: for example, an international consortium enlisting the most advanced expertise to develop such processes and products by favourable financing and investment funds to ensure that what has to be achieved for planetary survival is achieved promptly. Instead of inventive products and processes of mass homicide, which the money-sequence paradigm now selects for many hundreds of billions of dollars of public financing, the life economy favours what reduces pollution, waste and species destruction. Its basis in funding through available monetary instruments of public financing, not privatized debt, also ensures that these life-protective measures against money-sequencing do not bankrupt society in responding to money-sequence morbidities.

Needless to say, both before and after alternatives are in place to protect the life of societies' environmental hosts, the life-insulting products and technologies are effectively selected against in a life economy by tax policies to deter their continued use, as well as recover some of their costs to societies. Again this gatekeeping of money-demand flows is wholly within existing government and inter-government jurisdictions. It does not reduce market competition, but depathologizes it.

There are other types of manufacture which meet the most basic life-needs, but which the dominant paradigm's decision-structure is incompetent to develop. Vehicles powered by clean and renewable energy sources, for example, could hardly be more needed in increasingly overloaded and congested world cities. Countless millions of people are dying and diseased in rising numbers and rates in consequence of the fumes of fossil-fuel combustion engines. At the same time, carbon-dioxide loading is increasingly deforming climate patterns and endangering coastal life by its effects. Yet the global market system, despite under-one-per cent expenditures and token developments in this direction – entirely dependent on public authority for subsidies and selective laws to advance even this far – still remains without an alternative to fossil-fuel combustion engines which has long been known as a global survival imperative. Here again, the principles of a life economy are required to select a choice-path consistent with the conditions of existence itself.

In fact, even public sidewalks to walk on are beyond the dominant paradigm's capacities to develop without external instruction. Once rationality is permitted to open past the blinkers of the received market mind-set, vital life-requirements of unlimited number come into view. Insofar as they are not already provided by the evolution of the civil commons, each and all can be recognized, articulated and mandated into the decision-structures of society's money-creation, interest-rate and taxation processes by procedures constitutionally accessible to sovereign governments operating independently or collectively. There are many calls of the most urgent nature for marketable goods to protect and enable global life which the life-blind market does not and cannot respond to. In truth, virtually all of the systemic problems to be met are caused by global market commodities and processes themselves. It is here that the invasive channels of investment and reproduction must be steered by the monetary and fiscal instruments of public authority towards life-serving products – towards noiseless machines to still the ever-expanding motor-racket pervading the planet; for high-protein vegetarian fast-foods to reduce the many-times less efficient use of arable land by livestock grazing and the earth-wide slaughterhouse of fellow creatures; for priority research and development of physical systems to convert wastes of every sort into reusable manufacturing forms; and for more efficient water-recycling processes to convert waste water and sea-water into redeployable or potable forms increasingly lost by market depletion and pollution of existing sources.

No-one denies the sovereign rights to apply these monetary and fiscal instruments of steering society, even bankers who have plied and pulled them away from complicit political parties and public servants over time. What sustains the covert appropriation of these sovereign rights by private financial interests is silence – politicians in self-serving complicity with their election financers, bankers in the solemn secrecy of smoothly usurped social power, and corporate banking operations in pursuit of compound-interest payments for creating credit at will. Governments may praise themselves for abdicating their responsibilities to the public interest, and electorally financed politicians may join the new crusade to 'remake government' to fit corporate money sequences with 'no interference'. Occupied societies have always had their collaborators. The difference with a carcinogenic occupation is that the host body does not recognize the invader.

Servitude to alien forces we cannot see is, as with a superstition, a self-imposed condition. It is as reversible as cutting off people's limbs to please Allah, or foreign investors. To be specific, national banks are subject to national governments, and can be told what to do to serve the public interest, or be replaced by statutory direction (as we saw with Article 2 of the Maastricht Treaty or Article 18 of the Bank of Canada Act). The Bank of Canada, the Bank of England or the European Central Bank, as indeed the US Federal Reserve, have the established or preceding right to draw upon mandatory money reserves deposited by private banks for the purposes of sustaining the purchase of government or inter-government bonds at any interest rate they choose. They are all publicly owned banks, responsible to the common interest, and all of their chief executives and employees are government-appointed servants. In short, the existing instruments for serving the common interest are encoded in fundamental law.

That these legally instituted avenues have *not* been adopted while revenues for societies' social security, health, education and environmental infrastructures have been seized for redistribution to usury sequences is a bellwether indicator of the seriousness of the immune disorder and the disease. It is interesting to note in this connection that the transnational bank that has at the same time led the substitution of privatized government bonds for bank reserves is the Swiss-based Bank of International Settlements, an unaccountable committee of bankers which secretly determines the world's norms of money creations and supplies outside of any public scrutiny. The Bank of International Settlements was originally set up to bring German war reparations under banks' control before the 1929 Crash and Great Depression. It was later to hand over Czechoslovakia's gold to Hitler on his invasion of Prague in 1938.[77]

The reader may find the overarching pattern at work here difficult to believe – from the long experiment of 'structural adjustment programmes' in the Third World to invasion of the First World's public sector by the same site of expropriation, 'public debt'. Avoidance of dissonance and fear of recognizing the morbidity is how socially virulent sequences take hold. It is easier to accept the masking representation. 'Society was living beyond its means', 'we must compete' or – we may predict – 'social cohesion is by a common currency'.

Let us summarize.

Money supply, reduction, interest rate and reserves are all vested in the sovereign public authority of governments. But government politicians and market-indoctrinated bureaucrats looking for higher-paid employment in private corporations are subservient to corporate money sequences and media which finance political parties. That is why, at bottom, governments are continuously made to look foolish and incompetent, and why simultaneously the global market system has been 'unfettered' from accountability to the common life interests of societies. The global market paradigm has been programmed into their decision-codes as the only alternative. The distinction between the demands of money sequences and the requirements of life has in this way collapsed. The unseen master-switch of this subversion of the public sector's life-protective function is the covert acquisition by private financial institutions of control over the most basic financial instruments and powers of public authority.

The instituted resources for the reversal of this covert usurpation have already been won by a millennium of democratic development. The choice paths for social recovery are clear and available. The missing link remains social recognition of the systemic nature of the underlying disorder and the logic of its solution.

Epilogue: Depathologizing Competition

We have seen that global market competitiveness is conceived as the proper selector of what survives in the world, and what does not. 'We must compete harder' appeals to a structure of motivation which is required to accept the global market's money sequences at social-psychological level. The call to societies to prove themselves in the 'tough new global competition' relates to a very primitive impulsion. The primate which imagines itself to have won its individual, group and species place in the kingdom of life by life-or-death competition still moves to a primeval drum. You cannot sell the global market by lies and temptations alone. The 'competitiveness of the beast' is the atavistic substratum to which it ultimately appeals. This is a marker of fascisms of all kinds. 'Succeed or perish in the brutal global competition' is not far off *Mein Kampf*'s, 'Humanity as a whole must flourish. Only the weak and cowardly will perish.'[78]

'The triumph over communism' and 'the victory of market forces over protectionist barriers' have been propelled by the global market programme hitched to this preconscious motivation. On the individual level, the fact that you still survive and have money is the mark of your admission to the elect of the successful in the world market competition. This is the underlying appeal of the programme to those who are its creatures.

If we comprehend this pattern of competition and victory in terms of what it effects for or against life's development, however, we find a hidden correlation. The more that competitive money sequences advance across the world in regulation of social life and posting of gross quantitative gains, the more that both social and natural life-organization are diminished in their measures of diversity, range and health. Thus wherever we observe the 'victory of global market forces' after 1980, we observe also the reduction of species and environmental habitat, of public health indicators, of child nourishment, of universal education, of productive employment and of freedom from destitution. This is a startling generalization. But there are few exceptions to its grim hold.

With the pattern of global market competition now leading the countries of the world into progressively deregulated chaos, we find a wide spectrum of variations on an unseen global theme. This underlying theme is *the downsizing of life to upsize the sequences of money.* What appears to be nations competing against one another to sell to each other is, on the deeper level of global reality, *the market's money sequence of value competing against the natural and civil life-fabrics of the world.* This transnational process of defeating the claims of human labour, environments and social sectors to continued life in any other form but transient functions of expanding money sequences is the carcinogenic pattern. It does not invade and occupy social bodies without strong resistance. But whatever blocks or resists it is declared 'non-competitive'. If it resists directly with force of arms, it is 'terrorist'.

So 'increased competiveness' is an axial category which calls out for deeper examination. Let us begin with its meaning, a level of the civil commons which the global market media avoid.

All competition is a process of overcoming limiting conditions of some kind. Competition can be healthy or unhealthy in form. Competition is *healthy* when the overcoming of the limiting condition confronting the competitors *enables a wider and deeper range of life by the process and consequences of their competing.* Athletes are humanity's oldest and most transparent symbols of competitiveness. Their competitive feats are inscribed in matter and motion. They compete healthily when both they and their oppositions get better at what they compete at – running, jumping, throwing, lifting, feinting, and so on. At best, all achieve what they couldn't achieve before, and the margin of *'better'* is an *extension of the scope of life's capabilities.* Athletic competition is the paradigm of all competition because the margins of increase are clear, physical and commensurable. One knows what is better and what is not by a better time, a higher bar, a longer distance, a heavier weight, a better performance against identified benchmarks than before.

A similar decisiveness of betterment, or decline, can be discerned on the macro-level of social life-organization performances. Societies can get better or worse in such ratable measures as health and morbidity, literacy and illiteracy, value sensibility and blind ignorance. But global market competition has lost track of what it is doing, not recognizing what it is in fact, competing *against*. What global market competition is, at bottom, competing against without our realizing it is life's vital capacities themselves: invading, reducing and stripping them in a systemic pattern of turning the sequences of life into 'more productive' sequences of money. Humanity's primeval urge to overcome limits has in this way been harnessed to a programme that is consuming the life-substance itself, without clear social immune recognition of the advancing morbidity. For the reduction of living bodies and life-fabrics cannot be and is not computed in any calculus of the global market paradigm.

The way in which we can always tell *losses of life* from *gains of life* in any social life-host is by observing the parameters of life's reproduction and growth: its species biodiversity, its air, water and atmospheric qualities, its forest and other life resources, the disease-free health of society's members, their level of literacy and education, the rights of all to expression and association, and so on. There are many basic indicators of *life-gain* or *life-loss* which society, in the end global society, monitors and responds to in order to comprehend how well it is doing in the real life-and-death competition of planetary existence.

Nutrition levels, literacy rates, disease ratios, air quality, water purity, noise levels, biodiversity, forest cover, soil quality, physical fitness, public and green spaces, social and artistic communication venues, higher education graduates, housing, wildlife habitats, fish stocks, ozone-protection indices, and so on are all such *scorecards of humanity's life gains or losses*, and all are precisely identifiable by their *margins of change to more inclusive or diminished vital ranges.* Together these life-gains or losses tell us whether our lives and societies or our world is getting better, or worse. This is real life competition. It is what finally counts because it is winning or losing at life itself at the world level.

Winning is told by whether the lives of members of society and its environmental host are becoming more alive and comprehensive in their vital capacities. Losing is told by whether life's capacities are being reduced, degraded or extinguished. The money-count method of evaluation is a lapsed paradigm of competition. For it is in principle blind to life-losses, and counts only gains and debits of money-demand. Put in terms of the model, the capital or 'wealth that produces more wealth' which it seeks to expand is money capital, not life capital.

Competition becomes *pathological competition* when life is not *raised* to higher or more enabled levels of vital life compasses of thought, feeling and action, but is *reduced* to lower levels and, at worst, permanently disabled or destroyed. Nuclear war, for example, is a clearcut example of pathological competition because, once entered, it must destroy tens of millions of lives on both sides of its obliterative contest, as well as much of the life of the planet. We face a similar mind-lock in the global market competition of today. But rather suddenly, when there was no longer a satanic enemy to project evil onto that had to be destroyed, nuclear war or threat of nuclear war ceased to be a way of competing that sane people believed in as 'necessary' or 'inevitable'.

Global market competition has at this stage of social evolution become humanity's primary pathological competition. For it does not enable more comprehensive, vital life for humanity or the planet, but disables the world's species and environmental habitats, increasing hundreds of millions of malnourished, unemployed, homeless, insecure and money-subjugated people, and societies in general which have been variously stripped of their civil commons across the world – all in a period of greater technical powers and rising riches. We need not rediagnose the global pattern at work to conclude that life's sequences of growth and development are on a downward slide by self-regulating global market operations. This competition is pathogenic not only because its calculus of value rules out life's requirements, but because its programme prescribes the defunding of precisely what protects and fulfils these requirements. Yet all of this is said to be necessary '*to be more competitive*' – which it can only be from the standpoint of the disease invasion itself.

Once we recognize that the underlying logic of global market competition systemically selects against life's protection itself, we see that its pathology is virulent and progressive as an invasive disease is. It follows from this malignant pattern that social and planetary life-organization must resist what attacks it. This is not merely a morbidity to be regretted. It is, from a wider view, how life adapts and grows, through overcoming adversities to achieve more comprehensive ranges of capability. The secret of disease is that it is evolution's provocation. The secret of social disease is that consciously understood it is history's moving spring.

Notes and References

Chapter 1: The Ancient Taboo

1. See my 'Fascism and Neo-conservatism: Is there a Difference?' *Praxis International,* Vol. 4: No. 1 (1984), pp. 86–102.
2. Standardly, the state and its laws are *presupposed* as the expression of divine will and command, and no question as to their relationship even arises. This is as true of the impersonal Mandate of Heaven to which the secular rulers of the Chinese have traditionally laid claim, as it is of the unchallengeable Divine Right of Kings promulgated in pre-1800 Europe. We may be inclined to think that such a presupposed connection has largely disappeared with the modern Western separation of church and state, but almost no Western state has, in separating itself from the church, allowed itself to be disassociated thereby from God. To rationally challenge this connection – before testifying in court, while contesting an election, as a teacher of school, or on any public medium – is by no means yet an undangerous act. We may be closer to the mark in understanding this religious metaphysic of the established social order – note how the logic and language of sovereign, law, command, loyalty, obedience, judgement and punishment structure both spheres – if we understand religious absolutism and superstition as expressions of social absolutism and superstition, rather than the other way round.
3. It is extraordinary the length to which Socrates goes to avoid criticizing the system of military aggression, conquest and slavery upon which his society is based, even when these forms of life clearly violate his concern to restrain the appetites and to nurture the rational element inherent even in slave-boys (*Meno,* 82b–86a). A passage where this contradiction between allegiance to reason and subservience to the status quo (a contradiction which may provide the clue to Socrates' celebrated irony) emerges clearly in *The Republic,* II 372a–374e. Here Socrates, in a few lines, allows Glaucon to take the ideal republic from modesty, to luxury and swollen armies of labour, to robbery of neighbouring states and war ('no form of work whose efficiency is so important'), with no argument against any step of the way. By the end of the section, training for war has become Socrates' focal concern, and the breeding and education of a military class of guardians remains his preoccupation throughout the six subsequent chapters.
4. We do not, of course, mean to impute to the Pre-Socratics, cosmogonists and cosmologists a conscious intention to avoid trouble by avoiding social

philosophy (by which term we mean here and elsewhere to include political philosophy, or philosophy of the state). The Pre-Socratics' historical situation was one in which the constancy of ancient custom, conjoined with the forces of habit and established power, may well have been sufficient to rule out critical social thought as even a conceived possibility. However, it would be a mistake to suppose that unconceived implies inconceivable, and that the Pre-Socratics were *incapable* of questioning their social regimen. Even children are acute enough to question their forms of social life though they know no alternative, until their guardians put a stop to their queries. Herein may lie, indeed, the genetic structure of the generally successful suppression of social philosophy in the human condition.

5. Socrates has nothing critical to say about the state or the laws during or after his trial, according to the reports of both the *Apology* and the *Crito*. Indeed, he argues that the state and the laws are the source of life, his master, his sacred commander, his teacher, and his father and mother (50a–52b).

6. Socrates was not only legendarily provocative in his style (for which the young used to follow him about to watch the fun), but he was also allied with the Thirty Tyrants who were overthrown as Athen's rulers just four years before his trial.

7. Michel Foucault's words are of interest here:

> The history that bears and determines us has the form of a war rather than that of a language; relations of power, not relations of meaning. (*Power/Knowledge: Selected Interviews and Other Writings, 1972–77*, ed. Colin Gordon: Harvester, London, 1981.)

Foucault may construct a false disjunction here – if we conceive language and meaning to include war and power as basic elements – but his disjunction highlights what philosophers like to ignore: the structures of social power and struggle within which philosophical inquiry takes place.

8. Here are some of Lao Tzu's more regime-critical remarks in the *Tao-te-Ching* (translated by Wing Tsit Chan, *A Sourcebook in Chinese Philosophy*. Princeton University Press, Princeton, N.J., 1972, pp. 155–166):

> The more taboos and prohibitions there are in the world, The poorer the people will be ... (57)

> The courts are exceedingly splendid While the fields are exceedingly weedy; Elegant clothes are worn, Sharp weapons are carried, Foods and drinks are enjoyed beyond limit, and wealth and treasures are accumulated in excess. This is robbery and extravagance. This is indeed not Tao, ... (53)

> For a victory, let us observe the occasion with funeral ceremonies ... (31)

The *Bhagavad-Gita* is never so direct as this in its social criticism, but its implicit rejection of caste-ultimates and its explicit rejection of self-seeking behaviour ('To action alone hast thou a right and never at all to its fruit') might be illuminatingly compared to the standard acceptance of classes, and the uncritical equation of rationality to self-interest by English-speaking philosophers today.

9. Unlike modern philosophical materialists, the Carvaka's rejection of soul as anything more than the body distinguished by the attribute of intelligence carried with it radical social implications which its adherents explicitly embraced: namely, repudiation of the merit-justified caste system, the priesthood, and taboos against enjoyment in general. (See, for example, *Sourcebook in Indian Philosophy*, ed. S. Radhakrishnan and Samuel Moore, Princeton University Press, Princeton, N.J., 1971, pp. 227–36.)

10. We take this opportunity to emphasize the historical mutation of such concepts as cynic and anarchist – standing for philosophical positions which criticize and reject social convention and the state respectively–into accepted terms of abuse. The debasement of these concepts into labels of stigma indicates the extent to which philosophical opposition to the social order status quo is customarily discredited.

11. These famous words are Isaiah's (3:15), but this concern for the poor's oppression by the rich runs throughout the prophets: for example, Jeremiah (5:27–9), Ezekial (16:50), Amos (2:7; 8:4–8), Habakkuk (2:5–9) and Malachi (3:5). One might go so far as to say that class analysis originates with the old testament prophets, though their repudiation of the wealthy's exploitation of the needy is seldom officially noted. (Indeed, in the recent Krever Commission Inquiry in Ontario, it was observed that in Canada the mere citation of Isaiah by J.S. Woodsworth in the 1930s was enough to incur his prosecution for sedition. (Ross Dowson, *Ross Dowson* vs. *RCMP*, Forward Publications, Toronto, 1980, p. 51.))

12. The execution of Jesus as a political criminal is, again, a fact that is generally concealed: better for social rule that he is conceived as a religious apostate from colonized Jewry than a rebel against the Empire and Roman Law. As the biblical scholar Oscar Cullman has pointed out, if Jesus' crime had been religious and against Jewish law he would have been stoned for blasphemy, not crucified with his crime posted on the cross as required by Roman law. (*The State in the New Testament*, Scribners, New York, 1956, pp. 43 ff.)

13. In recent decades, in Central and South America especially, but also in South Africa and in outside supporting metropolitan centres, Christian churches have become unprecedently involved with people's movements against repressive governments and exploitative structures of corporate power. An extraordinary example of this identification with the struggle of people to expose and to remove the power-structures oppressing them, is the former Primate of El Salvador, Archbishop Romero, who made the following published comment after the killing of one of his priests by El Salvador security forces:

> When a dictatorship seriously violates human rights and attacks the common good of the nation, when it becomes unbearable and closes all channels of dialogue, of understanding, of rationality, when this happens, the Church speaks of the legitimate right of insurrectional violence. (Cited by Alan Riding, 'The Sword and The Cross', *The New York Review of Books*, Vol. xxviii, No. 9: May.)

Archbishop Romero was murdered with evident government collaboration not long after this statement, on March 24, 1980.

14. This more or less total compliance of Christian thinkers with the social given begins as early as Paul, who is quite clear about the duty of unqualified

subjection to all relations of established social power whatever: 'Let every man be subject to the powers that be' (Romans 13:1); 'The State is there to serve God for your benefit' (Romans 13:4); 'Wives should regard their husbands as they regard the Lord ... Slaves, be obedient to the men who are Called your masters' (Ephesians 5:23; 6:5); and 'For the sake of the Lord, accept the authority of every social institution' (I Peter 2:13).

Within such a sanctified framework of unquestioning obedience to the established order, it is not surprising that Church intellectuals to whom the positions of Paul constituted unimpeachable authority were so critically silent about social structure.

As Churchmen and theologians, Augustine, Aquinas, Scotus and Ockham were bound by the very premises of the institution for which they worked to unquestioning conformity to the social status quo. Even so far as they went, which was never so far as to critically investigate God's appointed social forms, they were not immune from censure.

Aquinas was imprisoned by his own family for two years for joining the more socially conscious Dominican Order in its early years, Scotus was banished from France for refusing to take the side of King Philip the Fair in a dispute over Church taxation, and Ockham was excommunicated by the Pope over his scholarly support of the legitimacy of apostolic poverty.

15. Hegel's dialectical method may be, as has often been argued, an inherently subversive one. The spirit of negation is its very meaning, however Hegel may himself have conceived the Prussian State as the Absolute's historical culmination. What is of particular interest here is that even though Hegel's dialectic contradicts in principle the absolutization of the social-institutional present, he is unable to refrain from so absolutizing the institutional edifice within which he lives, even though he must contravene his own method to do so. Hegel helps to reveal by his self-contradiction just how confined by the social given philosophy has traditionally been.

16. *An Inquiry Concerning the Principles of Morals*, ed. Charles W. Hendel, Library of Liberal Arts, Bobbs-Merrill, New York, 1957, p. 24.

17. *Discourse of the Origin and the Foundation of Inequality Among Mankind*, Part 2, paragraph 1.

18. See *The Social Contract and Discourse on the Origin of Inequality*, ed. Lester G. Crocker, Washington Square Press, New York, 1971, pp. 39, 135, 236, 145–6. For Rousseau's position that woman's submission to man is a law of nature, see his discussion throughout Book V of *Emile*, especially 'The Education of Women and Training for Womanhood' (1) and (2).

19. For Marx's precise laws of the economic determination of ideology, see my *The Structure of Marx's World-View*, Princeton University Press, Princeton, N.J., 1978, pp. 161–70.

20. Mill supports unequal voting and imperialism in his *Representative Government* where he argues for a plurality of votes for the managerial and professional classes (Chapter VIII), and where he defends British colonialism as a matter of free states governing dependencies (Chapter XVIII). He supports racism by his stated belief that there are backward states of society in which the race itself may be considered as in its non-age (*Collected Works of J.S. Mill*, ed. J.M. Robson, University of Toronto Press, Toronto, 1965, Volume XVIII, p. 224). And he shows himself insensitive to the lot of the oppressed – namely, slaves and serfs – in his claim that 'in ancient society in the middle ages, ... the

individual was a power in himself' (ibid., p. 268). I am indebted to Marvin Glass for the latter two points and citations.

21. Mill proposes no real explanatory model for the social process as a whole, whereas Marx's thought unprecedently subsumes the natural, technological, economic, legal, political and ideological factors by a more or less systematic sociohistorical theory. Marx also attempts to penetrate deep structures of social illusion, perhaps the philosopher's essential task, whereas Mill is inclined, as English-speaking philosophy generally, to take appearances at face value. Finally, Marx's development of substantive social alternatives is much deeper and more wide-ranging than the more conservative Mill's, attempting to outline the systematic transformation of the entire social order.

22. For a fuller analysis of this principle and its testing, see my 'The Unspeakable: Understanding The System of Fallacy of the Media', *Informal Logic*, Vol. X: No. 3 (Fall 1988), 133–50.

23. Philip Mirowski, *More Heat Than Light: Economics as Social Physics*. New York: Cambridge University Press, 1989, pp. 377–8.

24. The historically sustained press of neo-classical economics to construe itself as a physics amenable to the formalist reductions of mathematical equations which rule out all value problems by definition has increasingly dominated the discipline for over a century. For a detailed and sophisticated account of this research programme, see Philip Mirowski, *More Heat Than Light*, New York: Cambridge University Press, 1989.

25. The analogy is not remote from the facts of the world. 'Development by invasion', observes Berkeley geographer, Bernard Nietschmann, 'is done by all of the most populous states that together lay claim to 63 per cent of the world's peoples, and 43 per cent of the land area.' Nietschman's and others' documentation show that the ratios of land controllers to populations, the obey-or-be-killed relationship between them, the absolute prohibition of self-organization to construct an alternative, and the regularized extraction of super-profits from this arrangement in general resemble concentration-camp conditions for over 3000 million persons. (Bernard Nietschman, 'Economic Development By Invasion of Indigenous Nations', *Fourth World Journal*, Winter 1985–86 (1:2), pp. 89–126.) The 12 years since this article have marked a consolidation of this wealth-producing situation, with transnational trade agreements and IMF austerity programmes established subsequently to reduce social costs, expedite production and export, protect investment security, and prohibit 'process' discrimination against tariff-freed commodities extracted in this manner.

26. William Krehm, 'Social Immune Deficiency?' *Economic Reform* (8:2) June 1996, p. 4. Krehm identifies Leon Walras as the lead figure in the exile of value theory from economics but Arthur Marshall's and W.S. Jevous' revolution of economic theory by marginal utility analysis made the study of economic behaviour in terms of mathematically conceived preference schedules possible. In the current era, 'econometrics' has become dominant in the discipline, and mathematical functions have in this way displaced human beings and relations as the proper objects of economic science.

27. John Rawls, *A Theory of Justice*. Cambridge, Mass: Harvard University Press, 1968, pp. 142–3.

28. David Gauthier, *Morals By Agreement*. New York: Oxford University Press, 1986, p. 7.

dane illustration here is the pronouncement of the University of
o historian, Michael Bliss, who denounced the country of 'Canada',
qualifying attribute, for 'contributing next to nothing to bring down
the red regimes' and 'consistently supporting the oppressors of the Cuban
people'. ('Canada Will Rue Support For Castro', *Toronto Star*, March 22, 1996,
A19.) No professional historian publicly responded with methodological
concern for the absence of any factual evidence in Bliss's expression of the
dominant value programme, or for his 'presentist' opinions as a bylined
'historian'.

30. Digby J. McLaren, 'Reply to Colin Rowat', *Delta Newsletter of the Global
Change Programme* (Royal Society of Canada) Vol. 7: No. 3 (1996), 3; and
Ernst Weizzsacker, *Factor Four*. London: Earthscan Books, 1997.

31. George Grant, in a lesser-known work, implies a ruling class behind the
penultimate rule of technology when he asserts: 'Power is increasingly
concentrated, so that most people have to pursue their individual gain
within conditions set by the corporations, while the few who set the conditions
operate the calculus of greed, ambition and self-interest to their own ends'
(M. Oliver (ed.), *Social Purpose For Canada*. Toronto: University of Toronto
Press, 1961, p.4). But even here, Grant does not relate the march of
technology to the logic of profit maximization behind it. Rather he keeps them
as separate issues, and interprets the value programme of the money-to-more-
money sequence as the disordered motivation-structure of a corporate few.

32. The following text from a retired senior economist of the International
Monetary Fund is a revealing window on the closed circle of judgement within
which the creatures of this social value programme are confined in complete
disregard of the programme's effects on living societies and their members:

> What we had done over these years was to 'manufacture statistical indices
> – the RULC (Relative Unit Labour Cost) and several others – that would
> allow us to prove our point, and push a particular policy line, irrespective
> of economic realities ... Our previous 'mistakes' were never mentioned ...
> We went glibly on to ask for more ... devaluation of the local currency,
> removal of price controls even on the most basic essentials, accelerated
> reduction of wages, removal of exchange controls on external capital
> and current transactions, spectacular cuts in public sector wage bills, deep
> reductions in transfers to persons, in social services, including health
> and education, systematic increases in interest rates, restructuring of the
> taxation system to increase its regressiveness, and indiscriminate divestment
> of public enterprises. (Davison L. Budhoo, Open Letter of Resignation to
> the Managing Director of the International Monetary Fund, New York:
> New Horizons Press, 1990, cited in *Economic Reform*, Vol. 10: No. 7, July
> 1998, p. 10.)

Chapter 2: The Pathologization of the Market Model

1. In testimony given to the War Crimes and Crimes against Humanity Tribunal
at the 1989 World Summit in Toronto at which I was Chair of Jurists, a former
El Salvador death-squad officer testified: 'If we were told that someone was
a communist or subversive, then normally we would eliminate that
person'(Toronto, June 11, 1988). For an analysis of the relationship between

anti-communism and global market ideology and practice, see my 'Fascism and Neo-Conservatism: Is There a Difference?' *Praxis International*. Vol. 4: No. 1 (1984), pp. 7–24.

2. Adam Smith, 'Of Restraints Upon Imports From Foreign Countries of Such Goods As Can Be Produced At Home', *Book IV, Chapter II, An Inquiry into the Nature and Understanding of the Wealth of Nations*. New York : P.F. Collier and Son, 1909, pp. 351–2.

3. Milton Friedman, 'The Social Responsibility of Business Is To Increase Its Profits', *The New York Times Magazine*, September 13, 1970.

4. Adam Smith, 'Of the Agricultural Systems', Book IV, Chapter IX, *Wealth of Nations*, p. 46.

5. 'A Global Game of Monopoly', *The Economist*, March 27, 1993, p. 17.

6. Adam Smith, 'On the Extraordinary Restraints on the Importation of Goods', Book IV, Chapter III, *Wealth of Nations*, p. 352.

7. *Ibid*, 'Of the Accumulation of Capital', Book II, Chapter III (p. 272).

8. *Ibid*, p. 280.

9. *Ibid*, p. 279.

10. *Ibid*, 'Of the Expenses of the Sovereign or Commonwealth', Book V, Chapter I (p. 487).

11. *Ibid*, 'Of the Extraordinary Restraints on the Importation of Goods', Book IV, Chapter II (p. 383).

12. The logic of this infrastructural precipitation is first set into motion by John Locke's *Second Treatise on Government*, cited as the source of Adam Smith's own view of private property in *Wealth of Nations*. Locke provides a justification of private property – since canonical – which imperceptibly shifts from labour and use as the ground of private-property entitlement *to money*, which has no limits of possession, as a ground of private-property entitlement. I analyse Locke's argument as a metaphysical set in *Unequal Freedoms: The Global Market As An Ethical System*. Toronto: Garamond Press, 1998, pp. 87–92.

13. Friedrich A. Hayek, *The Road To Serfdom*. Chicago: University of Chicago Press, 1944, p. 37.

14. 'World Trade Threatens Massachusetts', *Earth Island Journal*, Fall 1997, p. 19.

15. United Nations Development Report 1997, cited by Victoria Brittain and Larry Elliott, 'World's Poor Lose Out to Corporations', *Guardian Weekly*, June 22, 1997.

16. Cited by Pierre Sane, Secretary-General of Amnesty International, 'Amnesty's Report Card From Hell', *Globe and Mail*, December 10, 1993, p. A21.

17. As an indicator of the effects of the global system on the 'freedom of the seller', consider the following facts about two very differently developed societies under the impact of its transnational regulatory regime: 'In the first three years of the US–Canada Free Trade Agreement, Canada lost 1.4 million jobs, including 500,000 manufacturing jobs, over 25% of the entire manufacturing sector. In Mexico, the [current] average hourly wage paid by US corporations is 63 cents. In the last ten years, as American and other foreign corporations moved into Mexico [and into Free Trade Zones], Mexican wages have been driven down by 60%.' *Citizens Concerned About Free Trade*, Saskatoon, Summer 1994.

18. Government interventions to subsidize corporations in the home of the 'global free market', the United States, is systemic and vast. The public owns

one-third of the United States and over four-fifths of Canada, but corporations control their rich mineral resources of timber, oil, and gas for their exclusive profit, which may be removed from the host society and invested anywhere else at will. At the same time, taxpayers furnish the money for roads and other infrastructure to enable these corporations to clear-cut, extract, and deplete publicly owned resources for a fraction of their market worth. The public also owns the airwaves used to transmit television, radio, and other communications. But private corporations control these as well, at little cost and with no accountability to the public interest.(The figures here are drawn from Ralph Nader,'Stop Americanizing Canadian Healthcare', *CCPA Monitor*, February 1996, p. 17.)

19. The investigative study by Mark Zepezauer and Arthur Naiman, *Take the Rich Off Welfare*, Tucson Arizona: Odonian Press, 1997, calculates an annual direct monetary subsidy to large corporations of $448 billion a year. These public hand-outs occur as guaranteed programmes of assistance to single mothers, children and the poor which have been in effect since the New Deal of the 1930s are abolished.

20. The US is thought to be the developed world's most successful economy in terms of employment at this time, with a rate of about 5 per cent (not counting the immense prison population, those who have stopped looking for work, and the estimated 40 millions who work for less than a living wage). The disciplining of the American working class to fit the global system went through a lengthy period of life reduction. By 1992, US wages for non-supervisory personnel had dropped 20 per cent over 20 years (Walter Russell Mead, *Harper's*, September 1992, p. 41). Even a leader of the global system, subsequently US Secretary of Labor, Robert Reich, acknowledged that 'the majority (four-fifths) of the population is losing out' under the new order. (Robert Reich, *The Work of Nations*. New York: Vintage Books, 1992, p. 282.)

21. In the 'highly competitive' commercial airlines business, for example, one firm, Boeing, owns two-thirds of the global market for commercial airplanes. The other one-third of the global market belongs to Airbus Industrie. Both firms are very heavily subsidized by US and European governments respectively. ('US, Europe Clash Over Trade Deal', *Guardian Weekly*, July 27, 1997, p. 8.)

22. *Tools for Peace*, Toronto, June 27, 1994.

23. These citations from the Trilateral Commission text are taken from Murray Dobbin, *The Myth of the Good Corporate Citizen,* Toronto: Stoddart, 1998, p. 162. See also Peter Steinfels, *The Neo-conservatives*. New York: Simon and Schuster, 1979.

24. Michael Walker of the Fraser Institute as cited in 'NAFTA: A New Economic Constitution', Canadian Union of Public Employees, February 3, 1993.

25. Smith writes: 'But in civilized society ... among the inferior ranks of people ... the scantiness of subsistence can set limits to the further multiplication of the species; and it can do this in no other way than by destroying a great part of the children which their fruitful marriages produce' (Adam Smith, 'Wages of Labour', Book I, Chapter VIII, *ibid*, p. 84). Note that Smith *anticipates* Social Darwinism in his theory of human selection.

26. 'Of the Expenses of the Sovereign or Commonwealth', Book V, Chapter I, *ibid*, p. 482.

27. Cited by Maude Barlow and Bruce Campbell, *Straight Through the Heart*. Toronto: HarperCollins, 1995, p. 37. In the case of Canada, 97.5 per cent of all foreign investment in 1997 went for takeovers of domestic firms, a year in which 'foreign investment' was typically trumpeted as the highroad to domestic prosperity (cited by Mel Hurtig, 'How Much Of Canada Do We Want to Sell', *Globe and Mail*, February 5, 1998, p. A23).

28. Cited by Maud Barlow, *Class Warfare*. Toronto: Key Porter Books, 1994, p. 62.

29. Cited by Geoffrey Hawthorne in 'Capitalism Without Capital', *London Review of Books*, 26 May, 1994, p. 12.

30. Cited by Madelaine Drohon, 'Perils of Privatization', *Report On Business Magazine*, May, 1996, p. 41.

31. For a combined empirical and logical analysis of this global structure of media control and its operations of selection and exclusion as an overall system, see my 'Understanding the System of Fallacy of the Mass Media', *Informal Logic*, Vol. 10: No. 1 (1988), pp. 133–50.

32. Before Somalia disintegrated into civil war, its people's traditional agricultural lands were taken over for oil drilling and agribusiness, turned to monoculture cash-crops and extraction for export, exhausted by single-crop and chemical farming, and, as across Africa, set into a cycle of desertification. (See, for example, Kristin Dawkins, *NAFTA, GATT, and the World Trade Organization: The Emerging New World Order*. Westfield, N.J.: Open Magazine Pamphlet Series, 1993, pp. 3–7.) In the former Yugoslavia, 'Secessionist tendencies ... gained impetus precisely during a period of brutal impoverishment of the Yugoslav population. ... A US financial aid package [preceded the impoverishment] in exchange for a devalued currency, the freeze of wages, a drastic curtailment of government expenditure, and the abrogation of the socially owned enterprises under self-management ... including the lay-off of more than 600,000 workers of a 2.6 million workforce ... [followed by] a decline of GDP by more than 50%' (Michel Chossudovsky, 'Dismantling Former Yugoslavia, Recolonizing Bosnia', Science for Peace International Conference on the Lessons of Yugoslavia, University of Toronto, March 20–23, 1997).

33. The extent to which transnational corporate agents control the legislative process of trade and investment with no public accountability is indicated by the construction of the apparently neutral *Codex Alimentarius* to regulate the minimum standards that can be applied to food and drug commodities (the closest these transnational regimes come to considering life requirements in their laws). Between 1989 and 1991, 2562 out of 2587 representatives came from corporations and 'the private sector', and 25 from public-interest groups. The *Codex* has the imprimatur of the UN Food and Agricultural Organization and the World Health Organization. Its standards include minimums of DDT residues 50 times greater than permitted under US law. These standards prevail if any government seeks to prevent the free entry of foreign commodities in accordance with its own laws. (Figures are drawn from David Korten, *When Corporations Rule the World*. San Francisco: Berrett-Koehler, 1995, p. 179.)

34. Private corporations in the US alone are estimated to cause $26 trillion of unaccountable damages a year to employees, consumers, environments and communities. (Ralph Estes, *Corporate Crime Reporter*, November 13, 1995, pp. 11–13.) Estes is a US professor of business management.

35. The author of these words is M.H. Ogilvie, a Professor of Law at Carleton University, in her 'Overcoming the Culture of Disbelief' published for the Centre for Renewal in Public Policy, Ottawa, 1995.

36. The US welfare state may seem an oxymoron to European consciousness, but its universal entitlements were precisely what the Trilateral Commission deplored in its 'Crisis of Democracy' position paper cited earlier. 'Previously passive and unorganized groups in the populace, blacks, Indians, Chicanos, white ethnic groups, students, and women', it stated, 'now embark on an effort to establish their claims to opportunities, positions, rewards, and privileges which they had not considered themselves entitled to before' (Dobbin, *The Myth*, p. 162). For more savage attacks on the universal entitlements of the welfare state, see the comments by syndicated columnists David Frum and William Kristol ahead.

37. Franklin Delano Roosevelt's 1944 State of the Union Address introducing this 'Second Bill of Rights', including the welfare provision for children abolished by the Clinton administration in 1996, declared 'the right' to 'a remunerative job', 'decent living', 'decent home', and 'adequate health care', and concluded: 'Unless there is security here at home, there cannot be lasting peace in the world ... we shall have conquered our enemies abroad, [and] yielded to the spirit of fascism here at home'.

38. Noam Chomsky, *The Restless Few and the Prosperous Many*. Berkeley, CA: Odonian Press, 1992, p. 15.

39. Perdue, *op. cit.*, p. 21.

40. Linda McQuaig, *Shooting the Hippo: Death by Deficits and Other Canadian Myths*. Toronto: Penguin Books, 1995, p. 108.

41. William Greider, *Secrets of the Temple: How the Federal Reserve Runs the Country*. New York: Simon and Schuster, 1989, p. 577.

42. *Ibid*, p. 577.

43. *Ibid*, p. 403.

44. *Ibid*, p. 397.

45. *Ibid*, p. 403.

46. *Ibid*, p. 137.

47. H. Mimoto and P. Cross, 'The Growth of the Federal Debt', The Canada Economic Observer (Statistics Canada), 1991.

48. Linda McQuaig, *op. cit.*, pp. 59–61.

49. Duncan Cameron and Ed Finn, *10 Deficit Myths*, Canadian Centre for Policy Alternatives, January 1996, p. 15.

50. US Department of Treasury, 'Monthly Statement of the Public Debt of the United States', Washington D.C.: US Government Printing Office, 1988.

51. Cameron and Finn, *op. cit.*, p. 15.

52. Roundtable Discussion, 'A Revolution or Business as Usual?' *Harper's Magazine*, March 1995, p. 45.

53. *Ibid*, p. 49.

54. James Laxer, 'In Toryland, the Rich Need More and the Poor Less', *Sunday Star*, December 10, 1995, p. A11.

55. Cameron and Finn, *op. cit.*, pp. 16–17.

56. Murray Dobbin, 'Warnings from Down-Under: New Zealand's social policy reforms', *Canadian Perspectives*, Winter 1995, p. 7. Boyce Richardson, 'Surviving the Miracle', *Canadian Forum*, March 1996, p. 14.

57. Jane Kelsey, *Economic Fundamentalism, the New Zealand Experiment*. London: Pluto Press, 1996.

58. All of these facts are drawn from a draft of the Multilateral Agreement on Investment, Paris, January 13 Draft, 1997. The draft in question includes reservations from specific countries on specific clauses – for example, Norway with respect to the MAI's inclusion of 'authorizations, licences and concessions for the prospection, exploration and production of hydrocarbons', a right of the home country which Norway's negotiators, mindful of Norway's reliance on public control of public oil resources for the funding of its social infrastructure, sought to exclude (*ibid*, Definitions 2.b.9). This analysis was presented under the title of 'The Multilateral Agreement on Investment: The Plan To Replace Responsible Government' to the *Interdisciplinary Conference on the Evolution of World Order: Building a Foundation of Peace in the Third Millennium.* Toronto, June 7–9, 1997.

59 . Tony Clarke, *The Corporate Rule Treaty.* Ottawa: Canadian Centre For Policy Alternatives, 1997, p. 9.

60. Pierre Sané, 'Amnesty International Report Card from Hell', *Globe and Mail*, December 10, 1993, p. A21.

61. Ed Finn, 'The New World Order', *Canadian Centre for Policy Alternatives*, November, 1996, p. 10.

62. Greenpeace Annual Review, 1994; 'East and South: The Facts', *New Internationalist*, September 1990, p. 12.

63. Richard Sandbrook, 'The Planet through Pollyanna's Eyes', *Globe and Mail*, April 16, 1994, p. D7.

64. John Leslie, *The End of the World.* New York: Lawrence and Wishart, 1996.

65. In 1950, the world caught 1900 million tons of fish a year. In 1989, the catch was 89 million tons (Tim Radford, 'Filled With More Than A Grain of Truth', *Guardian Weekly*, November 17, 1996, p. 19). Destruction of aquatic life not counted as fish stock is not included in these commercial counts.

66. Susan George, 'The Debt Crisis', International Physicians Against Nuclear War XI World Congress, October, 1993.

67. 'Russia's Welfare State', *Toronto Star*, November 26, 1995, p. F6, and Larry Elliott, 'Russia's Woes', *Guardian Weekly*, February 25, 1996, p. 12.

68. Hobsbawm, *op. cit.*

69. Simon Jenkins, *Accountable to None.* London: Hamish Hamilton, 1995.

Chapter 3: The Social Immune System and the Cancer Stage of Capitalism

1. The whole of anthropology can be understood as a decoding of tribal communities' beliefs and practices which confer survival advantage by protecting them from dangers and harms of all kinds which would otherwise compromise their capacities to reproduce in material conditions which constantly challenge them. Perhaps the most prolific contemporary expositor of this view and of countless examples of diet, sexual norms, rituals and so on which function to safeguard their community life-host is Marvin Harris, for example his classic short study, *Cows, Pigs, Wars and Witches: The Riddles of Culture.* Glasgow: Collins and Son, 1974.

2. Dorland's, for example, defines a taboo as follows: 'any of the negative traditions and behaviours that are generally regarded as harmful to social welfare' (*Dorland's Medical Dictionary* (27th edition). London: W.B. Saunders Company, 1994).

3. Frederick Cartwright and Michael D. Biddiss, *Disease and History*. New York: Dorset Press, 1991, pp. 35–6.

4. Stephen Hume, '"Bird Flu" – The Next Pandemic?', *The Vancouver Sun*, December 13, 1997, p. K9.

5. Malaria outbreaks and increase, for example, are at a record level in market-industrializing regions, with 300–500 million cases annually by 1997. But there is no tracking. Two entymologists ask: 'Can you get funding? Probably not. Funding for malarial pathogens and their vectors is at an all-time low. ... Money [is] the organizational goal.' (Leon G. Higley and David W. Stanley, 'The Dark Landscape of a World with Ten Ounces to the Pound', *American Entymologist*, Winter 1997, pp. 210–11).

6. The stripping of health and environment regulatory structures under rationales of 'competitive cost cutting', 'fighting deficits', and 'deregulation for heightened efficiency' is now such a pervasive practice in the global system that examples of its pattern and effects are too numerous to cite. But consider a cross-section. In the US 50,000 lives a year are now lost due to air pollution, while 100,000 people die prematurely due to toxics and trauma in the workplace, as corporations press for still more deregulation to lower their money costs in 'a brutally competitive global market' (Ralph Nader, 'It's Time To End Corporate Welfare As We Know It', *Earth Island Journal*, Spring, 1996, p. 36). In Russia since liberation to 'free market' regulation, there has been a 3000 per cent rise in cases of syphilis and an unmonitored skyrocketing of diseases of impoverishment for the 75 per cent of the population who now live in poverty without social services (Report of the World Health Organization, Tim Radford, 'Europe Faces Disease Invasion From East', *Guardian Weekly*, April 13, 1997, p. 7). In 'market reform' Ontario, one of the world's richest jurisdictions, an unprecedented 'public health crisis of air pollution' has emerged across the province which makes it dangerous for children and susceptible adults to be out of doors (Ontario Medical Association, Martin Mittelstaedt, 'Breathing Can Be Bad For Health, Doctors Warn', *Globe and Mail,* May 13, 1998, p. A3). 'Cancer cells are created not born. Current science estimates that, at most, 5–10% of cancer is caused by defective genes. ... The current system of regulating the use, release and disposal of known and suspected carcinogens – rather than preventing their generation in the first place – is intolerable' (Sandra Steingraber, *Living Downstream – An Ecologist Looks At Cancer and The Environment*. New York: Addison-Wesley, 1997).

7. The Harvard Working Group on New and Resurgent Diseases, 'Globalization, Development, and the Spread of Disease', Jerry Mander and Edward Goldsmith, *The Case Against the Global Economy'*. San Francisco: Sierra Club Books, 1996, pp. 160–3.

8. See, for example, Susan George, *A Fate Worse Than Debt*. San Francisco: Food First, 1988 and Michel Chossudovsky, *The Globalization of Poverty: Impacts of IMF and World Bank Reforms*. Penang, Malaysia: Third World Network, 1997.

9. For a systematic critique of the military paradigm of social self-defence, see my *Understanding War*. Toronto: Science for Peace and Samuel Stevens Press, 1989.

10. On November 11, 1994, Canada's House of Commons Committee on Foreign Affairs made the extraordinary announcement that the state of Canada's economy was more important than military defence to Canada's security

'because the threat to Canada's standard of living is now greater than the threat to its borders'. The announcement, however, was not communicated in any mainstream news media.

11. These conceptualizations are reported in Annmarie Adams, *Architecture in the Family Way: Doctors, Houses and Women.* McGill-Queens University Press, 1996.

12. In Yugoslavia prior to the 'ethnic cleansings', 1.9 million workers out of a total of 2.7 million were declared redundant under the US loan-pressured Financial Operations Act, and GDP subsequently declined by as much as 50 per cent under the massive 'privatization' programme (World Bank figures cited by Michel Chossoduvsky, *The Globalization of Poverty*, pp. 251–2). In Somalia, a *Los Angeles Times* report, carried by the *International Herald Tribune* on January 19, 1993, showed that two-thirds of Somalia's territory had been leased out to four transnational oil companies, a condition of lost grounds of life for Somalians that helped explain the primeval civil war which subsequently raged across the country. As in Yugoslavia, the restructuring and appropriative invasions of the global market system which caused the collapses of social fabric which issued in these horrific killing fields was not a connection that was permitted to circulate on 'the information highway'. Rather, conventional opinion was encouraged to believe that 'ethnic hatred' and 'warlords' were the causes of the disorders, which, in turn, required foreign interventions and armies of the global market's most powerful nation to resolve.

13. Russell Hardin argues for the 'rational' nature of contemporary ethnic conflict in his *One For All: The Logic of Group Conflict.* Princeton: Princeton University Press, 1995, p. 46.

14. The cycle involved here is described in systematic detail by Susan George, *Debt Boomerang: How Third World Debt Harms Us All.* London: Pluto Press, 1991, and Michel Chossudovsky, *The Globalization of Poverty.*

15. Ted Hyland, *Jesuit Centre for Social Faith and Justice*, September 30, 1993.

16. These figures are drawn from Walter Russell Mead, 'Essay', *Harper's Magazine*, September 1992, p. 41; Noam Chomsky, 'Notes on NAFTA', *The Nation*, March 29, 1993, pp. 14–18; Edward Luttwak, *London Review of Books*, April 7, 1994, pp. 3–5; and Geoffrey Hawthorn's 'Capitalism Without Capital', *London Review of Books*, May 26, 1994, pp. 12–13. Luttwak's book, *The Endangered American Dream: How to Stop the United States from Becoming a Third-World Country and Win the Geo-Economic Struggle for Industrial Supremacy*, New York: Simon and Schuster, 1993, documents the recent precipitous decline of worker income and job-security in the US in particular. Edward N. Wolff's, *Top Heavy. A Study of the Increasing Inequality of Wealth in America*, New York: Twentieth Century Fund Press, 1995, identifies in detail the shift of marketable and financial wealth to the richest sectors of the US population, in particular the top 1 per cent .

17. These figures are drawn from the *Globe and Mail Business Report*, July 16, 1993, p. B13; David Orchard 'The Flight Goes On', *Citizens Concerned about Free Trade*, Summer 1994, p. 2; Richard Grinspun, 'Mexico's Poor Also Pay For Speculators' Follies', *Americas Update*, March/April 1995, pp. 1–10; Editorial, 'Free Trade Boosters Ignore the Facts', *Ibid*, July/August 1995, p. 3; William Krehm, 'Shaking Off the Yoke', *Economic Reform*, October 1995, p. 7; 'Mexico's Woes', *Globe and Mail*, July 8, 1995, p. 7.

18. Murray Dobbin, 'Warnings From Down Under: New Zealand's Policy Reforms', *Canadian Perspectives*, Winter 1995, p. 5. Despite economist Dobbin's exposure of these statistical indicators of social life breakdown in New Zealand, Canadian mass media have aggressively propagated the 'New Zealand solution', which Canada's government is now in the process of emulating. For a detailed story of the stripping of New Zealand's social infrastructure and productive capacities for the benefit of decoupled private capital growth, see Jane Kelsey, *Economic Fundamentalism, The New Zealand Experiment*. London: Pluto Press, 1995.

19. John Pilger, 'The War Against Democracy', *The New Statesman and Society*, October 8, 1993, p. 80; Mike Trickey, 'Cultivating a Disaster', *Southam News*, November 25, 1995, p. B3; Larry Elliott, 'Russia's Woe', *Guardian Weekly*, February 26, 1995.

20. Patty Lee Parmalie, 'Learning to Live with Capitalism in East Berlin', *Z Magazine*, July/August, 1992, p. 24; Paul Koring, 'Leipzig Builds on Shaky Foundations', *Globe and Mail*, November 12, 1993, p. A11.

21. Michel Chossudovsky, 'Dismantling Former Yugoslavia, Recolonizing Bosnia', Science for Peace International Conference, University of Toronto, March 20–23, 1997.

22. Eric Hobsbawm, *The Age of Extremes*. London: Abacus Press, 1995, p. 411.

23. Kevin Phillips, 'The Tyranny of Traders', *Report on Business Magazine*, November 1994, p. 65, reported the ratio as 30–40:1 but within less than a year the McKinsey Global Institute reported the daily ratio of currency speculation to trade in goods and services as 50:1 ('Power of Financial Capital Overrides Governments', *Canadian Centre for Policy Alternatives Monitor*, April 1995, p. 8).

24. Joel Kurtzman, *The Death of Money*. New York: Simon and Schuster, 1993, pp. 89–91.

25. Chris Mihill, 'Poverty is the world's worst killer', *Guardian Weekly*, May 21, 1995, p. 1 (WHO source); Michael Valpy, *Globe and Mail*, February 3, 1995. 'Rights Violated, UN Advisor says', *Globe and Mail*, November 25, 1995, p. A10. Renée de Grace, *Save the Children* – Canada, October 1995, claims the rise in child poverty since 1989 is in fact 55 per cent.

26. Another source of these figures is Richard J. Barnet, 'Stateless Corporations: Lords of the World', *The Nation*, December 19, 1994.

27. See, for example, pp. 1401 and 1456.

28. J.K. Morris, D.G. Cook, A.G. Shaper, 'Loss of Employment and Mortality', *British Medical Journal*, April 30, 1994, pp. 1135–9. B.P. Dohrenwend, I. Levar *et al*, 'Socioeconomic Status and Psychologic Disorders', *Science*, Volume 255, pp. 946–52. R.L. Lin, C.P. Shaw, and T. Svoboda, 'The Impact of Unemployment on Health: A Review of the Evidence', *Canadian Medical Association Journal*, September 1995, pp. 529–39.

29. Sandi Ellis, 'Work and wealth for all', *Kitchener Waterloo Record*, November 9, 1995, p. A11. In the case of Canada, Statscan reports that the participation rate of the working-age population either working or looking for work has fallen to 64.4 per cent (*Globe and Mail*, December 2, 1995, p. A2). Judith Maxwell, Director of Canadian Policy Research Network, concludes in her independent research: 'Forty-one per cent of the Canadian population no longer feel connected to mainstream society' (Michael Valpy, *Globe and Mail*, November 17, 1995, p. A21).

30. Robert Y. McMurtry and Adalsteinn D. Brown, 'The Bank of Canada as a Determinant of Health', *Social Indicators Research*, Volume 6 (1997), pp. 1–9. The authors interestingly follow a chain of causal transitivity from central bank interest-rate increases to increased unemployment to rises in morbidity and mortality, showing the direct relationship of increased human disease in society *to* market regulation to preserve the value of money. In this way, we can see clearly the underlying, and we argue increasingly fatal, conflict between the money-sequence demands of the corporate market and the life-sequence demands of human society.

31. Morris, Cook and Shaper, *op. cit.*

32. This increase seems correlated to falling unemployment prospects and lack of social security. The US, for example, had over three-and-a-half times the teen-suicide rate as Sweden in 1994, as its full-time job prospects and real wages continued to decline (by 1.3 per cent), and as social spending was reduced still lower as a percentage of GDP (14.8 per cent in the US, 34 per cent in Sweden): *Canadian Centre for Policy Alternatives Monitor*, February 1995, p. 6. In New Zealand, teenage suicide doubled after social and educational spending was radically reduced between 1990 and 1992, and unemployment rates rose from the government-induced recession (Dobbin, *op. cit.*). In 1998, the Samaritans of Britain reported suicide attempts by girls in their teens and twenties at 'epidemic levels', with one in five attempting to kill herself before the age of 25 ('In Brief', *Guardian Weekly*, April 12, 1998).

33. As an instructor in philosophy of the environment to students specializing in environmental biology, I have found that there is no text at even the philosophical level which examines the relationship between the causal mechanisms of the global market and the reproduction and distribution of the world's species, despite the fact that the former daily alters the latter by destruction, depletion or pollution of life habitats.

34. Sue Branford, 'Asian Firms Buy Up Forest In Amazon', *Guardian Weekly*, July 7, 1996, p.5.

35. The Republican campaign to abolish the independent authority of the Environmental Protection Agency by wholesale rescindment of protective regulations and by control of Congressional committees by lawyers from major petrochemical, utility and resource-extractive corporations is anatomized in my *Unequal Freedoms: The Global Market as an Ethical System*. Toronto: Garamond Press, 998, pp. 224–5. The subsequent move by the Ontario Conservative Party to achieve the same effect was managed more successfully by leaving regulations intact, but removing their mechanisms of monitoring, research and enforcement for 'voluntary compliance' by the private corporations to whom the laws applied.

36. A.P. and Reuters, 'Earth Summit Leaves Nations Deeply Divided,' June 28, 1997.

37. John McMurtry, 'The Social Immune System and the Cancer Stage of Capitalism,' *Social Justice* (Special Issue: Public Health in the 1990s), Vol. 22: No. 4 (1995), pp. 1–25.

38. Colloquy, ' Global Roulette: In A Volatile World Economy, Can Everyone Lose?' *Harper's Magazine*, p. 43.

39. These 'shock treatments' include fiscal dismantling of occupational health and safety regulations and inspections, in a context where in the US alone an estimated 500,000 annual deaths are 'attributed to occupationally related diseases, the majority of which are caused by knowing and wilful

violation of occupational health and safety laws by corporations' (R. Kramer, 'Corporate Criminality' in E. Hochstedler (ed.) *Corporations as Criminals*, Beverly Hills: Sage Publications, 1984, p. 19). Trial Lawyer Gerry Spence observes that 'One in five major corporations has been convicted of at least one major crime – [or] serious civil misbehaviour', and observes in illustration that '240,000 of the million workers who worked with asbestos will die from asbestos-related cancer' (Gerry Spence, 'Corporate Crime', *With Justice for None*. New York: Random House, 1989, pp. 197–9). 'It is still not a crime,' he adds, 'to knowingly market an unsafe product or to conceal a hazard in the work place' (*ibid*, p. 213).

40. Cited by Bernard Lietaer, 'Money Traders Profit From Causing Currency Crises', *CCPA Monitor*, March 1998, p. 17.

41. Karl Marx, *Capital*, Volume III, Part V, Chapter XXIX.

42. This was a decision of the Nixon administration, to release the peg-currency of the dollar from the necessity of gold back-up after the US spent its treasury dry on the Vietnam War, which produced no productive good. This war, in turn, was itself a moment in the institution of the corporate global market, which cannot tolerate alternative to its regime if it is to draw all nations into its system, or keep those already in it who are impoverished by its operations.

43. William F. Hickson, *Economic Reform*, April 1996, p. 8. The mutual fund figure is Canadian.

44. Bernard Lietaer, 'Two Trillion In Currencies Now Being Traded Every Day', *CCPA Monitor*, March 1998, p. 16.

45. Cited by Ed Finn, *Canadian Centre For Policy Alternatives Monitor*, July/August 1996, p. 4.

46. William F. Hixson, *A Matter Of Interest*: *Re-examining Debt, Interest and Real Economic Growth*. New York: Praeger 1991, pp. xiii and 230.

47. Hixson, *ibid*, p. 177.

48. This quotation is from Ian Angell, a professor of information systems at the London School of Economics, cited by Richard Gwynne, 'Voice of Angell Provides Hard Truths', *Toronto Star*, October 6, 1996, p. A17. Notice that the 'acceptable' redistribution of wealth from 'the majority' and the consequent need to 'dismantle democracy' are headlined as 'hard truths'.

49. Ecumenical Coalition for Economic Justice, *Economic Justice Report*, Vol. 5: No. 2 (1994), p. 7.

50. Nate Laurie, 'The Economy: How Third World Debt Goes in Circles', *Toronto Star*, February 27, 1987, p. A19. R.T. Naylor, *Hot Money and the Politics of Debt*. Montreal: Black Rose Books, 1994.

51. Erik K. Peterson, 'Surrendering to Markets', *Washington Quarterly*, Autumn 1995, p. 109.

52. Norway declined membership in the Maastricht Treaty straitjacket of the European Union, required 50 to 80 per cent of its Petroleum Fund from North Sea oil extraction to be invested in publicly useful ventures or government bonds, contracted no foreign debt, and developed an official 'Solidarity Alternative' to the global market programme which targeted domestic demand, negotiated income controls and full employment as its linked economic-policy determinants. In consequence, Norway has an economy growing at twice the rate of the average of OECD partners, has an unemployment rate of 4 per cent compared to a European average of over 11 per cent , provides unemployment benefits up to three years, provides substantial income support for all children under 17, and strictly regulates

the use of natural resources (James D. Daniels, 'Norway's Oil Helps All, Alberta's Helps Mostly Business', *The CCPA Monitor*, July/August 1998, pp. 16–17).

53. To remind us of the pattern of increasing domination of economies by non-productive money sequences, we might note here that 'from 1951 to 1987 the real cost of wages in the US increased 4 times ... while interest returns increased 25 times' (Roger Schmitz, 'The Interest Is Killing Us', *Monetary Reform*, Fall 1996, p. 16).

54. *Canadian Centre for Policy Alternatives Monitor*, October 1995, p. 5.

55. Canada's 'Big Five Banks' – seeking in 1998 to monopolize further as two banks – have 'increased their market share of total assets held by investment dealers from zero per cent held in 1984 to 70 per cent in 1994 and of the trust and loan industry from 30 per cent in 1984 to 69 per cent in 1994' (cited from a submission by William Krehm of the Committee on Monetary and Economic Reform to the Hon. Douglas Peters, Secretary of State, Financial Sector Division, Department of Finance, August 30, 1996). The banks, however, now seek access to ownership of the insurance industry as well on the grounds that this is 'necesssary to compete' with larger banks in the international market where Canada rates comparatively low in asset control.

56. Maude Barlow and Tony Clarke, 'Canada: The Broken Promise', *The Nation*, July 15–27, 1996, p. 26, give many of the salient figures here.

57. H. Mimoto and P. Cross, 'The Growth of the Federal Debt', *The Canada Economic Observer* (Statistics Canada), 1991, pp. 3.1–3.18 and Linda McQuaig, *Shooting the Hippo: Death by Deficit and Other Canadian Myths*, Toronto: Penguin Books, 1995, pp. 53–62, 117. Other debt and tax figures which follow are taken from these sources.

58. Ken Epps, 'A Record Year for Team Canada', *The Ploughshares Monitor*, September 1995, p. 3. McQuaig, *ibid*, pp. 87–8.

59. From 1990 to 1997, the National Bureau of Statistics calculated the rise of total federal government liabilities to be from $343 billion in 1990 to $512 billion in 1997 (Bruce Little, 'Who Lent Canada All That Money?' *Globe and Mail*, May 11, 1998, p. A5).

60. The private creation of money demand by private financial institutions, banks and the financial-credit operations of major corporations is the best-kept secret of the market system. But as Lester Thurow observed after two years of deregulation by the Reagan administration, 96 per cent of all new money entering the markets of the US and Canada is created by private money-lending institutions. They create interest-bearing debts beyond the cash that exists, and these non-cash forms of money demand circulate, compound and grow without limit of reserves, which are fractional and diminishing towards zero (about 4 per cent in the US). 'The Federal Reserve Board,' reports Thurow, 'announced that it was giving up on its attempts to control the US money supply on the grounds that [banks and other money-lending institutions] ... had essentially taken over the government's role as the printer of money' (cited by William Henry Pope, 'The Re-Nationalization of Money', *Options Politiques*, February 1992, p. 33).

61. William Krehm, *A Power Unto Itself: The Bank of Canada*. Toronto: Stoddart, 1993.

62. Linda McQuaig, *Shooting the Hippo: Death By Deficit and Other Myths*. Toronto: Penguin Books, 1995, pp. 87–8.

63. The 'New Labour' government also distinguished itself by not reversing a single decision or policy of its predecessor, the Thatcher government, and by repudiating all Keynesian public spending – a fiscal self-emasculation of elected authority which followed from the handover of the government's monetary levers to the Bank of England which had long played a role in its private history prior to 1945 in lending money on a fractional-reserve basis to the British government on the basis of government gold. We can infer that it was in recognition of this commitment to obey Britain's ruling financial interests that Blair's party was supported by the press baron, Rupert Murdoch, not only in exchange for sustaining money-sequence policies, but for continuing protection of Murdoch's tax-havened media monopoly. (See, for example, John Grieve Smith, 'Jobs For The Boys, But Not Jobs For All', *Guardian Weekly*, July 20, 1997.)

64. Article 107 of the Maastricht Treaty states: 'Neither the ECB [European Central Bank] nor any national bank shall seek or take instructions from Community institutions or bodies from any government of a Member state or from any other body. The Community institutions and bodies and the governments of the Members States undertake to respect this principle and not to seek to influence the members of the decision-making bodies of the ECB or of the national central banks in the performance of their tasks.' (From Appendix 3, Maastricht Treaty, Treaty on European Union, text dated February 7, 1992 in Stephen Frank Overturf, *Money and European Union*. New York: St. Martin's Press, 1997.)

65. Alanna Mitchell, 'Rising Death Among Infants Stun Scientists', *Globe and Mail*, June 2, 1995, Statistics Canada News Release, June 1.

66. Susan George, *Proceedings of the World Congress of the International Physicians for the Prevention of Nuclear War, XI*, October 1993, p. 239. Ecumenical Council for Economic Justice, *Recolonization or Liberation: The Bonds of Structural Adjustment and Struggles for Emancipation*, Toronto: 1990, p. 12. For regional analysis of this problem from a health-care perspective, see Marc Epprecht, 'The World Bank, Health and Africa', *Z Magazine*, November 1994, pp. 31–8.

67. Bernard Lietaer, '$2 Trillion in Currencies Traded Every Day'.

68. Ecumenical Coalition for Social Justice, 'Cooling Hot Money', *Economic Justice Report*, Vol. 5: No. 2 (1994), p. 2; Ted Fishman, 'Our Currency in Cyberspace', *Harper's Magazine*, December 1994, p. 54; Kevin Phillips, 'The Tyranny of Traders', *Report on Business Magazine*, November 1994, p. 65.

69. Eric R. Peterson, 'Surrendering to Markets', *The Washington Quarterly*, Autumn 1995, p. 113.

70. Monsoor Ejazz, 'Economic Forecasting', CBC, 'Sunday Morning', September 25, 1995.

71. Fred Bergsten, 'The Corpse at the Summit', *Washington Post*, June 11, 1995, p. C-4.

72. Fuller argument here is provided in my 'The Unspeakable: Understanding the System of Fallacy in the Mass Media', *Informal Logic*, Fall 1988, pp. 130–50.

Chapter 4: The Life Code versus the Money Code: The Paradigm Shift

1. The detailed development of this point may be found in my *Unequal Freedoms: The Global Market as an Ethical System*. Toronto: Garamond Press, 1998, especially pp. 60–70, 76, 98.

2. '[E]conomics made a fateful choice in the 1930s and 1940s and chose ... a bifurcation in economic thinking between theoretical systems and the real world ... Economists had to speak the language of mathematical models ... [although in the words of A.C. Pigou,] Alfred Marshall "[saw them] as intellectual toys ... causing us to neglect factors that could not be worked up easily in the mathematical machine" ... By the time we get to the next generation of textbooks on price theory, all we have is an instructional book on mathematical techniques ... peculiar forms of escapism ... As the Report of the Commission on Graduate Education states it, ... "we might teach the language of mathematics but not the logic of mathematics, and end up valuing the grammar of the discipline, rather than its substance". ... [Thus] mathematical economics ... leads to the elimination from the field of study of the very questions which the real world of economic life demands that we, as a profession, ask.' (Peter J. Boettke, 'What Is Wrong With Neoclassical Economics (And What Is Still Wrong With Austrian Economics)', in Fred Foldvary (ed.) *Beyond Neoclassical Economics*. New York: Edward Elgar Publishing, 1996.)

3. These famous phrases come from Volume I of *Capital*, the First Preface and Chapter XXXII, 'Historical Tendency of Capitalist Accumulation'. That Marx who was above all concerned to liberate humanity from the capitalist machine should have employed the scientistic language of mechanics to reify coercive value prescriptions into independently operating 'laws' and their programming of people into the forger of human liberation indicates the lock-hold of this paradigm on even its adversaries.

4. Russia, for example, was liberated to enter the global corporate system under the tutelage of global market advisers, with every shock treatment and stripping of social life infrastructure soon accomplished to achieve 'the inevitable adjustments'. Its productive economy collapsed by 70 per cent, male life-expectancy dropped 11 years, the sharpest fall recorded in history, and 70 million pensioners are at risk. Raw material exports now account for 45 per cent of its GDP, up from 20 per cent in 1990. (See, for example, P. Seymour, 'Russia's Capital Punishment', *Guardian Weekly*, November 23, 1998, p. 2 and Sergei Rogov, 'Five Challenges For Russia', *Peace Magazine*, September–October, 1997, p. 8.)

5. See, for example, the seven-article series by the *New York Times*, 'The Downsizing of America', March 3–9, 1996.

6. The source of the estimate of US deaths by malpractice in the US for-profit medical system is the Harvard School of Public Health (cited by Ralph Nader, 'It's Time to End Corporate Welfare As We Know It', *Earth Island Journal*, Fall 1996, p. 37).

7. Thus the President of Educom, a transnational corporate consortium, observes (my emphasis): 'The potential *to remove the human mediation* [in education] ... and replace it with automation – smart, computer-based network-based systems – is tremendous. Its gotta happen' (cited by Tony Winson, Department of Sociology, University of Guelph, November 28, 1997). See also David F. Noble, 'Digital Diploma Mills: The Automation of Higher Education', *Monthly Review*, February 1998, pp. 38–52.

8. Cited in 'Earning Gap Grows Quickly', *USA Today*, February 16, 1996, p. A1.

9. Forum, 'Does America Still Work?' *Harper's*, May 1996, p. 36.

10. *Ibid*, p. 37.

11. While George Gilder celebrates the money sequence's triumphs of trillions of dollars of mergers and acquisitions and the doubling of the stockmarket's money value, it is important to emphasize that the richest 5 per cent of Americans own 72 per cent of all such stock, while the bottom 80 per cent of Americans own 2 per cent. (Holly Sklar, 'Upsized CEOs', *Z Magazine*, June 1996, p. 34.)

12. The evidence here is world-wide, as figures given elsewhere in this study indicate. But since Canada has been recognized by the UN in recent years to be the 'best country in the world to live', and since its international trade figures have increased dramatically during the same period, it offers a revealing case. During the 'globalization' period since 1989, all of these effects have in fact occurred. Its fabled fishstocks are exhausted, its forests are clearcut at increasing rates, its annual average income for wage and salary workers has dropped precipitously since 1990, and real unemployment is at the highest prolonged levels since the Depression.

13. Colin Graham, 'Will the Public Expect the Global Economy to Self-Destruct?', *The CCPA Monitor*, July–August 1998, pp. 20–1.

14. Maude Barlow and Bruce Campbell, *Straight Through the Heart*. Toronto: HarperCollins, 1995, p. 37.

15. Council of Canadians, *Canadian Perspectives*, Winter 1994, p. 22.

16. Will Hutton, 'High-Risk Strategy Not Paying Off', *Guardian Weekly*, November 12, 1995, p. 13. James Petras and Steve Vieux, 'The Minimum Wage President', *Z Magazine*, November 1994, p. 25.

17. Will Hutton, 'Social Policies that Destroy Jobs', *Guardian Weekly*, July 30, 1995, p. 2.

18. Russell Herbert Mead, 'Essay', *Harper's Magazine*, September 1992, p. 41.

19. Eric Hobsbawm, 'Golden Era Ends Forever', *Canadian Centre for Policy Alternatives Monitor*, July/August 1995, p. 15.

20. *Ibid.*

21. Larry Elliott, 'Russia's Woes', *Guardian Weekly*, February 25, 1996, p. 12.

22. Hobsbawm, *op. cit.*

23. 'Russia's Welfare State', *Toronto Star*, November 26, 1995, p. F6.

24. Van Smiley, 'Russian Roulette', *Report on Business Magazine*, January 1996, p. 52.

25. Victoria Brittain, 'Peace Games Spur Angolan Collapse', *Guardian Weekly*, June 23, 1996, p. 6.

26. On this base-line of real economic value – the capacity of an economic organization to provide the basic means of life-growth to its next generation with the resources available – the global market system shows itself to be less competent than even the widely reviled Soviet command economies which it replaced. In central Europe, for example, 'the number of children living in poverty has more than doubled in the 1990s' (Ian Traynor, 'Children Pay Price For Democracy', *Guardian Weekly*, April 27, 1997). This sharp decline is significant because it provides control and experimental conditions from which to judge the efficiency of opposing economic systems on this basic life parameter. The point is not to argue for a Soviet-style economy, but to observe how very inefficient the global market system is with respect to such *life* indicators, which it is structured to block out from view.

27. Maggie O'Kane, 'A Plague That Kills Millions – The Plague of Debt', *Guardian Weekly*, May 17, 1998, p. 1.

28. It is now well known after decades of repression that US cigarette corporations concealed massive scientific findings of the lethal and disease-causing properties of their commodities, targeting children and manipulating toxins to addict consumers (Milo Geyelin, 'Secret Tobacco Files To Be Released,' *Wall Street Journal*, April 22, 1998). The millions of terrible deaths and diseases in consequence are not yet perceived to connect to an economic model that expels life requirements from its framework of judgement.

29. Larry Elliott, 'Why the Poor Are Picking Up the Tab', *Guardian Weekly*, May 17, 1998, p. 14.

30. Wallace A.C. Peterson, 'Class Warfare American Style', Plenary Session of the Eighth World Congress of Social Economics, College of Charlston, South Carolina, July 31, 1996.

31. It is worth noting here that this life value is much more comprehensive in referent than the 'lifeworld' to which continental philosophers refer in contemporary discourse. Jurgen Habermas, for example, typically of philosophers whose analysis is confined to the linguistic plane of existence, means by the term only *the symbolic realm of life.* See, for example, Jurgen Habermas (trans. Thomas McCarthy), *The Theory of Communicative Action* (Volume 1), Boston: Beacon Press, 1984, p. xxxiv. Here, in contrast, the symbolic realm of life occupies only one of three planes of life.

32. Michael McCally MD, 'Next Steps After Rio + 5: A Physician Briefing on Health and the Environment', *Medicine and Global Survival*, Vol. 5: No. 1 (1998), p. 27.

33. 'More than 50% of the most frequently prescribed drugs in the US are derived from or patterned after substances derived from bacteria, fungi, plants, or animals. As of today, researchers have tested for only 2% of known plant species' (McCally, *ibid*, p. 37).

34. Herman E. Daly, 'Sustainable Growth? No Thank You', in *The Case Against the Global Economy*. San Francisco: Sierra Books, 1996, p. 194.

35. Daly, *ibid*, p. 196.

36. A graphic example of the block against recognizing the extent of life-destructive 'externalities' by money sequences of growth is provided by Lawrence Summers, the Chief Economist of the World Bank. He proclaims, with no relevant expertise in the life sciences, that there are 'no natural limits to [monetized economic] growth' and 'no limits to the carrying capacity of the earth'. The claim that there are, he states, 'is a profound error' (cited by Susan George, Associate Director of the Transnational Institute, in the *Globe Report on Business*, May 29, 1992, p. B15).

37. Andrew Coyne, 'Banks Prompt Strong Reactions', *Globe and Mail*, December 28, 1995, p. B5.

38. I am indebted to Daniel Morgenson of the Department of Psychology, Wilfrid Laurier University for this example.

39. The cognitive closure to negative externalities of industrial market processes is by no means confined to the Third World. It is a general blinker of the model in all its jurisdictions of implementation. Consider the following US example. In a CNN television discussion on November 26, 1996, a spokesman of the environmental health scientists of the US Environmental Protection Agency proposed new legislation to reduce air pollution, reporting that *166,000 US citizens die prematurely each year from air particulates from industrial effluents and exhausts.* His opponent, a representative of the corporations producing the effluents, insisted that further regulations were 'too costly'. The evidence

of the 166,000 deaths from the preventible air pollution depositing the deadly particulates was ruled out of view.

40. Another first-hand account of the Maquiladora 'free trade zones' of Latin America is given by Charles Bowden in 'While You Were Sleeping', *Harper's Magazine*, December 1996, pp. 44–52. The city is Ciudad Juarez on the border of Texas. 'Real wages have been falling since the 1970s – the working class [have suffered a drop] in their purchasing power of in excess of 50 per cent over an eight year period ... There are few environmental controls and little enforcement of those that exist ... yet industry is thriving ... it is a success story ... last year growth registered 12 per cent. ... The future is based on the rich getting richer, the poor getting poorer and industrial growth producing poverty faster than it distributes wealth.' For Bowden, in particular because of the many murdered teenage girls, the situation in Juarez is 'a living hell'. But every element of it is perfectly consistent with the market's self-regulating principles.

41. When federal health department scientists in Canada warned of the danger of these foods, the report was suppressed (Thomas Walkom, 'Mutant Food Products Hard to Swallow', *The Toronto Star*, June 2, 1998, p. A2). The world's largest producers of soya and milk, US transnationals like Monsanto Corporation, mix gene-altered soya with real soya and produce hormone-boosted milk at 40 per cent higher volume per unit of cost, and then threaten WTO trade action against any government which labels the products for 'discriminating against the process of production', a new transnational trade prohibition. Adulterated food in this way becomes illegal to identify.

42. I am indebted to Karen Finlay of the Department of Consumer Studies, University of Guelph for this finding of her research.

43. Myron Gordon, Faculty of Management Studies, University of Toronto, has stated that 'production is now secondary in the global market'. He provides a pace-setting figure of $800 millions for production costs, $800 millions for research, and $2 billion for advertising (Interdisciplinary Conference on the Evolution of World Order, Toronto, June 7–9, 1997).

44. A more developed account of the political economy of the armaments commodity may be found in my monograph, *Understanding War*, Toronto: Science for Peace, 1989. Lest it be thought that armaments are means of life in the sense of means of defending civilian populations from aggressors, we need to bear in mind that over three of four people killed by the armaments commodity in war are non-combatant civilians, and most of them are killed by their own governments (Ruth Leger Sivard *et al*, *World Military and Social Expenditures 1996*. Washington D.C., 1996).

45. We may think that after the end of the Cold War research into the leading weapons of mass destruction by US government programmes has effectively tapered off. But according to a 300-page document leaked in the summer of 1997, a massive secret programme to build a new generation of nuclear weapons, more extensive than at the height of the Cold War, has been funded to design and develop new warheads using computer-simulated detonations to avoid the restraints of signed test-ban treaties. The new programme is called, with now familiar Orwellian embellishment, 'The Stockpile Stewardship and Management Plan'. (Ed Vulliamy, reporting National Resources Defence Council, 'US in Secret New Nuclear Buildup', *Guardian Weekly*, August 24, 1997, p. 1)

At the same time, the publicly-funded US military-industrial complex controls over 70 per cent of the armaments market of the less developed countries, who expend up to 70 per cent of their public revenues on these weapons along with debt-interest payments to international money-lenders. ('External Debt and Military Spending', XI Conference of the International Physicians for the Prevention of Nuclear War, October 1993)

In these ways the money sequences combine to bleed impoverished societies dry of the little public wealth they possess.

46. Richard Norton-Taylor, 'Huge Subsidies Boost UK Arms Sales,' *Guardian Weekly*, May 28, 1995, p. 1.

47. United Press International, November 2, 1983.

48. Japanese banks which became heavily involved in international financing after the world-leading success of its planned productive ventures in automobiles and electronic manufacturing now hold an estimated $850 billion in bad debts (figure cited in Marcus Gee, 'The Real End of Japan Inc.,' *Globe and Mail*, April 18, 1998, p. D4).

49. The figures of child deaths are from UNICEF, September 1997, while those on child stunting are from UNFAO, September 1995.

50. '25% of Military Spending Would Cure World's Worst Ills,' *Canadian Centre for Policy Alternatives Monitor*, July/August 1995, p.18.

51. The following is a typical pattern of the relationship between state militaries equipped with advanced weapons commodities using these armaments to clear indigenous people off the land, a pattern as old as colonization and implemented also in such places as Guatemala, Somalia, East Timor and the Philippines. In the case of the global market invasion of the lands of the southern Mexican state of Chiapas, the story went as follows. Prior to the 1992 North American Free Trade Agreement, the Mexican government removed a constitutional provision protecting the communal lands of the Mayan people so that the land could be converted to corporate agribusiness production, and at the same time open South Mexico markets to the cheaper, subsidized corn and bean products of US corprorations. The Mayans resisted 'the death sentence of NAFTA', and the Mexican military proceeded to destroy the Chiapas farmers' villages and farms, latrines and water pipes with helicopters, tractors and armed personnel carriers, and also bombed them from the air with the latest napalm products. (John McMurtry, 'A Day in the Life of the New World Order', *Globe and Mail*, April 1, 1995, p. A17.)

52. After the massive defeat of the German armed forces in the Battle of Stalingrad in January 1943, Martin Bormann, the Deputy Fuhrer and the main linkage of the Nazi party with the industrial and financial cartels that ran the German economy, conceived a plan for post-War organization of German Nazis in Latin America, South Africa, Egypt and Indonesia called the 'Organization of Veterans of the S.S.,' or Odessa by acronym. A main element of the Odessa was the Gehlen Organization headed by General Reinhard Gehlen who was head of the Foreign Armies East in German Army Headquarters. He was responsible for all intelligence operations through East Europe and the Soviet Union, and in the remaining months of the war deposited the extensive files in a hiding place in the Bavarian Alps. After the war was over, he negotiated a secret treaty to work 'jointly with the Americans' on the basis of the detailed files and the services of some 4000 agents. 'By one estimate, some 70 per cent of the total intelligence flowing into NATO's military

committee and Allied headquarters (SHAPE) on the Soviet Union, the countries of East Europe, the rest of Europe and indeed the rest of the world was generated [from this source].' (Carl Oglesby,' The Secret Treaty of Fort Hunt'. *Covert Action Bulletin*, 35, Fall 1990, pp. 8–16.) Corroborating this heavily researched account, Lake Sagaris reports in her detailed study of Pinochet's Chile (Sagaris, *op. cit.*) that Nazi activity and influence in Chile was particularly widespread during Pinochet's military dictatorship from 1973–90 (cited in Graeme Mount, 'The Long Shadow of Chile's Fascism', *Literary Review of Canada*, October 1996, pp. 8–10).

53. Victor W. Sidel and Robert C. Wesley, 'Violence as a Public Health Problem: Lessons for Action Against Violence By Health-Care Professionals', *Social Justice*, 22:4 (1995), p. 161.

54. Holly Sklar, 'Outrageous Military Spending Continues', *Canadian Centre for Policy Alternatives Monitor*, April 1996, p. 7.

55. We have focused on the publicly-subsidized weapons commodities of state militaries. But recreational weapons are also a significant business with more guns than people in the US, and over 14,000 shooting deaths a year to confirm their function of killing human life. 'Most industry executives think the adult shooting market has become saturated, so with the failure of attempts to market guns to women shooters, the attention has switched openly and explicitly to children.' (Martin Kettle, 'Held to Ransom By The Gun Lobby', *Guardian Weekly*, April 5, 1998, p. 6.)

56. Here we see in clear expression what we will call the global market's death sequence of value affirmed as an optimum good. (Figures and quotations are cited in Glenn Frankel, 'US Aided Tobacco Firms in Asia Conquest', from the *Washington Post* in the *Guardian Weekly*, December 1, 1996, p. 15.)

57. That the corporate cigarette has been deliberately designed as a life-killing commodity is an assertion based on the now public facts that this commodity's production and marketing has long targeted children as young as 12 to become addicted at a more extreme level than heroin to a scientifically tested toxic chemical mix whose disease- and death-causing properties were known to be the single leading cause of preventable death and crippling disease world-wide. (I am indebted to molecular biologist Stan Blecher, University of Guelph, for the precision of this information.)

58. MIT Vegetarian Support Group, 'How Our Food Choices Affect Life On Earth,' *World-Wide-Web*, November 22, 1996, p. 1.

59. Together these economic operations of extraction and pollution 'lead to the extinction of plants and animals at about 1000 times the normal rate' (D.J. McLaren, 'Reply', *Delta: Newsletter of the Canadian Climate Change Program*, Vol. 7: No. 3 (1996), p. 3), with 'about $500 billion a year subsidizing the destruction of the oceans, atmospheres and land' (John Vidal, 'World Turning Blind Eye To Catastrophe', Reports of UN Environment Agency, British Panel on Sustainable Development, and World-Watch Institute, *Guardian Weekly*, February 7, p. 1). According to the Rio Plus Five Forum Earth Summit meeting in March 1997, these processes of life destruction and deterioration have not abated since the 178 nations pledged to 'clean up the world' five years previously, but have increased. Thus in 1997, while only 3 per cent of the earth's original temperate rainforest still stands, the UN's choice of the best country in the world to live, where one province alone contains over a quarter of the world's total supply, continues to clearcut forests at a 40 per cent higher rate than what its government estimates is sustainable

(Sierra Legal Defence Fund, 'Clearcut Future?' July 1997, p. 4). Here again we see the evidences of a value programme whose life-destructive consequences do not register to or inhibit its reproduction. At the same time, the money sequence of value grows as rapidly as the life sequence is depleted, with for example the number of the world's billionaires multiplying by more than 10 times since 1987 (Associated Press, July 14, 1997).

60. I sit on the Animal Care Committee of Canada's most intensive animal research institution, and also its subcommittee for protocol approval. I estimate that over 95 per cent of all publicly funded research done on animals is driven by the regulating money-sequence principle of reducing money costs for private corporate producers. No-one in the field has denied the estimate.

61. John Ralston Saul, *The Unconscious Civilization*. Toronto: House of Anansi Press, 1995, p. 11.

62. The *Wall Street Journal* reports, for example, that in February of 1998, the Japanese Parliament passed two bills, one that provided over US$100 billion for infusion of new capital into banks, and a greater amount to protect their depositors (cited by William Krehm, 'Donors of the Last Resort', *Economic Reform*, March 1998, p. 9). The hundreds of billions thus committed went to upholding the money sequence from collapse, while leaving declining infrastructure, unaffordable housing, and other life deficits unresponded to.

63. Andrew Simms, 'Double Standards on a Matter of Life or Debt,' *Guardian Weekly*, June 22, 1997, p. 23.

64. Three of these figures come from William F. Hixson, *A Matter of Interest: Re-examining Money, Debt, and Real Economic Growth*. New York: Praeger, 1991, pp. xix, xviii, and 270 respectively. The final figure comes from John Dillon, *Turning the Tide: Confronting the Money Traders*. Ottawa: Canadian Centre for Policy Alternatives, 1996, p. 67.

65. The facts which confirm all of these principles are best provided in Michel Chossudovsky's masterful study, *The Globalisation of Poverty*. Penang, Malaysia: Third World Books, 1997.

66. 'Caught in the Middle in Chiapas', *Globe and Mail*, March 24, 1995, p. A7.

67. Michel Chossudovsky, *The Globalization of Poverty*. Penang, Malaysia: Third World Books, 1997, pp. 193–205.

68. Jane Diaz-Limaco in Lima, 'Hint of Hope for Hostages in Peru', *Guardian Weekly*, January 5, 1997, p. 1.

69. UN Environment Program, *Canadian Press*, April 20, 1996.

70. World Health Organization, *Guardian Weekly*, May 21, 1995.

71. These figures are cited from, respectively, *Globe and Mail* Report on Business, July 25 and William Krehm, *Economic Reform*, July 1997, p. 3.

72. This account is drawn from Chossudovsky, *The Globalization of Poverty*, pp. 111–20.

73. Interest demands on public debt in Canada, for example, have escalated nearly eightfold in real terms between 1962–81 and 1981–95, requiring a corresponding dismantling of health, education and social security budgets to pay the compound-interest demands. In the US, as we have seen, it is estimated that at the 1967–87 rate of the interest-demand share of the US national income, all of the national income would be required to pay off compound-interest payments to money lenders by 2020 (William F. Hixson, *A Matter of Interest: Re-Examining Money, Debt, and Real Economic Growth*. New York: Praeger, 1991, pp. 177 and 176).

74. As the former Prime Minister of Australia, Malcolm Fraser, explains: 'Since the value of its [the US's] external debt, massive as it is, is written in US dollars, it is able to ignore the totality of that debt. It is also able to depreciate the value of the debt very significantly by depreciating the value of the US dollar (Malcolm Fraser, 'The US Pulls the Purse Strings', *The Australian*, October 10, 1996).

75. Even the IMF admits that the banking system itself provides by its publicly chartered lending powers almost 90 per cent of the money capital for currency speculators to attack national currencies, including the nations chartering the banks (figures cited by Roy Culpeper, 'Why We Have Currency Crises', *Report on Business*, December 27, 1997, p. 2).

76. Karl Marx, *Capital*, Volume 3: Chapter 29.

77. 'Capital Controversies', *The Economist*, May 23, 1998, p. 72.

78. 'The Way It Looks To Mr Yen', *Newsweek*, February 2, 1998, p. 56.

79. 'Asia's Avoidable Meltdown', *Guardian Weekly*, December 1997, p. 12.

Chapter 5: The Great Vehicle of the Civil Commons

1. I am indebted to Howard Woodhouse of the University of Saskatchewan who reported these facts to me from France where he was on sabbatical during 1995. In transglobal correspondence, a strike demonstration to protest against the provincial goverment's stripping of education, social assistance and environmental protection budgets brought out the largest crowd of supporters of a workers' demonstration in Canadian history, 250,000 people. It was reported widely in the media as 75,000, removing approximately 150,000 people from the protest.

2. 'From Abroad', *Times Higher Educational Supplement*, January 19, 1996, p. 19.

3. 'France is in Two Moods over Strike'. *Le Monde* report in *Guardian Weekly*, December 24, 1995, p. 9.

4. Tom Bueckle, 'Jobs Divide European Union Leaders', *International Herald Tribune*, March 29, 1996, p. 1.

5. 'Chirac Calls Snap Election in France', *Guardian Weekly*, April 27, p. 12 (emphasis added). The President of the French Republic is himself a symptom of the schizophrenic division between the market's money code demands and the requirements of society for the protection of the lives of its people. Chirac on December 12 1996 seemed to be asserting the opposite of what he had defended months before. Now he blamed the French people for being too 'conservative' and 'not responsible' for resisting the pace of 'market reforms'. ('Chirac Does A U-Turn On The French', *Guardian Weekly*, January 5, 1997).

6. John McMurtry, 'Europe dances to different tune', *Guardian Weeekly*, May 18, 1997.

7. Larry Elliott and Michael White, 'Brown Does A Conjuring Trick', *Guardian Weekly*, July 13, 1997, p. 7.

8. World Development Report 1995, *Workers in An Integrating World*. New York: Oxford University Press, 1996, p. 6.

9. *Ibid*, p. 110.

10. *Ibid*, p. 2.

11. 'Oxfam reports that in 1995–96, World Bank President James Wofensohn made a firm promise to increase social sector loans to developing countries from $4 billion to $5 billion a year for three years to provide vital health-care, nutrition, education and AIDS prevention. Bank lending figures for fiscal year 1997 now show that lending for health and education has instead plummeted to $2.5 billion' (Karen Hodgson, *Guardian Weekly*, May 24, 1998, p. 2).

12. Press Release, Office of the President, World Bank, 'World Bank Develops New System to Measure the Wealth of Nations', Washington, D.C., September 18, 1995, pp. 1–9.

13. 'Chileans Wrangle over Resources', *The Economist*, February 1996 (reproduced under this title in *Globe and Mail*, February 6, 1996, p. A11).

14. Drew Fagan, 'Gloves off debate sets stage for crucial southern primary', *Guardian Weekly*, March 1, 1996, p. 6.

15. 'Harsh language for party leaders', *New York Times*, February 19, 1996, p. A9.

16. 'For Workers, It's Still the Economy', *USA Today*, February 15, 1996, p. A10; *Globe and Mail*, March 22, 1996, p. A18.

17. Terence Corcoran, 'What's Wrong with Buchanan?' *Globe Report on Business*, February 24, 1996, p. B2.

18. Jeffrey C. Garten in 'Global Roulette', *Harper's Magazine*, June 1998, p. 40.

19. John McMurtry, 'The Social Immune System and the Cancer Stage of Capitalism', *Social Justice*, Vol. 22: No. 4 (1995), pp. 1–25.

20. Robert Reich, *Work of Nations*. New York: Vintage Books, 1992, pp. 3, 8.

21. 'The Downsizing of America', *New York Times*, March 8, 1996, p. A13.

22. Robert Reich, *Locked in the Cabinet*. New York: Alfred A. Knopf, 1997.

23. 'Economic Forecasting', Sunday Morning, *Canadian Broadcasting Corporation Radio*, September 25, 1995. (I am indebted to Maggie Laidlaw for her recording and transcription of this statement.)

24. R. Peterson, 'Surrendering to Markets', *Washington Quarterly*, Autumn, 1995, p. 111.

25. George Soros, *The Alchemy of Finance*. New York: Simon and Schuster, 1987, pp. 100–1.

26. George Soros, 'The Capitalist Threat', *Atlantic Monthly*, February 1997, p. 45.

27. Soros, 'The Capitalist Threat', pp. 46–7.

28. George Monbiot, 'The Tragedy of Enclosure', *Scientific American*, January 1994.

29. 'The unbridled plunder of the world's forests by giant timber firms', reports the Environment Investigation Agency of the United Nations Inter-Governmental Panel on Forests, 'is increasing at an alarming rate. ... The $100 billion timber industry is running out of control. ... Unless swift and decisive action is taken to control the intense pressures on the world's forests, the 20th century's legacy will be the extermination of most of the world's species and massive social disturbance.' The timber trade, the UN Agency reports, is 95 per cent dominated by multinational firms who now control 45 million hectares of rainforest. All log illegally as well as legally. Mitsubishi leads the 'forest rapists', Daishowa and Musa of Indonesia face charges of corruption. Samling of Malaysia, Hyundai of Korea, the US's Boise Cascade, rougier of France, Klunz and Karl Danzer of Germany and Macmillan-Bloedel of Canada are charged with systematically illegal practices. 'Deforestation is wiping out plant and animal species, increasing soil erosion and flooding and contributing to global warming', the UN report continues.

'27,000 species are made extinct each year in tropical forest alone.' (David Harrison, 'Loggers Out of Control in Forest Chainsaw Massacre', *Observer*, reproduced in the *Guardian Weekly*, September 15, 1996)

30. An excellent source of concrete examples of traditional commons within 'sustenance economies' is Maria Mies and Vandana Shiva, *Ecofeminism*. London: Zed Books, 1993.

31. Douglas Rushkoff, 'Free Lessons In Innovation', *Guardian*, April 9, 1998, p. 16.

32. Rushkoff, *ibid.* We should note here that it is not just a question of the civil commons being morally superior to the market because its principle of goods distribution is universalized. The civil commons is also *more cost efficient* than the market in the production of life-goods. Rushkoff observes this superior efficiency in the development of creative online technology by shareware. Richard Titmuss has investigated and generalized this superior competence in his classic study of blood banks (Richard M. Titmuss, *The Gift: From Blood to Social Policy*, London: Allen and Unwin, 1971). Ralph Nader among others has observed that public-sector health-care is vastly more cost efficient than for-profit market 'health maintenance', which in the US costs $1000 more per capita than Canada's public system, leaves 78 million people uninsured or grossly under-insured, and results in more deaths from medical malpractice than from traffic accidents, homicides and fires combined (Ralph Nader, 'Stop Americanizing Canadian Medicare', *CCPA Monitor*, February 1996, p. 16 and 'It's Time to End Corporate Welfare As We Know It', *Earth Island Journal*, Fall 1996, p. 37). David F. Noble has demonstrated that corporate training through private-sector telecommunications technology 'greatly expands administrative costs' with no gain in efficiency of educational dissemination ('Digital Diploma Mills: The Automation of Higher Education' (*OCUFA* [Ontario Confederation of Faculty Associations] *Bulletin*, Spring 1998, pp. 12–15), while I have argued that the for-profit market model and education are contradictory in principle ('Education and the Market Model', *Journal of the Philosophy of Education*, Vol. 25: No. 2 (1991), pp. 209–18). As we will see ahead, there are deep reasons in principle for this superior efficiency of civil commons institutions to the market in producing life goods.

33. The problem even here is that these international initiatives to save the environment can be used to further uproot the indigenous and the poor from their environments to, say, 'save tropical rainforests', a further deflection of the global market paradigm from facing the consequences of global market industrial destruction as the primary determinant of rapidly disappearing forest habitats.

34. E.P.Thompson writes: ' To be sure, this was not some generous and universalistic communal spirit. ... [It was] the bounded, circular, jealously possessive consciousness of the parish. The communal economy was parochial and exclusive: if Weldon's rights were "ours", then Brigstock men and women must be kept out' (E.P. Thompson, *Customs In Common: Studies in Traditional Popular Culture*. New York: The New Press, 1993, p. 179).

35. The defining pattern here has been the shift from and defunding of UN agencies protecting human rights and seeking to limit the control of multinational corporations (for example, the UN Centre and Code of Conduct for Transnational Corporations) to exclusive emphasis on IMF and other Bretton Woods institutions extracting interest payments and demanding open markets from poorer countries. (See, for example, any of the work by Martin Khor of the Third World Network of Penang, Malaysia.)

36. Ratios of external debt servicing + military spending to total government expenditures (ED + MS : TGS) provides a window on this pattern. The ratio is *over 65 per cent* for the United States, El Salvador, Indonesia, the Phillippines, and Columbia, for example (International Physicians for the Prevention of Nuclear War, XI Congress, October 1993).

37. There are now, according to David Gordon of the New School of Social Research, 17 million monitors and supervisors of the global market's regime in the US alone, not counting their secretaries, assistants and office staffs. They cost the economy $1.3 trillion in 1994, or *four times the total cost of US Social Security*. This cost of 'efficient' market administration is estimated to now be, on average, 20 per cent of the cost of all goods produced (Jack M. Beatty, 'What Election 96 Should Be About', *Atlantic Monthly*, May 1996 and David M. Gordon, *The Corporate System of Squeezing Americans*. New York: Simon and Schuster, 1996). In the sphere of activity where we can compare their performances, health-care, the US for-profit health-care system spends 22–24 cents on the dollar for administrative costs, while the Canadian non-profit, public system spends 10–11 cents on the dollar. That is, the 'market methods' which are everywhere declared 'necessary' for making the public sector 'operate more efficiently' are, in fact, twice as bureaucratically expensive as the non-profit, public system (Margaret Phillips, 'Canadian and US Health Care', *Canadian Perspectives*, 1995, p. 3). The public sector's 'bureaucratic bloat' is a secondary manifestation of the market money sequence's imperative for self-multiplying money revenues delinked from productive performance.

38. The constitutional objective of universities, for example, is normally worded in statute or other constitutional document of this institution as 'the advancement and dissemination of knowledge'. My experience has been that adhering to such a codified and constitutional objective as obliging all members of the institution is not a 'paper weapon', but a *civil commons given* on whose basis even a single individual can steer an institution from a course of action that does not comply with it. My experience has been similar with city plan legislation. In the cases with which I am familiar, a university was obliged to review and eventually forfeit a $55 million government-to-government contract as an executing agency with the Government of Indonesia, and a middle-sized city was required to pass an emergency control bylaw to protect all of its older buildings from lucrative developer contracts. These cases are observed here because they demonstrate the power of the civil commons infrastructure even in the form of codified purpose alone and one member of the commons upholding it. What lies behind is a history of institutional evolution and struggle for the common interest precipitated as stated shared ground upon which all successors stand whether yet conscious of it or not.

39. A constitutional lawyer representing citizens for The Defence of Canadian Liberty against the secretive, unconstitutional, and electorally unaccountable process of negotiation of the Multilateral Agreement on Investment among the 29 countries of the OECD described her official meeting with the Chief Negotiator for Canada as follows: 'Questions were not answered on the grounds of cabinet privilege ... whether or not some form of negotiation issue was ever forwarded to cabinet ... whether exemptions for first nations apply ... who directs the negotiations, makes decisions ... I came away struck by the enormity and extent of the power and the arrogance ... There was a distinct

impression that the unelected people running the government are our enemies.' (Connie Fogel, 'MAI Legal Challenge Report On Cross Examination of Federal Witnesses', via Council For Canadians, June 24, 1998.)

40. Along with these 'free trade agreements', a complementary method of transnational corporate takeover of domestic resources of poorer countries is by 'debt squeezing': where international banks and financial institutions loan money to these countries to keep up compound-interest loads in return for transnational corporate access to protected natural resources. By this method, 70 countries in Latin America, Asia, and Eastern Europe reformed their mining and forestry laws between 1992 and 1998 to open them up to foreign companies to extract resources not available in the past, with long leases, vast concessions, tax breaks, rights to evict communities and exemption from laws to enable the new global money-sequence invasion (figures from John Vidal, 'Baptism of Fire', *Guardian Weekly*, May 21, 1998, p. 23).

41. Resolution of the European Parliament via Rule 90(5) of Rules of Procedure, March 10, 1998. (I am indebted to Tony Clarke for this document who, in turn, received it from Gaby Kueper, Assistant to Wolfgang Kreissl-Doerfer, Green Group in the European Parliament.)

42. Tony Clarke, *The Corporate Rule Treaty*. Ottawa: Canadian Centre for Policy Alternatives, 1997, p. 9.

43. The statement was made on Friday April 3 in comments to Dutch NGOs. (I am indebted to an e-mail from Olivier Hoedeman for this quotation.)

44. 'OECD Head Unfazed By MAI Protests', Canadian Press, May 25 Release, 1998.

45. E.J. Dionne, 'Sidetracked on the Road to Global Growth', *Guardian Weekly*, June 7, 1998, p. 16.

46. It is sometimes held that a global economy with minimum standards would discriminate against nations because more developed nations could invoke these standards as a 'protectionist device' against imports from Third World nations. This argument is favoured by corporate spokesmen. In fact, representatives of Third World peoples argue that with such standards 'the Third World ... would be able to insist that those invited adhere to health and safety standards that prevail in the industrial countries' (Martin Khor, 'Global Economy and the Third World' in *The Case Against the Global Economy* (ed. Jerry Mander and Edward Goldsmith). San Francisco: Sierra Club Books, 1996, p. 58).

47. Geoffrey Chandler, 'Corporate Greed Set Against People's Need', *Guardian Weekly*, November 24, 1996, p. 12. (The author is described as 'Sir Geoffrey Chandler, a former senior director of the Royal Dutch Shell Group'.)

48. Paul Fireman, 'A Good Fit For All', *Report on Business*, January 1997, pp. 67–8.

49. John Pilger, 'Burma: Brutal Facts Lay Bare a Land of Fear', *Guardian Weekly*, May 12, 1996, pp. 22–3.

50. *Canadian Criminal Code*, Chapter 37, Section 6, 1.96.

51. The poverty figures are reported in John Vidal, 'The Global Formula For Dynamite', *Globe and Mail*, June 15, 1996, p. D4. The 100 manufacturers of torture instruments, 42 American, is reported in 'The 10 Top Censored Stories', *Utne Reader*, July–August 1998, p. 16. The *UN 1997 Human Development Report* notes the relative as well as absolute decline of life means for the poorest quintile of the world's people, more than halved since 1960, from 2.3 to 2.1, while the inequality ratio to the richest quintile more than

doubled, from 30:1 in 1960 to 78:1 in 1994 (David Harrison, 'Turning a Blind Eye to Pollution', *Observer* via *Guardian Weekly*, June 27, 1997).

52. Martin Walker, 'Europe This Week', *Guardian Weekly*, November 9, 1997, p. 6.

53. While the slow-motion European life-stripping continues with resistance most developed in France where the government of Lionel Jospin has steered the economy with life co-ordinates in view (for example, a 35-hour week, a tax increase on accumulated money wealth, and retention of public-sector investment), *The Economist* predictably recites the mantras of the global market, the magic syllables of masking, in opposing any sequence but money protection and growth – 'big cuts in taxes and social charges, fewer civil servants, greater labour-market flexibility, more support for free enterprise, more privatization, reforms of the welfare state ... call into question the sacrosanct minimum wage ... globalization ... an opportunity for our renewal'. Go over the list again. It is a catechism of the global cancer, every policy a continuance and increase of less costs for life and more for money sequence growth without limit ('The Rally of the French Right', *The Economist*, February 7, 1998, p. 51).

54. 'Answer to a Taxing Question', *Guardian Weekly*, June 14, 1998, p. 13.

55. Bernard Lietauer, '$2 Trillion In Currencies Traded Every Day', *CCPA Monitor*, March 1998, p. 16.

56. I refer here to the Maastricht Treaty's maximum deficit-to-GDP ratio of 3 per cent. This will have two predictable consequences: reduction of social spending to protect life, and increased protection to the value of European money held. This is in line with the logic of the cancer, regulating to protect money rather than life. It is the defence chosen by Europe against currency attacks by rogue money sequences, thus exposing itself to a less terrifying form of the disease to protect itself. The social immune option of a healthy social host would be to stop the currency attacks by a strict, transnational deterrent tax. But it is blinkered out because the mutant paradigm excludes whatever regulates money sequences, in proportion to their power to attack life. This is the inner code of the disease in succumbing public sectors.

57. When the Asian meltdown struck in January of 1998, I wrote the following letter to explain its cause. It was refused publication in 'Canada's national newspaper', the *Globe and Mail*, but provides a short summary explanation which is useful here. (It was soon after published as the lead letter in the *Guardian Weekly*, which is not controlled as a corporate advertising vehicle.)

> The meltdown of the 'miracle economies' of Asia has given rise to some perplexity. How could all of these economies which had 'the fundamentals right' suddenly collapse together overnight?
>
> Since the unregulated international financial system which caused these failures cannot be wrong, the fault must be the simultaneous and sudden sin of the economies involved. But people are beginning to disbelieve this fairy tale. They know something else is afoot.
>
> For just as the Multilateral Agreement on Investment (MAI) is being negotiated to open all the economies of the OECD still further to these deluges of unregulated money flows, the miracle economies themselves lie bleeding on the floor.
>
> So what does the International Monetary Fund do to rescue the failing system as it careens across continents leaving ever more broken societies

in its wake? It leads a publicly-funded rescue package to lend ever more billions to keep the hot money going – over US$100 billion at last count.

But make no mistake. It is not Indonesia or South Korea or Malaysia or any other country which is being 'bailed out' by this bottomless pit of emergency loans. It is this ruinously deregulated financial system itself and, more directly, the loan capital of international banks which stand to lose big from unpaid interest and debts if the money is not kept churning to them by the injection of countless billions into drained national accounts.

It is the foreign banks and creditors who lent the money who are, in fact, being bailed out. All that is being received by these mortally wounded societies is massive new debt to keep paying their external creditors back, along with a large dose of more financial deregulation to colonize them further.

At some point, the world's publics who are paying for this stripping of their societies to enrich the high-volume and velocity flood of deregulated money around the globe will awake from the nightmare imposed upon them by this mindless model of 'market freedom'. My bet is that we are beginning to already.

58. I am indebted to Alex Michalos, *The Tobin Tax*, Toronto: Science for Peace, for many of the points in this paragraph.

59. 'Illustration of an Assumed Investment of $10,000', *Templeton Growth Fund Limited Annual Report*, April 30, 1998, p. 3.

60. Peter Drucker, 'The Idol Rich', *Report On Business Magazine*, January 1998, p. 88.

61. In the 1998 Competitiveness Rankings by the World Economic Forum, the growth of child poverty, youth unemployment, environmental depletion and degradation, and every other indicator of societies in serious life-slippage – where 'successful economies' are in fact falling fast – is simply excluded from the index. This is how the value metric of the global market paradigm is systemically life-blind, and how nations which follow it can be hollowed out while believing they are ever more competitive.

62. The figures referred to above are drawn from across the special issue of *Newsweek* (February 2, 1998) devoted to the Asia financial crisis, 'How Big Is Asia?' *The Economist*, February 7, 1998, p. 72, *Wall Street Journal*, February 17, 1998 and Marcus Gee, 'The Real End of Japan Inc.' *Globe and Mail*, April 18, 1998, p. D4.

63. Kieran A. Kennedy, 'The Role of the State in Economic Affairs', *Studies*, Summer 1985, p. 131.

64. The Prime Minister of Malaysia described this uncontrolled money sequence's effects as follows: 'Markets can also become corrupt ... We are seeing the effect today – the impoverishment and misery of millions of people and their eventual slavery. ... Two decades of growth wiped out in two weeks. ... Vibrant economies have been reduced to begging for aid from the IMF ... [It is] a recipe for slavery' (Asia Pacific Conference, Vancouver, November as cited in Bob Djurdjevic, 'Wall Street's Financial Terrorism', *Chronicles* (Vol. 22, No. 3), March 1998. While the models of slavery and terrorism used by the Prime Minister and the reporter may hold, the largely unintentional effects are better understood as an aggressive disease of social life-organization.

65. Milton Friedman, 'A Monetary and Fiscal Framework for Economic Stability', *The American Economic Review*, Vol. 38 (1948), pp. 245–64. See also John H. Hotson, 'Ending the Debt Money System', *Challenge*, March–April 1985,

pp. 48–50 and 'Professor Friedman's Goals Applauded, His Means Questioned', *Challenge*, September–October 1985, pp. 59–61. This is apparently a position that the politically opportunistic Friedman has thought better to remain silent on in the present circumstances of the rule over societies of private corporate debt-holders and banks.

66. 'The colonies', said Franklin, 'would have gladly borne a little tax on tea and other matters, had it not been that England took away from the Colonies their money, which created unemployment and dissatisfaction' (cited by Patrick S.J. Carmack, 'The Money Masters', *Monetary Reform Magazine*, Fall 1997, p. 33). It was in this light that US President Thomas Jefferson later warned, 'I believe that banking institutions are more dangerous to our liberties than standing armies. Already they have raised up a monied aristocracy that has set the Government at defiance. The issuing power should be taken from the banks and restored to the people to whom it properly belongs' (cited in William F. Hickson, *Triumph of the Bankers: Money and Banking in the Eighteenth and Nineteenth Centuries*, Westport, CT: Praeger, 1993, p. 94). About 170 years later, Canada's Prime Minister William Lyon Mackenzie King declared, 'Until the control of the issue of currency and credit is restored to government and recognized as its most conspicuous and sacred responsibility, all talk of the sovereignty of Parliament and of democracy is idle and futile.... Once a nation parts with control of its credit, it matters not who makes the nation's laws. ... Usury once in control will wreck any nation' (cited in *Monetary Reform*, Summer 1996, p. 16).

67. See the preceding and subsequent statements by Franklin, Jefferson and King.

68. While African nations are bled at the average rate of four times their total health and education budgets by debt services to foreign money lenders, it is little known that the creation of money by government at low interest rates for private and public enterprises whose interest payments revert to public ownership is a long-established device of prosperous growth. We have seen that the success of the pre-revolutionary American colonies depended on this device, and that its prohibition by the British government precipitated the revolution. (See also John Kenneth Galbraith, *Money*, Boston: Houghton-Mifflin, 1975, pp. 45–89 on this hidden dimension of American politics.) It was also the means whereby the Canadian government after the Second World War paid back twice as high a debt as a percentage of GDP than is permitted by the European Union and maintained a robust growth rate at the same time. In exact contrast to the stripping of social sectors which governments across the world have collaborated with to 'pay back debts', central bank policies reduced foreign debt from 30.4 per cent of GNP to 6.3 per cent in seven years, and simultaneously reduced overall debt from 140 per cent of GDP to 26 per cent of GNP over a longer period, all the while increasing government expenditures on health, education, social security and other civil commons infrastructure (William Krehm, 'Let's Talk Bonds', *Economic Reform*, May 1996, p. 4).

69. The best narrative account of this legislation is given by Linda McQuaig in her *Shooting The Hippo*, Toronto: Penguin Viking, 1995. For direct observation of its continuous violation by giveaways of federal debt to commercial banks, removal of reserve requirements, unnecessary foreign borrowing and repression of alternative policies, see William Krehm, *A Law Unto Itself: The Bank of Canada*, Toronto: Stoddart, 1993.

70. These descriptions are taken from the Treaty itself. The Treaty's negative impact on the public provision of life-goods, the quintessential function of the civil commons, also proceeds from prohibitions of any public enterprise that competes with the priced goods of the corporate market (see, for example, Helen and William Wallace, *Policy-Making in the European Union*. Oxford: Oxford University Press, 1996, pp. 185–206).

71. One in six Europeans lives in poverty, the average rate of unemployment is 11 per cent, and child poverty in central Europe has more than doubled in the 1990s (Tom Buerkle, 'Poverty Afflicts One In Six Europeans', *International Herald Tribune News Service*, May 16, 1995 and Ian Traynor in Bonn, 'Children Pay Price For Democracy', *Guardian Weekly*, April 27, 1998, p. 4). There has been at the same time an overall reduction since the 1970s of 33 per cent in the share of GDP going to investment ('Euro's Coming Like It Or Not', *Guardian Weekly*, March 8, 1998, p. 12). The latter editorial comments, 'They (the member states) have driven their economies into the ground to fulfil their Maastricht vows.'

72. 'Rural Poland Faces Uncertain Future', *Le Monde* via *Guardian Weekly*, May 25, 1997, p. 14.

73. Theorists of the life economy are distinctively illuminating in their exposures of the insanity of the money-sequence paradigm. Some authors of this evolving leadership of the civil commons who have made an international written contribution are Susan George, Hazel Henderson, Maria Mies, Vandana Shiva, Terisa Turner and Marilyn Waring. A classic work in the area is Maria Mies and Vandana Shiva, *Ecofeminism*. London: Zed Books, 1993. The $16 trillion figure is from Hazel Henderson, 'The Price of Everything: the Value of Nothing', *Economic Reform*, June 1988, p. 3.

74. This position is not to be confused with Edmund Burke's or Alasdair MacIntyre's or other traditionalist standpoints which defer to hierarchy, presumed rank and repressive practices simply because they are long-established with no principled distinction between life-enabling and -disabling customs and practices. Because such standpoints cannot reject ancient caste systems, military institutions of war or suffocating traditions, however they may narrow and oppress the vital ranges of human existence, they are precisely opposed to the logic of value advocated here.

75. One example is Grameen, an Indian bank founded in 1983, a borrowers' co-operative funded 75 per cent by members and 25 per cent by the Indian government. It has two million clients, 94 per cent women and all below the poverty line on joining, with 48 per cent rising above subsequently (received from Accion information Internet, May 1998).

76. Pension and mutual funds are yet another money-into-more-money circuit which have been created by *government* decision and tax-money flows, and which are wholly unaccountable to social life-requirement. They are monolithic inputs into the segregated money-code sequences of the global market – by 1996 $350 billion in Canada, for example, and $4,000 billion in the United States in pension funds alone, and 'these swelling pension funds are expected to be the biggest suppliers of capital in global markets' (J. McNish, 'Bankers' Brawl', *Report on Business Magazine*, January 1996, p. 82). This is a threshhold development, considerably advanced since 1996, because it indicates the extent to which decoupled money sequences have been universalized in their hold. Pension and mutual funds are invested as the assets of the working class itself, whose membership does not noticeably

resist or observe this co-option of their savings and future into global market money-circuits. The programme in this way becomes a transclass pathology not only in motivation structure, but in actual monetary stock growth.

77. William Krehm, 'The Hidden Dossier of the BIS', *Economic Reform*, May 1996, p. 4.

Epilogue: Depathologizing Competition

1. The parallels in principle between market fundamentalism and fascism are explored in my 'Fascism and Neo-Conservatism: Is There A Difference?' *Praxis International*, Vol. 4: No. 1 (April 1984) pp. 86–102.

Index